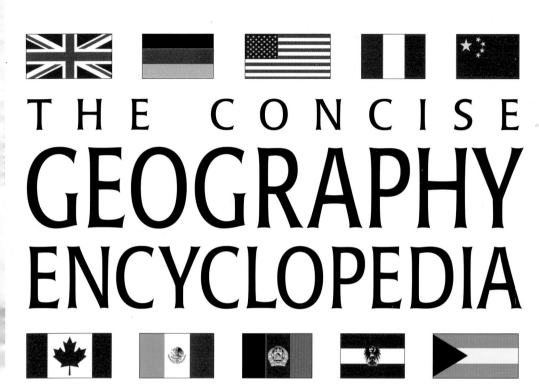

THE CONCISE
GEOGRAPHY
ENCYCLOPEDIA

KINGFISHER

a Houghton Mifflin Company imprint
222 Berkeley Street
Boston, Massachusetts 02116
www.houghtonmifflinbooks.com

First published as *The Kingfisher Geography
Encyclopedia* in 2003

Reprinted in a revised format in 2005
2 4 6 8 10 9 7 5 3 1
1TR/0605/SHE/CLSN/158MA/C

LIBRARY OF CONGRESS CATALOGING-IN-PUBLICATION DATA
Gifford, Clive.
The concise geography encyclopedia/Clive Gifford.—1st ed.
p. cm.
Includes index.
1. Geography—Encyclopedias. I. Title.
G63.G54 2005
910'.3—dc22 2004029249

ISBN 0-7534-5845-4
ISBN 978-07534-5845-7

Printed in Taiwan
PROJECT TEAM

Project Director and Art Editor Julian Holland
Editorial Team Julian Holland, Lynn Bresler
Designer Nigel White
Commissioned artwork Julian Baker
Picture Research Caroline Wood
Maps Anderson Geographics Limited, Warfield, Berks

FOR KINGFISHER

Managing Editor Paula Borton
Consultant Dr. Deryck W. Holdsworth,
Pennsylvania State University
Coordinating Editors Stephanie Pliakas, Caitlin Doyle
Art Director Mike Davis
DTP Manager Nicky Studdart
DTP Operator Primrose Burton
Senior Production Controller Deborah Otter

AUTHOR
Clive Gifford

CONSULTANT
Clive Carpenter

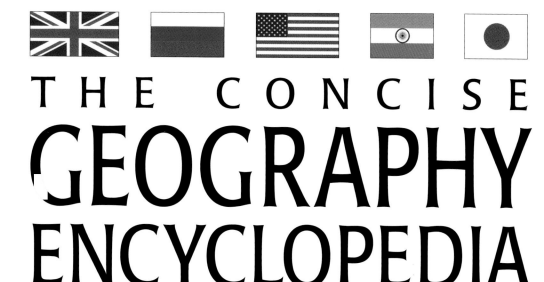

THE CONCISE
GEOGRAPHY
ENCYCLOPEDIA

KINGFISHER
BOSTON

CONTENTS

Chapter 5

Africa

Chapter 6

Oceania and Antarctica

COUNTRIES OF THE WORLD

Every part of Earth's land surface belongs to or is claimed by one of its 193 independent countries. The oldest country with defined borders is San Marino, which was established in A.D. 301. East Timor became the newest independent nation in 2002.

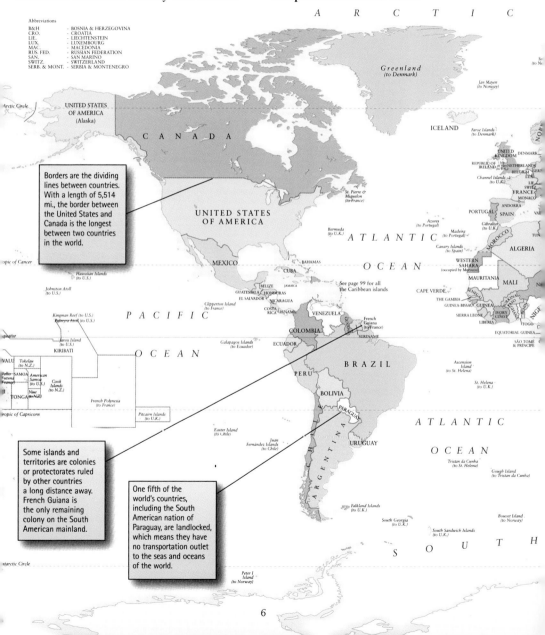

Abbreviations

B&H — BOSNIA & HERZEGOVINA
CRO. — CROATIA
LIE. — LIECHTENSTEIN
LUX. — LUXEMBOURG
MAC. — MACEDONIA
RUS. FED. — RUSSIAN FEDERATION
SAN. — SAN MARINO
SWITZ. — SWITZERLAND
SERB. & MONT. - SERBIA & MONTENEGRO

Borders are the dividing lines between countries. With a length of 5,514 mi., the border between the United States and Canada is the longest between two countries in the world.

Some islands and territories are colonies or protectorates ruled by other countries a long distance away. French Guiana is the only remaining colony on the South American mainland.

One fifth of the world's countries, including the South American nation of Paraguay, are landlocked, which means they have no transportation outlet to the seas and oceans of the world.

6

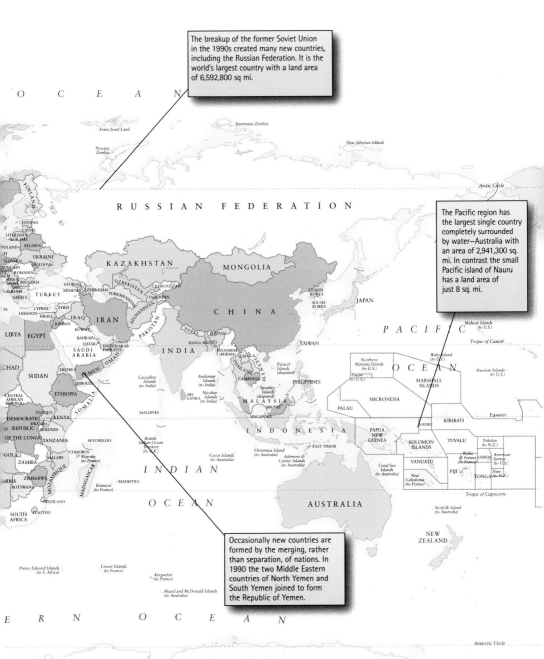

The breakup of the former Soviet Union in the 1990s created many new countries, including the Russian Federation. It is the world's largest country with a land area of 6,592,800 sq mi.

The Pacific region has the largest single country completely surrounded by water—Australia with an area of 2,941,300 sq. mi. In contrast the small Pacific island of Nauru has a land area of just 8 sq. mi.

Occasionally new countries are formed by the merging, rather than separation, of nations. In 1990 the two Middle Eastern countries of North Yemen and South Yemen joined to form the Republic of Yemen.

EARTH STATISTICS

PLANETARY DATA

Estimated age	4.6 billion years	Orbital period (year)	365.24 days
Diameter at the equator	7,909 mi.	Rotational period (day)	23 hours and 56.1 minutes
Diameter at the poles	7,883 mi.	Average temperature	57°F
Circumference at the equator	24,841 mi.	Surface area	316,240,920 sq. mi.
Circumference at the poles	24,795 mi.	Land area	92,161,140 sq. mi. (29.1%)
Average distance from the Sun	92.75 million mi.	Total water area	224,079,780 sq. mi. (70.9%)
Distance between Moon and Earth	238,328 mi.	Ocean area	207,859,960 sq. mi.

THE WORLD'S OCEANS BY AREA

Pacific	103,068,880 sq. mi.
Atlantic	53,667,200 sq. mi.
Indian	45,526,600 sq. mi.
Arctic	8,202,600 sq. mi.

THE WORLD'S MAJOR SEAS BY AREA

South China Sea	1,844,252 sq. mi.
Caribbean Sea	1,706,860 sq. mi.
Mediterranean Sea	1,551,860 sq. mi.
Bering Sea	1,406,284 sq. mi.
Gulf of Mexico	956,598 sq. mi.
Sea of Okhotsk	946,740 sq. mi.
East China Sea	744,380 sq. mi.
Hudson Bay	763,840 sq. mi.
Sea of Japan	624,650 sq. mi.
Andaman Sea	494,574 sq. mi.
North Sea	356,686 sq. mi.
Black Sea	283,378 sq. mi.

DEEPEST POINTS OF OCEANS AND SEAS

Pacific Ocean	36,082 ft.
Atlantic Ocean	28,169 ft.
Caribbean Sea	24,667 ft.
Indian Ocean	23,760 ft.
Gulf of Mexico	17,033 ft.
South China Sea	16,417 ft.
Mediterranean Sea	16,309 ft.
Arctic Ocean	15,271 ft.
Bering Sea	13,412 ft.
Sea of Japan	12,250 ft.

MAJOR RIVERS BY LENGTH

Nile, Africa	4,135 mi.
Amazon, South America	3,998 mi.
Chang Jiang (Yangtze), Asia	3,906 mi.
Mississippi-Missouri, North America	3,732 mi.
Yenisey-Angara, Asia	3,732 mi.
Huang (Yellow), Asia	3,388 mi.
Ob-Irtysh, Asia	3,354 mi.
Paraná-Río de la Plata, South America	3,026 mi.
Congo, Africa	2,914 mi.
Lena, Asia	2,728 mi.
Amur-Argun, Asia	2,694 mi.

WORLD'S HIGHEST MULTIPLE WATERFALLS

Angel, Venezuela	2,205 ft.
Tugela, South Africa	3,100 ft.
Utigordfoss, Norway	2,619 ft.
Mongefoss, Norway	2,534 ft.
Mutarazi, Zimbabwe	2,494 ft.
Yosemite, U.S.	2,419 ft.
Espelandsfoss, Norway	2,301 ft.
Ostre Mardolafoss, Norway	2,417 ft.
Tyssestregene, Norway	2,115 ft.
Cuquenán, Venezuela	1,899 ft.

MAJOR LAKES BY AREA

Caspian Sea, Asia-Europe	230,516 sq. mi.
Superior, North America	41,057 sq. mi.
Victoria, Africa	43,090 sq. mi..
Huron, North America	36,952 sq. mi..
Michigan, North America	35,836 sq. mi.
Tanganyika, Africa	20,398 sq. mi.
Great Bear, North America	19,716 sq. mi.
Baikal, Asia	18,910 sq. mi.
Malawi/Nyasa, Africa	18,352 sq. mi.
Great Slave, North America	17,670 sq. mi.

LARGEST ISLANDS BY AREA

Greenland	1,348,872 sq. mi.
New Guinea	509,039 sq. mi.
Borneo	461,507 sq. mi.
Madagascar	363,965 sq. mi.
Baffin	295,162 sq. mi.
Sumatra	293,636 sq. mi.
Honshu	142,878 sq. mi.
Great Britain	135,185 sq. mi.
Ellesmere	131,867 sq. mi.
Victoria	131,563 sq. mi.

HIGHEST MOUNTAINS BY CONTINENT

Asia, Mount Everest	29,070 ft.
S. America, Aconcagua	22,831 ft.
N. America, Mount McKinley	20,320 ft.
Africa, Mount Kilimanjaro	19,335 ft.
Europe, Elbrus	18,506 ft.
Antarctica, Vinson Massif	16,062 ft.
Oceania, Puncak Jaya	16,019 ft.

WORLD'S 10 HIGHEST MOUNTAINS

Everest, Himalayas	29,070 ft.
K2, Karakoram	28,244 ft.
Kanchenjunga, Himalayas	28,146 ft.
Lhotse, Himalayas	27,862 ft.
Makalu, Himalayas	27,763 ft.
Cho Oyu, Himalayas	26,847 ft.
Dhaulagiri, Himalayas	26,735 ft.
Manaslu, Himalayas	26,699 ft.
Nanga Parbat, Himalayas	26,699 ft.
Annapurna, Himalayas	26,487 ft.

10 LARGEST COUNTRIES BY AREA

Russian Federation	17,075,400 sq. mi.
China	9,326,411 sq. mi.
Canada	9,220,910 sq. mi.
United States	9,166,601 sq. mi.
Brazil	8,456,511 sq. mi.
Australia	7,617,931 sq. mi.
India	2,973,190 sq. mi.
Argentina	2,736,690 sq. mi.
Kazakhstan	2,717,300 sq. mi.
Algeria	2,381,741 sq. mi.

10 COUNTRIES WITH HIGHEST HUMAN POPULATION

China	1,284,303,705
India	1,045,845,226
United States	280,562,489
Indonesia	232,073,071
Brazil	176,029,560
Pakistan	147,663,429
Russian Federation	144,978,573
Bangladesh	133,376,684
Nigeria	129,934,628
Japan	126,974,628
World Population	6,135,000,000

POPULATION OF WORLD'S LARGEST CITIES (URBAN AREAS)

Tokyo, Japan	26,444,000
Mexico City, Mexico	18,066,000
São Paulo, Brazil	17,962,000
New York City, U.S.	16,732,000
Mumbai (Bombay), India	16,086,000
Los Angeles, U.S.	13,213,000
Kolkata (Calcutta), India	13,058,000
Shanghai, China	12,867,000
Dhaka, Bangladesh	12,519,000
Delhi, India	12,441,000
Buenos Aires, Argentina	12,024,000
Jakarta, Indonesia	11,018,000
Osaka, Japan	11,013,000
Beijing, China	10,839,000
Karachi, Pakistan	10,032,000

HIGHS AND LOWS

DRIEST RECORDED PLACE ON EARTH
Calama in Chile's Atacama Desert has zero average annual rainfall.

WETTEST RECORDED PLACE ON EARTH
Tutunendo, Colombia, with 471 in. average annual rainfall.

COLDEST RECORDED TEMPERATURE
Vostok station, Antarctica (-128°F)

HOTTEST RECORDED TEMPERATURE
Al Aziziyah, Libya (136°F)

THE ARCTIC, NORTH AMERICA, AND CENTRAL AMERICA

THE ARCTIC

The Arctic is the area circling the North Pole and extending south to include the Arctic Ocean and the northernmost parts of three continents: Asia, Europe, and North America. Surrounding the North Pole and extending outward is a gigantic ice sheet, bigger than all of Europe. Much of this polar ice cap floats on the Arctic Ocean. The ice cap recedes in the summer, with large chunks breaking off to form icebergs. In the winter, when the temperatures can fall as low as -76°F, it increases in size again. Despite the hostile climate and living conditions, the Arctic is home to a number of large mammals, including polar bears, walrus, and seals. It has also been inhabited for thousands of years by peoples such as the North American Inuits and the European Lapps (Samis).

▼ Part of Greenland covered in glacial ice meets the sea near the settlement of Cape York, 124 mi. south of Qaanaaq.

GREENLAND

Greenland is the world's biggest island. It is a dependency of Denmark but is 50 times bigger. Much of the land is covered by a huge ice cap.

Area: 840,000 sq. mi.
Population: 56,376
Capital: Nuuk (13,700)
Main languages spoken: Inuktitut, Danish
Main religion: Lutheran
Currency: Danish krone
Main exports: minerals, (lead, zinc, coal, chrome, copper), fish and fish products
Government: self-governing dependency of Denmark

▼ The small village of Savissivik lies on the west coast of Greenland. It was originally founded by Inuit people who made iron tools using the iron contained in meteorites discovered in the area.

Greenland lies mainly within the Arctic Circle, and its landscape is dominated by a giant ice sheet that covers 80 percent of the island. The action of glaciers has created a complex coastal landscape with many fjords and offshore islands. Almost all of Greenland's small population live on the coast, particularly on the southwestern side, where the climate is not as bitterly cold as in the interior. Only one percent of the island's total area can be farmed; hardy vegetables, such as beets and turnips, are grown, and small herds of sheep, goats, and reindeer are raised for their meat. The Arctic waters around the coast provide good catches of salmon, cod, and shrimp, and fish processing is Greenland's major industry. The island has no railroads and only 93 mi. of roads. Dogsleds remain the main form of land transportation. The people of Greenland are a mixture of descendants of Inuit, Danish, and Norwegian settlers. Although Denmark is around 1,300 mi. away, all Greenlanders are Danish citizens. After a long campaign the island was

Qaanaaq

Baffin Bay

Greenland
(to Denmark)

Ittoqqortoormiit

Illulissat

Sisimiut

Davis Strait

■NUUK

Paamiut

Qaqortoq

allowed to rule itself from 1979 on, although Denmark remains in control of foreign affairs. A 31-member parliament, called the Landsting, is elected every four years. Following a referendum in 1982 Greenland withdrew from the European Union, which it had joined in 1972.

NORTH AMERICA

The third-largest continent, North America lies completely in the Northern Hemisphere. Its 9.86 million sq. mi. of land stretches deep into the Arctic Circle and extends southward through Central America to join South America. The continent consists of three large countries—Canada, the United States, and Mexico—as well as a cluster of smaller countries in Central America. Young, folded mountains run almost the entire length of the continent's western side and contain a number of volcanoes. A large proportion of this western area has been shaped by the movement of the plates of Earth's crust. Much of North America is uninhabited, especially the land in the far north, while many of the region's 491.5 million population live in large towns and cities. Fertile land exists throughout the continent, and many of the countries have large reserves of minerals and fossil fuels. Economically the continent is dominated by the U.S., the world's richest and most powerful nation. The Central American nations tend to be poorer and reliant on trade and aid from the U.S. and, to a lesser extent, Canada and Mexico.

▲ The Chrysler Building was built between 1928 and 1930 and is just one of New York City's many skyscrapers.

▼ A bison grazes on a grassy plain in Wyoming close to the Rocky Mountains. This 2,000-mi.-long mountain chain runs from the southwestern U.S. to British Columbia in Canada.

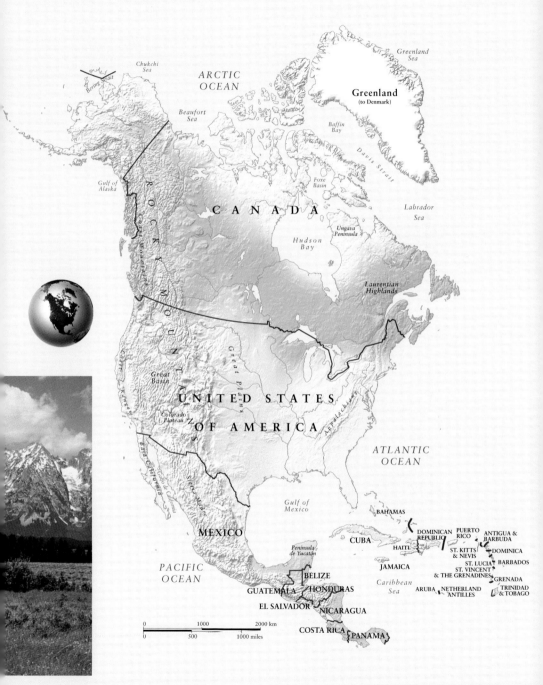

ARCTIC
OCEAN

Chukchi
Sea

Bering Strait

Beaufort
Sea

Greenland
Sea

Greenland
(to Denmark)

Baffin
Bay

Davis Strait

Gulf of
Alaska

R O C K Y   M O U N T A I N S

Coast Mountains

C A N A D A

Foxe
Basin

Hudson
Bay

Ungava
Peninsula

Labrador
Sea

Laurentian
Highlands

Great
Basin

Great Plains

U N I T E D   S T A T E S

Colorado
Plateau

Z   O F   A M E R I C A

Appalachians

ATLANTIC
OCEAN

Columbia River

Sierra Madre

Baja California

Gulf of
Mexico

MEXICO

Peninsula
de Yucatán

Golfo de California

PACIFIC
OCEAN

BAHAMAS

CUBA

DOMINICAN
REPUBLIC

PUERTO
RICO

ANTIGUA &
BARBUDA

HAITI

ST. KITTS
& NEVIS

DOMINICA

JAMAICA

ST. LUCIA
ST. VINCENT
& THE GRENADINES

BARBADOS

Caribbean
Sea

GRENADA

BELIZE

ARUBA

NETHERLAND
ANTILLES

TRINIDAD
& TOBAGO

GUATEMALA

HONDURAS

EL SALVADOR

NICARAGUA

COSTA RICA

PANAMA

0   1000   2000 km
0   500   1000 miles

13

CANADA

With the longest coastline of any nation, Canada is a huge country that occupies the northernmost part of North America and extends deep into the Arctic Circle.

Area: 3,560,200 sq. mi.
Population: 31,902,268
Capital: Ottawa
(1,094,000)
Main languages spoken: English, French
Main religions: Roman Catholic, United Church, Anglican
Currency: Canadian dollar
Main exports: motor vehicles, other machinery and transportation equipment, mineral fuels, lumber, newsprint and wood pulp, foodstuffs (particularly cereals)
Government: confederation with parliamentary democracy

▼ The St. Lawrence river runs from the most easterly of the Great Lakes, Lake Ontario, through the Canadian cities of Montreal and Quebec (pictured) before emptying into the Gulf of St. Lawrence. The river provides a vital shipping link between the industrial centers of the Great Lakes and the Atlantic Ocean.

Canada is the second-largest country in the world—only Russia is bigger. It has long coasts with the Arctic, Atlantic, and Pacific oceans and shares two separate land borders with the U.S. To the east it borders Alaska, while its main border is to the south and extends almost 4,000 mi. Canada has a varied landscape that includes rugged mountain ranges, ice-covered wastelands, fertile prairies, and temperate lowlands and plains. Islands account for almost one sixth of its total land area, with Baffin Island being the fifth-largest island in the world.

A LAND OF LAKES AND TREES

Canada contains more lakes and inland waters than any other country in the world. Within its borders lie over 30 lakes with an area bigger than 507 sq. mi. Canada's longest river is the Mackenzie river, which runs for 1,075 mi., but the St. Lawrence is the most important for trade and shipping. This river helps form more than 2,480 mi. of linked waterways connecting the Great Lakes to the Atlantic Ocean. It is estimated that as much as 25 percent of the world's entire freshwater sources are found in Canada. Forests cover more than 35 percent of the entire country. Trees, such as pine, spruce, cedar, and maple, are especially common.

PEOPLE AND RESOURCES

Canada is one of the world's least densely populated countries with an average of nine people per square mile. Huge areas, especially in the cold north, are unpopulated. Most people live in a fairly narrow belt in the southern part of the country where the climate is milder than the icy, harsh north. Although Ottawa is its capital, Canada's two largest cities are Toronto, with a population of 4.75 million, and Montreal, with a population of 3.5 million. Canada was settled by English- and French-speaking peoples. Today people of European origin form more than two thirds of its population. The country has rich mineral resources and large areas of fertile farmland.

▲ The Athabasca glacier lies in the northern Rocky Mountains, and its meltwaters feed the 763-mi.-long Athabasca river, which runs though the Canadian province of Alberta. In the past this river was an important transportation route for fur traders.

▲ The fox squirrel (*Sciurius niger*) is found in the western parts of Canada bordering Montana and Washington.

ARCTIC
OCEAN

Beaufort
Sea

Banks
Island

Queen
Elizabeth
Islands

Ellesmere Island

Baffin
Bay

Victoria
Island

Baffin Island

Mount
Logan
19,850 ft.

Mackenzie

Great Bear
Lake

Foxe
Basin

Rocky Mountains

Coast Mountains

Great Slave
Lake

C A N A D A

Ungava
Peninsula

Labrador
Sea

Lake
Athabasca

Hudson
Bay

Labrador

Reindeer
Lake

Saskatchewan

Lake
Winnipeg

Newfoundland

Laurentian
Highlands

St. Lawrence

St. Pierre
& Miquelon
(to France)

| 0 | 1000 | 2000 km |
| 0 | 500 | 1000 miles |

Great
Lakes

OTTAWA

ATLANTIC
OCEAN

EASTERN CANADA

Eastern Canada includes the industrial and farming heartlands of Quebec and Ontario, Canada's biggest city—Toronto—and its seat of government in Ottawa.

▲ Canada's parliament buildings are found in the eastern Canadian city of Ottawa. First opened in 1866, the buildings show British influence, with the tower bearing a striking resemblance to the Houses of Parliament buildings in London, England.

▼ Built in 1976, the 1,815-ft.-high CN Tower is the most notable landmark in the busy Ontario city of Toronto—Canada's largest city, with a population of four million. The tower receives around two million visitors every year.

Canada is divided into ten provinces and three territories. Six of these provinces form eastern Canada: Ontario, Quebec, New Brunswick, Prince Edward Island, Newfoundland and Labrador, and Nova Scotia.

SHAPED BY GLACIERS

Canada was shaped mainly by glaciation. The glaciers that remain in the north are remnants of an ice sheet that once covered Canada. Glaciation is responsible for many geographical landmarks—from the low, rolling hills on Prince Edward Island and Nova Scotia to the magnificent Niagara Falls, which lie between Lake Erie and Lake Ontario. Eastern Canada is made up of three geographical regions: the Canadian Shield, the Appalachian mountains to the east, and, between the two, a rich agricultural area called the Great Lakes–St. Lawrence lowlands. The Canadian Shield takes its name from the hard bedrock of gneiss and granite that lies underneath the surface. This rock is estimated to be more than three billion years old and occupies half of Canada. It extends south from Hudson Bay down through the provinces of Ontario and Quebec to reach the northern shore of Lake Superior. Scraped by the advance and retreat of glaciers, the region contains many rivers and lakes and tends to have a thin soil that supports boreal evergreen forests.

THE ATLANTIC PROVINCES

The four Atlantic provinces are Prince Edward Island, Newfoundland and Labrador, New Brunswick, and Nova Scotia. Valleys full of fertile soil mean that farming is a key industry in all four provinces. The smallest Canadian province is Prince Edward Island, which lies in the Gulf of St. Lawrence and has an area of just 2,185 sq. mi. Half of the island is covered in dense forests, although farming and fishing are the most important industries for the island's 135,000-strong population. Newfoundland and Labrador is the newest Canadian province. It joined Canada in 1949 and consists of Labrador, the mainland area, and the large island of Newfoundland, which has been the traditional center of Canada's fishing industry and is one of the world's richest fishing grounds. New Brunswick is almost rectangular in shape with an area of 28,355 sq. mi. Large fishing grounds in the Bay of Fundy and the Gulf of St. Lawrence as well as mines and some manufacturing factories, sustain many of the province's

▲ Seal Cove is a fishing village in the Atlantic province of New Brunswick. It is situated on Grand Manan Island in the Bay of Fundy.

729,498 people. Mostly covered in forests, logging and timber products are a vital part of the province's economy. Forests also cover a large part of Nova Scotia. Bordering the Atlantic Ocean, Nova Scotia was founded by French settlers in 1605. The area has a long history of ship- and boatbuilding, supplemented by fishing and mining for coal and other minerals. Its largest settlement, Halifax, is a major port.

THE POWERHOUSE PROVINCES

Ontario and the southern part of Quebec are Canada's agricultural and industrial centers. Half of all Canadians live in this region, where around 70 percent of all Canada's manufactured goods are made. Around the shore of Lake Ontario is Canada's industrial heartland—the Golden Horseshoe. Industries use transportation links provided by the lake and the St. Lawrence Seaway. Southern Ontario has large stretches of prime agricultural land.

CENTRAL GOVERNMENT

Ottawa, Ontario, is home to Canada's national government. Canada is a federal union, which means that power is divided between the provinces and the central government. The Canadian parliament has two houses: the Senate, whose members are appointed and serve until the age of 75, and the House of Commons, whose members are elected once every five years.

FRENCH-SPEAKING CANADA

Canada has two official languages: English and French. This reflects the patterns of settlement that saw British and French arrivals from the 1600s on. French-speaking Canadians live in the Atlantic provinces and throughout Canada, but they are concentrated in Quebec—the area that French fur traders and farmers first settled. Lying to the east of Ontario, Quebec is blessed with good farmland and rich mineral reserves. Although the capital of the province is the city of Quebec, its largest settlement is Montreal—a busy port and financial center.

WESTERN CANADA

Rich in natural resources, western Canada features mountainous British Columbia and the three "prairie provinces" of Manitoba, Saskatchewan, and Alberta.

▲ Grizzly bears are found in western Canada, especially in more mountainous regions. They are one of the largest meat-eating land creatures, but they are also an endangered species.

▼ Vancouver is Canada's third-largest city and is situated on the Canadian mainland opposite Vancouver Island. It has a large natural harbor, which has helped make it the center of British Columbia's sea trade.

Three of western Canada's four provinces are dominated by the Great Plains, which run through large parts of Alberta, Saskatchewan, and Manitoba. The plains feature fertile soils and large deposits of fossil fuels. Manitoba, the flattest of the three provinces, is known as "the land of 100,000 lakes," with many lakes being created through glaciation. There are many rivers and lakes in the northern half of Saskatchewan, while the Rocky Mountains and their foothills extend into the southwestern corner of Alberta. The northern regions of all three provinces tend to be heavily forested, and timber industries are a major contributor to the local economies. British Columbia is the only Canadian province with a Pacific coastline and is more mountainous, with two enormous mountain ranges running along much of its length.

BRITISH COLUMBIA

British Columbia is separated from Alberta by the Rocky Mountains, which run throughout its length and continue north into the Yukon Territory. West of the Rockies lie heavily forested lands, natural grasslands, and large numbers of lakes. Another mountain range, the Coast Mountains, define much of the province's coastal area, with glaciation having carved out many islands and fjords. The Queen Charlotte Islands to the north and the 285-mi.-long Vancouver Island are the largest islands. The province's landscape is naturally beautiful and sustains much wildlife, including grizzly and black bears, elks, and waterfowl. The animals' habitat is preserved in the form of 675 parks or protected areas, which attract more than 23 million visitors every year. A feature of the province is its large forests, which contain a big percentage of Canada's commercially sold wood—trees that can be used for timber, pulp, paper, and other industries. Wood processing, mining, tourism, and service industries are the biggest employers of the province's 3.9 million people. Most of the population live in the southwest, with 60 percent living in just two cities: Victoria and Vancouver, Canada's third-largest city.

▲ The Maligne river flows from the Canadian Rocky Mountains through Jasper National Park in the province of Alberta.

Victoria is the province's capital and is located on Vancouver Island. It is built on the site of the first permanent European colony, which was established in 1843. Facing the Pacific Ocean and the Far East, British Columbia is increasingly trading and building commercial ties with Japan, South Korea, and other Asian nations. Although most people in the province are of British origin, there are also more than 60,000 inhabitants of Indian descent, around 200,000 Native Americans, and North America's largest Chinese community outside of San Francisco, California.

WARM SUMMERS—COLD WINTERS

Some distance from both the Pacific and Atlantic oceans, the three "prairie provinces" have a continental climate. This means large differences between warm summer and cold winter temperatures. For example, Manitoba's largest city, Winnipeg, records an average January temperature of -4°F, and average temperatures in July are 68°F higher. In southwestern parts of Alberta, the closest of the three provinces to the Pacific Ocean, mild winds from the Pacific—called the chinook—tend to raise the cold winter temperatures a bit.

▲ Canada is the world's largest producer of barley, an important cereal crop. More than 90 percent of the country's total production of 12.6 million tons is grown in western Canada. It is grown on Canada's Great Plains and is harvested with automated machinery.

▼ Lying on the eastern slopes of the Rockies and famous for its spectacular mountain scenery, Banff National Park is also Canada's oldest national park, first opened in 1883.

All three provinces receive low rainfall averaging between 15–18 in. per year but enjoy a large number of sunny days in both the summer and the winter. The town of Estevan in Saskatchewan is considered the sunshine capital of Canada, with an average of more than 2,500 sunshine hours per year. The most eastern parts of the fourth province, British Columbia, also feature a continental climate, but much of this province is affected greatly by its closeness to the Pacific Ocean. Warm, moist air from the Pacific not only helps create milder winters but also brings heavy rainfall, between 52–152 in. per year.

FARMING AND FUELS

The warm summer conditions, along with the large expanses of flat, fertile plains, have made the three "prairie provinces" highly productive farming areas. Alberta, for example, is the largest beef-producing province in Canada. Only 13 percent of this meat is used within the state, half is shipped to other parts of Canada, while a further 30 percent is traded with the U.S. Saskatchewan produces more than half of the wheat grown in Canada and also has large farmlands devoted to growing rye, flaxseed, and other crops. Manitoba's central location in Canada has made it an important trading, transportation, and distribution center for farming and food products. Around 60 percent of its population live in and around the capital city of Winnipeg. Food production and packaging are major industries in all three provinces, while fossil fuels are exploited, particularly in Alberta, which supplies 90 percent of Canada's natural gas needs, and Saskatchewan. More than 18,000 active oil wells in Saskatchewan produce around one fifth of Canada's total oil output.

NORTHERN CANADA

Northern Canada consists of three sparsely populated
territories: Yukon, the Northwest Territories, and Nunavut.
Four fifths of these territories are wilderness areas.

▲ Northern Canada is
the main home of the
polar bear. Since 1973
hunting restrictions
have helped it survive.

▼ Cutting a hole in the
ice, this Inuit fisherwoman
fishes for arctic char.

The three
territories of northern
Canada are among the most
sparsely populated regions in the world.
In the Northwest Territories and Nunavut
there is one person for every 37 sq. mi.,
while in Yukon there is one person
per 11 sq. mi. Yukon occupies
186,661 sq. mi., yet over half
of its entire population lives
in a single town, Whitehorse.
Icy tundra occupies large
parts of these territories
to the north, and
permafrost is widespread. Many of northern
Canada's peoples are either Native American
Indians or traditional Arctic people such as
the Inuit. Hunting, fishing, trapping, mining,
and forestry are the main sources of work.

NUNAVUT

The boundaries defining Canada's two
territories were redrawn in 1999, creating
the newly formed Nunavut territory.
Nunavut is the most northerly region
in Canada and includes the thousands
of islands in the Arctic Ocean that
form the Arctic archipelago.
Nunavut is a self-
governing homeland
for the Inuit people,
who form 85 percent
of the territory's
total population
of around 26,000.
Nunavut means
"Our Land" in
the Inuit language.
More than one
third of Nunavut's
population is under
15 years of age.

UNITED STATES OF AMERICA

The U.S. is the third-largest and the most powerful country in the world. A world leader in manufacturing industries, it has an abundance of natural resources.

Area: 3,539,200 sq. mi.
Population: 280,562,489
Capital: Washington, D.C. (3,997,000)
Main languages spoken: English, Spanish
Main religions: Roman Catholic, Baptist, Methodist
Currency: U.S. dollar
Main exports: machinery and transportation equipment (particularly road vehicles), chemicals, food, scientific and related equipment
Type of government: federal republic with strong democratic tradition

▼ Independence Day in the U.S. commemorates the adoption of the Declaration of Independence in 1776. Held every 4th of July, it is celebrated with large fireworks displays such as this one over Florida's largest city, Miami.

The United States of America gets its name from its administrative divisions. Each of its 50 states has its own courts and government, which wield much local power. Mainland U.S. consists of 48 states that share borders and occupy the width of North America, stretching from the Pacific Ocean to the Atlantic Ocean. Alaska, which borders western Canada, and the Pacific islands of Hawaii are the remaining two states.

Two large mountain ranges dominate the country's landscape. To the west the Rocky Mountains form a high altitude spine, with some peaks rising to more than 13,000 ft. To the east the Appalachian mountain system runs almost parallel to the Atlantic Ocean for approximately 1,500 mi. The Appalachians are older, lower in height, with large parts covered with forests. In between much of the land consists of giant plains crossed by many rivers. The U.S.'s longest river is the Mississippi. Its main tributary is the Missouri, and together they make up the third-longest river in the world. To the north the U.S. shares a border with Canada. The countries share ownership of the Great Lakes, the series of lakes that run along their border.

The United States is rich in natural resource—from metals, such as lead and iron, to oil and timber. More than one fifth of the world's known reserves of coal lies within its borders. Large parts of the plains running through the center of the country have fertile soils that are used to grow corn and other cereal crops on a huge scale and as grazing land for the U.S.'s 100 million cattle.

◄ The bald eagle is the national bird of the U.S.

AMERICA'S PEOPLE

Populated by Native Americans for many thousands of years, the first Europeans arrived and settled particularly along the U.S.'s eastern coast in the 1600s and 1700s. The Revolutionary War (1775–1781) finally resulted in the nation freeing itself from British rule. The new country encouraged settlers and immigrants for many decades, and the U.S. today is a "melting pot" of different peoples and cultures. Approximately 69 percent of people are of European origin, with 13 percent African-Americans, 12 percent Hispanics, four percent Asians, and two percent Native Americans.

▲ The U.S.'s landscape varies greatly and includes flat, temperate grasslands, rugged mountains, and arid wilderness regions such as this area of New Mexico.

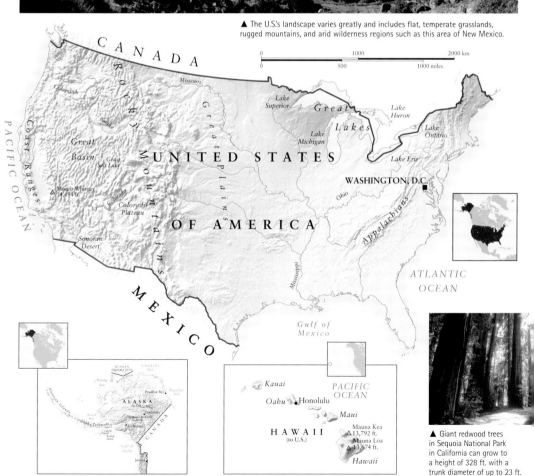

▲ Giant redwood trees in Sequoia National Park in California can grow to a height of 328 ft. with a trunk diameter of up to 23 ft.

23

EASTERN U.S.

The site of the first European arrivals to
the United States, the eastern U.S. is as
rich in land resources as it is in history.

▲ The eastern seaboard of the U.S. has many excellent
natural harbors around which ports and fishing settlements
developed such as Rockport on Cape Ann peninsula
in Massachusetts.

The eastern U.S. borders the Atlantic Ocean with a long, irregular coastline. Two eastern U.S. states, Pennsylvania and New York, have shorelines with the two most easterly Great Lakes, Erie and Ontario. The geography of the region alters as you travel both south and inland. The Atlantic coastal plain broadens as the land runs southward, while the Appalachians mountain system lies inland. Running almost parallel to the Atlantic coast, the Appalachians extend more than 1,400 mi. from the Canadian province of Quebec southward through the eastern U.S., where they reach as far south as Alabama. They form many mountain ranges, including the Green Mountains of Vermont, the Catskill Mountains in New York state, and the Blue Ridge Mountains, which run through Georgia, North Carolina, West Virginia, and Virginia. The Appalachians are some of the oldest mountains to be found anywhere in the world. Their heavily eroded formations are rich in mineral deposits, including coal, iron ore, and zinc. The region includes the six northeastern states known as New England, as well as the mid-Atlantic states of New Jersey, Delaware, Maryland, Pennsylvania, and Virginia. West Virginia sits inland and is the only one of the eastern states not to have a shoreline with either a Great Lake or the Atlantic Ocean. Some forest areas of these states have been cleared for farmland and for the many large towns and cities that house the region's 69 million people. However, 75 percent of West Virginia is covered in trees, while 60 percent of Virginia, 55 percent of Pennsylvania, and 43 percent of Maryland remain forested. Although there are extensive farmlands in many eastern states, manufacturing industries and services are extremely important to state economies.

▲ This marble statue
of former U.S. president
Abraham Lincoln is the
centerpiece of the Lincoln
Memorial, a building
located in Potomac Park
in the capital city of
Washington, D.C.

▼ The White House
in Washington, D.C.
was designed by Irish-
American architect
James Hoban and was
originally called the
Executive Mansion.

GOVERNMENT

The U.S. system of government splits powers between the 50 states and a national government called the federal government. Both state and national government have powers to collect taxes, borrow money, build roads, and provide welfare services. In addition, the national government has powers to make foreign policies and treaties with other nations, provide military forces, and print money. The Capitol building in Washington, D.C. is the home of Congress, the lawmaking body of the United States, and is split into two houses, the House of Representatives and the Senate. The members of both houses are chosen by public elections and both houses meet separately. Pennsylvania Avenue links the Capitol building with the White House, the home of the president of the U.S.

NEW YORK CITY

The giant metropolis of New York started life as a fur-trading post positioned on the mouth of the Hudson river. It is now one of the world's largest, busiest, and richest cities and is a world center for finance and business. It sits on both the mainland and a collection of 50 islands, the largest being Manhattan. For the past 200 years it has been the main gateway into the U.S., and many immigrants have settled here, giving it a mixed racial background.

▼ The fall season in the states of New England sees the leaves of the deciduous trees there turn beautiful shades of orange, yellow, and red. This autumnal scene is from Vermont.

MIDWEST AND THE GREAT LAKES

A major location for manufacturing and trade and home to the world's largest cereal-farming operations, this region plays a major part in the U.S. economy.

▲ Cities like Detroit and Chicago have been synonymous with manufacturing industries such as the production of motor vehicles. This Chicago-based Ford assembly plant manufactures around 250,000 vehicles per year.

Most of the land that makes up the U.S. is part of a giant plateau that runs from the Rocky Mountains in the west across the interior of the country. South and North Dakota and northwestern Nebraska are also home to a region of rugged rock masses and hills called badlands. They are caused by erosion, assisted by short periods of heavy rains followed by long periods of droughts. A large part of the interior consists of the Great Plains, while a region called the Corn Belt, stretching from western Ohio to the central part of Nebraska, is one of the largest crop-growing regions in the world.

THE GREAT PLAINS
The Great Plains occupy a large area of southern Canada and extend south to cover the land east of the Rocky Mountains and west of the Mississippi river. The Great Plains was once one of the largest areas of grassland in the world, supporting herds of bison estimated to total more than 50 million. The rich, fertile topsoil in the area was heavily exploited by farmers from the 1800s on.

▼ Almost one fifth of all wheat grown in the U.S. comes from the state of Kansas. Approximately half of the wheat grown in Kansas is exported overseas.

▲ Built on the southwestern shores of Lake Michigan, Chicago is the U.S.'s third most populous city behind New York and Los Angeles. Its location makes it a vital junction for air, water, and land transportation.

Years of overfarming saw the creation of large dust bowls as the topsoil eroded. However, modern farming and irrigation techniques have seen North America's grasslands return to intensive farming, both in rearing livestock and in growing crops. A little over 75 percent of the world's wheat exports are produced in this region.

THE MISSOURI AND MISSISSIPPI
The Missouri river flows across the central U.S. It is second in length only to the Mississippi, which it flows into just north of St. Louis. Together, the Missouri and the Mississippi travel almost the length of the country and drain much of the central interior. The Mississippi is an important transportation link with barges and ships carrying bulk cargo. The Missouri is harnessed by the Missouri River Basin Project to irrigate large areas of farmland and to provide energy via hydroelectric power plants.

THE GREAT LAKES
The Great Lakes were formed during the last Ice Age when glaciation helped

▶ The bison is the largest land mammal in North America. Around 50 million bison roamed the central U.S. before the arrival of European settlers with guns in the 1800s.

to scour and hollow out broad and deep depressions from valleys. The resulting five large lakes (Michigan, Erie, Ontario, Huron, and Superior) hold an estimated 20 percent of the world's freshwater and 90 percent of the freshwater of the U.S. They all join to form a giant drainage system. The water flows from Lake Superior through the other lakes before entering the sea in the Gulf of St. Lawrence. Together, the lakes drain a region approximately 300,000 sq. mi. in size, known as the Great Lakes Basin. Around one fifth of the United States' population live within this area.

NATIVE AMERICANS
Native American peoples had lived throughout much of North America for thousands of years before the arrival of Europeans. Although early contact tended to be peaceful, gradually tensions built up, and conflicts occurred as the settlers wanted more land to farm and to exploit mineral resources. By the 1800s crisis point had been reached. The buffalo herds on which many Native American tribes depended had been killed in their millions, and thousands of settlers were arriving. Wars erupted as the different Native American tribes attempted

to keep control of their tribal lands. Many of these conflicts occurred in the Midwest and in the states surrounding the Great Lakes. The 1890 massacre of Sioux men, women, and children at Wounded Knee in South Dakota signaled the end of the conflict. Today Native Americans account for no more than two percent of the country's population. They live in greatest numbers in the four adjoining southern states of Oklahoma, New Mexico, Arizona, and California. Each of the states has populations of more than 200,000 Native Americans.

▼ A shopping mall found in the city of Columbus. The state capital of Ohio since 1816, Columbus is Ohio's most populous city.

THE SOUTH

The southern United States has a distinctive nature created by its landscape, its economy, culture, and character of its people.

▲ The White Sands National Park lies in the south-west of New Mexico. These white gypsum sand dunes are shifted by winds to create ever-changing landscapes.

The southern states of the U.S. have a varied geography and climate. Some have a warm, temperate climate, while others, such as Louisiana and Florida, have a subtropical climate with hot, humid summers and, in most places, mild winters. In the states that surround the Gulf of Mexico on average between five and eight tropical storms or hurricanes reach some part of the Gulf coast each year.

▲ New Orleans, Louisiana, is known for its rich mixture of cultural influences, which reflect the varying periods when it has been a French and Spanish colony. Here, a jazz band strikes up in the Vieux Carré, also known as the French Quarter of the city.

▼ The Mesa Montosa lies in New Mexico. The river, the Rio Chuviscar, originates in this landform and eventually flows into the larger Rio Conchos across the border in Mexico.

THE LANDSCAPE

The Appalachian mountains extend into the southern U.S., reaching North Carolina, Georgia, and Alabama. Other major mountain ranges include the Cumberland Mountains and Plateau and the Ouachita Mountains. Florida's eastern coastline faces the Atlantic, and its west side faces the warmer waters of the Gulf. Louisiana and Texas have long coastlines, while Alabama and Mississippi have only small Gulf shores.

THE MISSISSIPPI

The Mississippi is the largest river in the south and the longest in the U.S. It flows through the central southern states before its final journey through southern Louisiana, after which it empties into the Gulf of Mexico near New Orleans. The river's final course has changed many times in the past few thousand years and has created a giant river delta measuring around 11,000 sq. mi. The Mississippi also deposits sediment elsewhere. Large alluvial plains extend on both sides of the river. These have been created over long periods of time and measure between 37–74 mi. in width. With the plains low-lying, the risk of flooding is battled in many ways,

including storage reservoirs, dams, and large embankments or levees, which run for around 1,600 mi. along its length.

THE COTTON BELT
Cotton is the world's largest nonfood crop and is used to make textiles. In 2001 the U.S. was the world's second-largest producer of raw cotton, most of it grown in the Cotton Belt, which sweeps across the southern states. This region provides ideal climatic conditions for cotton. Today Mississippi, Arkansas, Louisiana, and Texas are still leading producers.

SLAVERY
As farms and plantations grew early settler farmers turned to slavery to create a larger workforce. Millions of black Africans were imported by slave traders into the South. By 1790 black people made up one

third of the South's population. Controversy grew around the morality of slavery, and the issue split the U.S., with the North opposing it. In 1860–1861 11 southern states withdrew from the rest of the U.S. to form the Confederate States of America. This was the start of The Civil War (1861–1865). The southern states lost the war, and their economy suffered. Although slavery was abolished, conditions barely improved for many decades, and many African-Americans migrated to the industrial North.

▼ An inhabitant of the Appalachian mountains region of North Carolina plays his banjo. Folk songs from the Appalachian mountains originated from Celtic folk music introduced by 18th- and 19th-century settlers from the British Isles.

WESTERN U.S.

From the high volcanic mountains of the north to the Grand Canyon and the flat, dry deserts in the south, western U.S. has a dramatic range of scenery.

▲ Organ Pipe National Park in Arizona is one of a number of national parks that preserve portions of the Sonoran Desert. The park, which covers more than 326,040 acres of land, is named after the rare organ pipe cactus.

▲ Convict Lake is found in the eastern Sierra Nevada mountains. The 0.81-mi.-long lake is named after a gunfight in 1871 involving c_ ed prisoners on its shores.

The western U.S. is a land of contrasts. It contains major centers of population, including San Francisco and Los Angeles, as well as some of the least inhabited areas. It is home to some of the most high-tech regions and centers in North America, while other parts of its land are owned by native peoples. Geographically the region contains a number of the United States' highest and lowest, as well as wettest and driest, places. This part of the U.S. is made up of different geographical regions. Inland the giant Rocky Mountains separate a lot of the western U.S. from states farther east. To the south large areas of desert stretch across the border into Mexico. The large state of California has a complex geography partly created by a major fault line in Earth's tectonic plates called the San Andreas Fault. The fault runs through around 651 mi. of the state. California has an enormous central valley flanked by the Sierra Nevada mountains and ranges of coastal mountains. Lower-lying areas of California are found in the central valley and along the Pacific coast, west of the coastal mountains, as well as to the southeast in flat, desert areas that includes the Mojave Desert. North of central California is the region known as the Pacific Northwest, which runs from northern California through Oregon and Washington state. It features coastal ranges of mountains and the Cascade Range farther inland. East of California and the Pacific Northwest much of the landscape consists of what geographers call intermontane (between mountain) basins and plateaus, including the Great Basin—an area of broad valleys and rugged mountain blocks covering almost 200,000 square miles.

HOT AND COLD, DRY AND WET

To the north and south of the western U.S. lie vastly different landscapes. Much of Arizona and parts of Nevada and southern California are covered in hot, arid deserts. The largest desert in the region is also the largest in all of North America. Called the

◄ One of the western U.S.'s most notable landmarks, the Golden Gate Bridge, is found in San Francisco, California. Completed in 1937, the bridge's main span measures 4,198 ft. in length and is suspended from two cables hung from towers 743 ft. high.

Sonoran Desert, it covers an area around 192,200 sq. mi. Death Valley is an extremely dry desert area in California and Nevada that receives just two inches average rainfall per year. There the highest temperature ever was recorded in the U.S.: 134°F. In contrast temperatures in the northern states of Idaho, Oregon, and Washington are much lower, averaging between 45°F–54°F, and with a record low in Idaho of -60°F. These states are crossed by a series of mountain ranges with peaks above 13,094 ft. Parts of Washington and Oregon are among the wettest places in the U.S., receiving more than 80 in. of rainfall each year. Large forests are found in all three states, and forestry forms an important part of their economy.

A THRIVING STATE
California, the state with the biggest population, is home to 34 million people, many of whom are drawn to this state for the glamour of its major entertainment industries and its high-tech region, nicknamed "Silicon Valley." California is also a leading food producer. Half of the nation's fruit and vegetables and 15 percent of its milk are produced within its borders.

▼ Surfers are attracted to the Californian coastlines and its large waves.

◄ In less than one century Los Angeles has grown from a town of 50,000 people to a metropolitan area, which in 2000 had 13,213,000 residents. It is famous as the home of Hollywood—the heart of the U.S. movie industry.

ALASKA

The largest and most northern part of the U.S, the vast, icy wilderness of Alaska was bought from Russia in 1867.

Lying at the northwestern tip of the North American continent, Alaska is separated from the Russian Federation by the seas that course through the Bering Strait. The 663,267 sq. mi. state includes frozen tundra to the north, large taiga forests, hundreds of small lakes, and a southern peninsula that stretches out westward. Beyond it lies the Aleutian Islands, a long island chain. Alaska has a rugged geography with large mountain ranges bordering the Pacific and running inland. In total, the state has 39 mountain ranges that hold 17 of the 20 highest peaks in the entire United States.

▲ Built in the 1970s, the Trans-Alaska Pipeline runs for 798 mi., carrying crude oil from Alaska's northern coast to the city of Valdez in the south.

▼ At 20,320 ft. above sea level, Mount McKinley is the highest point in all of North America. The mountain is known to Native Americans as Denali, which means "the high one."

PEOPLE AND ECONOMY

It was across the Bering Strait at least 30,000 years ago that the first people were thought to have entered North America. Descendants of these first arrivals include the Inuit and Aleut peoples, who today make up around one tenth of Alaska's total population of 634,892. Oil and petroleum exploitation dominate the Alaskan economy, producing almost one third of its income. Forestry and fishing are the state's other key resources, while tourism is also on the rise. Visitors are attracted to Alaska's harsh landscapes and its national parks, which contain a rich range of wildlife, including black, brown, and polar bears and large herds of caribou (moose).

▶ Alaska is home to the world's largest population of gray wolves.

HAWAII

Hawaii is the name given to a group of 132 atolls and islands, along with the largest island in the group. In 1959 these Pacific islands became the 50th state of the U.S.

The islands of Hawaii form a 1,488-mi.-long arc through the Pacific Ocean. Some smaller islands are coral atolls, but most of the islands are the topmost parts of giant volcanoes that extend more than 29 ft. up from the Pacific Ocean floor and break the water's surface. Only the volcanoes found on the island of Hawaii, known as the "Big Island," are thought to be still active, although the region experiences earthquake activity. The landscape of the Hawaiian islands is a dramatic mixture of volcanic peaks, steep cliffs, sandy beaches, and deep valleys covered in forests. The climate is tropical, with the northeast trade winds bringing rain. Large parts of the islands are covered in lush, tropical vegetation. Apart from Hawaii, there are seven other large islands. One of these, Oahu, is home to over two thirds of the islands' 1,224,398 population, as well as the islands' largest and capital city, Honolulu. The people of Hawaii are ethnically diverse, with those of European (31 percent), Japanese (20 percent), Filipino (14 percent), and Polynesian (13 percent) descent the largest groups. Fishing is important to the economy in Hawaii; however, tourism is the islands' single biggest industry and is worth more than $10 billion every year.

▼ The beautiful weather, sandy beaches, and excellent surfing in the waters of the Pacific attract many tourists from all over the world to the islands of Hawaii.

BERMUDA

The most northerly coral islands in the world, Bermuda lies in the Atlantic Ocean around 558 mi. off the coast of the U.S. It remains a British dependency.

Area: 20 sq. mi.
Population: 63,960
Capital: Hamilton (6,000)
Main language spoken: English
Main religions: Anglican, Methodist
Currency: Bermudian dollar
Main exports: fuel for shipping and aircrafts, reexported pharmaceuticals
Type of government: self-governing dependency of U.K.

Bermuda consists of more than 150 islands that have a base of volcanic rock with coral formations lying above. The population relies on collecting and storing rainfall for their water supply. The island chain has a mild, humid climate aided by the warm Gulf Stream ocean current. The islands are covered in rich vegetation, including mangrove hedges and many flowering plants. Yet there is very little agricultural land, and flowering lilies are Bermuda's only agricultural export. Tourists, although falling in numbers throughout the 1990s, are still a major contributor to the economy, with more than 80 percent of visitors coming from the U.S. The remainder of Bermuda's economy is reliant on service industries such as insurance. Discovered in 1503 by Spaniard Juan Bermudez, the chain of islands came under British rule in 1684. Although still a dependency of the U.K., Bermuda became self-governing in 1968. The population, who are mainly descendants of former black slaves or Portuguese or British settlers, enjoy a high standard of living and in 1995 rejected a move for full independence.

CENTRAL AMERICA

Bounded by the Pacific Ocean to the west and the Caribbean Sea to the east, Central America is a land bridge, known as an isthmus, that links the rest of North America with the South American continent. It is dominated by the country of Mexico, south of which lies a further seven countries: Belize, Guatemala, Nicaragua, El Salvador, Honduras, Costa Rica, and Panama. Around 40 percent of the land area of these countries is covered in rain forests that harbor a rich variety of wildlife. Much of Central America, from southern Mexico southward, is mountainous, and the region is one of the most active volcanic areas in the world. Water falling from high land is harnessed to generate almost half of the region's electricity via hydroelectric power. Farming is the main activity of the majority of Central Americans, with many crops, such as corn and beans, grown on small family farms. Approximately half of all farm products are exported out of the region. The five most important export products are: coffee, cotton, sugar, beef, and bananas. Central America has been inhabited by a series of ancient civilizations, including the Aztec, Maya, Olmec, and Toltec. The region has seen many wars and conflicts since the arrival of Spanish explorers in the 1500s.

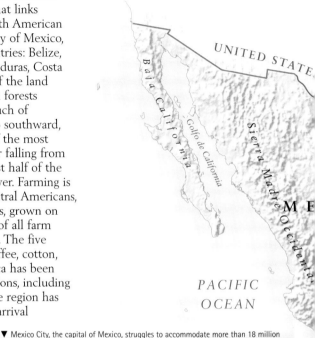

▼ Mexico City, the capital of Mexico, struggles to accommodate more than 18 million inhabitants. Many people live in slums without sanitation. The lack of environmental controls contributes to one of the world's worst air problems.

▲ The Mayan pyramid of Altun Ha in Belize is one of many ancient sites found in Central America. It attracts millions of tourists every year, providing the relatively poor region with much-needed income and employment.

AMERICA

Río Grande

Sierra Madre Oriental

C O

MEXICO CITY

Gulf of Mexico

Península de Yucatán

BELMOPAN

BELIZE

GUATEMALA

HONDURAS

GUATEMALA CITY

TEGUCIGALPA

SAN SALVADOR

EL SALVADOR

NICARAGUA

MANAGUA

Lago de Nicaragua

Caribbean Sea

SAN JOSÉ

PANAMA CITY

COSTA RICA

PANAMA

COLOMBIA

◄ The blue morpho butterfly with its spectacular metallic-blue wings is found in Costa Rica's forests and feeds mainly on fallen fruit.

0   1000 km
0   500 miles

MEXICO

Around one fifth of the size of the U.S. with which it shares a major land border, Mexico is the most populous Spanish-speaking nation in the world.

Area: 742,500 sq. mi.
Population: 103,400,165
Capital: Mexico City (18,268,000)
Major language spoken: Spanish
Main religion: Roman Catholic
Currency: Mexican peso
Main exports: manufactured goods (including machinery and transportation equipment), crude petroleum, agricultural goods (particularly sugar, fruit, and meat)
Type of government: federal republic

▼ The center of Mexico City is the Zócalo, or Plaza of the Constitution. It contains the huge Metropolitan Cathedral, which was built in the 1600s and added to in the 1800s.

Mexico is at its broadest to the north where it borders the U.S. It ends in land borders with Guatemala and Belize and in a square-shaped area jutting into the Gulf of Mexico called the Yucatán peninsula. The Yucatán is formed of limestone rocks and is low-lying, with an average height above sea level of 98 ft. Mexico's second peninsula, Baja California, is very different. It extends 760 mi. south from California, creating the Gulf of California and bordering the Pacific Ocean on its western side. Much of Baja California consists of mountains more than 9,821 ft.

THE CENTRAL PLATEAU

The center of Mexico is a huge, high plateau that is open to the north but bounded by two large mountain chains: the Sierra Madre Oriental to the east and the Sierra Madre Occidental to the west. This plateau forms around half of Mexico and slopes down from the west to the east. To the south the plateau rises to form a region that is crossed by many mountains

▲ Cancún is a major vacation resort found just off the east coast of the Yucatán peninsula. Growing from a small island village in the 1970s, it now has more than 30,000 hotel rooms and attracts tourists from around the world.

and volcanoes. Lying between the cities of Veracruz and Puebla is Citlaltépetl, a volcano that is the country's highest point. On the far side of the mountain ranges from the plateau the land forms huge, low-lying coastal plains. The plains facing the Gulf of Mexico are fringed with swamps, lagoons, and sandbars. Mexico's largest lake is Lake Chapala, which covers approximately 670 sq. mi. and is found near Guadalajara, Mexico's second-largest city. The country's longest river, the Rio Grande (also known as the Rio Bravo del Norte), forms more than 1,240 mi. of border between Texas and Mexico before emptying into the Gulf of Mexico.

▲ A busy market day for local Mexicans in the south of the country. Mexican markets, known as *mercados*, exist all over the country and are a major way in which goods are traded between local people.

HOT AND COLD LAND

From snow-covered mountain peaks to hot, dry deserts and lush, wet rain forests, Mexico has a varied range of landscapes and climates. Climate changes with both the height of the land and its latitude. Land below 2,979 ft. is known as *tierra caliente* (hot land), between 2,979–5,892 ft. is *tierra templada* (temperate land), and above 5,892 ft., *tierra fría* (cold land). Mexico City lies in the *tierra templada* and has a cool, dry climate with only a small variation in temperature. In the north of Mexico temperature extremes are much greater, with a maximum of more than 113°F. This intense heat, along with low rainfall, creates vast desert and semidesert areas. Much of central and southern Mexico is also dry, and rainfall is heavy only in the tropical regions to the far south and southeast. The wettest areas are to the south and in the Yucatán; they can receive more than 120 in. of rainfall per year.

MEXICO'S PEOPLE

Mexico has been home to a number of ancient civilizations, including the Olmecs, the Maya, and the Aztecs. The Aztecs settled in Mexico around A.D. 1200 and built their capital city, Tenochtitlán, where Mexico City now stands. Most of their civilization was destroyed by the Spanish in the early 1500s. Native Americans make up approximately 30 percent of Mexico's population of 103.4 million. The largest group are mestizos, people of mixed Spanish and Native American origin, who form around 60 percent of the population. The mixture of European and Native groups contribute to Mexico's rich culture.

▼ Ancient Mayan people lived throughout large parts of Mexico and left behind many impressive structures and sites. This ancient Mayan pyramid is called the Temple of the Inscriptions. It is found at Palenque, 68 mi. southeast of the city of Villahermosa.

37

GUATEMALA

Guatemala is a mountainous country that experiences both earthquakes and volcanic activity. It contains the largest continuous area of rain forest in Central America.

Area: 41,900 sq. mi.
Population: 13,314,079
Capital: Guatemala City (3,366,000)
Main languages spoken: Spanish, Mayan languages
Main religion: Roman Catholic
Currency: quetzal
Main exports: coffee, sugar, bananas, vegetable seeds, legumes
Type of government: republic

▼ Lying between Mazatenango and Guatemala City, Lake Atitlán fills part of a large sunken crater, or caldera, created by an enormous volcanic explosion.

Almost two thirds of Guatemala are covered in mountains. There are two main mountain ranges that cross the country. To the north is a series of older mountains that have been heavily eroded yet still stand almost 10,000 ft. in height in some places. To the south the mountains are younger and contain more than 30 volcanoes, three of which are still active. Soil mixed with volcanic ash has washed down from the Sierra Madre mountains to create a narrow plain of excellent growing land along Guatemala's Pacific coast. Although it lies in the tropics, the cooler seas it borders and its range of high- and low-lying land create a number of different climates. On the Pacific coast temperatures tend to average over 86°F, while in the highlands above 5,900 ft. temperatures between 50°F–60°F are more common. The dry season is when most of the country's 850,000 tourists visit. Most tourists are from the U.S. and Mexico.

EL PETÉN

Approximately one third of Guatemala is made up of low-lying land in the northern region called El Petén. This area consists of plains and small, knobby hills made largely of limestone rocks. Dense rain forests cover most of the region, providing habitats for a great variety of creatures, including the jaguar. This big cat is the largest predator in Central America. Few rivers run through El Petén since most of the rainfall it receives drains underground. Transportation links are sparse, although a major road and airport connect the region's main town, Flores, with the rest of the country.

THE PEOPLE OF GUATEMALA

Guatemala was the center of the ancient Maya civilization, which flourished between A.D. 300 and A.D. 900. Almost half of all Guatemalans are descendants of the ancient Maya and other native Indian peoples, while just over half are mestizos—people of mixed Indian and European origins. Farming dominates the lives of 60 percent of the workforce. Cereals and fruits are grown for local use, and coffee is the most important export crop. The country is also one of the world's largest producers of cardamom seeds, a popular spice. After many decades of dictators ruling without elections, as well as violent civil wars, Guatemala is currently peaceful but faces problems in health care and education. For example, 39 percent of adult women cannot read or write.

◄ Approximately 1.7 percent of Guatemala's rain forests, home to a large range of wildlife, is removed every year for its timber and to clear new land for farming.

BELIZE

Bordering the Caribbean Sea, the small country of Belize contains a varied mixture of landscapes and peoples. It became independent in 1981.

Area: 8,800 sq. mi.
Population: 262,999
Capital: Belmopan (9,000)
Main languages spoken: English, Spanish, Mayan, Garifuna (Carib)
Main religions: Roman Catholic, Protestant
Currency: Belize dollar
Main exports: sugar, orange and grapefruit juice, bananas, fish, clothes
Type of government: parliamentary democracy

► Keen-billed toucan

Known as British Honduras until 1973, Belize is a country of two distinct geographical sections. The northern half, which borders Mexico, is mainly low-lying and contains many swamps close to the coast. The southern half begins with grassy savannas and rises to mountain ranges. Over 40 percent of Belize is covered in forests that flourish in the country's subtropical climate. The forests provide hardwoods such as mahogany, rosewood and chicle, the gum of which is used to make chewing gum. Off Belize's coastline is a chain of coral reefs and small sandy islands called cays.
Running for approximately 1,809 mi., this chain is the largest coral reef in the Western Hemisphere. Several hundred thousand tourists visit Belize every year, mainly for its beaches and the reef but also for its historic sites. Belize was once a part of the Mayan empire, and many ancient sites remain. Its people are a mixture of many cultures, with mestizos and creoles accounting for 75 percent. More than half of the people live in rural areas, where they work in forestry or grow sugarcane, citrus fruits, corn, and rice. Although Belmopan is the official capital city, Belize City is much larger, and around 20 percent of Belize's total population live there.

▼ El Castillo is part of an ancient Mayan site found in the mountainous west of the country.

HONDURAS

The third-largest country in Central America, Honduras is dominated by mountain ranges. It borders Nicaragua, Guatemala, and El Salvador.

Area: 432,00 sq. mi.
Population: 6,560,608
Capital: Tegucigalpa (980,000)
Main language spoken: Spanish
Main religion: Roman Catholic
Currency: lempira
Main exports: coffee, bananas, shrimp and lobsters, zinc, frozen meat
Type of government: republic

Honduras has a long coastline with the Caribbean Sea and a short coast alongside the Pacific Ocean. The Caribbean coast features several important ports, including Le Ceiba and, offshore, the Bay Islands (Islas de la Bahia), which are popular tourist destinations. The country's lowland areas are found near the coasts and in large river valleys that crisscross the highlands of Honduras. Much of the country is mountainous. The highest mountains are found in the western and central areas and were created by volcanic activity. In the hot, humid lowland areas rain forests cover large stretches of land. On the mountains forests of oak and pine trees dominate.

A DEVELOPING NATION

Honduras is less industrialized than its neighbors, and its people are among the poorest in the Western world. Foreign aid and investment have helped to set up food-processing plants, as well as industries producing rum, cooking oil, cement, and paper. The country's mountains contain vast deposits of metal ores, particularly, silver, zinc, lead, and gold. Underground mines have been excavated to extract these metals for industry. Most people farm land or work for owners of large plantations on which bananas, coffee, and exotic fruits and flowers are grown for sale overseas. Honduras was once the world's leading exporter of bananas, and this crop still accounts for almost 25 percent of the country's income. Much of the highland areas are unsuitable for farming, but the terrain allows 80 percent of the country's electricity to be generated by hydroelectric plants, harnessing the power of falling water.

▲ Discovered by Christopher Columbus in 1512, the Bay Islands lie in the Caribbean Sea off the north coast of Honduras and attract many tourists and divers.

▶ Many Hondurans work on plantations owned by foreign companies growing coffee and bananas. These women, employed by the U.S.-owned Chiquita company, are washing bananas.

EL SALVADOR

The smallest nation in Central America,
El Salvador's landscape is a mixture of
lowlands and high volcanic mountains.

Area: 8,000 sq. mi.
Population: 6,353,681
Capital: San Salvador
(1,381,000)
Main language spoken:
Spanish
Main religion: Roman
Catholic
Currency: colon
Main exports: coffee,
paper and paper products,
clothing, pharmaceuticals,
sugar
Type of government:
republic

E l Salvador is bordered
to the east and north by
Honduras and to the west by
Guatemala. Behind its 198-mi.-long
coast with the Pacific Ocean the land
forms a narrow coastal plain before rising
to a large central plateau dominated by
several chains of mountains, around 20
volcanoes, and deep valleys. More than
280 rivers and large streams flow across the
country, mostly carrying water to the Pacific
Ocean. Of all the Central America nations
south of Mexico, El Salvador has the least
amount of forests. In the past much of
the land would have been covered in trees,
but many years of clearing the land for
agriculture now mean that only around
six percent of the land remains forested.

NATURAL RESOURCES

El Salvador's mountainous backbone
has been settled by native Indian people
for many thousands of years. The slopes
of the volcanic mountains were covered
in nutrient-rich soils that have attracted
farmers since the earliest times. El Salvador
has little in the way of mineral resources
such as gold, iron, or oil. The mountains
and hills, however, do help generate much
of the country's electricity. Fast-falling

▼ Pineapples are one of a
number of fruits, including
avocados, mangoes, and
papaya, grown in the rich
soils of El Salvador.

▲ San Salvador is El Salvador's capital and largest city.
The World Bank estimates that 48 percent of the country's
entire population live in extreme poverty. Many of these
people live in slums in San Salvador and other cities.

water turns turbines in hydroelectric
power plants to generate around two thirds
of El Salvador's electricity. A further ten
percent is created by a large geothermal
power plant. This taps into the heat
below Earth's surface.

RICH AND POOR

El Salvador is the most densely
populated country in Central America
with an approximate average of 794 people
per square mile. The vast majority are
mestizos—people of mixed native Indian
and European descent. For many years
just 14 families owned 75 percent of
the country's land, but reforms are now
changing that, and small plots of land are
being handed over to many more people.
After a devastating 13-year civil war that
ended in 1991 the gap between the rich
and poor remains large, with wealth
still concentrated in the hands of a few
people. The U.S. is El Salvador's main trading
partner and is responsible for 40 percent of
its imports and 20 percent of its exports,
which include clothing, machinery, and cash
crops such as fruits, coffee, and sugarcane.

NICARAGUA

Nicaragua is considered one of the most beautiful countries in Central America, but earthquakes and human conflict have left their mark.

Area: 46,400 sq. mi.
Population: 5,023,818
Capital: Managua (1,039,000)
Main language spoken: Spanish
Main religion: Roman Catholic
Currency: gold cordoba
Main exports: cotton, coffee, meat, chemicals, sugar
Type of government: republic

▼ Nicaragua's capital city, Managua, lies on the southern shore of Lake Managua. The city was badly damaged by earthquakes in 1931 and 1972. Parts of its center have never been rebuilt.

Nicaragua has a varied landscape with dramatic variations in terrain throughout the country. The eastern region of Nicaragua, bordering the Caribbean Sea, is known as the Mosquito Coast (Costa de Mosquitos). Partially covered in rain forests and featuring many lagoons and river deltas, this area is a coastal plain that extends more than 43 mi. inland from the sea. The western side of Nicaragua has a drier climate and is mainly savanna grasslands and some forests. In between are two long chains of mountains that contain more than 40 volcanoes. These volcanoes are partly responsible for the great amount of earthquake activity that Nicaragua experiences. In 1992, for example, a large earthquake made 16,000 people homeless. Nicaragua has a tropical climate with a wet season between May and October. Parts of Nicaragua receive more than 124 in. of rainfall each year. The eastern side of Nicaragua has been hit by hurricanes on many occasions. In 1998, for example, Hurricane Mitch (which also devastated El Salvador and caused a lot of damage in Honduras) took the lives of over 1,800 Nicaraguans and also destroyed much of the country's banana, sugar, and coffee crops.

LIVING NEAR THE LAKES

The southern part of Nicaragua is dominated by a giant basin in which lie Lake Managua and Lake Nicaragua, the largest lake in Central America. Lake Nicaragua is 110 mi. long and is 36 mi. wide at its widest point. The lake contains more than 400 islands, and their picturesque location makes them popular visitor destinations. It is the only freshwater lake in the world to contain a number of sea fish, including swordfish and sharks. Research shows that these fish came from the Caribbean Sea and made their way to the lake via the San Juan river, one of four main rivers that flow from the lake. Most of Nicaragua's population live and work in the lowlands between the Pacific Ocean and the shores of Lake Nicaragua and Lake Managua. The soil in this region is rich in nutrients, and crops, including cotton, corn, rice, bananas, and beans, are grown for local markets and for export.

TROUBLES

Nicaragua has suffered from many natural disasters such as hurricanes and earthquakes. It has also experienced many years of civil war, local conflicts, and unrest. The Somoza family, who ruled for more than 40 years, was overthrown in 1979, and the Sandinista government that replaced them was removed from power in 1990. Years of troubles have left Nicaragua's public services in poor condition, and shortages of food and clean water are common. To generate revenue Nicaragua is developing more industries, as well as exploiting its natural reserves of gold, silver, and copper.

COSTA RICA

Costa Rica is one of the most peaceful and prosperous of the Central American nations. Growing coffee is the mainstay of rural life in this country.

Area: 19,600 sq. mi.
Population: 3,834,934
Capital: San José (983,000)
Main language spoken: Spanish
Main religion: Roman Catholic
Currency: Costa Rican colon
Main exports: bananas, coffee, textiles and clothing, fish, flowers
Type of government: republic

Costa Rica spans the width of the narrow Central America isthmus. The land on both coasts tends to be low-lying. The eastern side receives more rain than the western, but both coastal areas have a number of mangrove swamps and white, sandy beaches. The land rises from the coasts in the center and south, with high, rugged mountains created by volcanic activity. Between the main mountain ranges lies a large plateau on which the majority of Costa Ricans live. The country has a tropical climate with relatively heavy rainfall. Its rain forests cover around one third of its land and help provide homes for an abundance of plant and animal life.

PEOPLE AND PROSPERITY

Costa Rica's population is unusual in the region in that they are mainly of European descent. Native Indians account for less than one percent of the total population, while around three percent of people are black. Agriculture occupies most of its workforce, with sales of bananas and coffee earning the country around 50 percent of its income. Costa Rica generates the majority of its electricity using hydroelectric power. The mining of metal ores, particularly bauxite, is becoming more important, as is tourism. Since its 1948 civil war Costa Rica has largely been a nation at peace. It has the most extensive welfare state in Central

▲ Costa Rica was the first country in the region to grow and export coffee. Coffee growing on plantations supports around half of the population and has been the country's leading export for more than 100 years.

America. Compulsory education is free up until the age of 15, and Costa Rica is home to the University of Central America. The country has a well-developed health care system to which it devotes almost 25 percent of its total expenditure. As a result, Costa Ricans have a life expectancy of just over 76 years, the best in Central America. However, the country does have economic problems. Reduced U.S. aid, the rising price of imported oil, and falling prices for coffee and bananas, which it exports, have caused large debts to build up.

▲ The macaw is just one of 725 different species of birds found in Costa Rica.

► Here is a local fruit market in Costa Rica. Bananas are one of the country's major export earners.

PANAMA

The small country of Panama links the continents of North and South America. Its 50-mi.-long canal also links the Pacific and Atlantic oceans.

Area: 29,300 sq. mi.
Population: 32,882,329
Capital: Panama City (1,202,000)
Main languages spoken: Spanish, English
Main religions: Roman Catholic, Protestant
Currency: balboa (U.S. currency is also legal tender)
Main exports: bananas, shrimp, coffee, clothing, fish
Type of government: constitutional republic

Panama occupies a relatively narrow strip of land, known as an isthmus, bordered by the Caribbean Sea to the east and the Pacific Ocean to the west. Two sets of mountains run the length of Panama, and between these ranges are many low-lying hills, lakes, and more than 400 rivers and streams. Panama has a tropical climate with particularly heavy rainfall on its eastern side. There lush rain forests grow, and Panama is home to more than 2,000 species of tropical plants. On its western, Pacific side the land tends to receive less rainfall, and scrub forests are common. The scrub forests of Darien National Park in the south of Panama are virtually uninhabited and untouched by humans. Panama's coastline is indented by many bays and lagoons.

THE PANAMA CANAL

One of the biggest engineering feats in the world, the Panama Canal was finally opened in 1914. The canal and its dredged entrances stretch 50 mi. through Panama, linking the Atlantic and Pacific oceans. To sail between these oceans without using the canal involves a 7,440-mi.-long trip around the southernmost tip of South America. More than 14,000 individual journeys through the canal are made by ships every year, and the tolls that are paid are a major source of income for Panama. Traffic can travel in both directions, and three sets of giant locks raise and lower the water level, altering it by 85 ft. during the course of the journey. The canal was built by the U.S., which assisted Panama in obtaining independence from Colombia in 1903. At the end of 1999, following a 20-year handover period, full control of the canal was passed to Panama.

AN INTERNATIONAL GATEWAY

The Panama Canal has made the country an international gateway for shipping, trade, and finance. Panama has a free-trade zone around the canal, and tax-free banking attracts customers from all over the world. Panama also has one of the largest fleets of merchant ships in the world. Most of these ships are registered in Panama but are owned by foreign companies.

The warm climate and fertile soil allow the rural population of Panama to grow enough food for the country to be largely self-sufficient. Rice, corn, and beans are the main staple crops, with bananas, coffee, and sugar grown for export abroad. Shrimp is also an important export product.

▲ Due to its shipping and banking interests and also because of the revenue collected from running the Panama Canal, Panama City, the country's capital, is one of the wealthiest cities in the entire Central American region.

▲ The Miraflores Locks on the Panama Canal raise or drop 55 ft.—the difference between the elevation of the waters of Miraflores Lake and the Pacific Ocean.

THE CARIBBEAN AND SOUTH AMERICA

THE CARIBBEAN

The Caribbean islands form a broken bridge of land 1,984 mi. long between the South American country of Venezuela and the southeastern U.S. state of Florida. The islands form a boundary separating the Atlantic Ocean from the Caribbean Sea. The region's climate is largely tropical, with most islands experiencing a wet season between June and November. The Caribbean is also one of the regions most at risk from the threat of hurricanes. The Carribean is comprised of three groups of islands. The Bahamas are the most northerly; the Lesser Antilles, which include the islands of Antigua & Barbuda, Grenada, and Trinidad & Tobago are the most easterly; while the Greater Antilles contain the largest islands such as Cuba, Jamaica, and the large island of Hispaniola shared by the states of Haiti and the Dominican Republic. The region is named after some of the earliest known inhabitants of the area, the Carib people. In 1492 Christopher Columbus and his crew became the first European visitors when they landed in the Bahamas. He mistakenly thought he had reached Asia, which led to the region being called the West Indies. In the centuries since Columbus's discovery most of the Caribbean has seen colonial rule by the Spanish, French, British, Danish, and Dutch.

▶ These Cuban workers are harvesting tobacco, a major crop in Cuba and several other Caribbean islands. Cuba, with a land area of 42,800 sq. mi., comprises almost half the total land area of the Caribbean region.

◀ The landscape and climate of the U.S. Virgin Islands make it a popular tourist destination. Sandy beaches often fringed with palm trees are found throughout the Caribbean.

Gulf of
Mexico

Andros Island

BAHAMAS

CUBA

G r e a t e r

*Cayman Islands
(to U.K.)*

Turks & Caicos Islands
(to U.K.)

ATLANTIC

OCEAN

HAITI **DOMINICAN
REPUBLIC**

Hispaniola

JAMAICA

A n t i l l e s

*Puerto Rico
(to U.S.)*

Virgin Islands (to U.S.)

*Netherland Antilles
(to Netherlands)*

*British Virgin Islands
(to U.K.)*

*Anguilla
(to U.K.)*

*St. Martin
(to France &
to Netherlands)*

**ST. KITTS
& NEVIS**

*Montserrat
(to U.K.)*

**ANTIGUA
& BARBUDA**

Guadeloupe (to France)

DOMINICA

Martinique (to France)

ST. LUCIA

BARBADOS

**ST. VINCENT &
THE GRENADINES**

L e s s e r A n t i l l e s

*Aruba
(to Netherlands)*

C a r i b b e a n

S e a

0   400   800 km
0   200   400 miles

*Netherlands Antilles
(to Netherlands)*

GRENADA

Tobago

**TRINIDAD
& TOBAGO**

Trinidad

▼ Vacation cruise ships dock at New Providence island in the Bahamas. Many Caribbean islands depend on tourism for a large part of their revenue.

CUBA

Cuba is the largest, most varied, and one of the most beautiful of all Caribbean islands. Long but narrow, it lies just 89 mi. south of the state of Florida.

Area: 42,800 sq. mi.
Population: 11,224,321
Capital: Havana (2,268,000)
Main language spoken: Spanish
Main religion: Roman Catholic
Currency: Cuban peso
Main exports: sugar, minerals (nickel and chromite), fish products, tobacco
Type of government: communist state

▼ This old steam train is carrying harvested sugarcane to a refinery. Sugar is an important export for Cuba, and in 2000 36 million tons were produced.

Cuba extends approximately 781 mi. roughly east to west, and its widest point measures 118 mi. It is separated from mainland United States by the Straits of Florida and from the island of Hispaniola by the Windward Passage. Its closest neighbor is Jamaica, 86 mi. away. Hundreds of natural bays, reefs, and peninsulas give Cuba a shoreline of 2,316 mi. Its territory includes one major island, the Isla de la Juventud (Island of Youth), and many tiny islets.

Cuba is less mountainous than its neighbors in the Greater Antilles, with around one fourth of its land covered in high elevations. The main mountain system of the Caribbean crosses southeastern Cuba, where it is called the Sierra Maestra. Most of the remainder of Cuba is lowlands. Cuba is part of a limestone platform related to the limestone areas of the Yucatán peninsula in Mexico, in Florida, and in the Bahamas. The country's longest river, the Cuoto, runs west to east and passes 12 mi. north of Bayamo. However, only small boats are able to navigate it.

▲ Tobacco grown in Cuba is used to make the country's world-famous cigars. In 1998 Cuba exported 180 million cigars. Today only the most expensive are hand rolled.

FARMING IN CUBA

Around 80 percent of Cuba's soil has been created by the action of rainfall on red limestone, producing deep, fertile soil. Around 20 percent of the land is covered with forests of pine and mahogany. Much of the remainder is pastureland for the country's 4.6 million cattle or cropland. Cuba has a mostly hot climate with heavy seasonal rainfall, and many crops flourish, including rice, coffee, citrus fruits, and tobacco, which is used to make its world-famous cigars. The country's chief crop, however, is sugar and has been so for over a century. Cuba is the world's third-largest sugar producer, and sugar sales account for almost 50 percent of its exports.

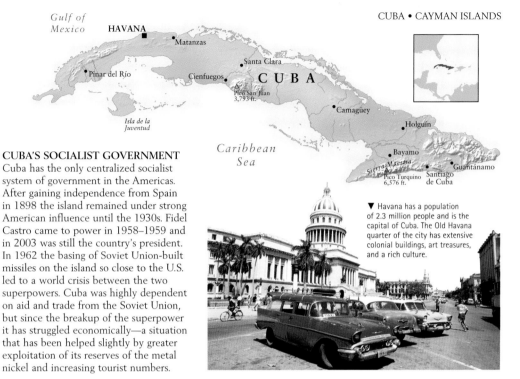

Gulf of Mexico

HAVANA ■
● Matanzas

● Pinar del Río

Cienfuegos ● ● Santa Clara

C U B A

△ Pico San Juan 3,793 ft.

Isla de la Juventud

● Camagüey

● Holguín

Caribbean Sea

● Bayamo

Sierra Maestra ● Guantánamo

Pico Turquino 6,576 ft. ● Santiago de Cuba

CUBA'S SOCIALIST GOVERNMENT

Cuba has the only centralized socialist system of government in the Americas. After gaining independence from Spain in 1898 the island remained under strong American influence until the 1930s. Fidel Castro came to power in 1958–1959 and in 2003 was still the country's president. In 1962 the basing of Soviet Union-built missiles on the island so close to the U.S. led to a world crisis between the two superpowers. Cuba was highly dependent on aid and trade from the Soviet Union, but since the breakup of the superpower it has struggled economically—a situation that has been helped slightly by greater exploitation of its reserves of the metal nickel and increasing tourist numbers.

▼ Havana has a population of 2.3 million people and is the capital of Cuba. The Old Havana quarter of the city has extensive colonial buildings, art treasures, and a rich culture.

CAYMAN ISLANDS

World-renowned for its beautiful beaches, the three islands that comprise the Caymans lie approximately 180 mi. northwest of Jamaica.

Cayman Islands (to U.K.)

Little Cayman *Cayman Brac*

Grand Cayman

Caribbean Sea

George Town ● ● Bodden Town

Area: 102 sq. mi.
Population: 36,273
Capital: George Town (25,000)
Main language spoken: English
Main religions: Anglican, Roman Catholic
Currency: Cayman Islands dollar
Main exports: manufactured consumer goods, turtle products
Type of government: dependency of U.K.

The Cayman Islands consist of Cayman Brac, Little Cayman, and Grand Cayman, the largest of the group. All three islands are low-lying, feature excellent beaches, and are fringed by spectacular coral reefs that are home to a rich range of marine life. Mangrove swamps cover a little under one third of the land, although there are no natural streams on any of the islands. Among the vegetation found on the islands are coconut palms and banana, mango, and breadfruit trees. Turtles raised on a government turtle farm provide food, shell, and leather, which is sometimes fashioned into souvenirs for the Cayman's large number of tourist visitors. Cayman Brac is approximately 12 mi. long and 1 mi. wide. Its land is riddled with caves and

dozens of shipwrecks, which are popular sites for divers. Little Cayman is only around 5 mi. long, and much of its area is given over to a wildlife sanctuary for iguanas and wild birds. More than half of the Cayman Islands' population is located in its capital, George Town, where more than 500 bank offices from many countries take advantage of the Cayman Islands' low levels of taxation. The Caymans were administered by Jamaica from 1863. When Jamaica became independent in 1962, they remained a British dependency. The governor of the islands, who represents Great Britain, works with a legislative assembly that consists of 18 members, 15 of whom are elected.

JAMAICA

Jamaica is a mixture of mountainous and lowland regions that are relatively densely populated. It lies around 90 mi. km south of Cuba.

Area: 4,200 sq. mi.
Population: 2,680,029
Capital: Kingston (672,000)
Main language spoken: English
Main religions: Protestant, Roman Catholic
Currency: Jamaican dollar
Main exports: bauxite, agricultural products, food, beverages, tobacco
Type of government: parliamentary democracy

▼ Kingston's bustling Coronation Market is where many Jamaicans sell a wide range of farm produce, including peppers, bananas, tobacco, yams, and mangoes. Jamaica grows almost the entire world supply of allspice.

J amaica has beaches like many other Caribbean islands, but much of its land is mountainous. In the northwest limestone rock forms a series of steep ridges and flat basins that have many sinkholes. To the northeast the land rises to form the island's main mountain range. Called the Blue Mountains, the highest of its summits, Blue Mountain Peak, is also the highest point in the Caribbean. The lowlands are largely covered in farms, with sugar being the country's major crop. In 2000 around 2.5 million tons were produced. Agriculture employs around one fifth of the Jamaican workforce, and the island has over 440,000 goats and a similar number of cattle. Mining is one of Jamaica's most important industries. Bauxite—an ore from which aluminum is extracted—has been mined on the island since the 1950s, and aluminum ore and products account for more than 60 percent of the country's exports. Tourism is vital, with over 1.5 million visitors to the island in 2001.

KINGSTON

Kingston is the capital of Jamaica and is the largest English-speaking city in the entire Caribbean. It is the center of government of the island, which is divided into 14 parishes. The city was founded in 1692 after an earthquake destroyed much of the capital at that time, Port Royal. Kingston is situated on one of the largest natural harbors in the world and is overlooked by a highland area. The city is a busy port, a manufacturing center for clothing and food processing, and a tourist destination for cruise ships. The city's architecture is a mixture of traditional colonial buildings, modern tower blocks, rich mansions, and poor slum areas. Reggae music developed particularly in the deprived areas of Kingston and made reggae musician Bob Marley a world-famous Jamaican.

THE BAHAMAS

One of the most prosperous states in the region, the Bahamas are a collection of 700 islands, plus 2,000 rocky islets, located in the northwestern Caribbean.

Area: 3,900 sq. mi.
Population: 300,529
Capital: Nassau (220,000)
Main language spoken: English
Main religions: Baptist, Roman Catholic, Anglican
Currency: Bahamian dollar
Main exports: petroleum, crayfish, machinery and transportation equipment, salt
Type of government: independent commonwealth

An island archipelago, the Bahamas are spread over 144,460 sq. mi. of ocean, with the closest neighboring landmasses being the state of Florida and, to the south, Cuba. Most of the islands are low-lying with mangrove swamps and reefs around their edges. The islands have no rivers but contain many tropical plants including orchids and jasmine, as well as a rich bird life. Thousands of tourists are attracted to the Bahamas for

the scenery, beaches, and warm climate. Average daily temperatures rarely slip below 64°F, even in the winter. Only around 40 of the 700 islands are inhabited. Andros is the largest of the islands, while Grand Bahama is the site of much of the Bahamas' industry, especially around the town of Freeport. Over half of the Bahamas' population live in Nassau, its capital.

◀ Beautiful palm-fringed beaches, clear seas, and a year-round warm climate attract visitors to the Bahamas.

TURKS & CAICOS ISLANDS

The Turks & Caicos are two island groups whose cays and islands rise more than 6,550 ft. from the sea floor. They are a British crown colony.

Area: 193 sq. mi.
Population: 18,378
Capital: Cockburn Town (5,000)
Main language spoken: English
Main religions: Anglican, Methodist
Currency: U.S. dollar
Main exports: salt, lobster, fish
Type of government: dependency of U.K.

The Turks & Caicos Islands are an extension of the Bahamas chain and consist of eight major islands and over 30 largely uninhabited cays. The two island groups are separated by a 22-mi.-wide trench called the Turks Island Passage, which is over 7,202 ft. deep. Much of the land is sandy and rocky and covered in scrubs and cacti. The Turks Islands get their name from the turk's head cactus that grows on the islands. The climate is warm and constant, averaging between 75–90°F throughout the year. Rainfall averages between 22–29 in. per year, and drinking water is relatively scarce. Irrigation and careful management of the

available water allow crops, including beans, corn, and citrus fruits, to be grown. In 1678 salt traders from Bermuda started to clear much of the island to create salinas—salt-drying pans—in which salt was dried and then taken on ships and traded. Salt remained a key industry until the 1960s, but today tourism, fishing, and financial services are the main sources of revenue.

HAITI

Occupying the western third of the tropical island of Hispaniola, Haiti has few natural resources, and agriculture forms the basis of its economy.

Area: 10,600 sq. mi.
Population: 7,063,722
Capital: Port-au-Prince (1,838,000)
Main languages spoken: Haitian Creole, French
Main religions: Roman Catholic, Protestant, voodoo
Currency: gourde
Main exports: textiles and clothing, handicrafts, coffee, manufactures
Government: republic

Haiti is mountainous, with five distinct mountain ranges separated by deep valleys and plains. The lowland areas are densely populated, with around 80 percent of the country's population living in rural areas. Around one third of Haiti's land can be farmed, and most farms are small plots on which families grow only enough to feed themselves. The most common subsistence crops are corn, bananas, and cassava. Larger estates and plantations exist where crops, including coffee, sisal, and sugar, are grown for export. Much of Haiti's farmland suffers from soil erosion, and large tracts of its forest areas have been removed to create new farmlands and to produce charcoal. Ninety-five percent of its people are descendants of black slaves employed

▶ Haitians are the poorest people in the entire Caribbean. Many live in slums, such as Cité Soleil, around the fringes of Haiti's capital city, Port-au-Prince.

to grow sugarcane by the Spanish and the French colonial powers. In 1804 a slave revolt enabled Haiti to gain independence from France, and it became the first independent nation in the Caribbean.

DOMINICAN REPUBLIC

Occupying the western two thirds of Hispaniola, the Dominican Republic is the second-largest and second-most-populous country in the Caribbean.

Area: 18,700 sq. mi.
Population: 8,721,594
Capital: Santo Domingo (2,629,000)
Main language spoken: Spanish
Main religion: Roman Catholic
Currency: Dominican peso
Main exports: nickel, raw sugar, coffee, gold
Government: republic

The Dominican Republic is a mountainous country, with large areas of fertile lands in valleys between the peaks and in the lower-lying lands near the coast. A wide range of crops is grown on these lands, including tobacco, sugar, and cocoa. In 2000 1.29 million tons of fruits and berries were harvested. The Dominican Republic has the largest and fastest-growing economy in the Caribbean. Large reserves of ores containing nickel and gold are mined, while construction and telecommunications industries have expanded at a rapid rate. Tourism has also increased in importance, with many vacation cruise ships stopping in its natural harbors. The country has established a

number of free-trade zones within its borders. Overseas companies employ more than 200,000 people, making clothes, footwear, and electronic goods. The land was twice visited by Christopher Columbus, and the city of Santo Domingo was established in 1496 by his brother, Bartholomew. It is the oldest European settlement in the entire Americas. Today Santo Domingo is the capital of the Dominican Republic, with more than 2.6 million inhabitants in its metropolitan area.

PUERTO RICO

The most easterly of the Greater Antilles Islands, Puerto Rico is a mountainous island with a tropical climate and rich plant life.

ATLANTIC OCEAN

Puerto Rico (to U.S.)

San Juan
Bayamón • Carolina
Cerro de Punta 4,389 ft. • Caguas
Mayagüez • *Cordillera Central*
Ponce
Isla de Culebra
Isla de Vieques

Caribbean Sea

Area: 5,324 sq. mi.
Population: 8,721,594
Capital: San Juan (2,629,000)
Main languages spoken: Spanish, English
Main religion: Roman Catholic
Currency: U.S. dollar
Main exports: chemicals and chemical products, food (particularly sugar, coffee, and vegetables)
Government: dependency of U.S.

Puerto Rico is separated from the Dominican Republic by a stretch of the Caribbean called the Mona Passage. Part of a key shipping lane to and from the Panama Canal, the island has benefited from shipping and trade industries, especially since its capital city, San Juan, is located on the site of one of the largest natural harbors in the Caribbean. Around three fifths of the country is mountainous, with coastal lowlands in which dairy farming and coffee growing are the most important farming activities. The island was claimed by the explorer Christopher Columbus in 1493 and was

a Spanish colony until 1898 when the U.S. gained control. Many U.S. businesses have invested in the island, and the economy is increasingly reliant on manufacturing and service industries. Eighty-nine percent of the island's exports go to the U.S.

▶ These Puerto Ricans are working in a rum distillery on the island. Rum uses sugar as its principal ingredient, and the alcoholic drink is exported to many countries.

VIRGIN ISLANDS

Lying east of Puerto Rico, these islands form the economically strong dependency of the U.S. and the smaller, less prosperous British Virgin Islands dependency.

for three fourths of revenue. The economy of the U.S. Virgin Islands is also largely based on tourism, with more than one million visitors per year. Bought from Denmark by the U.S. in 1917, the U.S. Virgin Islands consist of many small, hilly, volcanic islands. A giant oil refinery located on St. Croix accounts for almost all of the islands' exports.

Virgin Islands (U.S.)

Area: 171 sq. mi.
Population: 123,498
Capital: Charlotte Amalie (28,000)
Main language spoken: English
Main religions: Baptist, Roman Catholic
Currency: U.S. dollar
Main exports: refined petroleum, rum, watches, fragrances
Type of government: dependency of U.S.

British Virgin Islands

Area: 59 sq. mi.
Population: 21,272
Capital: Road Town (8,500)
Main language spoken: English
Main religions: Anglican, Roman Catholic
Currency: U.S. dollar
Main exports: fish, gravel, fruit
Type of government: self-governing dependency of U.K.

The largest of the British Virgin Islands, Tortola is the location of the island group's capital, Road Town. Most of the islands are of volcanic origin, with the exception of the second-largest, Anegada, which is a coral and limestone atoll. The islanders engage in rum making, raising livestock, and fishing, but tourism accounts

ATLANTIC OCEAN

British Virgin Islands (to U.K.)
Anegada
Virgin Gorda
St. Thomas
Tortola • Road Town
Charlotte Amalie • St. John

Virgin Islands (to U.S.)

St. Croix • Christiansted
Frederiksted •

Caribbean Sea

ST. KITTS & NEVIS

The first British colonies in the Caribbean since the 1620s, St. Kitts & Nevis is a federation formed by a pair of islands separated by a two-mile-wide channel.

Area: 139 sq. mi.
Population: 38,736
Capital: Basseterre (12,000)
Main languages spoken:
English, English Creole
Main religion: Protestant
Currency: East Caribbean dollar
Main exports: electronic goods, sugar, foodstuffs
Type of government: constitutional monarchy

Both the islands of St. Kitts & Nevis were formed by volcanic activity, and both feature a high volcanic peak at their center. The islands bask in a tropical climate with high rainfall, but both have been hit by a number of hurricanes that have caused widespread damage. Although much land has been cleared for farming, there are large areas of rain forests, wetlands, and grasslands in which a great variety of plants and creatures live. St. Kitts & Nevis has little mineral or energy resources. Almost all fuel for energy has to be imported, mainly in the form of oil from Mexico and Venezuela. St. Kitts, the larger of the two islands, is also the home of the capital,

Basseterre, which is an important port and receives much trade from cruise ships. Charlestown is the largest town on Nevis. Once inhabited by Carib and Arawak Indians, the population of St. Kitts & Nevis is now almost entirely of African or mixed African-European descent. The islands gained independence from Great Britain in 1983, and in 1998 a vote for Nevis to withdraw from the federation just failed to gain the necessary two-thirds majority.

Below: A worker harvests sugarcane on the Caribbean island of St. Kitts. Sugar is a major export earner for the federation of St. Kitts & Nevis.

ANGUILLA AND MONTSERRAT

Anguilla is a flat limestone coral island, while Montserrat is more mountainous and features seven active volcanoes. Both are British dependencies.

Anguilla

Area: 60 sq. mi.
Population: 12,446
Capital: The Valley (800)
Main language spoken: English
Main religions: Anglican, Roman Catholic
Currency: East Caribbean dollar
Main exports: lobsters, fish, livestock, salt
Type of government: dependency of U.K.

Montserrat

Area: 32 sq. mi.
Population: 8,437
Temporary capital: Plymouth (2,000)
Main language spoken: English
Main religions: Anglican, Methodist
Currency: East Caribbean dollar
Main exports: electronic components, food, cattle
Type of government: dependency of U.K.

First occupied by British settlers in 1650, the present-day population of Anguilla is mainly descendants of African and European peoples. Anguilla's income is derived from lobster fishing, salt mining, and tourism. It has a dry, sunny climate.

Montserrat's economy has been more varied than Anguilla's, with vegetable farming,

cotton growing, and manufacturing industries producing local crafts, motor vehicle parts, and electronic components. The island is dominated by a series of active volcanoes. In 1997 eruptions of the Soufrière volcano east of Plymouth destroyed the capital.

ANTIGUA & BARBUDA

Colonized by Great Britain from the 1600s before becoming independent in 1981, Antigua & Barbuda is a nation almost totally dependent on tourism for its income.

Area: 170 sq. mi.
Population: 67,448
Capital: St. John's (24,000)
Main languages spoken: English, English Creole
Main religion: Anglican
Currency: East Caribbean dollar
Main exports: re-exported petroleum products, fruit
Type of government: constitutional monarchy

Antigua & Barbuda consist of three islands. Antigua is by far the most important, being the largest and where an estimated 98 percent of the population live. The remainder inhabit Barbuda, a low-lying coral island, while a tiny third island lies uninhabited. Unlike most of the other members of the Leeward Islands group, Antigua has no forests, few trees, and no rivers. With only a few springs, droughts occur, even though approximately 40 in. of rain falls every year. Few native animals exist, but the islands are home to over 100 species of birds. After the closure of the sugar farming industry in the 1970s the islands have come to depend on their beaches to lure tourists, as well as developing a finance and banking industry. Two military bases on Antigua have been leased to the U.S. Ninety percent of Antigua & Barbuda's population are the descendants of black slaves brought to the islands. The population has recently been increased by some 3,000 refugees fleeing a volcanic eruption on nearby Montserrat.

GUADELOUPE

Two contrasting islands, one a high-peaked volcanic island, the other a lower-lying coral island, form the majority of the land of Guadeloupe.

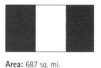

Area: 687 sq. mi.
Population: 435,739
Capital: Basse-Terre (54,000)
Main language spoken: French
Main religion: Roman Catholic
Currency: euro
Main exports: bananas, sugar, rum
Type of government: dependency of France

Guadeloupe is an archipelago made up of two major islands, Basse-Terre and Grande-Terre, and a number of smaller islands. On Basse-Terre the summit of the active volcano, Soufrière, is one of the wettest landmarks in the Caribbean and can receive more than 320 in. of rain in a year. In contrast the coastal areas of the islands tend to receive around 52 in. While Basse-Terre is home to Guadeloupe's capital, Grande-Terre is more heavily populated, with Pointe-à-Pitre being the main port and commercial center. Guadeloupe depends heavily on tourism and aid from France.

DOMINICA

A mountainous, volcanic island with many hot springs, Dominica has a great variety of wildlife and a large number of protected parks and reserves.

DOMINICA

Portsmouth • Marigot

Caribbean Sea

ATLANTIC OCEAN

ROSEAU • Berekua

Area: 290 sq. mi.
Population: 70,158
Capital: Roseau (26,000)
Main languages spoken: English, French patois
Main religions: Roman Catholic, Protestant
Currency: East Caribbean dollar
Main exports: bananas, soap, fresh vegetables, limes, coconuts
Type of government: parliamentary democracy

A high ridge forms the backbone of Dominica, which slopes down toward the sea and contains more than 300 rivers and streams. The mountains are covered in dense woodlands, thickets, and rain forests, much of which is protected in a series of national parks and reserves. Dominica has a varied plant and animal life, with more than 130 species of birds. Many creatures, including opossums, iguanas, crabs, and freshwater shrimp, are collected as food.

Much of the island's electricity is generated from a hydroelectric plant found in the center of the island. Dominica was one of the few Caribbean islands whose native Indian inhabitants managed to stop becoming a colony of a European nation until the late 1700s. Around 3,000 descendants of the Carib Indians still live on the island.

MARTINIQUE

Martinique is one of the most beautiful and rugged islands in the Caribbean, with volcanic peaks, dense rain forests in the mountains, and narrow, fertile valleys.

Martinique (to France)

ATLANTIC OCEAN

Montagne Pelée 4,582 ft. △ • Sainte-Marie

• Le Robert

Fort-de-France

• Rivière-Pilote

Caribbean Sea

Area: 436 sq. mi.
Population: 422,277
Capital: Fort-de-France (101,000)
Main language spoken: French
Main religion: Roman Catholic
Currency: euro
Main exports: bananas, refined petroleum, rum
Type of government: dependency of France

The island of Martinique has an average elevation of more than 2,950 ft. above sea level. Narrow plains around the coast and a plain in the center of the island are the only flat areas. Its highest point, the volcano Montagne Pelée, destroyed the town of St. Pierre, killing more than 28,000 people in 1902. Around one third of the island remains covered in forests, with large amounts of tropical hardwoods. Colonized by the French in 1635, the island remains

a dependency of France. France maintains an oil refinery on the island in which crude oil from Venezuela and Trinidad & Tobago is processed and shipped elsewhere. The majority of its population are of either African or mixed African-European descent. Agriculture and service industries, particularly tourism, are the main sources of income.

St. Lucia

Explored by Spain and then France, the volcanic island of St. Lucia became a British territory in 1814 and became independent in 1979.

Area: 236 sq. mi.
Population: 160,145
Capital: Castries (57,000)
Main languages spoken: English, French patois
Main religion: Roman Catholic, Protestant
Currency: East Caribbean dollar
Main exports: bananas, other foodstuffs, live animals, chemicals and chemical products
Type of government: parliamentary democracy

St. Lucia's mountains are heavily wooded and contain many fast-moving streams and rivers. The legacy of its volcanic origins can be found at many points around the island. A volcanic crater and bubbling mud pools releasing sulfur gases are found in Soufrière, a town that is overlooked by twin volcanic peaks. To the south of the island lies an area that contains a chain of 18 volcanic domes and a number of craters. The island has many fine beaches, some of which are covered in black volcanic sand in the southwest. St. Lucia is the second-largest producer of bananas in the Caribbean. The seas around the island are exploited relatively heavily, with 1,795 tons of fish, especially tuna, dolphin, and kingfish, caught in 2000.

▼ Overlooking Jalousie Plantation harbor on the western side of St. Lucia are the Pitons. These two volcanic domes have elevations of 2,617 ft. and 2,460 ft.

St. Vincent & The Grenadines

St. Vincent & the Grenadines consist of one main island, St. Vincent, and the northern part of the chain of 600 islands and islets called the Grenadines.

Area: 131 sq. mi.
Population: 116,394
Capital: Kingstown (28,000)
Main languages spoken: English, French patois
Main religions: Anglican, Methodist, Roman Catholic
Currency: East Caribbean dollar
Main exports: bananas, flour, rice
Type of government: constitutional monarchy

The island of St. Vincent makes up 89 percent of the area and 95 percent of the population of the nation. The island is rugged with little flat land, and its northern one third is dominated by an active volcano called Soufrière, which erupted a number of times during the 1900s. The central and southern sections of the island fall sharply from mountainous heights to the sea, with rocky cliffs and black sand beaches on the eastern side. Most of the islands of the Grenadines are less rugged and tend to be surrounded by coral reefs. Several of the Grenadines, including Mustique and Bequia, have become exclusive resort islands for

◀ On Dominica fishermen use seine nets to catch schools of fish that swim near beaches.

wealthy foreign visitors. Bananas are the most important farm crop, and there are also small food-processing, cement, clothing, and rum-making industries. St. Vincent & the Grenadines are less wealthy than many of its Caribbean neighbors and have a high rate of unemployment (22 percent in 2001).

BARBADOS

The most easterly of all Caribbean islands, Barbados is around 21 mi. long, with an economy based on agriculture, tourism, and other service industries.

Area: 166 sq. mi.
Population: 276,607
Capital: Bridgetown (136,000)
Main languages spoken: English, Bajan (English Creole)
Main religions: Roman Catholic, Protestant
Currency: Barbados dollar
Main exports: sugar, chemicals, food and beverages, construction materials
Type of government: parliamentary democracy

Barbados is formed from coral limestone and is largely flat with a few rolling hills in the north. The west coast has a number of white-sand beaches, while the east coast has a rocky shoreline. Sugarcane production accounts for more than 80 percent of the cultivated land. Oil found on the island provides around one third of the country's energy needs. Founded in 1628, Bridgetown is the island's capital and commercial port. Ninety percent of the population are of African descent, and roughly one third of Barbados' people, known as Bajans, live in or around Bridgetown. The original inhabitants of Barbados were Arawak Indians, who are believed to have been driven off the island by the warlike Carib Indians around 1200. The island lay deserted until a colony was established in 1627 by British settlers. Barbados has been independent from the U.K. since 1966, and tourism now employs one third of the workforce. Remnants of traditional British customs and buildings have earned it the nickname "Little England" by its Caribbean neighbors.

▶ Cars head through an arch in Bridgetown, the capital of Barbados and the island's largest port.

GRENADA

Grenada consists of one major island and several of the southern Grenadine islands, including Carriacou. It is famous for its spices and agricultural produce.

Area: 131 sq. mi.
Population: 89,211
Capital: St. George's (36,000)
Main languages spoken: English, French patois
Main religions: Roman Catholic, Protestant
Currency: East Caribbean dollar
Main exports: fish, cocoa, nutmeg, bananas, clothing
Type of government: parliamentary democracy

Grenada's geography is quite varied, with a hilly interior covered in lush vegetation, deep valleys through which fast-flowing streams run, several mountain lakes, and 45 beaches around its coastline. Its tropical climate features 60 in. of rainfall per year on its coasts and more than double that amount on the mountain slopes. Created by volcanic activity, the island has a rich, black soil in which many crops flourish. Grenada is known in the Caribbean as the "Isle of Spice" and is the world's largest producer of nutmeg and mace. It also produces large amounts of cinnamon, cloves, pepper, and ginger. Limes, cocoa, and bananas are also grown. Grenada was a French colony from 1650 until it was captured by British forces in 1762. Gaining independence in 1974, two military coups, one in 1979, the second in 1983, were followed by U.S. forces invading the island and establishing a new government.

▲ A plantation worker separates strands of the spice mace from cloves.

Tourism has since become important after an international airport was built in Point Salines near the capital, St. George's.

TRINIDAD & TOBAGO

One of the few Caribbean nations with oil reserves, the two islands of Trinidad & Tobago are the most southerly islands in the Caribbean.

Area: 2,000 sq. mi.
Population: 1,163,724
Capital: Port-of-Spain (54,000)
Main languages spoken: English, English Creole
Main religions: Roman Catholic, Protestant, Hindu
Currency: Trinidad & Tobago dollar
Main exports: petroleum, ammonia, iron, and steel
Type of government: parliamentary democracy

Lying close to the coast of Venezuela, where the Orinoco river empties into the Atlantic Ocean, Trinidad is a geological extension of South America. Trinidad's major resources are fossil fuels. Large reserves of oil and natural gas have been exploited both on the island and just offshore. In the southwest of the island lies one of the world's largest sources of natural asphalt, used for road building. Unlike most Caribbean nations, Trinidad & Tobago's population come from a great range of backgrounds. Those of African and East Asian descent each form around 40 percent. There are also many people of European, Chinese, and South American origin.

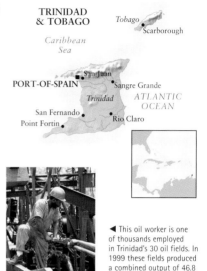

◀ This oil worker is one of thousands employed in Trinidad's 30 oil fields. In 1999 these fields produced a combined output of 46.8 million barrels.

NETHERLANDS ANTILLES AND ARUBA

The Caribbean dependencies of the Netherlands are clustered into two places—east of the Virgin Islands and just off the northern coast of Venezuela.

Netherlands Antilles

Aruba

Area: 309 sq. mi.
Population: 214,258
Capital: Willemstad (119,000)
Main languages spoken: Dutch, Papiamento (in Curaçao and Bonaire), English (in Dutch Windward Islands)
Main religion: Roman Catholic
Currency: Netherlands Antilles guilder
Main exports: refined petroleum, consumer goods.
Type of government: dependency of the Netherlands

Area: 75 sq. mi.
Population: 70,441
Capital: Oranjestad (21,000)
Main languages spoken: Dutch, Papiamento
Main religion: Roman Catholic
Currency: Aruban guilder
Main exports: refined petroleum, fish
Type of government: dependency of the Netherlands

The Netherlands Antilles consists of two contrasting island groups. The islands of Curaçao and Bonaire lie off the Venezuelan coast, while 496 mi. north the second group, including Saba and St. Eustasius, are found. Crude oil and petroleum products account for more than 80 percent of the Netherlands Antilles' imports and exports. The same industry is important to Aruba, which lies just 16 mi. off the Venezuelan coast. Aruba is flat, and its western side has been heavily developed for tourism. Agriculture is limited on the islands because soils are poor and water is often limited, but peanuts and tropical fruits are among the crops grown.

▶ Willemstad, with its Dutch-style buildings, is the main town on Curaçao.

SOUTH AMERICA

S outh America is the fourth-largest continent, with a total surface area of 11,048,958 sq. mi. It extends from the Caribbean Sea southward, a distance of 4,588 mi., to Cape Horn, and its maximum width is 3,199 mi. The Brazilian Shield and the smaller Guyana Shield to the north, as well as the Patagonian Shield to the southwest, are the oldest geological parts of the continent. Running along the entire western edge of the continent is the much younger Andes mountain range, with many peaks more than 19,680 ft. A large part of the interior is a series of basins in which three large rivers—the Amazon, the Orinoco, and the Paraguay-Paraná—drain much of the continent's water into the Atlantic Ocean. The largest lowland region of South America is the enormous Amazon basin, the world's largest river basin, covering an area of more than four million sq. mi. Much of its extent is covered in lush, tropical rain forests. South America has been inhabited for many thousands of years with advanced native cultures, including the Chavin, Moche, Chimu, and Inca civilizations. The continent's population is now over 345 million—a figure that more than doubled between 1960 and 2000.

▲ These small houses are made of adobe mud bricks and lie on the shore of Lake Titicaca, which straddles the border between Bolivia and Peru.

Caribbean Sea

Orinoco

Llanos

VENEZUELA

Guiana Highlands

GUYANA

SURINAME

French Guiana (to France)

COLOMBIA

ECUADOR

Amazon

Amazon

A M A Z O N

B A S I N

Tapajós

B R A Z I L

Juruá

Purus

P E R U

Represa de Sobradinho

Mato Grosso Do Sul

BOLIVIA

Brazilian Highlands

A

N

D

Atacama Desert

Pilcomayo

Gran Chaco

PARAGUAY

Paraguay

Uruguay

Salado

E

S

▲ Aconcagua 22,831 ft.

Juan Fernández Island

Paraná

URUGUAY

ARGENTINA

Río de la Plata

PACIFIC OCEAN

C

H

I

L

E

pampas

Patagonia

ATLANTIC OCEAN

Falkland Islands (Islas Malvinas) (to U.K.)

Tierra del Fuego

Cape Horn

South Georgia (to U.K.)

ATLANTIC OCEAN

▲ Native South Americans, such as this Ecuadorian girl, are now far outnumbered in the continent by other ethnic groups, including people of European descent.

0   500   1000 km
0   250   500 miles

▲ A native Indian market gets underway in Peru. Many people in the Andean nations of South America rely on local markets in order to barter and exchange produce and goods.

◄ The Andes mountain system dominates the landscape of the western countries of South America. This beautiful, colored lake, called Laguna Verde, lies in the Bolivian Andes.

61

VENEZUELA

During the 1900s Venezuela underwent a transformation from one of the poorest South American countries to one of the wealthiest.

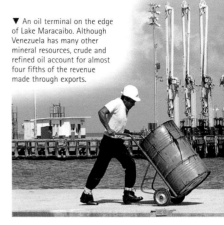

▼ An oil terminal on the edge of Lake Maracaibo. Although Venezuela has many other mineral resources, crude and refined oil account for almost four fifths of the revenue made through exports.

Area: 340,600 sq. mi.
Population: 24,287,670
Capital: Caracas (3,177,000)
Major language spoken: Spanish
Main religion: Roman Catholic
Currency: bolivar
Main exports: petroleum and petroleum products, basic manufactured goods, bauxite, aluminum, chemicals
Type of government: federal republic

▼ The flat, grassed plains of the Llanos in central Venezuela provide good grazing ground for large livestock herds. The cattle ranchers, or cowboys, are called *llaneros*.

Venezuela shares borders with Brazil, Colombia, and Guyana. Its coastline meets the Caribbean Sea to the north and the Atlantic Ocean to the east, in which around 70 islands belonging to Venezuela lie. Mainland Venezuela has a number of geographical regions. In the center are low-lying grassland plains called the Llanos. The rugged granite Guiana Highlands are in the south and are only sparsely inhabited. Much of the north of Venezuela is made up of narrow coastal plains and large mountains, including two branches of the Andes. These define part of the Venezuela-Colombia border and include the country's highest peak, Pico Bolivar (16, 391 ft.). Between these two mountain ranges lie the lowlands surrounding Lake Maracaibo. Most of the Llanos and Guiana Highlands are drained by the 1,699-mi.-long Orinoco river.

OIL AND LAKE MARACAIBO

Lake Maracaibo is a large inlet of the Caribbean Sea lying in northwest Venezuela. It extends south from the

Gulf of Venezuela for around 130 mi. Many rivers flow into this stretch of water, some of which are also important transportation routes for shipping. The waters in the north of Lake Maracaibo are salty and stagnant as the tides mix seawater with freshwater. In the south the water is fresh. The discovery of oil reserves in and around the lake has transformed the Venezuelan economy. The first productive oil well was drilled in 1914. The oil reserves are huge and are one of the largest supplies outside of the Middle East.

HISTORY AND PEOPLE

Venezuela was inhabited by Native Indian peoples for many centuries before the arrival of Europeans. Until the early 1800s Venezuela was controlled by Spain. The population of Venezuela reflects its colonial past, with people of mixed Native American and European descent (mestizos) making up two thirds of the population. A small number of Native Americans still maintain their traditional way of life deep in Venezuela's forests. The most notable group is the Yanomami, who live in the remote forests of the Orinoco river basin in southern Venezuela and across the border in northern Brazil.

▼ Angel Falls is the waterfall with the highest drop in the world. The falls, which are located in the Guiana Highlands, drop a long 3,205 ft.

COLOMBIA

Colombia is troubled politically, but it is a country blessed with rich wildlife, fertile land, and large mineral resources.

Area: 401,000 sq. mi.
Population: 41,008,227
Capital: Bogotá (6,957,000)
Main language spoken: Spanish
Main religion: Roman Catholic
Currency: Colombian peso
Main exports: petroleum products, coffee, chemicals, textiles and clothing (The illegal export of cocaine and marijuana produces the greatest revenue.)
Type of government: republic

Colombia's short border with the southernmost part of Panama marks the northern end of the South American continent. The western part of the country is mostly mountainous with three large ranges from the Andes mountain system: the Cordillera Occidental, Central, and Oriental. Between the three ranges are several large valleys. The Magdalena river flows north through the eastern part of these valleys. In addition to the three chains of Andes mountains, the landscape of the western part of Colombia is also marked by an isolated mountain range to the north of the region. Containing Colombia's highest peak, Pico Cristóbal Colón (18,492 ft.), it is the highest coastal mountain range in the world. More than half of Colombia consists of lowland areas. The more northerly lowlands are the Llanos, which are the low-lying plains that run east into and throughout much of Venezuela.

South of the Llanos are further lowlands that form part of the Amazon river basin and tend to be covered in thick rain forests. Many of the region's rivers provide a key—and sometimes only—transportation link to isolated areas in the lowlands.

COLOMBIA'S CLIMATE

Colombia's climate is mainly tropical with not much change throughout the year since the country lies close to the equator. However, there is a lot of variation in temperature and rainfall based on altitude and also based on location near the mountain ranges, some of which cast a rain shadow over nearby lowlands. Above around 9,840 ft. the climate is cold, with temperatures ranging from -0.4°F–55°F. Mountain peaks in the Andes that extend above 14,760 ft. are permanently capped in snow and ice. Generally Colombia receives moderate-to-heavy rainfall with no completely dry season.rainfall with with no completely dry season.

◄ Colombia's capital city, Bogotá, sprawls over a sloping plain at the base of two mountains. The city features two of the oldest universities in South America: the University of Santo Tomás (founded in 1580) and the Xavier Pontifical University (founded in 1622).

GUYANA

Guyana means "land of many waters" in local native Indian language, reflecting the many rivers that cross its area. It gained independence from the U.K. in 1966.

Area: 76,000 sq. mi.
Population: 698,029
Capital: Georgetown (280,000)
Main languages spoken: English, Amerindian dialects
Main religions: Christian, Hinduism, Islam
Currency: Guyanan dollar
Main exports: sugar, gold, rice, bauxite, timber
Type of government: republic

Guyana is a country of dense interior rain forests, many parts of which have been barely touched by humans. Ninety percent of its people live on a relatively narrow coastal plain bordering the Atlantic Ocean. Parts of this plain have been formed by land reclaimed from the sea, creating over 120 mi. of dikes and canals. Rice, sugar, coconuts, corn, and coffee are grown on the coastal plain, which is never more than 40 mi. wide. Guyana's longest river is the Essequibo, which measures 626 mi. and is partly navigable by small boats along stretches of its length. Diamond-digging industries occur on parts of many of Guyana's rivers, while mining for bauxite is Guyana's chief mineral resource. The Dutch were the first colonial power to reach Guyana, where they established settlements along the Essequibo river in 1615. They grew a range of crops, including sugarcane and cocoa, and imported slaves from Africa. During the early 1800s Great Britain took over the Dutch colonies of Berbice, Demerara, and Essequibo, which became British Guiana in 1831. Slavery was outlawed in 1834, and the great need for plantation workers led to a large influx of immigrants, mainly from the Indian subcontinent. Today around half of the population is of East Indian descent, and around 43 percent are of African descent.

▲ A Guyanan forestry worker in the process of felling a tree. Forests cover around four fifths of the country's land.

▶ Situated in central Guyana, Kaieteur Falls is between 295–344 ft. at its top and falls 741 ft. Over time the falls have eroded a gorge around 5 mi. long.

SURINAME

Previously called Dutch Guiana, the independent
republic of Suriname has a small population that
is one of the most varied in South America.

Area: 62,300 sq. mi.
Population: 436,494
Capital: Paramaribo
(240,000)
Main languages spoken:
Dutch, Sranang English,
Hindustani
Main religions:
Protestant, Roman
Catholic, Islam
Currency: Surinamese
guilder
Main exports: bauxite,
shrimp and fish, rice,
aluminum
Type of government:
republic

▼ Suriname's largest
industry, the mining,
processing, and exporting
of the aluminum ore
bauxite, forms the basis
of its economy. Here
barges carrying bauxite
arrive at Suralco refinery.

Suriname consists of three distinct
geographical areas: a coastal plain
that is narrow and marshy in places, a
small plateau area that is covered in savanna
grasslands and forests, and a large tract of
dense rain forests. The rain forest makes
up around 90 percent of the country, and
few roads penetrate it. Unlike its immediate
neighbors, French Guiana to the east and
Guyana to the west, Suriname has a number
of huge lakes, including one of the largest
artificial lakes in South America just south
of Brokopondo, created by damming a river
for hydroelectric power. Only a small portion
of Suriname's land is used for agriculture,
with rice being the major crop. The British
established plantations on the banks of the
Suriname river in 1651 and founded the
settlement on which Suriname's capital city,
Paramaribo, now lies. In 1667 Great Britain
and the Netherlands exchanged lands in
the Americas. The English swapped their
territories in Suriname. In exchange they
received the territory of New Amsterdam,
which is now known as New York City.
The Dutch imported many slaves to work
on plantations, not just
from Africa but from many
parts of Asia, and this has
given the country its varied
cultural background. Around 37 percent
of the population are Asian Indians, while
31 percent are Creoles, and 15 percent are
of Indonesian origin. There are also sizeable
populations of Chinese, as well as descendants
of native tribes. The Netherlands granted
Suriname independence in 1975 but remains
a major aid donor, providing 80 percent
of Suriname's tourists. Many Surinamese have
emigrated to the Netherlands. The country
has suffered from a lack of political stability,
with the military often intervening in affairs.

FRENCH GUIANA

An overseas dependency of France, French Guiana consists of a narrow belt of flat land at the coast that rises to higher ground blanketed in lush rain forests.

Area: 34,400 sq. mi.
Population: 182,333
Capital: Cayenne (66,000)
Main language spoken: French
Main religion: Roman Catholic
Currency: euro
Main exports: timber and wood products, bauxite
Type of government: dependency of France

French Guiana is situated on the northeast coast of South America and is bordered by Brazil to the south and the east and by Suriname to the west. An area bounded by the Maroni river is under dispute between Suriname and French Guiana. Most of the country is covered in rain forests that rise from low elevations near the coast to mountains that lie on the frontier with Brazil. The rain-forest region is largely uninhabited by humans but has a rich variety of wildlife, including many species of monkeys, tapirs, anteaters, ocelots, and caimans, a relative of the crocodile family. French Guiana has a tropical climate with high humidity and heavy rainfall, especially in its interior. The heaviest rain falls from January to June, and the average rainfall in the country's capital, Cayenne, on the coast, is approximately 152 in. Cayenne is the country's largest town and its chief port. French Guiana exports bananas, sugar, aluminum ores, and timber. With only one percent of the country's land devoted to agriculture, many foods have to be imported.

The French first established a colony in Cayenne in 1637, and French Guiana remains the last remaining colony on mainland South America. From 1852 until the 1950s it was notorious as the place where France sent its most hardened convicts. Penal colonies were established in Cayenne and on a nearby small islet in the Atlantic Ocean known as Devil's Island. Most of French Guiana's population live near the coast and are people of mixed white, Native American, and black African origin called creoles. Small numbers of Native Americans live in the rain forests and highlands of the country's interior, which is largely untouched by modern life.

▲ Almost nine tenths of French Guiana are covered in rain forests that provide timber, oils, fibers, and foods for many of the dependency's population.

▲ An *Ariane 4* rocket blasts off from Kourou satellite launch base in French Guiana in May 2002. Kourou is the launch site for European Space Agency projects, and the town nearby has grown to become the second largest in French Guiana.

67

ECUADOR

Ecuador is the smallest Andean country but has a varied landscape. It also governs the world-famous Galapagos Islands in the Pacific Ocean.

Area: 106,900 sq. mi.
Population: 13,447,494
Capital: Quito (1,616,000)
Main languages spoken: Spanish, Quechua
Main religion: Roman Catholic
Currency: U.S. dollar
Main exports: petroleum, bananas, shrimp, coffee, cocoa
Type of government: republic

▼ Quito is located on the slopes of a volcano in a valley among the Andes. The oldest of all South American capital cities, Quito has many well-preserved Spanish colonial buildings, including 86 churches.

Ecuador has three distinct geographical areas: two sets of lowlands split by a highland region that runs through the country from north to south. The highland region consists of two chains of mountains that are part of the Andes. The mountains contain 22 peaks that are over 13,000 ft. in elevation, as well as around 30 mountains of volcanic origin, including the 19,342-ft.-high cone volcano Mount Cotopaxi—one of the highest active volcanoes in the world. To the west of the highlands are the coastal lowlands bordering the Pacific. The northern coastal lowlands are largely covered in tropical rain forests, while to the south the land is more arid, and vegetation is more sparse. East of the Andes mountains lies Ecuador's Amazon basin lowlands, which are covered in dense rain forests.

ECUADOR'S ECONOMY

Ecuador's economy is based mainly on agriculture, fishing, and oil. Over 310,000 tons of fish are caught every year, although overfishing now threatens certain marine life. Ecuador's oil industry produces around 400,000 barrels per day, making oil the single largest export earner. Ecuador's rugged countryside allows it to produce over 70 percent of its electricity from hydroelectric power plants. A number of metals are mined, while the government of Ecuador controls a large salt-mining industry. Guayaquil, in the south of the country, is Ecuador's main industrial center and its biggest port. Quito, in the north, remains the governmental and cultural capital.

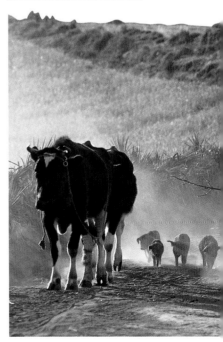

ECUADOR'S PEOPLE

Like all of the Andean nations, Ecuador was colonized by the Spanish and only obtained independence in the 1800s. Wars with Peru between 1904 and 1942 saw the country lose a lot of territory. Unlike most South American countries, the Native American population is large; pure-blooded Quechua Indians make up 25 percent of the population. Most speak the Quechua language used in the times of the Inca civilization. People of mixed European and Native American descent make up a further 65 percent of the population. Ecuador is the most densely populated South American country, with an average of approximately 126 people per square mile.

GALAPAGOS ISLANDS

Ecuador's major island territories lie around 620 mi. from its coastline in the Pacific Ocean. The Galapagos Islands comprise 19 islands and many islets and rocks, most of which are formed from lava piles. Lava rock forms the islands' shorelines, with higher ground containing

▲ Found on the Galapagos Islands, the giant tortoise can grow to lengths of just over 3 ft., weigh over 550 lbs., and live for over 100 years.

▼ Ecuadorians herd some of the country's 2.1 million sheep down from the slopes of the inactive volcano Chimborazo, the country's highest point. Permanently snow-capped from around 15,000 ft. upward, the volcano gets its name from the Quechua Indian for "mountain of snow."

▲ Around 60 percent of Ecuadorians live in towns and cities. The country's most populous city, Guayaquil, contains over two-and-a-half million people.

most of the islands' plant life. Although some remains of Inca pottery have been found in places, the Galapagos are believed to have been uninhabited for most of their existence. Isolated from other landmasses, the islands are home to a large number of unusual species of plants and creatures not found elsewhere. Most of the Galapagos Islands' animals are thought to have originated long ago in South and Central America, but they have adapted and evolved into separate species. For example, the marine iguana is the only iguana that swims and feeds on seaweed. Other unusual creatures include flightless cormorants and giant tortoises, which can weigh over 550 lbs. and are believed to be the longest-living land creatures. Ecuador has had to control visitor numbers to the islands in order to conserve their future welfare. Laws ban further settlements and development.

PERU

Peru is the third-largest country in South America and has a long Pacific Ocean coastline. The interior features the Andes and rain forests.

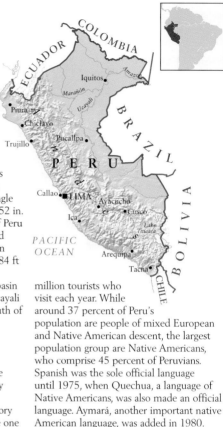

Area: 492,200 sq. mi.
Population: 27,949,639
Capital: Lima (7,594,000)
Major languages spoken: Spanish, Quechua, Aymará
Main religion: Roman Catholic
Currency: new sol
Main exports: copper, fish and fish products, zinc, coffee, petroleum, lead
Type of government: republic

▼ Local Aymará Native Americans fish the waters of Lake Titicaca. The Aymarás use boats built out of reeds and rushes in the same way as their ancient ancestors did. Lake Titicaca is a large lake of over 3,237 sq. mi. that, at an altitude of over 12,464 ft., is the highest navigable lake in the world.

Peru can be divided into three geographical regions: the coast, a jungle interior, and, in between, the highlands, or sierra. Peru's narrow coastal region runs the country's entire length, around 1,500 mi. This region is mostly dry, although many of the valleys near the coast are farmed using modern irrigation techniques. In contrast the jungle interior receives heavy rainfall—up to 152 in. in places. This region covers over half of Peru and is divided into highland and lowland regions. The highland area on the eastern side of the Andes is between 1,607–9,184 ft in altitude. Thick with rain forests, the lowlands are part of the Amazon river basin and include Peru's longest rivers, the Ucayali and the Marañón, which join 50 mi. south of Iquitos to help form the Amazon river.

PEOPLE OF THE INCA EMPIRE

Peru has been home to a number of ancient native civilizations, including the Nazca, Chimú, and Chavin. The country was also at the center of the great Inca empire. Remains of the Incas' former glory are one of the biggest attractions for the one million tourists who visit each year. While around 37 percent of Peru's population are people of mixed European and Native American descent, the largest population group are Native Americans, who comprise 45 percent of Peruvians. Spanish was the sole official language until 1975, when Quechua, a language of Native Americans, was also made an official language. Aymará, another important native American language, was added in 1980.

BOLIVIA

Most of the people of Bolivia, one of the poorest South American nations, live on a high plateau, called the Altiplano, between the Andes mountain ranges.

Area: 418,700 sq. mi.
Population: 8,445,134
Capitals: La Paz (1,499,000) and Sucre (183,000)
Major languages spoken: Spanish, Quechua, Aymará
Main religion: Roman Catholic
Currency: boliviano
Main exports: zinc, soybeans, petroleum, gold, natural gas, tin
Type of government: republic

Bolivia is a landlocked country, with no sea or ocean coastline. It borders five South American countries: Peru and Chile to the west, Brazil to the north and east, and Paraguay and Argentina to the south. The largest expanse of water is formed by Lake Titicaca, which sits on the border with Peru. The country's most notable highland areas consist of two mountain ranges that run roughly south to north through the west of the country. The more westerly of these two mountain ranges includes a number of active volcanoes. The more easterly range in which Bolivia's twin capital cities of La Paz and Sucre are situated, is more populated. Its eastern slopes are covered by dense forests. This region is the wettest part of the Bolivian Andes, with around 54 in. of rain per year, mostly falling in just three months. To the north and the east the land descends into part of a huge lowland area called the Oriente. This is made up of low alluvial plains, large swamp areas, and tropical forests.

THE ALTIPLANO

Lying between the two Andean mountain ranges

◀ Life in rural areas is often very harsh. Almost half of the Bolivian workforce grow crops or raise livestock for a living.

at around 12,000 ft. above sea level is a large, high-altitude plateau called the Altiplano. Approximately 500 mi. long, the plateau is almost 200 mi. wide at its broadest point. The northern half of the region receives moderate rainfall, while the southern region is dry. Cold winds sweep the entire plateau, keeping average temperatures under 54°F.

This harsh landscape actually provides homes for the majority of Bolivians. Many live in towns, work in the mining region based around Oruro, or farm the land and raise herds of alpacas and llamas. Successive Bolivian governments have urged people to move from the Altiplano to the Oriente, where the discovery of fossil fuels and the possibility of large-scale forestry and growing tropical crops could provide a boost to the economy. The population has increased, especially in and around the main town of the Oriente, Santa Cruz, but most people who live on the Altiplano are reluctant to leave their homelands.

MINING AND NATURAL GAS

Spanish explorers in the 1500s discovered reserves of silver, and the mine established at Potosí became famous as the world's largest. The boom in silver ended, and now Bolivia has large-scale tin production. For the first half of the 1900s Bolivia was the world's largest tin producer. Natural gas is Bolivia's biggest export and accounts for more than 50 percent of the money Bolivia earns from overseas.

BRAZIL

The largest country in South America, Brazil has a
rapidly industrializing economy, a growing population,
and incredibly rich wildlife and mineral resources.

Area: 3,265,100 sq. mi.
Population: 176,029,560
Capital: Brasilia (2,073,000)
Major languages spoken:
Portuguese, Spanish,
English, French
Main religion: Roman
Catholic
Currency: real
Main exports: iron and
steel products, nonelectrical
machinery, iron ore, road
vehicles, wood and wood
products, coffee
Type of government:
federal republic

▼ The Amazon basin
covers over one third
of Brazil, and large parts
of the rain-forest-covered
region remain unsurveyed
or have only been recently
explored. The Amazon
forest contains the largest
single reserve of biological
organisms in the world.

B razil shares a border with every country
in South America, except for Chile
and Ecuador. The country is a federal
republic divided into 26 separate states,
with a federal district based in the city
of Brasilia. The country has a great variety
of landscapes over its huge area, but there
are a small number of major geographical
regions. To the north and east lie the
Guiana Highlands, which run into Guyana
and Suriname. This region of mountains
and valleys include Pico da Neblina. With
an elevation of 9,886 ft., this mountain is
the country's highest peak. Most of north
and west Brazil is home to a large part of
the Amazon basin, containing the Amazon
and its hundreds of tributary rivers, plus
the largest rain forest region in the world.
In the center and south of the country
are the Brazilian Highlands. This area is
a large plateau of rock that is divided by
low mountain formations and has been
weathered over thousands of years to create
deep river valleys. Much of the Highlands
are covered in scrubland or forests.

▲ The ornate opera house in Manaus was built in 1896.
Situated on the Negro river, Manaus is the capital of
Amazonas state and home to half the state's population.

DEFORESTATION IN THE AMAZON

The rain forest is shrinking, mainly
owing to human impact. Deforestation to
clear lands for mining, farming, or for timber
and other products has seen over 15 percent
of the rain forest destroyed since the early
1970s. As much as 13,650 sq. mi. have been
lost in individual years. There deforestation
has become an international issue, with
initiatives designed to slow or halt the
cutting down of trees.

ATLANTIC OCEAN

Mount Roraima
9,217 ft.

VENEZUELA

Guiana Highlands

SURINAME

French Guiana
(to France)

GUYANA

COLOMBIA

△ Pico da Neblina
9,886 ft.

Negro

A m a z o n

Amazon

Marajó

Macapá

Belém

São Luís

Fortaleza

Japurá

Manaus

B a s i n

Amazon

Natal

Juruá

S e l v a s

Purus

Madeira

Tapajós

Irirí

Xingu

Tocantins

São Francisco

Recife

PERU

Rio Branco

Porto Velho

B R A Z I L

Teles Pires

Araguaia

Represa de
Sobradinho

BOLIVIA

Guaporé

Juruena

Jauru

*Mato Grosso
Do Sul*

Cuiabá

BRASÍLIA

Goiânia

*Brazilian
Highlands*

Salvador

PARAGUAY

Paraguay

Campo Grande

Paraná

Campinas

Belo Horizonte

Vitória

Nova Iguaçu

São Paulo

Rio de Janeiro

Santos

Curitiba

ARGENTINA

Uruguay

Pôrto Alegre

URUGUAY

Lagoa dos Patos

Lagoa
Mirim

▲ Found in many parts of central and southern America but most common in Brazil, the jaguar is the largest wild cat species in either North or South America.

BRAZIL'S PEOPLE

Almost half of Brazil's population are under 20 years old, and the population has more than tripled in the last 60 years. Brazilians are a mix of different origins, with the Native Americans who first settled the country now less than one percent of the population. Most of the early European settlers were from Portugal, and from the 1500s to the 1800s they brought between three and four million black Africans to Brazil as slaves. People of mixed descent from European, African, and Native American backgrounds comprise the majority of the population. Brazil also has the largest population of Japanese outside of Japan. Arriving mainly as poor farmers in the 1920s, over two million people of Japanese origin now live in Brazil. Massive migration from rural to urban areas has occurred. Some Brazilians are very wealthy, but income is distributed with huge inequalities—and millions are desperately poor. Large shantytowns surrounding major cities see people living in squalor with little water or sanitation.

BRAZILIAN CITIES

Brazil has many major cities: São Paulo is the country's most populous city, with approximately 17,834,000 people, while Rio de Janeiro is its most famous city and its cultural center. Neither is the official capital, a role given to the purpose-built city of Brasilia, constructed in the 1950s to encourage people to move into the Brazilian interior. Brasilia now houses the national seat of government and many foreign embassies.

PARAGUAY

A relatively unknown and isolated country, Paraguay is divided into two geographical regions. The eastern half is the more populous.

Area: 153,400 sq. mi.
Population: 5,884,491
Capital: Asunción (1,302,000)
Main languages spoken: Spanish, Guaraní
Main religion: Roman Catholic
Currency: guaraní
Main exports: soy flour, cotton, oilseed and vegetable oil, timber
Type of government: republic

▼ Oxen are used as beasts of burden throughout rural Paraguay. Ninety percent of the country's roads are unpaved, and car ownership is low—14 vehicles per 1,000 people as compared to 140 per 1,000 in Argentina.

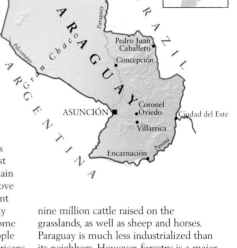

Paraguay's borders are largely created by rivers such as the Parana, Paraguay, and the Pilcomayo, which form much of the border with Argentina. The Paraguay river also divides the country into two very different geographical regions. To the east is the Paraneña region, which increases in elevation to form a series of low-lying mountains near the border with Brazil. To the west lies the Chaco region. This is a huge plain averaging around 410 ft. in altitude above sea level. It covers more than 60 percent of the country, and in the summer rainy season large parts are flooded and become temporary swamplands. Paraguay's people are mainly descendants of Native Americans. Agriculture is the key occupation of most of Paraguay's workforce. Half of the country's population live in rural areas, growing a wide range of crops, including cotton, sugarcane, wheat, bananas, and sweet potatoes. Livestock raising, especially cattle, is very important. There are over nine million cattle raised on the grasslands, as well as sheep and horses. Paraguay is much less industrialized than its neighbors. However, forestry is a major industry worth seven percent of the country's exports. Asunción is Paraguay's capital and its largest city. Founded by Spanish settlers in 1537, it is built on low-lying hills overlooking the Paraguay river at the point where it joins the Pilcomayo river. It is the chief manufacturing city of the country.

URUGUAY

The smallest country in southern South America, Uruguay is a land of rolling plains and low-lying hills. Most of the land is used to raise livestock.

Area: 67,000 sq. mi.
Population: 3,386,575
Capital: Montevideo (1,329,000)
Main language spoken: Spanish
Main religion: Roman Catholic
Currency: Uruguayan peso
Main exports: meat and other animal products, live animals, textiles and clothing, vegetables
Type of government: republic

Uruguay is one of the few countries in South America that does not have a tropical or subtropical climate. Its location some distance from the equator and its position facing the Atlantic Ocean give the country a warm temperate climate with relatively high rainfall (around 38 in. per year) and average temperatures of 50°C in the winter and 72°C in the summer. Cold wind storms, called *pamperos*, can occur during the winter, but few parts of Uruguay ever experience frost. The natural vegetation is tall prairie grasslands with relatively few forest areas. Almost 90 percent of the country is suitable for agriculture, but only one tenth of this land is used for growing crops such as corn, wheat, and rice. Much of the remaining land supports the giant herds of livestock, particularly cattle and sheep, that roam Uruguay's plains. For such a relatively small country Uruguay is a major sheep-farming nation and is the world's second-largest exporter of wool.

Uruguay's people bear few traces of the original Native American inhabitants. Less than ten percent of the population are either solely or part Native American. The large majority of people are immigrants from Europe or from Brazil and Argentina. Uruguay's capital city, Montevideo, sprawls along the northern banks of the Río de la Plata and is the center of Uruguayan business and food- and wool-processing industries. Large-scale migration from

▲ A market stall in the Barrio Reus district of Montevideo, Uruguay's capital city. Montevideo is Uruguay's main port and is the site of its state university.

the country to the city means that around half of the entire country's population live in or close to the city. Uruguay was the first South American country to establish a state welfare system and has a high level of literacy (97 percent) and good health care.

▼ A shepherd tends his flock in eastern Uruguay. The country has around 16 million sheep.

ARGENTINA

The second-largest country in South America, Argentina's territory includes large areas of rich pastureland where some of the largest cattle herds in the world graze.

Area: 1,056,000 sq. mi.
Population: 37,812,817
Capital: Buenos Aires (12,106,000)
Main languages spoken: Spanish, English, Italian
Main religion: Roman Catholic
Currency: Argentine peso
Main exports: meat, wool, cereals, manufactured goods, machinery and transportation equipment
Type of government: republic

▼ Ushuaia is the capital of the Argentinian province of Tierra del Fuego, Antarctica, and South Atlantic islands. Founded in 1884 and with around 29,000 inhabitants, Ushuaia lies at a latitude of 54.8°S, making it the southernmost large settlement in the world.

Forming the southeastern part of South America, Argentina is a large plain that rises in elevation from the Atlantic Ocean westward to the country's border with Chile. There some of the highest peaks of the Andes are found, including Aconcagua, with an elevation of 22,831 ft. The Andean region of Argentina is sparsely inhabited by miners and sheep herders. To the north, where Argentina borders Bolivia and Paraguay, lies the Gran Chaco region, which contains large forested areas and swamplands. South of this are the large rolling plains of the Pampas region, where Argentina's largest city, Buenos Aires, is located. Farther south lies Patagonia, a vast, inhospitable region shared with Chile.

ARGENTINA'S CLIMATE
Because Argentina is a long country— approximately 2,065 mi. from north to south—its climate varies greatly. In the northeast there is a small tropical region, while the Gran Chaco has subtropical temperatures. Most of Argentina has a temperate climate that gets colder farther south. Rainfall varies greatly, with Argentina's capital city, Buenos Aires, averaging around 38 in.

▲ Argentina is one of the foremost polo-playing nations. Many of the world's best polo ponies are thoroughbred horses from either Argentina or the southwestern U.S.

▼ Southern Patagonia has a cold and very dry climate with less than 10 in. of rainfall per year. The region is split between Chile and Argentina.

per year. To the south and the west much less rain falls, and the semiarid climate restricts the types of plants that can grow there. In the Argentinian Andes hot, dry winds, called *zondas*, travel across the mountains, absorbing moisture but not forming clouds and rain.

PATAGONIA
The southernmost region of Argentina, Patagonia is a vast, frequently windswept plain with an area of approximately 303,030 sq. mi. Much of the region experiences a dry climate, but the northern portion of the region is warm enough to be able to support large farms growing alfalfa grass, vegetables, and some fruit, as well as raising huge flocks of sheep. Argentina has approximately 13.7 million sheep, many millions of which are found in Patagonia. Tourism has become important in the region. Argentina has more than 20 national parks, a number of which are located in Patagonia, along with wildlife reserves and other protected areas. However, Patagonia's biggest impact on the country's economy is increasingly due to its reserves of oil, natural gas, and coal, as well as metal ores such as iron, tungsten, lead, and gold.

▲ Buenos Aires is Argentina's largest city and became its capital in 1816. The city is a major transportation terminus in South America, and it has the largest railroad center and is the continent's largest port.

THE PAMPAS
The Pampas get their name from a Quechua Indian word meaning "flat surface" and are a vast series of largely treeless plains that cover most of central Argentina. The region is split in half based on climate. The Humid Pampas runs from the coast inland and receives moderate-to-heavy rainfall. The soils are deep, heavy, and rich. Farther inland the Dry Pampas is a larger area but supports fewer people and has less crop-growing land. Originally covered in grassland vegetation, most of the Pampas region has been turned into farmland, with huge pastureland and ranches for the country's large herds of cattle, which number over 49 million.

CHILE

Chile is a nation of natural extremes in its landscapes and especially its climate. Volcanoes, icy wastelands, and temperate plains are all part of this highly developed country.

Area: 289,100 sq. mi.
Population: 15,498,930
Capitals: Santiago (5,551,000). Valparaiso (811,000) is the legislative capital
Major language spoken: Spanish
Main religions: Roman Catholic, Protestant
Currency: Chilean peso
Main exports: copper, iron ore, zinc, silver, food products, paper and paper products
Type of government: republic

▼ Founded in 1849, Punta Arenas lies on the stretch of water, known as the Straits of Magellan, which links the Atlantic and Pacific oceans. The city's 116,000 inhabitants work in industries processing and transporting oil, mutton, wool, and timber.

Chile shares borders with Argentina, Peru, and Bolivia and has the longest Pacific coastline of any South American country. About 2,300 mi. west of its coast in the southern Pacific Ocean lies Easter Island, which is owned by Chile. Several other small islands in the Pacific are also under Chilean control. Chile owns the western part of the island group of Tierra del Fuego.

A CHANGING LANDSCAPE

Around 2,666 mi. long but averaging only 109 mi. in width, Chile's landscape is dominated by the Andes mountains, which run the country's entire length. Northern Chile includes one of the driest places in the world, the Atacama desert. South of this area lies a large temperate region where most of Chile's towns, cities, and farmland are found. Farther south the mild climate gives way to a cold, windswept region. Rainfall is high there, reaching as much as 163 mi. per year.

THE CHILEAN PEOPLE

The great majority of Chile's people are mestizos. Native Americans make up around one tenth of the population, and most live in the Andes and along the southern coast. Almost 90 percent of all Chileans live in central Chile, with more than one third living in and around the capital city of Santiago. Valparaiso is the country's main port.

▲ Magellanic penguins breed on the southern Chilean coast and islands including Tierra del Fuego.

SOUTH ATLANTIC ISLANDS

Lying in the icy waters of the south Atlantic Ocean
are a number of largely barren, ice-covered islands that
include South Georgia and the South Sandwich Islands.

▲ The third-largest
penguin species, the
gentoo penguin is found
on the South Sandwich
Islands, where it nests
on rocky shorelines.

South Georgia is the largest of the
south Atlantic islands and lies around
800 mi. southeast of the Falkland Islands.
Largely covered in ice, it is mountainous
with a rugged coastline. The small
population consists mainly of military
personnel and scientists, who reside
in a small settlement formerly used by
whalers. The South Sandwich Islands
are a group of six glacier-covered volcanic
islets 470 mi. southeast of South Georgia.
British ownership of these islands and
South Georgia is disputed by Argentina.

ST. HELENA AND DEPENDENCIES

A small, isolated collection of islands makes up
the British dependency of St. Helena and includes the
islands of St. Helena, Ascension, and Tristan da Cunha.

Area: 46 sq. mi.
Population: 7,266
Capital: Jamestown
(1,500)
Major language: English
Main religions: Anglican,
Baptist
Currency: local issue
of U.K. pound
Main exports: tinned and
frozen fish, handicrafts
Government:
dependency of U.K.

A rugged, mountainous island created
by volcanic activity, St. Helena sits in
the South Atlantic Ocean around 1,200 mi.
from the west coast of Africa. Large cliffs
face the ocean on its north, east, and west
sides, while deep valleys are carved into its
mountainous interior. About one fourth of
the island's population lives in Jamestown,
a natural harbor and port for shipping.
Potatoes, corn, and flax are grown, but
most of the economy is subsidized by the
United Kingdom, with additional revenue
generated through the port. Ascension lies

Ascension Island
(to St. Helena)

Georgetown • The Peak
2,818 ft.

▲ St. Helena was
the last place of exile
for the French leader
Napoleon Bonaparte.

St. Helena
(to U.K.)

Jamestown • ▲
Diana's Peak
2,699 ft.

Tristan da Cunha
(to St. Helena)

Edinburgh •
Queen Mary's Peak
6,760 ft.

◇ Inaccessible Island

Nightingale Island

over 700 mi.
northwest of
St. Helena and
is used as a military base. Its rugged,
volcanic landscape provides habitats for
thousands of sea turtles and sooty terns.
The small population of the volcanic islands
of Tristan da Cunha grow potatoes and catch
crayfish. The main island is dominated by
a volcano that last erupted in 1961, causing
the island to be evacuated.

▶ The slopes of Green
Mountain on Ascension
is one of the few places
where fruit and vegetables
are grown on the island.

FALKLAND ISLANDS

Located in the southern Atlantic Ocean, the Falkland Islands are a dependency of the U.K. Their ownership is disputed by Argentina, which calls them Islas Malvinas.

Falkland Islands
(Islas Malvinas)
(to U.K.)

ATLANTIC OCEAN

West Falkland

East Falkland

Weddell Island

Port Stephens

Port Howard

Mount Usborne
△ 2,312 ft.

Goose Green

Darwin

Stanley

Bluff Cove

Area: 4,700 sq. mi.
Population: 2,317
Capital: Stanley (1,800)
Main language spoken: English
Main religion: Anglican
Currency: U.K. pound
Main exports: sheep products, fish
Type of government: dependency of U.K.

▼ With a permanent population of around 20 people, Port Howard is the second-largest settlement on West Falkland island. It is the base of Port Howard Farm, which has around 45,000 sheep.

The Falklands consist of two main islands, East and West Falkland, and approximately 200 smaller islets. The two major islands are hilly, and their coastlines are heavily indented with many drowned river valleys that form natural harbors. The climate is cool, very windy, and wet. The average winter temperature is 35°F, while the average summer temperature is approximately 50°F. Rain falls on around 250 days of the year, with almost constant winds averaging 19 mph. The islands' vegetation reflects the harsh conditions, with few trees and mainly grasses and low-lying scrub bushes. The grasslands act as pastureland for the main farming activity on the island—sheep raising. East Falkland is the site of the islands' biggest settlement, Stanley. Ninety percent of all Falkland Islanders live in this town, which contains the islands' only hospital. Many of the older buildings in Stanley were constructed from locally quarried stone and timber salvaged from shipwrecks. Timber today is just one of many items that has to be imported. Situated on the site of a large natural harbor, Stanley is the main terminal for imports of food, coal, oil, and clothing, as well as exports of wool and sheepskins. A dependency of the United Kingdom, disputes over the ownership of the islands with Argentina have continued for many decades. Negotiations came to crisis point in April 1982 with the invasion of the islands by Argentina. A bloody ten-week war ended with British military forces reoccupying the islands. In 2002 the United Nations called on both countries to reenter negotiations over the islands' future.

EUROPE

EUROPE

Europe is considered an individual continent, but it is actually part of the Eurasian landmass that extends eastward through Asia. Its landscape varies from icy, rugged mountain ranges, such as the Alps, to temperate forests and warm regions, particularly around the Mediterranean Sea. Europe is the second-smallest continent, and its land area is not that much greater than the country of Australia. However, its population of more than 700 million makes it the second-most-populous continent and the most densely populated of all. The birthplace of modern industry and exploration, a number of European countries, particularly Spain, France, Great Britain, Portugal, and the Netherlands, claimed lands all over the world as colonies from the 1400s on. Rich in history that extends back thousands of years, Europe has many divisions of language and nationality and over 60 native languages. The continent has seen a lot of conflict and changing boundaries. The most recent redrawing of borders came in the 1990s with the reunification of East and West Germany into one nation, the splitting of Czechoslovakia into Slovakia and the Czech Republic, and the breakup of the former country of Yugoslavia into a series of states. Europe's largest nation is also its most easterly. The Russian Federation emerged from the breakup of the Soviet Union in the early 1990s.

▲ The capital of the Russian empire for over two centuries, St. Petersburg is the Russian Federation's second-largest city. It is located on the delta of the Neva river and contains many elaborate buildings, including this church, the Church of Our Savior.

◄ Many countries in southern Europe border the Mediterranean Sea, which provides thousands of tons of fish every year. They are sold at markets such as this one in Marseille in the south of France.

0   500   1000 km

0   250   500 miles

Novaya Zemlya

North Cape

*Barents
Sea*

Vesterålen
Lofoten

*Norwegian
Sea*

*Kola
Peninsula*

*White
Sea*

N
O
R
W
A
Y

S
W
E
D
E
N

Gulf of Bothnia

FINLAND

R U S S I A N

F E D E R A T I O N

*North
Sea*

Gulf of Finland

Saaremaa

ESTONIA

Gotland

LATVIA

DENMARK

Öland

*Baltic
Sea*

LITHUANIA

Bornholm

Russ. Fed.

NETHERLANDS

BELARUS

GERMANY

LUXEMBOURG

POLAND

UKRAINE

CZECH
REPUBLIC

SLOVAKIA

Carpathians

SWITZ.

LIECH.

AUSTRIA

MOLDOVA

A
L
P
S

SLOVENIA

HUNGARY

ROMANIA

*Sea of
Azov*

Caspian Sea

MONACO

CROATIA

CRIMEA

SAN
MARINO

BOSNIA-
HERZEGOVINA

C a u c a s u s

*Ligurian
Sea*

Apennines

UNION OF
SERBIA AND
MONTENEGRO

BULGARIA

Black Sea

*Corsica
(to France)*

Adriatic Sea

MACEDONIA

VATICAN CITY

*Sardinia
(to Italy)*

ITALY

ALBANIA

*Tyrrhenian
Sea*

GREECE

*Aegean
Sea*

*Ionian
Sea*

Peloponnese

Sicily

MALTA

Rhodes

Crete

U r a l   M o u n t a i n s

▲ The red deer
is found mainly
in forest areas in
northern Europe.

► Europe is one of the most industrialized continents, and
this steelmaking plant is located in the Ruhr Valley in western
Germany's central and southern territory, one of the largest

ICELAND

Lying in the North Atlantic Ocean, Iceland is a young, volcanic island. Its population relies largely on the fishing industry for trade.

Area: 38,700 sq. mi.
Population: 279,834
Capital: Reykjavik (175,000)
Major language spoken: Icelandic
Main religion: Evangelical Lutheran (Church of Sweden)
Currency: Icelandic krona
Main exports: frozen fish, shrimp and lobsters, salted fish, fresh fish, aluminum
Type of government: constitutional republic

ICELAND

Iceland is just 178 mi. east of Greenland and 495 mi. northwest of Scotland. Most of its landscape consists of a rocky plateau dotted with mountains. Its entire area averages between 1,964–3,110 ft. in height above sea level. Around 15 percent of the land is covered in ice or snowfields. The coastline is indented with deep bays, steep cliffs, and fjords on the east and northwest, while the south coasts tend to be more low-lying. Geologically, Iceland is a very young country still in the process of formation. The island sits on a major geological fault—the mid-Atlantic rift—which makes it one of the most volcanically active countries in the world.

THE ICELANDIC PEOPLE
Celtic people from Ireland and Norse people from Scandinavia were Iceland's first settlers, and almost all of the country's population are descendants of these peoples. The island was first controlled by Norway, and then Denmark,

▲ Sea fishing contributes more than 70 percent of all export income to the Icelandic economy. The biggest customers are the United Kingdom and Germany.

before becoming independent in the 1900s. Almost all electricity and much heating is generated by abundant hydroelectric and geothermal power.

▲ Thermal springs are found in various parts of Iceland and are harnessed to heat many buildings. Erupting hot water springs, called geysers, got their name from an example found on Iceland called Geysir.

▶ More than half of Iceland's population live in Reykjavik, its capital city. The center of Iceland's fishing and fish-processing industries, Reykjavik is also home to Iceland's only university and the world's oldest ongoing lawmaking body, the Althing (established in A.D. 930).

NORWAY

A mountainous and rugged country, Norway is the most northerly and westerly of the mainland Scandinavian nations and one of the most sparsely populated in Europe.

Area: 118,900 sq. mi.
Population: 4,525,116
Capital: Oslo (787,000)
Major language spoken: Norwegian
Main religion: Evangelical Lutheran (Church of Norway)
Currency: Norwegian krone
Main exports: petroleum and natural gas and their products, machinery and transportation equipment, metals and metal products
Type of government: hereditary constitutional monarchy

▼ The first major discovery of oil was made at the Ekofisk field in the North Sea in 1969, making a great difference to the Norwegian economy. Today Norway is Europe's largest oil producer, producing around 3.2 million barrels per day.

Norway is a long, narrow country that runs northeast to southwest along the Scandinavian Peninsula. A portion of the North Sea, called the Skagerrak, separates Norway from Denmark, and it shares a long land border with Sweden and much shorter, northerly borders with Finland and the Russian Federation. Norway's territory also includes the island of Jan Mayen and the island group of Svalbard in the Arctic Ocean. The mainland consists of a large number of high plateaus called *vidder*. In the far north they are still covered in glaciers. The Norwegians mainly live along the coast, including the cities of Bergen, Stavanger, and Trondheim, or in the southeast in and around the capital, Oslo.

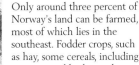

A COUNTRY OF WATER

Norway's western coastline is so indented that in a country which measures 1,643 mi. long, the coastline measures 13,235 mi. Along most of the coastline lie hundreds of islands known as the *skerryguard*. These islands provide some shelter from the open sea, allowing Norwegians to use the fjords and bays as natural harbors. Most of this coastline is free of ice, despite lying in northern latitudes, due to the warm Gulf Stream current. Much of Norway's landscape has been shaped by the glaciation. It has hundreds of rivers and streams and thousands of lakes.

FARMING AND FISHING

Only around three percent of Norway's land can be farmed, most of which lies in the southeast. Fodder crops, such as hay, some cereals, including rye, oats, and barley, and root vegetables, are common crops. Pigs, sheep, and cattle are all raised. No part of Norway is too far from the sea, and Norwegians have long relied on the sea for fishing, port trade, transportation, and boat- and shipbuilding industries. Norway has one of the largest fleets of merchant ships in the world, and its fishing industry catches around 2.6 million tons of fish each year.

SWEDEN

Sweden has a highly developed welfare state and
advanced industries that help give its population
a very high standard of living.

Area: 158,900 sq. mi.
Population: 8,876,744
Capital: Stockholm
(1,626,000)
Major language spoken:
Swedish
Main religion: Evangelical
Lutheran (Church of
Sweden)
Currency: Swedish krona
Main exports: machinery
and transportation
equipment (mainly motor
vehicles and electrical
machinery), paper
products, chemicals,
iron and steel products
Type of government:
constitutional monarchy

▼ The northern area of
Sweden is part of a region
called Lapland (Samiland),
which extends into
Norway, Finland, and
Russia. Lapland has an
Arctic climate, and
dogsleds are still used in
areas for transportation.

The kingdom of Sweden is the largest of
the three Scandinavian countries and the
most populous. Its eastern coast faces the
Gulf of Bothnia and the Baltic Sea, while its
much shorter western coast is an outlet to
the North Sea. Sweden's main land border
is with Norway, and to the west the country
is mountainous just like its neighbor. To the
northwest the Kölen Mountains contain
Sweden's highest points. In central,
eastern, and southern regions the
landscape is less rugged and consists
mainly of plateaus and rolling lowlands.
Periods of glaciation have left behind
many lakes. Sweden has more than 4,000
lakes over .39 sq. mi. in size, while its
largest, Lake Vänern, occupies 3,463 sq.
mi. Sweden also has many rivers, most
of which flow eastward, emptying into
the Gulf of Bothnia and the Baltic Sea.

SWEDEN'S CITIES

Sweden's largest city, Stockholm, is one
of the most elegant and picturesque capital
cities in the world. It is also Sweden's
second-biggest port and the country's
largest industrial area. Stockholm is home
to the country's national lawmaking body,
the Riksdag. Just outside Stockholm
is the official residence of the country's
monarchy. Sweden's largest port is the city
of Gothenburg found on its western coast.

FINLAND

Finland is a low-lying country of lakes and forests.
Physically isolated and remote from much of Europe,
Finland joined the European Union in 1995.

Area: 117,900 sq. mi.
Population: 5,183,345
Capital: Helsinki (936,000)
Major languages spoken:
Finnish, Swedish
Main religion: Evangelical
Lutheran (Church
of Sweden)
Currency: euro
Main exports: metal
products and machinery,
paper and paper products,
chemicals and chemical
products
Type of government:
constitutional republic

Lying between Russia to the east
and Sweden to the west, Finland also
shares a land border with Norway to the
north. The western coast of Finland faces
Sweden, separated by the Gulf of Bothnia.
The Gulf of Finland, to the south, flows into
the Baltic Sea. Most of Finland is relatively
level, with an average elevation of between
393–622 ft. The coast of Finland is marked
by thousands of mainly small islands. Many
of these are found in the southwest, where
an island chain called the Turun, or Turku,
archipelago extends west and joins the
Åland Islands. The Åland Islands are made
up of over 6,500 rocky reefs and granite
islands of which only 35 are inhabited.
The landscape of Finland was greatly altered
by glaciation. Experts estimate that glaciers,
several miles thick, forced Earth's crust
downward by many feet. Since
the glaciers and their weight have
disappeared much of Finland is
rising up from the sea at rates
of as much as 0.4 in. per year.

THE LAND OF THE
MIDNIGHT SUN
The north of Finland, a little
over a quarter of its territory,
lies within the Arctic Circle.
In its most northerly region,
the sun does not set for 73 days
in the summer and shines for 24
hours a day. This gives the region
its nickname of 'The Land of
the Midnight Sun'. In the same
area, during the dark winter period called
Kaamos in the Finnish language, the sun
does not rise above the horizon for 51 days.

LAKES AND FORESTS
Finland's scenery is dominated by large
forests, which cover three fourths of its
land. More than 1,100 species of trees and
plants are found in Finland. While some
deciduous trees, such as aspen and elm,
are found in the south, the vast majority

▲ A member of the Lapp
(Sami) people fishes in the
Arctic by cutting a hole in
the ice through which he
can extend his fishing line.

▶ Koli National Park is
located on the western
shore of Lake Pielinen
approximately 59 mi. east
of Kuopin. Over 120,000
visitors a year come to
admire the views and
hike through the park.

of its trees are coniferous and include pine
and spruce. These forests provide habitats
for a range of wildlife, including wild geese
and mammals, including the Arctic fox,
lynx, and wolf. Finland's forests are its
most important natural resource. In 2000
almost 30 percent of money gained from
exports came from its forests, including
timber, young trees, wood chippings, and
paper. Wood is one of only two naturally
occurring fuels. The other is peat, which
is mostly found in large peat bogs in the
northern third of the country. Finland has
around 87,000 lakes that make up around
ten percent of its land area. The largest
of its inland waterways is Saimaa in
southeastern Finland, which measures
approximately 2,730 sq. mi. Part
of a complicated network of natural
waterways, which includes 120 other
lakes containing a total of 14,000 islands,
the waters of the Saimaa flow to Lake
Ladoga in Russia, the largest
lake in Europe.

DENMARK

The smallest and most densely populated of the
Scandinavian countries, Denmark consists of
a peninsula and 406 islands.

Area: 1,400 sq. mi.
Population: 5,368,854
Capital: Copenhagen
(1,332,000)
Main language spoken:
Danish
Main religion: Evangelical
Lutheran (Church of
Sweden)
Currency: Danish krone
Main exports: machinery,
pig meat, pharmaceuticals,
furniture, textiles and
clothing
Type of government:
consitutional monarchy

Mainland Denmark occupies
the Jutland Peninsula, which
extends north from Germany
almost 211 mi. into the North Sea.
The portion of the North Sea that
lies between Sweden and Denmark's
eastern coast is called the Kattegat,
and the arm of the North Sea thst
separates Norway from northwest
Denmark is called the Skagerrak.
In the south of Jutland Denmark has
a 36-mi.-long border with Germany.
The Jutland Peninsula makes up around
70 percent of Denmark's land area. The
remainder is made up of a large series
of islands mostly found to the east of
Jutland. The country is responsible for
two self-governing territories: the Faroe
Islands and the world's biggest individual
island, Greenland.

A LOWLAND, TEMPERATE COUNTRY

Denmark is one of the lowest and flattest
countries in the world. Almost the entire
country is low-lying, with an average
elevation of only 98 ft. above sea level.
The 365 sq. mi. island of Bornholm, lying
east of Denmark in the Baltic Sea, is an
exception since it is covered with rocky
hills. The western coast of Jutland
is indented with lagoons, spits,
and sandbars. Fjords
cut into parts of

the eastern coast. The largest fjord,
Limfjorden, slices right through the
northern part of the Jutland Peninsula and
broadens into a complex series of inland
waterways. Denmark's climate is temperate
with mild summers, when temperatures can
reach 77°F, and cold, rainy winters, when the
average daily temperatures hover around the
freezing point. Winter temperatures are up to
50°F warmer than average for this latitude.
The warming effect of the Gulf Stream,
which sweeps northward along the west
coast of the country, is the reason for
Denmark's milder-than-typical climate.

▲ The Tivoli Gardens
is a large area in the
center of Copenhagen
that was opened in 1843.
It includes concert halls,
cafés, flower gardens,
and an amusement park.

▶ Nyhavn Canal in
Copenhagen is lined with
picturesque buildings—
many dating back to the
1500s. Most immigrants
to Denmark and just over
one fourth of the entire
Danish population live in
or around Copenhagen.
The city is situated on
the island of Sjaelland.

A FARMING NATION

Denmark's manufacturing and service industries are very important to the economy, although the country has few mineral resources. Almost two thirds of its land is used for farming. Centuries of cultivation have improved the land's ability to grow crops, particularly cereals, of which wheat, followed by barley and rye, are the most important. Much of Denmark's farmland is used to support livestock, especially pigs and cattle. In 2000 Denmark had 11.6 million pigs, 1.85 million cattle, and produced over 4 million tons of barley. It also has a large fishing fleet of around 2,500 vessels, which catch over one million tons of fish every year.

THE DANES

Denmark has been occupied for thousands of years but took its name from the Danes—a people from Sweden who colonized the region in around A.D. 500. Denmark's oldest town, Ribe, 16 mi. southeast of Esbjerg, was an international trading center as far back as A.D. 850. The Danish people stem almost entirely from the Danes and other Scandinavian peoples, who make up 96 percent of its population. Communities of people of German origin are found close to Denmark's border with Germany, and there are small numbers of Turks, Iranians, Pakistanis, and some refugees from countries such as the former Yugoslavia and Somalia. Denmark's people enjoy one of the highest standards of living in the world.

▲ The south Denmark island of Fyn has large expanses of fertile land on which cereal crops and fruit are grown. Together with a number of neighboring islands, Fyn makes up a Danish county with a population of almost 500,000.

FAROE ISLANDS

Lying in the North Atlantic Ocean halfway between Norway, Iceland, and Scotland, the Faroes are a group of islands that are a self-governing territory of Denmark.

Area: 540 sq. mi.
Population: 46,011
Capital: Tórshavn (16,700)
Main languages spoken: Faroese, Danish
Main religions: Evangelical Lutheran (Church of Sweden), Plymouth Brethren
Currency: Faroese krone
Main exports: fish and fish products
Type of government: self-governing dependency of Denmark

The Faroe Islands are clustered closely together and are separated by deep fjords. The islands were shaped by volcanic action and subsequent erosion, which has created sharp cliffs and towering stacks on a number of the islands and has deposited a relatively thin layer of soil in many places. Almost constant high winds mean that the islands have few naturally occurring trees, although some have been planted in artificially sheltered areas. Large flocks of seabirds are found on the islands' coasts, while a thick grass layer in many areas provides food for sheep. However, the majority of Faroe Islanders are engaged in fishing industries. The seas around the islands are rich in fish, including cod and haddock, and the prospects of offshore oil

exploration have increased following an agreement signed in 1999 between Denmark and the United Kingdom.

IRELAND

One of the most westerly European nations, the
Republic of Ireland occupies much of the island of
Ireland and consists of farmland, lakes, and mountains.

Area: 26,600 sq. mi.
Population: 3,883,159
Capital: Dublin
(1,009,000)
Main languages spoken:
English, Irish (Gaelic)
Main religion: Roman
Catholic
Currency: euro
Main exports: machinery
and transportation
equipment, chemical
products, food products
(particularly dairy products
and meat), manufactured
goods
Type of government:
parliamentary republic

The Republic of Ireland is located on
the most westerly part of the Eurasian
landmass and, like Great Britain, was once
part of the European mainland. Great
Britain and Ireland became separated
only around 11,000 years ago owing to
melting glaciers and rising sea levels.
Ireland's landscape consists of a large
central plain almost completely
surrounded by highlands near the coast.
The plain is relatively low, averaging
around 295 ft. in height and broken in
many places by low hills, lakes, and
rivers. The country's main river is the
Shannon, which rises in the north of
the country and forms a long estuary
south of Limerick. A broad, slow-moving
river, at 231 mi. in length, the Shannon
is the longest river in the British Isles.

THE EMERALD ISLE
Ireland's climate is moderated by
the warm waters of the North Atlantic
Drift, which help make the winters milder
than other places in a similar latitude.

The average daily
temperature in the winter
is between 40°F–45°F—as much as 57°F
warmer than comparable places of a similar
latitude. The opposite effect occurs in the
summer, when average temperatures are

▲ Found in the center
of Dublin, St. Patrick's
Cathedral was founded
in 1191, although a church
had been on its site since
the A.D. 400s. At 298 ft.
in length, St. Patrick's
is one of the largest
cathedrals in Ireland.

▶ Much local community
life in Ireland centers
around the local pubs
and bars, where stories
are told and local, Celtic
folk music is played.

▲ A sheep market in the town of Ballinrobe, 16 mi. south of Castlebar in County Mayo. In 2001 there were over 5.3 million sheep in the Republic of Ireland.

A CHANGING ECONOMY

For a long period Ireland's economy relied on traditional methods of agriculture, with crops such as sugar beets, potatoes, and cereals grown. Pigs were kept in their hundreds of thousands, while sheep grazed on the pastures of the mountain slopes, and cattle were raised in the center and south of the country. Agriculture remains important, but Ireland's economy is changing dramatically. Farming has been modernized with financial assistance from the European Union, of which the country is a part. Less than seven percent of its workforce is now employed in agriculture. Many more people work in new manufacturing industries, such as electronics and computing, and in the food, drink, and clothing industries. Ireland's beautiful landscape, history, and culture have been heavily promoted to foreign visitors, and in 2000 over 6.7 million tourists visited the country.

▲ An Irish peat cutter removes chunks of peat, which has been used for many centuries as a fuel. Peat is the remains of dead, rotted plants that have been squeezed together. When it is burned, peat generates heat. Several power plants in Ireland are powered by peat.

kept to a relatively cool 59°F–63°F. With the warming ocean currents and Atlantic winds come plenty of rain. It tends to rain on two out of three days throughout the year, and average rainfall can be as high as 98 in. in the mountains of the southwest. This heavy rainfall helps promote the thick grass, moss, and wild plants and flowers that cover much of the country and give Ireland the nickname "the Emerald Isle." Peat bogs, which occupy around ten percent of the land, are homes for rare wild plants but are threatened owing to peat's continued use as a fuel to generate power and also as a fertilizer. Many small mammals, including stoats, hare, and foxes, along with over 120 species of native birds, inhabit the country.

TRADITIONAL LIFE

All of Ireland has a long tradition of settlement stretching back at least 9,000 years. Around 2,400 years ago Celts arrived from mainland Europe. Since that time Ireland was often isolated from the rest of Europe—for example, it was never part of the Roman Empire—which led to its people developing a rich and different culture and language called Gaelic. English has taken over from Gaelic as the most widely spoken language and, although still taught in schools, is only the first language of a dwindling number of people in rural areas. Other elements of Irish culture still flourish in Celtic art, literature, and various forms of music.

▶ Found on the western coast of Ireland, the Cliffs of Moher are a series of shale and sandstone cliffs that reach heights in excess of 655 ft.

UNITED KINGDOM

A union of four countries—England, Scotland, Wales, and Northern Ireland—the densely populated United Kingdom lies off the coast of northwest Europe.

Area: 93,300 sq. mi.
Population: 58,778,002
Capital: London (7,640,000)
Main languages spoken: English, Welsh, Scottish, Gaelic
Main religions: Anglican, Roman Catholic, other Christian, Islam
Currency: pound sterling
Main exports: electrical equipment, chemicals, road vehicles, petroleum and petroleum products
Type of government: constitutional monarchy

▲ The London Eye towers 442 ft. over the Thames river. More than 15,000 passengers can travel in its pods each day.

▲ London was the first city to have a subway. The London Underground opened in 1863 and now serves more than 260 stations.

▶ The prehistoric stone circle of Stonehenge in southern England was built between 3200 and 1000 B.C. It is one of the most important prehistoric monuments in Europe.

The United Kingdom's territory consists of the island of Great Britain, a northeastern portion of Ireland, and a large number of smaller islands off its coast. Due to the warming effect of the Gulf Stream, the country has a temperate climate with relatively high rainfall and milder winters than usual for its latitude. Its location, at a point where many seas and air currents meet, means that its weather is extremely changeable. In general the south of the country tends to be warmer, and the west of the country tends to receive more rainfall.

A VARIED LANDSCAPE

For such a small area the landscape of the U.K. has great variation, from lowland areas barely above sea level to rugged mountain ranges in Scotland, Wales, and the north of England. Around half of Scotland consists of the Highlands and a large number of islands off its coast, while Wales' landscape is dominated by the Cambrian mountains, which run through much of the principality from north to south. Northern Ireland is a region of rolling plains with some low mountains. Northern England features hills and low mountain ranges, while most of the rest of the country is relatively flat with occasional areas of gentle hills.

The U.K. has a large number of rivers crisscrossing its land—most of the major cities are sited on rivers; for example, London is located on the Thames, and Newcastle is on the Tyne. The longest river is the Severn (219 mi.), which flows from central Wales to southwest England. Scotland's heavily indented coastline, and its

many lakes—known as lochs—reveal the past action of glaciers that have greatly shaped the country's landscape.

Glaciation also scoured out river valleys to form the lakes in the scenic Lake District of northwest England.

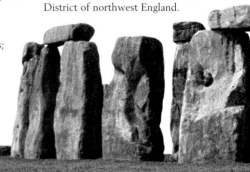

▼ At a height of 799 ft., Number One, Canada Square—known as the Canary Wharf building—is the tallest in the United Kingdom. It is a landmark in the Docklands area of London, which has been redeveloped since the 1980s from old, disused docks and warehouses to become a major financial, media, and business center.

The Lake District is also the home to England's highest point, Scafell Pike. Mount Snowdon is the highest point in Wales, and Ben Nevis is the highest point in Scotland and all of the British Isles. The U.K.'s largest lake is Lough Neagh in Northern Ireland, which is located just 12 mi. west of Belfast.

FLORA, FAUNA, AND FARMING

Most of the U.K. was once covered in forests, but thousands of years of human settlement and activity have reduced these areas dramatically. Although replanting programs have been in place since the early 1900s, the U.K. has one of the lowest levels of tree cover in Europe. Coniferous trees, such as pine, are found in Scotland, while the most common trees elsewhere are beech, ash, oak, and chestnut. The largest animal found in the wild is the red deer, found in Scotland and on Exmoor in southwestern England, while smaller mammals found in the wild include foxes, voles, shrews, mice, and squirrels. The hedgerows, moors, and coasts of the U.K. provide habitats for many species of birds, but all fauna and much of the U.K.'s rich collection of wildflowers have suffered from habitat destruction and air and water pollution. Around seven percent of the U.K. is under a degree of protection as national parks. These include Snowdonia in North Wales, the Lake District, and areas of the North York Moors, nine miles south of Middlesbrough. Much of the U.K. is farmed, with belts of cropland and large areas of pastures on which livestock herds are grazed. Although only one percent of the workforce is employed in agriculture, the U.K. is self-sufficient in 60 percent of all types of food and animal feed.

▲ Canals, such as the Trent and Mersey in the Midlands of England (opened in 1777), were built to transport materials and goods during the Industrial Revolution. Today the majority of canals are used for leisure cruising.

THE FIRST INDUSTRIALIZED NATION

The United Kingdom was the first country in the world to undergo an industrial revolution. Based on industries, including coal, iron, steel, and textiles, the U.K. became wealthy through inventing and pioneering the machines and factory processes used in industry. However, coal mining, steelworking, shipbuilding, and other heavy industry have been in decline for many years.

In their place have come fast-growing service industries and high-tech companies, medicine and chemical manufacturers, industrial researchers, and engineering firms. Aided by large offshore oil and natural gas reserves, the U.K. is the fourth-biggest economy in the world today and is a major international trading power.

CROWDED ISLANDS

The United Kingdom is Europe's fourth-most-populous nation after Russia and Germany yet is less than half the size of France, which has a smaller population. The population density is around 640 people per square mile, with 90 percent living in or around major towns and cities. In the past century the urban areas of the U.K. have sprawled outward, creating both new towns, such as Milton Keynes, halfway between London and Birmingham, and large urban areas called conurbations such as the many towns around Birmingham. The majority of the population of each of the three countries of Great Britain are situated in the south. The south coast of Wales includes the cities of Swansea, Cardiff, and Newport, while Scotland's two largest cities of Glasgow and Edinburgh are both south of the Highlands. The southeast is the most densely populated portion of England and is dominated by London. Founded by the Romans in A.D. 43, London is one of the world's foremost cities. Its prosperity is founded mostly on services, such as insurance, finance, and trading, while its many historic buildings and parks attract millions of tourists every year.

▲ Sitting on a giant volcanic rock that towers over Scotland's capital city, Edinburgh Castle has been the main Scottish royal fortress for many centuries.

▼ The United Kingdom has the largest energy resources of any member of the European Union, most of which is in the form of oil and natural gas situated off the country's east coast in the North Sea.

◄ The Millennium Stadium is the national stadium of Wales and hosts concerts and sports events. It has a sliding roof and seats over 72,000 spectators.

▲ Over 11 million cattle, including this Highland Breed, are raised in the U.K. The outbreak of foot-and-mouth disease in 2001 caused more than one million cattle to die.

THE U.K.'S PEOPLE

In the past the U.K.'s position as an island nation lying close to mainland Europe saw it undergo periods of both isolation and invasion. Migration by Celtic people, occupation by the Romans, and waves of invasion and settlement by Danes, Saxons, Vikings, and the Normans have all left their mark. Most of the U.K. population descended from these invaders and settlers. Sizable communities of other ethnic groups do exist, including people from former British colonies in Africa, the Caribbean, and south Asia, as well as Chinese, Jewish, and European peoples. Although Celtic languages still exist, especially in Wales, the dominant language is English, which is primarily a blend of Anglo-Saxon and Norman French.

FOUR COUNTRIES IN ONE

The U.K. has a complex political history. England and Wales were united by the 1500s, and the 1707 Act of Union formed the Kingdom of Great Britain, including Scotland. For a period from 1801 to the 1920s Great Britain and all of Ireland were ruled as one nation. Wales, Scotland, and Northern Ireland have their own national identity, different elements of culture, and a degree of government devolved away from the U.K. national government based in London. In 1999 the Scottish Parliament and the National Assembly for Wales were opened, giving these two countries more control over their own affairs.

The Northern Ireland Assembly, held in the city of Belfast, has been troubled by problems between the Protestant majority and the Catholic minority. The U.K. head of state is officially the monarch, but power is held by the prime minister, usually the leader of the majority political party in the House of Commons in Westminster, London.

A COLONIAL POWER

From the 1600s to the 1900s the U.K. was one of the world's major colonial powers, with the British empire laying claim to territory on every continent and exploiting its colonies' resources and peoples in order to grow wealthy and powerful. Most of its former colonies are now independent but are part of a loose alliance of states known as the Commonwealth. The U.K. still controls a number of dependencies as far away as the Falkland Islands in the south Atlantic and Turks & Caicos in the Caribbean. Closer to home are the Isle of Man, lying between Ireland and Great Britain, and the Channel Islands, lying off the northern coast of France. Both of these dependencies have their own legal systems, but the U.K. government is responsible for their external affairs. The U.K. continues to exert international influence through its close relationship with the U.S. and as a member of the European Union.

▲ The symbol of the Celtic cross is found at standing signs and statues, especially in Scotland and Northern Ireland.

▼ Giant's Causeway on the north coast of Northern Ireland was formed over 50 million years ago from volcanic lava that cooled to form over 40,000 basaltic pillars.

BELGIUM

One of the Benelux countries (along with Luxembourg and the Netherlands), Belgium is an industrialized nation in which 97 percent of its people live in urban areas.

Area: 11,700 sq. mi.
Population: 10,274,595
Capital: Brussels
(1,134,000)
Main languages spoken:
Flemish (Dutch), French,
German
Main religions: Roman
Catholic, Protestant
Currency: euro
Main exports: machinery
and transportation
equipment, chemicals
(particularly plastics),
food, diamonds, iron
and steel, textiles
Type of government:
parliamentary democracy

▲ Work building the City Hall in Belgium's capital city of Brussels started in 1402. The imposing tower is 314 ft. high.

► The Atomium stands in Heysel Exhibition Park in Brussels and has become a symbol of the city. Designed for the 1958 World's Fair, the 393-ft.-high structure is an aluminum model of a carbon molecule magnified 165 billion times.

The north of Belgium has a similar landscape to the Netherlands. It is a flat coastal plain, barely rising more than a few feet above sea level and is laced with river deltas and canals. Most of the coastline is marked by a belt of giant sand dunes that are among the largest in Europe. South of the coastal plain is a central plateau region that contains the country's best farming land. The southeastern area of the country is part of the Ardennes region, a rocky, heavily forested region with an average elevation of 1,506 ft. Belgium's main river, the Meuse, is linked with other rivers and canals, giving the country almost 992 mi. of inland waterways, most of which can be traveled by large boats.

A TRADING NATION

Belgium's location between a number of European countries, plus its access to the oceans via the Scheldt estuary, on which the port of Antwerp lies, has made it a major trading

nation. Belgium's manufacturing industries include metalworking, steel, cloth, and carpet making, and heavy engineering. Much of the electricity required by these industries is supplied by nuclear power, which generates almost two thirds of Belgium's electricity. Lacking large reserves of raw materials, Belgium imports many of them raw and exports finished or semifinished goods. Millions of tons of imports and exports pass through the port of Antwerp. Situated around 50 mi. inland from the North Sea, Antwerp is one of the largest ports in Europe.

LANGUAGE DIVISIONS

Belgium is divided into three federal districts that reflect, in part, its centuries' old language divisions between its Flemish or Dutch-speaking people, known as Flemings, and its French-speaking people, called the Walloons. Flanders, its northern district, is principally home to the Flemings, while the southern district, Wallonia, is populated mainly by French speakers. Bilingual signs in Flemish and French are common throughout the country, while a small German-speaking minority lives in the extreme east of the country. The third district, the land in and around Brussels, its capital city, has a mixed population. Brussels is home to one tenth of Belgium's population and is an international business center. The city is also the administrative center of the European Union and home to the major headquarters of the North Atlantic Treaty Organization (NATO).

▲ The picturesque city of Ghent, located in western Belgium, lies at the joining point of two rivers. These rivers, along with many canals, crisscross the city, dividing it into many small islands linked by more than 200 bridges.

LUXEMBOURG

A tiny nation bordering Germany, the Netherlands, and France, Luxembourg is a center for finance and for the European Court of Justice.

Area: 998 sq. mi.
Population: 448,569
Capital: Luxembourg (82,000)
Main languages spoken: Luxembourgian, English, German, French
Main religion: Roman Catholic
Currency: euro
Main exports: machinery and transportation equipment, plastics and rubber, textiles, processed food
Type of government: constitutional monarchy

Luxembourg's landscape can be divided into two areas. The northern one third consists of densely forested hills and many narrow valleys with fast-flowing streams. The southern two thirds have a more gentle landscape of meadows, vineyards, and forests. The southwest is heavily industrialized with large iron and steelworks and some chemical and food-processing plants.

The people of Luxembourg enjoy the highest standard of living in Europe. Almost one third of Luxembourg's workers are foreigners, many of them employed by more than 200 banks, including the European Investment Bank, which are based in the country. Luxembourg is also home to the European Court of Justice. Most of the country's population speak two or three languages.

French is the main language used in the courts, while German is the language used in newspapers and literature. For centuries Luxembourg was ruled by other countries, and it finally regained complete independence in 1890.

THE NETHERLANDS

Lying between Germany and Belgium with a long North Sea coastline, the Netherlands is one of the lowest-lying countries in the world.

Area: 13,100 sq. mi.
Population: 16,067,754
Capitals: Amsterdam (1,105,151); The Hague—seat of government (442,799)
Main language spoken: Dutch
Main religions: Roman Catholic, Protestant
Currency: euro
Main exports: machinery and transportation equipment (particularly motor vehicles), food (mainly meat and dairy products), chemicals and chemical products, petroleum
Type of government: parliamentary democracy under a constitutional monarch

Geographically, the Netherlands can be divided into two regions, the Low Netherlands to the north and west and a smaller region of gently rolling land, called the High Netherlands, to the southeast. The average elevation of the High Netherlands is below 164 ft. Because the Netherlands has no high hill ranges or mountains, the climate varies little from area to area, with only a slight difference in temperatures and rainfall between the coast and inland areas. The Netherlands has a temperate maritime climate shared by much of northwestern Europe. The winters are mild, while the summers are kept cool by westerly winds. Rainfall averages around 29 in. per year.

BELOW SEA LEVEL

The country derives its name from the Dutch word for low-lying land, and around one fourth of its land lies below sea level. Much of the Netherlands has been reclaimed from the sea or fortified to stop rivers from submerging the surrounding area. From the 1200s

on barriers were built to stop water from getting in, and windmills were used to pump out excess water. By the 1800s the Netherlands had over 9,000 windmills. Polders are areas of drained land surrounded and protected by embankments called dikes. Today there are over 5,000 polders in the Netherlands, the largest of which was the result of the Zuyder Zee works, during which time the inland sea, the Zuyder Zee, became a lake and 1,023 sq. mi. of land were created.

▶ Opened in 1996, the Frasmus Bridge provides a link over the river at the major European port of Rotterdam. Rising to a height of 455 ft. and spanning a width of 2,619 ft., the bridge took seven years to construct. Its steel deck contains lanes for motor vehicles, a tram track, two footpaths, and two cycle paths.

▲ 25,071 acres of fruit, vegetables, and flowers were grown under glass in the Netherlands in 2000. Over one tenth of this (2,853 acres) is devoted to growing peppers, which are shown here being harvested for export.

Without dikes and dams the most densely populated part of the Netherlands—around half of the country's land area—would be submerged by the North Sea and the country's rivers.

EUROPE'S LARGEST PORT

Located at the center of the most industrialized and populated area in the world is the port of Rotterdam. Originally a fishing village, Rotterdam was seriously damaged in the two world wars but has since developed into the world's largest port and is a major oil refining and trading center. It has a prime location 19 mi. inland from the North Sea and lies at the mouths of two important European rivers, the Rhine and the Meuse. Tens of thousands of cargo barges, loaded and unloaded at Rotterdam, travel the Rhine, taking raw materials and goods into France, Germany, and the heart of Europe. In 2000 397 million tons of goods traveled through Dutch ports, particularly Rotterdam. Shipping is not the only way goods are transported. Giant pipelines carry oil and petroleum products to other parts of the Netherlands, to Antwerp in Belgium, and also to Germany.

▶ The picturesque city of Amsterdam with its well-preserved buildings, 160 canals, and hundreds of bridges is a popular tourist destination for foreign visitors.

THE DUTCH PEOPLE

The Netherlands is one of the world's most densely populated nations, with 1,227 people per square mile. A proportion of the country's population are immigrants from Turkey, Morocco, and former Dutch colonies, including parts of Indonesia, Suriname, and the Netherlands Antilles. Half of the country is farmed, and Dutch farming is among the most advanced and intensive in the world. The Netherlands has one of the 20 largest and most powerful economies based on its transportation and trade services, including tourism and the engineering, chemical, and electronics industries.

GERMANY

The third-largest economy in the world, Germany lies at the heart of Europe and is a vital part of the European Union.

Area: 135,200 sq. mi.
Population: 83,251,851
Capital: Berlin (3,310,000)
Major language spoken: German
Main religions: Protestant, Roman Catholic
Currency: euro
Main exports: road transportation equipment, chemicals and chemical products, other machinery, electrical equipment, plastics
Type of government: federal republic

Germany extends from the Alps in the south to a northern coastline that borders both the North Sea and Baltic Sea, a maximum distance of 543 mi. The country's territory extends into islands in both seas, most notably the islands of Rügen, Hiddensee, and Fehmarn in the Baltic, and the East and North Frisian Islands in the North Sea. The country shares 2,245 mi. of borders with nine countries: France, Luxembourg, the Netherlands, and Belgium to the west; Switzerland and Austria to the south; Denmark to the north; and Poland and the Czech Republic to the east.

LOWLANDS AND UPLANDS
Germany's landscape is varied and can be split into three main geographical regions. A large lowland belt lies to the north and

▼ Heavy industry, such as this chemical factory near the Elbe river, remains an important part of the German economy, although services and light industries, such as electronics, contribute more to the economy.

▲ A horseshoe bend in the Saar river. This river starts its life in the northern Vosges mountains of France and meanders in a northwesterly direction through Germany before becoming a tributary of the Mosel river.

consists of dry, sandy plains with moors (bogs) and heaths. The second major area is the Central Uplands. Dividing the north from the south, it consists of hill and mountain ranges, river valleys, and plateau areas. The south consists mainly of hills and mountains and is heavily forested.

THE RHINE AND OTHER RIVERS

Germany's biggest river is the Rhine, which flows from the Alps in Switzerland through or along the boundaries of Austria, Liechtenstein, France, Germany, and the Netherlands before emptying into the North Sea. The Rhine acted as a natural boundary in historic times and is now a vital transportation link. In 1992 the 106-mi.-long Main-Donau-Kanal opened. This links the Danube with the Rhine, allowing heavy cargo to be carried through the center of Europe. Apart from the Rhine and Main, a further ten major rivers flow through Germany, including the Elbe and Ems. All provide important transportation links for industries along their banks.

GERMANY'S FORESTS

Germany is a heavily populated industrial country, but it is also large enough to have huge forested areas. Around 30 percent of Germany is forested. Half of all Germany's forested areas is owned by the state or by the local community, while farmers and forestry companies manage and harvest fast-growing coniferous trees for timber, paper, and other wood-based products. Germany's most famous forest, the Black Forest, covers an area of over 3,162 sq. mi. and attracts thousands of tourists to view its scenery and picturesque lakes.

▼ A major financial and commercial center that hosts many international trade fairs every year, Frankfurt is also the home of the European Central Bank. The city's airport is also among the busiest in Europe.

▲ A giant beer hall in Munich is in full swing as the city's Oktoberfest celebrates Germany's food, drink, and entertainment.

▼ The church of Ramsau is situated in the mountainous area of southeast Germany. It lies close to a mountain lake.

TRANSPORTATION AND CITIES

Germany has excellent land, sea, and air transportation links. More goods and people travel by road than any other mode, with 403,000 mi. of roads, including 7,068 mi. of highways. Many of the country's major cities are linked by high-speed rail links along which InterCity Express (ICE) trains travel at 174 mph. Regular flights between the major cities don't take much more than one hour. Germany has a large fleet of oceangoing merchant ships that sails from ports such as Bremen and Hamburg, the country's biggest port and fourth-largest urban area.

CONFLICT AND DIVISION

Germany has spent many more years as separate states than it has as one nation. Around 3,000 years ago a number of tribes settled in the Rhine and Danube river valleys. The Romans named the area Germania after one of these tribes, the Germani.

Until the 1800s the region was home to many different states but was unified into one nation in 1871. Germany suffered greatly after its defeat at the end of World War I in 1918. Under Adolf Hitler the country was again defeated at the end of World War II in 1945. Germany was then divided into four zones occupied by the U.K., France, the U.S., and the Soviet Union. By 1949 the occupation zones had become two separate nations. The Soviet occupation zone became the German Democratic Republic, or East Germany. The Federal Republic of Germany, or West Germany, comprised the three remaining zones. Both nations joined the security organizations of their previous occupying powers—West Germany was a part of NATO, while East Germany belonged to the Warsaw Pact. Germany was reunited in 1990 after the breakup of the Soviet Union. West Germany's 11 *lander*, or states, were joined by five new additions from East Germany: Brandenburg, Mecklenburg-West Pomerania, Saxony, Saxony-Anhalt, and Thuringia. Since then Germany has had to deal with the economic and social issues that come with reuniting two sets of people who have spent more than 40 years living apart.

FRANCE

The largest country in Western Europe, France
has a long history of political, economic, and
cultural influence that continues to this day.

Area: 210,700 sq. mi.
Population: 59,765,983
Capital: Paris (9,658,000)
Main language spoken:
French
Main religion: Roman
Catholic
Currency: euro
Main exports: machinery
and transportation
equipment, agricultural
products (particularly
food and wine), chemical
products, plastics
Type of government:
republic

▼ The TGV high-speed
train travels at speeds of
up to 186 mph, linking
Paris with major cities
throughout France.

Sixty percent of
France lies below
155 ft. in elevation.
Much of this land
consists of gently
rolling plains with
occasional rocky
outcrops and hills and
large river valleys. To the
northwest of the country the
regions of Brittany and Normandy
are more hilly and have heavily
indented coastlines. France
contains a number of distinct
highland areas. To the northeast the
Vosges are a series of gently rounded
summits over 200 million years old. South
of the Vosges are the Jura mountains, which
extend into Switzerland and reach 5,598 ft.
at their highest point. The Jura and Vosges
are dwarfed by the French Alps found in
the east of France. Peaks include Mont
Blanc, the second highest in Europe. The
south-central highland plateau, called the
Massif Central, was formed around 300
million years ago. Covering
around 15 percent of the

country, it was disturbed
by the formation of the
Alps 65 million years ago.
Volcanic activity ceased in
the region around 10,000
years ago, leaving behind
many extinct cones, outcrops, and pointed
hills called *puys*. A number of France's
major rivers begin their life in the Massif
Central, including the Loire. This and other
rivers, including the Seine and the
Rhône, have carved out large
valleys and have helped
create fertile lands.

▲ The European Parliament building in Strasbourg, in northeast France, opened in 1999. Members of the European Parliament are elected by voters of countries in the European Union.

▼ Outdoor eating and drinking at sidewalk cafés is a feature of life in France. This café is located on the Champs Elysées, a famous broad avenue in Paris that runs from the Arc de Triomphe—a distance of 1.17 mi.

INDUSTRY AND THE ENVIRONMENT

Although it was slow to industrialize, France has become a major industrial power since World War II. It has been aided by large reserves of minerals, including some of the richest deposits of iron ore in Europe. Coal, particularly from the north and the east, was once plentiful but is dwindling. France is one of the countries most committed to using nuclear power to supply its electricity needs. Seventy-seven percent of its electricity is generated from nuclear power plants. The country is also a key engineering center of Europe, with many companies devoted to producing machinery, cars, and defense products. The water and air pollution

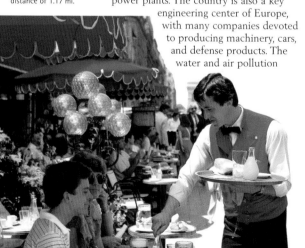

caused by these industries have had a detrimental effect on the country's environment. France's 37 million acres of forests and woodlands have suffered some acid rain damage but not as much as some of its eastern neighbors.

THE CULTURAL CAPITAL

As the world's most popular visitor destination with over 75 million arrivals in 2000, tourism is a vitally important part of the French economy. People travel all over the world to visit its many attractions—from the pilgrimage center of Lourdes at the foot of the Pyrenees and its winter ski resorts in the Alps to the unspoiled countryside of its river valleys and the warmth and glamour of coastal towns such as Nice. Paris is the number-one destination. More than just France's capital, the city exerts a dominant influence in government, business, and culture over the rest of the country. Paris dwarfs all other French cities. Its metropolitan area is the home of one fifth of the country's people and is around seven times more populous than France's next largest city, Marseille. The Île de la Cité is a small island on the Seine river first populated by a Celtic tribe over 2,200 years ago. Paris has since developed around this point, with the river winding its way through the city.

The city has had a long and turbulent history. It was occupied during both world wars and became the focal point of the French Revolution (1789–1799), which overthrew the succession of kings and queens who had ruled France for over 1,300 years. The legacy of France's long history can be found throughout Paris in such famous sites as Notre Dame cathedral, the Sorbonne university, and the Louvre museum.

FRANCE'S PEOPLE

Over 90 percent of French people were born in the country, are white, and speak French. In the distant past France was a trading crossroad and was settled by waves of different people, including Celts, Visigoths from Italy, and Vikings. The ancient Greeks started a trading colony in what is now the major city and port of Marseille over 2,600 years ago, while much of France later came under the control of the Roman Empire. A colonial power in the 1700s–1900s, much of North Africa, parts of West Africa, the Caribbean, Southeast Asia, and many islands in the Pacific all came under France's colonial rule. Although almost all of its colonies are now independent, large numbers of people from former French colonies, especially from North Africa, are now resident in France along with sizable communities of Portuguese, Italian, Spanish, and Turkish people.

▲ French cakes and sweets are frequently enjoyed by the French and visitors alike. This food stall is part of a market in the city of Nice in southeast France.

MONACO

Bordering the Mediterranean Sea and completely surrounded by France, Monaco has a largely rugged landscape and a mild climate.

Area: 1 mi.
Population: 31,987
Capital: Monaco (34,000)
Main languages spoken: French, Monegasque, English, Italian
Main religion: Roman Catholic
Currency: euro
Main exports: chemicals, plastics, electronic goods
Type of government: constitutional monarchy

Although land reclaimed from the sea has increased its area by 20 percent since 1964, Monaco remains the second-smallest nation in the world. Less than one fourth of Monaco's population was born in the country. Its population has grown, due to a large number of celebrities, businesspeople, and athletes attracted by low taxes settling there. Light industries, including cosmetics and clothing, are dwarfed in economic importance by the nation's banks and insurance industries. Monaco has been ruled by one family, the Grimaldis, for over seven centuries. The National Council of 18 elected members helps run the country.

▶ Attracted by Monaco's mild climate and its status as a tax haven, millionaires have made their homes among the luxury apartments that overlook the Mediterranean Sea.

Head of the Grimaldi family, Prince Rainier III died in 2005, having been Europe's longest-serving monarch.

SWITZERLAND

The most mountainous country in all of Europe,
Switzerland's people speak a number of
languages and enjoy a prosperous life.

Area: 15,400 sq. mi.
Population: 7,301,994
Capital: Bern (Berne)
(316,000)
Main languages spoken:
German, French, Italian,
Romansh
Main religions: Roman
Catholic, Protestant
Currency: Swiss franc
Main exports: machinery,
electronics, chemical
products, precision
instruments, watches,
jewelry
Type of government:
federal republic

▼ The Reuss river in
the Swiss city of Luzern
is crossed by seven
bridges. The town
is a German-
speaking
center.

Switzerland borders
France to the west,
Lichtenstein and Austria
to the east, Germany to
the north, and Italy to the
south. It has a landscape
of high mountain peaks
and lush green valleys and
plateaus, with around 20 percent of
its land covered in forests. The country's
main rivers, which include the Rhine
and the Rhône, flow in different directions
and finally empty into three different seas,
the North Sea, the Mediterranean Sea, and
the Black Sea. To the west winds from the
Atlantic Ocean carry much moisture and
cause rainfall. In the east the climate is drier
and has sharper differences in temperature.
Generally the lower-lying areas of plains and
valleys enjoy a temperate climate, while the
low-lying region south of the Alps receives
warmer weather.

THE MOUNTAINS OF SWITZERLAND

Over two thirds of its area are covered in
two sets of mountain ranges. Lying to the
west, the Jura mountains form a natural
border between Switzerland and France.
Between the Alps and the Jura mountains
lies the Swiss Plateau, a region with an
average elevation of 1,293 ft. and dotted
with many low hills. The country is home
to one fifth of the entire Alps mountain
system, which runs roughly east to

west across much
of the south and central
regions. The Alps are at
their most spectacular
along Switzerland's
southwestern border with Italy.
Famous peaks over 14,000 ft. include
the Matterhorn and Dufourspitze.

FARMING, TRADE,
AND TRANSPORTATION

Swiss farming and industry have had
to adapt to the country's landscape and
location in order to prosper. The terrain
makes farming difficult, yet the Swiss
people are self-sufficient in certain farm
products, including beef, dairy products,
and wheat. Swiss dairy products, including
cheeses and chocolate, are exported around

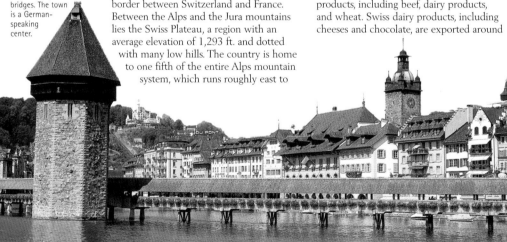

the world. Apart from fast-flowing rivers to generate hydroelectric power, Switzerland has few natural resources for industry. The country depends on importing raw materials, processing them, and using them for manufacturing goods, particularly small items of high value, including watches, medicines, electronics, scientific instruments, and handicraft products. Transporting raw materials in and finished goods out of the country relies on rivers and good road and rail links. Switzerland has worked with other nations to build a number of road and rail tunnels through its mountainous borders. Although Switzerland is landlocked, it has a national fleet of over 170 vessels that operate from foreign ports or from Basel, a city located on the Rhine.

MANY LANGUAGES

Even though Switzerland is a small country, its people speak a variety of languages. German is spoken by 65 percent of the population, French by 18 percent, and Italian by four percent. Swiss-German is very different from regular German, but because it is not a written language, regular German is used for newspapers and other print media. French is most often spoken and used in and around Geneva and in the west. Romansh is the fourth official language, although it is only spoken by less than two percent of the population.

A NATION APART AND AT PEACE

Switzerland has remained neutral in wars and conflicts for almost two centuries. Internally the country has remained stable and grown wealthy as a financial and banking center. These and other service industries employ over half of the workforce. The country has become the home of a number of major world organizations, including the Red Cross and the World Health Organization, both of which have their headquarters in the city of Geneva. The European headquarters of the United Nations is also sited in Switzerland, although the country only voted to join the UN in 2002. In 2001 over three fourths of voters rejected the proposal to join the European Union.

▲ Switzerland's famous Emmenthal cheese is pressed for around 20 hours, and the holes found in the cheese occur owing to gases trapped inside.

▼ The town of Lauterbrunnen is located 62 mi. east of Lausanne in a steep river valley that contains famous waterfalls, including the Trümmelbach and the Staubbach falls.

AUSTRIA

Famous for its mountain scenery and its historic and cultural sites, Austria is a landlocked country dominated by the foothills and mountains of the Alps.

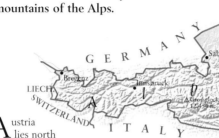

Area: 31,900 sq. mi.
Population: 8,19,929
Capital: Vienna (2,066,000)
Main language spoken: German
Main religions: Roman Catholic, Protestant
Currency: euro
Main exports: machinery and transportation equipment, chemicals, paper and paper products, iron and steel
Type of government: parliamentary democracy

▼ Traditional dancing at a winter ball in Vienna. The winter ball season is a major part of Viennese social life and lasts for around seven weeks, from New Year's Eve onward.

Austria lies north of Italy and Slovenia and south of Germany and the Czech Republic. The Alps sweep across much of its extent, covering more than two thirds of its land area. The mountain barriers are broken in many places by passes, including the Brenner Pass, 19 mi. south of Innsbruck and a major route between Austria and Italy. The country has a temperate continental climate, with temperatures varying according to altitude. The summers tend to be relatively short and mild, while the winters are cold and last three months or more in the valleys.

Austria is crossed by a number of rivers, including the Danube and its tributaries such as the Inn. Broad green valleys covered in lush meadows and pastureland frequently separate the mountains, while dense forests cover large portions of the mountains' lower slopes. Almost all of the croplands in Austria are situated in the northeast, while dairy farming is common in the mountain valleys.

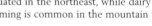

ELECTRICITY AND INDUSTRY

The fast-flowing rivers and mountainous landscapes help Austria generate vast amounts of hydroelectric power, enabling it to sell excess energy to neighboring countries. More than 70 percent of Austria's electricity is generated this way, much of which is used by industry to produce iron, steel, and aluminum. Such raw materials are used in manufacturing industries to build ships, machine tools, and motor vehicles. A feature of Austrian industry is the large number of factories and companies making and selling craft goods, including porcelain, fine glassware, jewelry, and traditional clothing. Much of Austria's industry

is centered around Vienna, the capital of the country. Around one fifth of the country's population live in Vienna, which is counted as one of the nation's nine *Bundesländer*, or provinces.

HISTORY AND GOVERNMENT

People have lived in Austria since prehistoric times, but the country rose to prominence from the 1200s onward under the rule of one family, the Hapsburgs. The country became the center of a vast empire, which, at its peak, included Hungary and many other nations such as Spain and the Netherlands. The cities of Vienna and Salzburg became major European centers of culture and the arts. Two world wars devastated the country and left it occupied by Soviet, U.S., British, and French forces. Austria regained its independence in 1955 and, in 1995, joined the European Union.

▲ The Tirol province of Austria is highly mountainous, with over 300 peaks above 9,821 ft. in elevation. Between the peaks are lakes, dense forests, and lush meadows that attract many walkers in the summer and winter sports enthusiasts in the winter. The largest city in the Tirol is Innsbruck, with a population of around 183,000.

LIECHTENSTEIN

The world's sixth-smallest nation, Liechtenstein is perched between the Rhine river and the Alps. Its neighbor, Switzerland, provides many of its services.

Area: 62 sq. mi.
Population: 32,842
Capital: Vaduz (5,000)
Main language spoken: German
Main religions: Roman Catholic, Protestant
Currency: Swiss franc
Main exports: machinery and transportation equipment, metal products, dental products, hardware
Type of government: hereditary constitutional monarchy

Liechtenstein is not as mountainous as its neighbors, Austria and Switzerland. During the winter it may experience heavy snowfall and temperatures below 32°F, but its summer is warm, with maximum temperatures as high as 82°F, allowing grapes and corn to be cultivated. On the plain near the Rhine river livestock is raised. First formed in 1719, the tiny principality has managed to stay independent and has flourished, giving its inhabitants one of the highest standards of living in the world. Low tax rates have attracted foreign businesses and banking, while sales of postage stamps generate almost one tenth of the country's income. Liechtenstein has no airport; the closest is found in the Swiss city of Zurich. Like its neighbor, Switzerland, Liechtenstein is not a member of the European Union.

HUNGARY

A landlocked country in central Europe, Hungary has a mixed economy and one of the most beautiful capital cities in Europe.

Area: 35,700 sq. mi.
Population: 10,075,034
Capital: Budapest (1,812,000)
Major language spoken: Hungarian
Main religions: Roman Catholic, Calvinist, Lutheran
Currency: forint
Main exports: industrial goods, consumer goods, machinery, food (cereals, meat, and dairy products)
Type of government: parliamentary democracy

▼ The Elizabeth Bridge is one of many bridges that cross the Danube river, linking both sides of the city of Budapest. The bridge was first completed in 1903 and then rebuilt between 1961 and 1964.

The Danube river divides Hungary in two. To the east lies the low-lying Great Plain, or Great Alföld, which covers more than half of Hungary. West of the Danube is a hilly region called Transdanubia. It contains the Bakony Mountains, which are close to Lake Balaton, the largest freshwater lake in central Europe. Hungary has a continental climate with cold, cloudy winters, late summers, and heavy rainfall in the spring and summer.

AGRICULTURE

The black-colored soils of the Great Plain are very rich in nutrients. Coupled with its mild, dry climate in which rainfall is heavy during the growing season, Hungary's farms have flourished. Fruit growing, wine making, and cereal and vegetable planting are the biggest users of cropland.

THE MAGYARS

In the past Hungary was a large country, but its land area shrunk after World War I when it lost its border provinces. Today over 95 percent of Hungarians are Magyars, descendants of a mixture of tribes that settled in Hungary over 1,100 years ago. The ancient Magyars had a strong culture, much of which is still kept alive today, especially in the towns and villages of the Great Plains.

BUDAPEST—QUEEN OF THE DANUBE

Hungary's capital, Budapest, is, in fact, an amalgam of three individual cities with long histories—Obuda became the first center of Hungary in the 900s; Buda, on the western bank of the Danube, was the former royal capital of the Hungarian empire; Pest, on the eastern bank, grew as a center of trade and industry.

POLAND

A large nation in northern central Europe, Poland's present borders were fixed in 1945 after the end of World War II.

Area: 117,600 sq. mi.
Population: 38,625,478
Capital: Warsaw (2,282,000)
Major language spoken: Polish
Main religion: Roman Catholic
Currency: zloty
Main exports: manufactured goods, machinery and transportation equipment, consumer goods, food (particularly poultry, eggs, pork, fruit, and vegetables)
Type of government: republic

The Republic of Poland borders seven other nations. Its land consists mainly of plains with low hills to the north, while the southern third of the country is mainly occupied by highland areas. Along the country's southern border are the Carpathian mountains. The Tatras, a mountain range within the Carpathians, is a protected national park and contains peaks over 7,860 ft. in height. The range is one of 28 national parks within Poland's borders.

PEOPLE AND WORK

Poland has substantial mineral and agricultural resources. It has the world's fifth-largest reserves of coal, in addition to deposits of copper, sulfur, zinc, lead, and silver. Its industrial region around Katowice is one of Europe's largest. The country contains around eight million beef and dairy cattle and 19 million pigs. Forests cover around 30 percent of Poland, but the forestry industry has been damaged by high levels of pollution from heavy industries.

POLAND'S RIVERS

Poland has over 2,480 mi. of navigable rivers and lakes. The Oder river flows through the west of Poland forming part of its border with Germany. Over 560 mi. long, it is joined by a canal to the Vistula, or Wisla,—Poland's longest river. Many of Poland's important cities, including Kraków and the capital, Warsaw, lie on its banks.

▼ Wawel Castle lies in the city of Kraków, one of the most ancient settlements in Poland. The castle overlooks the Vistula river and for centuries was the site where Polish kings were crowned.

CZECH REPUBLIC

A small, hilly country at the center of
Europe, the people and settlements of the
young Czech Republic have a long history.

Area: 30,400 sq. mi.
Population: 10,256,000
Capital: Prague (1,202,000)
Major languages spoken:
Czech, Slovak
Main religions: nonreligious
(nearly half), Roman Catholic,
athiest, Protestant, Orthodox
Currency: Czech koruna
Main exports:
manufactured goods
(including textiles), industrial
machinery, motor vehicles,
chemicals, fuel
Type of government:
republic

▼ Prague Castle is the
home of the President of
the Czech Republic. Much
of Prague's older buildings
have survived many
conflicts, including
numerous wars and
Soviet occupation.

On January 1, 1993 the
former federal republic
of Czechoslovakia was
dissolved, and two new nations
were created: the Czech Republic
and Slovakia. The Czech Republic
is the larger, more populous, and more
industrialized of the two nations. It is
actually the most industrialized of the
former communist nations of central
Europe. The country is landlocked and
lies 200 mi. from the Adriatic Sea and
202 mi. from the Baltic Sea. It shares
borders with four nations: Germany to
the west and north, Poland to the north
and east, Austria to the south, and Slovakia
to the southeast. Mountain ranges form
a large part of its borders, including the
Carpathians, which separate the country
from Slovakia, and the Sudetey mountains,
which run west of the city of Ostrava and
form most of the border with Poland. Most
of the country inside this ring of low
mountains consists of a large basin called
the Bohemian Massif. The country is split
into two regions—to the east lies Moravia,
and to the west lies Bohemia.

COLD WINTERS AND
WARM SUMMERS
The Czech Republic
has a humid, continental
climate and does not
experience the modifying
effects of ocean air masses. As a result,
the winters tend to be colder and the
summers warmer than in other European
nations at similar latitudes. Easterly winds
from Siberia force the temperatures down
to below freezing during the winter, and
snowfalls are often heavy on the high
ground. A little under two thirds of the
country is covered in forests, particularly
of spruce, pine, and beech trees, and
494 million ft.^{3} of timber was produced
in 2001. Farming has been modernized,
and cereal crops and root vegetables are
the most widely grown. In 1999 there
were 16,600 sq. mi. of cultivated land.

SLOVAKIA

A small, landlocked country in central Europe,
Slovakia was formed from the separation of
the two halves of Czechoslovakia in 1993.

Area: 18,800 sq. mi.
Population: 5,422,366
Capital: Bratislava
(464,000)
Major languages spoken:
Slovak, Hungarian
Main religions: Roman
Catholic, Protestant
Currency: Slovak koruna
Main exports:
semimanufactured
products, machinery and
transportation equipment,
chemicals, manufactured
goods, food
Type of government:
republic

Slovakia is bordered by five nations: Poland, Austria, the Ukraine, Hungary, and the Czech Republic. Much of the country is mountainous to the north and west, while the southern region consists of fertile lowlands on which crops, such as corn, wheat, and potatoes, are grown. Slovakia has a continental climate with warm summers and cold winters. Eighty-six percent of the country's people are Slovaks—a distinct ethnic group that has lived in the region for more than 1,000 years. People of Hungarian origin make up a further 11 percent of the population, reflected in the fact that Slovakia's capital, Bratislava, was the capital of the Kingdom of Hungary from the 1500s until the 1700s.

INDUSTRY AND ENVIRONMENT
Slovakia has reserves of copper, lead, iron, and lignite (brown coal) but has to import most of its oil and natural gas. Hydroelectric power from plants located on the Váh and other rivers provides an important source of energy, while Slovakia is also building nuclear power plants. A large scale hydroelectric project at Gabcíkovo, 25 mi. southeast of Bratislava, which involved damming the Danube river, has caused environmental concerns. Slovakia has high levels of industrial pollution, which have affected its forests and inland waterways. Around three in ten of all Slovakian workers are employed in industries such as iron and steelmaking and motor vehicle manufacturing. Many thousands more work in food-processing factories producing products such as beer and sheep's cheese. Most of the country's industry is centered around the capital city, Bratislava, or to the southeast around the city of Kosice.

▶ The Tatra, or Tatry, mountain range is the highest range of the Carpathian mountains, which lie along the Poland–Slovakia border. The range consists of more than 300 peaks, and its lower slopes are heavily forested with pine and spruce trees that provide habitats for animals, including bears and eagles. A popular year-round leisure destination, visitors come to hike its mountain trails and to view its many picturesque mountain lakes.

SPAIN

The fourth-largest nation in Europe, Spain was once the center of a giant colonial empire and possesses a rich culture, history, and fine architecture.

Area: 192,800 sq. mi.
Population: 40,077,100
Capital: Madrid (3,969,000)
Main languages spoken: Castilian (Spanish), Catalan, Galician, Basque
Main religion: Roman Catholic
Currency: euro
Main exports: transportation equipment, agricultural products, machinery
Type of government: constitutional monarchy

Spain is the fifth-most-populous nation in Europe. It shares land borders with Portugal, Gibraltar, and two nations in the Pyrenees mountains: France and Andorra. Spanish territory includes the Balearic and Canary islands and three smaller island groups off the coast of Africa. Spain has a long Atlantic coastline to the north and northwest of the country, and on its eastern side it borders the Mediterranean Sea.

CLOSE TO AFRICA

Spain occupies four fifths of the Iberian Peninsula, the European landmass closest to Africa. It is separated from North Africa by the Straits of Gibraltar—the Mediterranean's narrow outlet to the Atlantic Ocean. Spain administers two small areas in the north African country of Morocco called Ceuta and Melilla. Close to the straits on the Spanish mainland is the British dependency of Gibraltar. This 16 sq. mi. territory is home to almost 28,000 people, most of whom are engaged in tourism and shipping. Spain and the U.K. have been contesting the dependency's sovereignty for many years. A referendum in November 2002 saw Gibraltarians vote in favor of staying as part of the U.K., but negotiations are expected to continue in the future.

THE MOUNTAINS AND THE MESETA

Spain has a number of large mountain ranges that cross different parts of the country, as well as a huge central plain, called the Meseta, which occupies almost half of the Spanish mainland. To the north lie the Pyrenees and, westward, the Cordillera Cantabrica mountains, which run close to Spain's northern coastline with the Atlantic

▲ Flamenco originated in southern Spain in the 1700s and is an exciting mixture of dance, guitars, and percussion instruments.

before veering southward toward northern Portugal. To the east mountains run southeast from the Cordillera Cantabrica toward the Mediterranean Sea, while south of the central plain lies the Sistemas Béticos. The Meseta covers an area of around 81,900 sq. mi. and has an average elevation of 2,296 ft. It contains the oldest geological features of the Iberian Peninsula. Much of the plain is treeless, and water is drained by two major rivers, the Duero and the Tagus, and their tributaries. A series of block mountains, called Sistema Central, occurs in the middle of the Meseta. There is a marked difference in soil quality between the east and west parts of the Meseta. The underlying limestone rocks of the eastern plains have been weathered to form richer soils and provide good agricultural areas.

CLIMATE AND FARMING

Most of Spain has an essentially warm Mediterranean climate that varies with altitude and location. While temperatures in parts of northern Spain fall below 32°F in winter, Málaga, on the south coast, has an average daily winter temperature of 57°F. Most of the country receives less than 24 in. of rainfall each year, and droughts frequently occur in the Meseta. Farmers in many regions rely on irrigation systems to transport water to their fields, and the problem of desertification is growing. Spain is traditionally an agricultural nation that grows a wide range of crops, from sugar beets and cereals to citrus fruits and grapes. The country has industrialized rapidly in the past four decades, but farming and food processing remain very important. Spain is also one of the world's leading wine makers.

▲ The Guggenheim museum was opened in the industrial city of Bilbao in 1997 and within a year had received 1.3 million visitors. Covered in titanium sheets, it is a supreme example of modern architecture.

▼ These Spaniards are harvesting grapes near the southern city of Málaga. In 2000 Spain produced just over six million tons of grapes.

▲ The layout of the city of Toledo is dominated by the Alcázar, a fortress palace built in the 1300s and since renovated on several occasions. Toledo lies in central Spain on the Tagus river not far from Madrid.

▼ The giant cone of the volcano El Tiede lies at the center of Tenerife, the largest of the Canary Islands. El Tiede reaches an elevation of 12,195 ft. and is the highest point in the islands and Spain.

A VARIETY OF CULTURES

Until the 1400s many waves of settlers had helped make Spain a patchwork of different states with varying cultures. Following the Roman conquest of the native Iberian people settlers and invaders from northern Europe arrived, as well as Muslim people from North Africa. Between the 800s and 1300s the land was a flourishing center of Islamic arts, culture, and science that influenced the architecture and society for centuries afterward. Spain has been very influential in European art, architecture, literature, and music, and traditional art forms and entertainment have survived to this day. Several regions in Spain have maintained their own distinct culture and identity, including the Basques in northern Spain and the Catalans in the east and

northeast of the country. After the Spanish Civil War (1936–1939) Spain was ruled by a dictator, General Francisco Franco, until 1975. During his leadership minority languages and customs were banned. Separatist movements in the Basque region and Catalonia, which had existed before Franco's rise to power, strengthened in their demands for independence from Spain. Democratic elections and a new constitution were established in the late 1970s. The separatist movements still exist, but Basque, Catalan, and Galician languages are all recognized and taught in schools.

CITY LIVING

With a move to more manufacturing and service industries has come a migration of Spaniards from the countryside to towns and cities. Around three fourths of Spaniards now live in towns and cities— of which Madrid is the biggest, as well as being the capital and seat of government. Unusually for a European capital city, Madrid, which sits in the center of the Meseta, is neither located on one of the country's major rivers nor on the coast, like Barcelona, Spain's second-largest city. Barcelona is a major Mediterranean port and the center of a large and densely populated industrial region.

A MAJOR COLONIAL POWER

In the late 1400s Spain became united as one nation under the rule of Queen Isabel and King Ferdinand. At around the same time some of the first major explorations of other continents by Spanish sailors were underway. These resulted in Spain building up a large colonial empire. By 1600 Spain controlled parts of North and South America, much of Central America, and a number of Caribbean islands. The Spanish empire also included Portugal, the Netherlands, Austria, and parts of France, Germany, and Italy. Conflicts from the mid-1600s onward caused Spain to lose its European territories by 1714 and, by 1850, almost all of its South American colonies.

A TOURISM GIANT

Spain is one of the world's top-five tourist destinations, and in 2000 the revenue from tourism was over $30 billion. Half of all visitors come from Germany and the U.K., lured by the warm climate, the beaches of the Mediterranean, particularly those of the Costa del Sol, Costa Blanca, and Costa Brava, and major cities of culture and history such as Barcelona, Madrid, and Valencia. The country's two main island groups—the Balearics in the Mediterranean and the Canary Islands in the Atlantic—have also become major tourist destinations. The Canaries are the remains of steep-sided volcanic cones, and their land is rugged with relatively sparse vegetation. Year-round sunshine and mild winters not only

attract many tourists but also enable bananas and tomatoes to be grown for export. The Balearics include the islands of Majorca, Minorca, and Ibiza, which have become popular vacation destinations. Development on a huge scale has transformed large parts of both groups of islands and has led to environmental concerns.

▲ Café customers sit and enjoy the views found in the Plaza Mayor in the center of Spain's capital, Madrid. The plaza was built in the early 1600s and was originally used by royalty to watch plays, bullfights, and royal pageants.

ANDORRA

A small, mountainous principality in the Pyrenees, Andorra has existed as a separate state since 1278 and relies on tourism and its status as a tax haven.

Area: 174 sq. mi.
Population: 68,403
Capital: Andorra la Vella (21,000)
Main languages spoken: Catalan, French, Castilian
Main religion: Roman Catholic
Currency: euro
Main exports: motor vehicles, electrical machinery
Type of government: parliamentary coprincipality

Andorra lies in the eastern Pyrenees, bordering both France and Spain. Its land consists of sharp mountain peaks, mountain slopes, and a series of valleys. Andorra has a large number of natural sources of hot water known as thermal rock springs. The summers are dry and relatively warm, but in the winter snowfall and cold temperatures mean that its mountain slopes are covered with snow for many months. Only four percent of its land can be cultivated; much of the remainder is forested. Andorra relies on its snowfall to lure winter visitors in their millions. Visitors at other times are attracted by its charm and tranquillity. Andorra's heads of state are the coprinces

—French and Spanish authorities who in modern times have been the Spanish Bishop of Urgel and the French president. In 1993 Andorra introduced a new constitution that gave its inhabitants free elections and the right to join trades unions. In the same year Andorra joined the United Nations, although France and Spain still remain responsible for its defense. Native-born Andorrans make up only around 30 percent of the population. Most of the remainder are immigrants from France and Spain. Andorra la Vella is the highest capital in Europe.

PORTUGAL

Lying on the far west of southern Europe, Portugal is a long, rectangular-shaped country. It is one of the most rural countries in Western Europe.

Area: 35,400 sq. mi.
Population: 10,084,215
Capital: Lisbon (3,942,000)
Main language spoken: Portuguese
Main religion: Roman Catholic
Currency: euro
Main exports: textiles and clothing, machinery and transportation equipment, footwear, cork, chemicals
Type of government: republic

▼ Built on seven hills around the estuary of the Tagus river, Lisbon is a major European city and important deep-water port.

Portugal occupies the southwestern part of the Iberian Peninsula and shares borders in the north and east with Spain, while facing the Atlantic Ocean to the south and west. Northern Portugal is mountainous. The highest part is a highland region that in winter is snow-covered and popular for skiing. Much of the forests that cover around 35 percent of the country are also found in the north. Portugal's major river, the Tagus, rises in western Spain and divides Portugal into its northern and southern regions. The Douro and the Guadiana rivers, both of which also flow into Spain, are the other major rivers. South of the Tagus the land is much flatter and more low-lying. Much of it consists of vast plains that are divided from the south coast by a mountain range. The south coast region, known as the Algarve, is popular as a tourist destination.

TRADITIONAL FARMING

Around ten percent of Portugal's population are engaged in farming, while almost one fourth live in rural areas. The dry soil and climate of the southern part of the country have allowed olives, grapes, and fruits to flourish, and Portugal is renowned worldwide for the production of table wine and two fortified wines, madeira and port, named after the city of Oporto. Cereal grains are grown, and

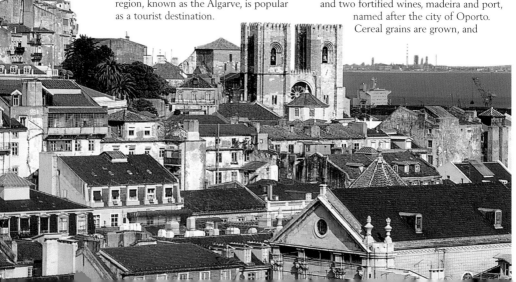

◄ Over 12 million tourists visit Portugal every year, and a large proportion of them come to the Algarve region in the south of the country. It is renowned for its wide, sandy beaches and warm climate.

livestock are raised on the flatter uplands, as well as on the plains near the coast. Traditional agricultural methods are still practiced in large parts of Portugal. As a result, wild birds and animals have been able to flourish without losing their natural habitats. In the last 20 years Portugal has undergone major economic changes. In particular it has increased its levels of light manufacturing industries, including clothing, footwear, and paper and food processing.

A SEAFARING NATION

Portugal's long coastline with the Atlantic has meant that—for hundreds of years— many of its people have relied on fishing and trade to make a living. This is still partly the case today, with major ports, such as Lisbon and Oporto, and large fishing fleets. Trawlers fish the Atlantic for cod, hake, mackerel, halibut, and anchovies, while sardines account for one third of all fish catches. In more shallow waters near the coast oysters and other shellfish are harvested. From the 1400s onward Portuguese explorers traveled the world, and the country became a colonial power, with colonies in Africa, the Caribbean, South America, and Asia. In 1999 Portugal relinquished control over the last European colony in the Far East when it handed Macau back to China. Today most of Portugal's trade is conducted with other members of the European Union.

▶ Portugal is the world's leading producer of cork, the thick bark of a particular evergreen oak tree that grows in abundance in the country.

ISLANDS AND ADMINISTRATION

Portugal first won its independence from Moorish Spain in 1143 and was ruled by a monarch until 1910, when it became a republic. Portugal is divided into seven administrative regions, which include the Atlantic island groups of Madeira and the Azores. Madeira consists of three small islands and one main island on which its capital, Funchal, is located. Covered in subtropical and tropical plants, Madeira, a popular vacation destination, is around 620 mi. southwest of Portugal. The Azores are a group of nine volcanic-formed islands and smaller islets. They lie just over 744 mi. west of Lisbon.

▲ This distinctively styled pottery is from Sintra, a small collection of towns and villages on the slopes of the Sintra mountains around 15 mi. from Lisbon.

ITALY

Unified as one country in 1860, Italy is now a major European industrial country with a large agricultural base.

Area: 113,500 sq. mi.
Population: 57,715,625
Capital: Rome (2,651,000)
Major language spoken: Italian
Main religion: Roman Catholic
Currency: euro
Principal exports: machinery and transportation equipment, electrical machinery, precision machinery, chemicals, textiles, clothing and shoes, processed metals
Type of government: republic

▼ The city of Naples was founded around 2,600 years ago by the ancient Greeks. Today it is one of Italy's largest ports and the center of industry in southern Italy. Mount Vesuvius, an active volcano, is closeby.

Much of Italy extends into the Mediterranean Sea as a long peninsula. It is bordered by five nations to the north: France, Switzerland, Monaco, Austria, and Slovenia, while within its territory are two tiny independent states, San Marino and Vatican City. In the northeast is Italy's largest plain, the Plain of Lombardy, which is drained by Italy's longest river, the 404-mi.-long Po river. Running along the west coast from Genoa to Naples are a series of lowlands separated by mountains and plains. This region, along with the Plain of Lombardy, has Italy's most fertile soil and are the most populated parts of the country.

SICILY

Italy's territory includes Sicily, the largest island in the Mediterranean, which is separated from the mainland by the Straits of Messina. Most of Sicily is a plateau of between 656–1,640 ft., with higher mountains to the north and several isolated volcanic peaks. The most famous of these is Mount Etna, which, at 10,998 ft., is Europe's highest active volcano. Sicily's warm, dry climate allows large crops of citrus fruits, grapes, and olives to be grown. Fishing is extremely important to the island economy, with around one fourth of all Italian fishing vessels based in Sicily.

SARDINIA

North of Sicily, the island of Sardinia is also mountainous, with its best farmland where a large plain lies on the southwest. Cereals, olives, tobacco, and grain are the chief crops, while the mining industry extracts lead, copper, zinc, and salt from the island. Sardinia's population of more than 1.5 million live in a number of towns mostly situated around the island's coast.

NORTH-SOUTH DIVIDE

Italy is divided into 20 administrative regions, but geographers and economists talk of two Italys: the north and the south.

The north is the industrial heart of the country, producing chemicals, iron, steel, textiles, electrical goods, and cars. Major industrial cities in the north, including Milan and Turin, are home to giant Italian companies, like Olivetti and Fiat. Northern Italy is one of the most prosperous regions in Europe. This is in contrast to the south of the country, which is poor with high unemployment. There traditional agriculture and small-scale industries are the dominant way of life. Poverty has forced many southern Italians to migrate to the north.

▲ The Marmolada Massif is part of the Dolomites mountain range in northern Italy. The highest peak in the Dolomites, the Marmolada Massif, is also home to the biggest glacier in the eastern Alps.

▼ Tomato pickers hard at work harvesting their crop. Italy is the second-largest grower of tomatoes in the world and processes much of its crop into sauces and pastes used in Italian cuisine.

SAN MARINO

The third-smallest nation in Europe, San Marino was
established in the A.D. 300s and is completely surrounded
by Italy. It relies on tourism for much of its income.

Area: 23 sq. mi.
Population: 27,730
Capital: San Marino (5,000)
Main language spoken:
Italian
Main religion: Roman
Catholic
Currency: euro
Principal exports: wine,
wheat, woolen goods,
furniture, ceramics
Type of government:
republic

Located in central Italy in the
Apennine mountain range, San
Marino is a tiny country with a maximum
length of around nine miles. Its landscape
is dominated by Monte Titano, which has
three individual peaks. Each of these peaks
is topped by a medieval fortress: la Rocca,
la Cresta, and Montale. The land to the
northeast of the mountain slopes gently
toward the Romagna plain, while to the
southwest there are a number of hills.
Several large streams run through San
Marino, including the Ausa and Marano.
The country is crowded, with an average
population density of over 1,197 people
per square mile. Hewn out of the steep
slopes of Monte Titano is the nation's

capital, also
called San Marino.

Agriculture and stone quarrying
were important in the past, but today
San Marino relies on tourism for around
three fifths of its income. The spectacular
location of San Marino's settlements and
their history, along with the mild climate,
lure 2.5 million tourists within its borders
every year. Three fourths of these are
Italians, and many tourists arrive via
the Italian city of Rimini, the closest
airport to San Marino.

VATICAN CITY

The world's smallest independent state, Vatican City
is encircled by the city of Rome. It is home to the head
of the Roman Catholic church, the pope.

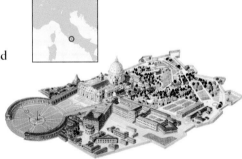

Area: 108.7 acres
Population: 880
Capital: Vatican City
(880)
Main languages spoken:
Italian, Latin
Main Religion: The
Vatican is the
headquarters of the
Roman Catholic church.
Currency: euro
Main Exports: none
Type of government:
theocracy

Vatican City lies near the Tiber river
and is cut off from Rome by its
medieval walls. All food, goods, and
energy supplies have to be imported.
Vatican City's economy is unlike any
other nation in the world. Money comes
from investments and from the churches
and followers of Roman Catholicism around
the world. In addition, admission charges
and sales of literature and souvenirs to the
hundreds of thousands of tourists who visit
provide a large proportion of the state's
income. The Vatican's form of government
is a theocracy. The person elected pope
for life by the Roman Catholic church has
supreme control over the country's laws and
government. Security is the task of the 100-
strong Vatican army called the Swiss Guard.

▶ Built in the 1500s, St. Peter's Basilica in Vatican City
is one of the world's largest religious buildings.

SLOVENIA

Part of former Yugoslavia, Slovenia is a small, scenic, and mountainous country that gained its independence in 1991.

Area: 7,800 sq. mi.
Population: 1,932,917
Capital: Ljubljana (250,000)
Main languages spoken: Slovenian, Serbo-Croatian
Main religion: Roman Catholic
Currency: tolar
Main exports: machinery and transportation equipment, chemicals, foodstuffs
Type of government: republic

▼ A market in progress in the Slovenian capital city of Ljubljana. Located on the banks of two rivers, the city has been a major transportation center for many centuries. Today it is an industrialized city with large heavy engineering and paper, soap, and chemical factories.

Slovenia borders Italy to the west, Hungary to the east, Austria to the north, and Croatia to the south. The country has a small 29-mi.-long coastline with the Adriatic Sea. Much of the northern and western parts of Slovenia are occupied by mountains, which are heavily forested on their lower slopes. Almost half of Slovenia is covered in forests, which still provide habitats for small numbers of bears, wolves, and lynx. The eastern portion of the country lies on a barren limestone plateau. Over millions of years the erosive actions of rainwater in this region have formed some of the most impressive cave systems in Europe, including the 12-mi.-long Postojna caves.

Slovenia has a continental climate with cold winters and warm summers. Forty-five percent of the country's population live in small farming communities, where cattle and sheep raising are the most important activities. In the northeast of Slovenia, where the climate is warmer, wine making is an important industry. Brown coal, lead, zinc, and uranium are among the minerals found within its borders, and Slovenia has a small but flourishing manufacturing industry. Despite being ruled by other nations for long periods of their history, the Slovenian people, over 85 percent of whom are descendants of Slavs, have retained much of their rich culture and craft skills. Slovenia's people enjoy relatively high standards of living, health care, and education. The country has the lowest number of prisoners as a proportion of its population, with just 630 in prison in 2001.

MALTA

Strategically located in the Mediterranean Sea between Europe and North Africa, Malta has been an important trading center for more than 2,000 years.

Gozo
Rabat
(Victoria)
Comino
Mediterranean Sea

Sliema ■VALLETTA
Rabat ■ Birkirkara

MALTA Malta

Area: 124 sq. mi.
Population: 397,499
Capital: Valletta (82,000)
Main languages spoken: Maltese, English
Main religion: Roman Catholic
Currency: Maltese lira
Main exports: machinery and transportation equipment, manufactures (mainly textiles, clothing and footwear), chemicals
Type of government: parliamentary democracy

The Maltese archipelago consists of three inhabited islands—Malta, Gozo, and Comino—and two uninhabited islands. They lie in the middle of the Mediterranean Sea around 56 mi. south of the Italian island of Sicily and more than 155 mi. from the coast of North Africa. Malta is the largest of the islands. Measuring 17 mi. by 9 mi. at its greatest extent, the island's 85-mi.-long coastline is rocky and contains many low cliffs, bays, and natural harbors. There are also a number of sandy beaches, which, along with the country's warm, dry climate and long history, attract over one million vacationers every year. Away from the coast Malta's landscape is one of mainly low hills, with small farming fields cut into the hill slopes as terraces. Crops are grown on the terraces, including feed for livestock, flowers, and citrus fruits. Malta has no rivers and little surface water. It relies on desalination plants, which produce freshwater from seawater, for its water supply. Lying northwest of Malta and linked by a regular ferry service, the island of Gozo is less populated but has more fertile soils in which grapes, other fruits, and vegetables are grown. The Maltese islands' strategic location has seen them occupied by the ancient Phoenicians, Greeks, Romans, Normans, Arabs, and Turks. The last colonial power to control Malta was Great Britain, from which Malta became independent in 1964. Shipping and trade remain vitally important to the Maltese economy. Malta has few natural resources and has to import fuel, raw materials, and many foodstuffs.

▼ Lying on the southeastern coast of Malta, the harbor and town of Marsaxlokk has been a site of the Maltese fishing industry for many centuries.

CROATIA

Founded in A.D. 800 and part of Yugoslavia during the 1900s, Croatia lies on the crossroad between central Europe and the Mediterranean countries.

Area: 21,800 sq. mi.
Population: 4,390,751
Capital: Zagreb
(1,081,000)
Main language spoken:
Croatian
Main religions: Catholic, Orthodox
Currency: kuna
Main exports: basic manufactures, machinery, chemicals, fuels, food
Type of government: parliamentary democracy

▼ The ancient historic town and port of Dubrovnik is one of the most scenic settlements in all of Croatia. Originally founded in the A.D. 600s, it is overlooked by Mount Srjd and features heavily fortified stone city walls.

Croatia borders Slovenia and Hungary to the north, while its eastern border with Serbia is partly defined by the Danube river. Croatia wraps around the northern and western sides of Bosnia & Herzegovina and extends along the Adriatic Sea with one 12 mi. break, giving Bosnia & Herzegovina a short Adriatic coastline. The remaining Croatian territory, which includes the city of Dubrovnik, is cut off from the rest of Croatia and has a short border with Serbia & Montenegro. The western part of Croatia is known as Dalmatia and is a rocky and relatively barren land. Changes in sea level have drowned mountain valleys, creating many steep islands and small, rocky peninsulas. This western part of Croatia experiences a Mediterranean climate, while the remainder of the country's climate is continental with colder winters. Croatia's large river, the Sava, flows into the Danube. Around one fifth of the country is devoted to agriculture, with the most fertile region in the east. Pigs, chickens, and dairy cattle are raised, while cereal crops cover almost two thirds of the land. Other important produce includes sunflower seeds, soybeans, and sugar beets. The country has rich mineral resources, including oil and coal, and today, following the damaging conflicts of the 1990s, much aid and investment is being introduced into rebuilding its former industries.

BOSNIA & HERZEGOVINA

Bosnia & Herzegovina became independent of Yugoslavia in 1992 and is now rebuilding following a devastating civil war.

Area: 19,700 sq. mi.
Population: 3,964,388
Capital: Sarajevo (552,000)
Main language spoken: Serbo-Croatian
Main religions: Islam, Catholic
Currency: convertible mark
Main exports: food, timber, basic manufactures
Type of government: republic; partial democracy

▼ The city of Mostar is surrounded by high, barren mountains. Formerly home to Roman Catholic Croats, Bosnian Muslims, and Serbs, the city was heavily damaged during the civil war, and today Serbs no longer live there.

Bosnia & Herzegovina lies in the Balkans bordering Serbia & Montenegro and Croatia. The country's rugged landscape is very mountainous in the north, while to the south there are flatter, more fertile regions. Cereal crops and flax are grown in the north, while tobacco, fruit, and cotton are important in the south. Large parts of the country lie on a barren limestone plateau. Underground rivers flow through this area, and there are many mineral springs. Almost half of the country is covered in forests of oak, beech, and pine trees. Since the time of the Roman Empire many different religious and cultural groups have settled here. The country's main ethnic groups today are Croats, Serbs, and the largest group, ethnic Bosnians, most of whom are Muslims. Following the savage civil war many people emigrated, and the population dropped by one fourth.

The country is now made up of two self-governing states, the Muslim-Croat Federation and the Serbian Republika Srpska. Bosnia & Herzegovina is now trying to revive its industries.

SERBIA & MONTENEGRO

A union of two semiindependent republics, both of which were a part of the former Yugoslavia, Serbia & Montenegro have a varied landscape and climate.

Area: 34,100 sq. mi.
Population: 9,979,752
Capital: Belgrade (Serbia) (1,687,000)
Capital: Podgorica (Montenegro) (131,000)
Main languages spoken: Serbo-Croatiain, Albanian
Main religions: Orthodox, Islam, Roman Catholic
Currency: dinar (Serbia); euro (Kosovo); dinar, euro (Montenegro)
Main exports: basic manufactures, food, machinery and transportation equipment, chemicals
Type of government: republic; partial democracy

Serbia & Montenegro occupy a strategic location in the Balkans, bordering the Eastern European countries of Hungary, Romania, and Bulgaria, as well as sharing borders with five Balkan neighbors. Serbia is the larger of the two states, occupying 86 percent of the country, but Montenegro has a coastline with the Adriatic Sea. To the north, which experiences a continental climate, there are large plains and some low hills. Limestone hills and basins lie east, while to the southwest mountains act as a barrier between the interior and the coast, which experiences a warm Mediterranean climate. Only half of the population live in cities, of which Belgrade is the largest. Serbs are the biggest ethnic group, comprising around 60 percent of the population, with Muslim Albanians making up around 17 percent. Almost all of the five percent of

▼ Serbian refugees from Kosovo work on a farm in the central region of Serbia & Montenegro.

the population who are Montenegrins live in Montenegro. The country's resources allow it to produce all of the electricity that it needs from large coal reserves and hydroelectricity. Serbia & Montenegro also have large reserves of bauxite, iron, copper, and lead. Industries have been disrupted by the bitter civil war. Its ending may have brought a degree of peace but, as yet, little prosperity. The country's people are among the poorest in Europe, with as many as two thirds living below the poverty line.

MACEDONIA

A landlocked nation with great scenic beauty, the former Yugoslav republic of Macedonia was once at the heart of the ancient Greek Empire.

Area: 9,900 sq. mi.
Population: 2,054,800
Capital: Skopje (444,000)
Main languages spoken: Macedonian, Albanian, Serbo-Crotian
Main religions: Eastern Orthodox, Islam
Currency: denar
Main exports: basic manufactures, machinery and transportation equipment, food products, chemicals
Type of government: republic

Macedonia is bordered by Bulgaria, Albania, Serbia & Montenegro, and Greece. Much of the country is covered in steep-sided hills and mountains with deep valleys and large forested areas. Macedonia has 34 mountain peaks that exceed 6,560 ft. and four major lakes, of which Lake Ohrid is the largest. Macedonia's longest river, the Vardar, runs for 187 mi. through the country. It starts in the northwest and flows into southern Greece, where it is called the Axiós river, before draining into the Aegean Sea. The country's capital and largest city, Skopje, lies on the Vardar. Rebuilt after an earthquake destroyed much of the city in 1961, Skopje is an important market center for neighboring farmlands. It is also the country's main industrial region, where metal production and metalworking, chemicals, and assembling goods are key industries. Sheep and chickens are the most common livestock, while there are over 80,000 beehives producing honey and beeswax.

One of Macedonia's most thriving industries is alcohol production. In 2000 the country produced more than 35 million gallons of wine, 39 million gallons of brandy, and over 208 million gallons of beer. A part of the former nation of Yugoslavia, Macedonia became independent in 1991, but disputes with Greece over its name and flag followed, which led to its adoption of the temporary nation name of the Former Yugoslav Republic of Macedonia. Two thirds of the country's population are Macedonian Slavs, while Albanians comprise 23 percent. There are small populations of Turks, Serbs, and Romany peoples. Tensions between its different ethnic groups and an influx of many refugees from other Balkan countries are among the country's most pressing problems.

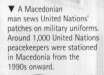

▼ A Macedonian man sews United Nations' patches on military uniforms. Around 1,000 United Nations peacekeepers were stationed in Macedonia from the 1990s onward.

ALBANIA

One of the poorest and least developed nations in Europe, Albania remained isolated from the outside world for much of the 1900s.

Area: 10,600 sq. mi.
Population: 3,544,841
Capital: Tirana (279,000)
Main languages spoken: Albanian, Greek
Main religions: Islam, Albanian Orthodox, Roman Catholic
Currency: lek
Main exports: manufactured goods, chromium and copper, food and tobacco, manufactures
Type of government: republic

▼ Founded in the 1600s and lying on the Ishm river, Tirana is Albania's capital and largest city.

Albania is found on the western part of the Balkan Peninsula facing the Adriatic Sea, with Serbia & Montenegro to the north, Macedonia to the east, and Greece to the south. The country can be divided into two geographical regions. To the west is an area of coastal lowlands. Although some of this land is marshy, much of it contains fertile soils and is heavily farmed, as well as being the most densely populated part of the country. Much of the rest of Albania consists of highlands and mountains. Albania's major rivers begin their life in the mountains and flow in a western direction, emptying into the Adriatic Sea.

Half of the country's workforce is employed in agriculture, with wheat, corn, potatoes, and sugar beets being the major crops, while there are some 1.9 million sheep. Albania's population is one of the least mixed in Europe, with only two percent of people not ethnic Albanians. Much of the 1900s was spent in isolation from the rest of the world under a communist dictatorship. As a result, the country is less developed, and despite its reserves of metals, gas, and oil, its industry and economy lags behind the rest of Europe. Albania's people are among the poorest in Europe, and many young Albanians emigrate to seek work. There are more ethnic Albanians overseas than in the country.

GREECE

Greece is one of the oldest civilizations in Europe, although it only gained independence from Turkey in 1832.

Area: 50,500 sq. mi.
Population: 10,645,343
Capital: Athens (3,120,000)
Major language spoken: Greek
Main religion: Greek Orthodox
Currency: euro
Principal exports: textiles, food, beverages, tobacco, petroleum products, minerals, cotton
Type of government: parliamentary republic

▼ Lying on the Saronic Gulf, the city of Piraeus first served as a port for the city of Athens, around five miles inland, almost 2,500 years ago. Developed in the 1900s, Piraeus is now Greece's largest port.

Greece is a highly fragmented landmass, with a coastline that measures over 2,480 mi. The country occupies the southernmost part of the Balkan Peninsula and curves around the northern and eastern edge of the Aegean Sea. Its land borders are to the north with Albania, Macedonia, Bulgaria, and Turkey. Two large gulfs almost split the southern portion of the mainland, the Peloponnese Peninsula, from the rest of mainland Greece. Much of the country consists of highland areas. The Pindus mountains is Greece's largest mountain range. Greece's mountains are young and are still being built, which results in many earthquakes. Most of Greece has a Mediterranean climate with mild, rainy winters and subtropical, dry, and warm summers.

FAMILY FARMING

Only 22 percent of Greece's territory consists of arable land. The rest is rocky scrubland, both mountains and forests. Greek agriculture employs almost one fifth of the country's workforce. Most farms are small and family-owned, and warm weather crops, including olives, grapes, and citrus fruits, are grown. The leading export crop is tobacco, with cotton, olive oil, and Greek cheeses also important.

THE ISLANDS OF GREECE

One fifth of Greece's land area consists of over 2,000 islands, of which only 154 are inhabited. These are divided into many groups, including the Ionian Islands and the Cyclades. A number of Greece's islands lie just off the coast of Turkey. With an area of 5,168 sq. mi., Crete is the largest of the Greek islands. Three mountain ranges run across the island, forming a spine, and create the deep and scenic gorges for which Crete is famous. Home to the Minoan civilization from 3500 B.C., Crete was also one of the major birthplaces of the ancient Greek civilization, which became centered around the modern day capital of Athens. The Olympic Games, which started in ancient Greece over 2,500 years ago, returned to Athens in 2004.

BULGARIA

A mountainous country bordering the Black Sea in southeastern Europe, Bulgaria has had a long and colourful history.

Area: 42,700 sq. mi.
Population: 7,621,337
Capital: Sofia (1,187,000)
Major language spoken: Bulgarian
Main religions: Bulgarian Orthodox, Islam, nonreligious
Currency: lev
Principal exports: chemicals and plastics, food, beverages, tobacco, textiles
Type of government: republic

Bulgaria is a country with varied scenery. Plateaus, plains, hills, and mountains are all found in its territory. The two largest mountain ranges are the Balkans, which run west to east through the center of the country, and the Rhodope mountains to the southwest. Bulgaria's climate is temperate with marked differences between the four seasons. To the south and around the Black Sea the temperatures are milder in the winter and warmer than average in the summer, reaching a daily average of 84°F in July and August.

A COUNTRY IN TRANSITION

Bulgaria was ruled by the Turkish Ottoman Empire from the late 1300s until 1878 before becoming fully independent in 1908. A communist ally of the former Soviet Union until 1990, the country has since become a multiparty democracy. Its economy is recovering after major crises in 1995, 1997, and 1999, and Bulgaria is still readjusting to economic independence, which has meant that cheap supplies of high quality coal, oil, and iron from the Soviet Union are no longer available. Farming and industry are in the process of being reorganized to become more competitive, and tourism is being promoted. Eighty-four percent of the country's population are Bulgars— ethnic Bulgarians—while ten percent are of Turkish origin. There are also smaller minority groups, including Macedonians and Romany peoples. Seventy percent of people live in towns and cities.

▲ There are an estimated 1,000 wolves living in the wild in remote parts of Bulgaria. Other large mammals found in the country include wildcats, elks, and bears.

▶ Bulgaria's National Assembly building lies in the center of its capital city of Sofia. It was built in three stages between 1884 and 1928 from plans by the Austrian architect, Yovanovich.

ESTONIA

Dense forests, low hills, and a lengthy coastline
are key features of the smallest and most
northern of the three Baltic states.

Area: 17,400 sq. mi.
Population: 1,415,881
Capital: Tallinn (401,000)
Main languages spoken:
Estonian, Russian
Main religions:
Evangelical Lutheran,
Russian Orthodox
Currency: kroon
Main exports: chemicals
and mineral fuels, food
products, textiles and
clothing, wood and paper
Type of government:
republic

E stonia borders
its Baltic state
neighbor of Latvia
to the south and the
Russian Federation to
the east. It faces the
Baltic Sea to the west
and an arm of the Baltic,
called the Gulf of Finland,
to the north. Estonia is a low-lying
country, with two thirds of its land below
164 ft. in elevation. Its land is crossed by
around 7,000 streams and rivers, as well
as more than 1,000 lakes, which together
make up around five percent of the
country's area. Lake Peipus is Estonia's
largest lake. It forms much of the Estonian
border with Russia and is Europe's fifth-
largest freshwater lake. A further ten
percent of Estonian territory comes in the
form of islands lying a short distance off
its Baltic coastline. The two largest islands
are Saaremaa, where livestock raising is
the main activity, and Hiiumaa, on which
most of its workforce, many of whom are
of Swedish origin, fish for a living. Trees
cover around 45 percent of the country
and provide habitats for many creatures,
as well as the raw materials for Estonia's
large timber, furniture making, and paper
industries. Metalworking, engineering,
and the mining and processing of oil
shale into fuels and chemicals are the
country's chief industries.

Estonia's small population
gives the country one of
the lowest densities in
Europe, with just 81
people per square mile.
The country derives its
name from a people called the Ests who
settled in the region around 2,000 years
ago. Around two thirds of the population
are native Estonians whose language and
descent are closely related to the Finns.
Russians form the largest minority group,
comprising 28 percent of the population.
Seven out of ten
Estonians live in major
towns and cities such
as the capital, Tallinn,
the industrial city of
Narva, and Pärnu,
a popular summer
vacation resort
with a warmer
climate than
much of the
country.

▲ Tallinn dates back to
the 1200s when crusading
knights built a castle on
the site. The city has
developed and retained
many charming historic
buildings, which have
survived fires and wars.
Tallinn is visited by several
hundred thousand foreign
tourists every year.

► A sailing boat in the
choppy waters of the Bay
of Tallinn. The waterfront
of Estonia's capital city
is in the background.

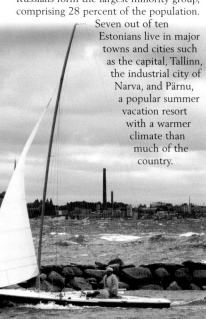

LATVIA

Latvia is the most industrialized of the Baltic states. A flat, wooded, and marshy country, it uses its coastline for trade and fishing.

Area: 24,900 sq. mi.
Population: 2,366,515
Capital: Riga (756,000)
Main languages spoken: Lettish, Lithuanian, Russian
Main religions: Lutheran, Roman Catholic, Russian Orthodox
Currency: lat
Main exports: timber and paper products, textiles, food and agricultural products, machinery
Type of government: republic

▼ Lying on the southern shore of the Gulf of Riga, the capital city of Riga is Latvia's major port and is home to around one third of the entire country's population.

Latvia is a low-lying country, with 98 percent of its territory below 656 ft. in elevation. It borders Belarus and the Russian Federation to the east, and a large part of its coast curves around to form much of the Gulf of Riga. Sheltered from the Baltic by the large Estonian island of Saaremaa, the Gulf of Riga provides warm water harbors, including Liepaja, Ventspils, and the country's largest port and capital city, Riga. Latvia has thousands of small rivers and streams, only 17 of which are longer than 56 mi. The longest is the Daugavapils, which begins its life in northwestern Russia and flows through Latvia, emptying into the Gulf of Riga. Frozen from December to April and with a series of rapids and shallows, the river is not navigable by large shipping. It is, however, used to provide hydroelectricity and to float timber to transport it from Latvia's wooded interior

to the ports on its coast. Over half of Latvia's forests consist of pine trees, while forests of oak are also common. Trees cover around 40 percent of the country's land and contribute to a sizable timber industry. Apart from peat from the bogs that cover almost one tenth of the country and limestone and dolomite rocks for building, Latvia has few natural resources. It is reliant on the Russian Federation for imports of oil and other fuels, although oil has recently been discovered in the east of the country. Dairy and livestock farming occupy many Latvians in rural areas, while three fourths of its people live in towns and cities. Around 57 percent of the population are Latvians, with Russians forming a large minority of over 30 percent. Smaller minorities of Ukrainians, Belarussians, and Poles exist.

INDEPENDENCE AND GOVERNMENT

Latvia has been ruled by foreign powers, including Sweden and, later, Poland, for most of its history. In the 1700s the country was absorbed into the large Russian empire of Peter the Great. It seized independence in 1919 and remained independent until the Soviet Union took control after World War II. Since independence in 1991 the country has restored the 1922 constitution, and the government is headed by a president elected by the Saeima, a 100-member parliament elected by free vote for terms of four years. Latvia will join the European Union in 2004.

LITHUANIA

The most southerly of the Baltic states, Lithuania
has a short west-facing coastline. Most of its
people work in heavy industry or farming.

Area: 25,200 sq. mi.
Population: 3,601,138
Capital: Vilnius (579,000)
Main languages spoken:
Lithuanian, Polish, Russian
Main religion: Roman
Catholic
Currency: litas
Main exports: textiles,
chemicals, mineral
products, machinery
Type of government:
republic

▼ Lithuanians pray
in front of the altar of a
church containing an icon
of the Virgin Mary. Around
72 percent of Lithuanians
are Roman Catholic.

Lithuania borders Latvia
to the north, Belarus to
the south and east, and Poland
to the southwest. Its land is
mainly a series of plains and low
hills dotted with many lakes and
crossed by over 20 rivers. The largest river,
the Neman, is around 580 mi. long and
drains much of the country. Lithuania's
short coastline with the Baltic Sea is the
location of much of the world's amber,
the fossilized resin from prehistoric trees
used to make jewelry. It is also the site of
the Courland Spit, a 59-mi.-long bank of
sand dunes stretching south from the port
of Klaipéda and enclosing the Courland
Lagoon. Over one fourth of the country
is forested, and it has five national parks
and four national wildlife reserves.
Lithuania was a powerful independent state
700 years ago, but from the 1500s onward

it became part
of Poland and, later, Russia.
It declared independence
in 1918, only to become
occupied by the Soviet
Union from 1944 until 1991, when it again
achieved independence. Native Lithuanians
comprise 82 percent of the population.
Poles and Russians (around seven percent
each) make up the largest minorities.

BELARUS

A flat, low-lying nation with many lakes in the north and large marshlands in the south, Belarus became independent from the former Soviet Union in 1991.

Area: 80,200 sq. mi.
Population: 10,335,382
Capital: Minsk (1,719,000)
Main languages spoken: Byelorussian, Russian
Main religion: Eastern Orthodox
Currency: Belarussian ruble
Main exports: trucks and tires, diesel fuel, synthetic fibers, refrigerators, fertilizer, milk and dairy products
Type of government: republic

The mountain range that runs diagonally through Belarus forms a ridge that divides the country into two areas of lowlands. The northern area has a number of gentle hills and many of the country's 11,000 small lakes. South of the ridge lies a large marshy plain drained by the Pripet river and its tributaries. This region comprises the largest area of unreclaimed marshland in Europe. To the west where Belarus borders Poland lies the Belovezhskaya Forest. Much of this forest is protected to create Europe's largest nature reserve, the home of the otherwise rare wisent, or European bison.

DEVASTATED TWICE

Over two million Belarussian people lost their lives during World War II, which devastated many of its towns and cities. In 1986 the Chernobyl nuclear power station in neighboring Ukraine exploded, and 70 percent of the radioactive fallout landed on Belarus territory. Close to three million people were seriously affected, and soil, streams, and rivers were contaminated. Around 15 percent of the country's forests and 20 percent of its farmland remain too radioactive for their products to be used. The cost of cleaning up the region, rehousing people, and dealing with the long-term effects of the world's biggest nuclear accident has put severe strain on the country's health service and economy, despite aid from other nations and charities.

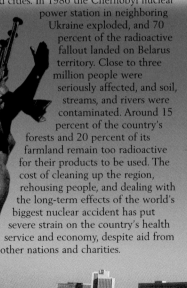

▼ A monument overlooks part of the Belarussian city of Minsk. The nation's largest settlement, almost all of Minsk was reconstructed from 1944 onward. The city has barely changed since independence.

A DECLINING ECONOMY

An estimated one fifth of the country's workforce is engaged in agriculture, but industry contributes more to the economy. When it was part of the former Soviet Union, many heavy industrial factories and processing plants were built in Belarus to process the raw materials extracted from other parts of the Soviet Union, especially the Ukraine. As an independent nation and one with relatively few mineral resources, Belarus has struggled since independence. It has largely kept its old Soviet-style economy and has privatized or modernized very little of its industry to make it more competitive in the world market. As a result, production has declined, and the country faces huge economic problems. Its main industrial center is in and around the capital city, Minsk. In Minsk many products, including farm machinery, motor vehicles, machine tools, and electrical goods, are manufactured and assembled. The country retains close ties with Russia, which it relies on for around three fifths of its imports and almost half of its exports. Russia provides more than $1 billion in aid through relief from debts and cheap supplies of oil and gas.

MOLDOVA

Moldova is the smallest and most densely populated of
the former Soviet republics. The country is landlocked
and is one of the poorest nations in Europe.

Area: 13,000 sq. mi.
Population: 4,434,547
Capital: Chisinau (662,000)
Main languages spoken:
Moldovan, Russian
Main religion: Eastern
Orthodox
Currency: Moldovan leu
Main exports: food and
agricultural goods,
machinery, textiles, metals
Type of government:
republic

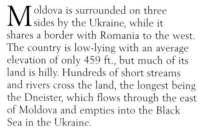

Moldova is surrounded on three
sides by the Ukraine, while it
shares a border with Romania to the west.
The country is low-lying with an average
elevation of only 459 ft., but much of its
land is hilly. Hundreds of short streams
and rivers cross the land, the longest being
the Dneister, which flows through the east
of Moldova and empties into the Black
Sea in the Ukraine.

A FARMING NATION

More than seven tenths of Moldova's
land is covered in a rich black soil that
can be farmed. Wheat, tobacco, corn,
and sunflower seeds are among the main
crops, while grapes tend to be grown in
the south of the country. Moldova's
wine-making industry is one of the few
industries that has flourished since the
country gained independence in 1991.
Agriculture is the leading employer of
Moldova, providing work for 39 percent
of the country's workforce and generating

many of its exports. Food processing
accounts for 42 percent of the country's
industrial output. With only limited
mineral resources and poor transportation
links, the country's economy has struggled,
and Moldavians are among the poorest
people in Europe. Moldova was once
part of Romania, and almost two thirds
of its people are of either Moldavian or
Romanian descent. Two large minorities—
Ukrainians and Russians—make up a
further one fourth of the population.
Many of the Russians and Ukrainians
live east of the Dniester river in an
autonomous republic within Moldova.

▲ A church wedding
takes place in the country's
capital city of Chisinau.
Many Moldavians are
followers of the Romanian
Orthodox church.

► Moldavians harvest
potatoes in a small field.
Most agriculture in Moldova
is farmed by cooperatives of
people working together.

ROMANIA

Achieving independence in 1878, Romania is a country with a Black Sea coastline. Its land is a mixture of mountains and lowlands.

Area: 88,900 sq. mi.
Population: 22,317,730
Capital: Bucharest (1,998,000)
Main languages spoken: Romanian, Hungarian, German
Main religions: Romanian Orthodox, Roman Catholic, Protestant
Currency: Romanian leu
Main exports: textiles, mineral products, chemicals, machinery, footwear
Type of government: republic

▼ A large portion of Bucharest was demolished in the 1980s to build the huge Palace of the People (now Parliament Palace). Even though parts of the building remain incomplete, it is the second-largest administrative building in the world behind the United States' Pentagon.

Romania borders Hungary to the northwest, the Ukraine to the north, Moldova to the east, Bulgaria to the south, and Serbia & Montenegro to the west. It also has a strategically important coastline on the Black Sea. The Danube river flows along most of the border with Bulgaria, providing an important transportation route for inland shipping. The Danube forms a large delta as it empties into the Black Sea.

MOUNTAINS, FORESTS, AND FARMING

Much of north and central Romania is covered by two large mountain ranges. Running east to west are the Transylvanian Alps, which include the country's highest point, the 8,344-ft.-high Varful Moldoveanu. North of these mountains is a large, hilly plateau that is bordered to the north and east by the Carpathian Mountains. Forests cover more than one fourth of the country and provide homes for a wide range of wild animals, including wolves, deer, bear, wild boars, and lynx. Forty five percent of

Romania's land is suitable for agriculture.

NATURAL RESOURCES

Most of the raw materials used in Romania's industries are imported, and its once important oil and natural gas reserves are fast dwindling. Romania's major natural resources are its fertile soils and its fast-moving rivers, which are harnessed for hydroelectricity generation. The country also has deposits of lead, zinc, and sulfur. Much of Romania's industrial and agricultural exports are transported out of the country's biggest port, Constanta. Lying in the northeast, the city of Iasi has a population of more than 320,000, making it Romania's second-largest city after Bucharest, the capital.

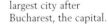

UKRAINE

Bordering the Black Sea to the south, the Ukraine is one of the most economically powerful of the former Soviet states.

Area: 23,100 sq. mi.
Population: 48,396,470
Capital: Kiev (2,488,000)
Major languages spoken: Ukrainian, Russian
Main religions: nonreligious (about 55%), Ukrainian Orthodox, Ukrainian Catholic
Currency: hryvna
Main exports: ferrous metals, machinery, minerals, chemicals
Type of government: constitutional republic

▼ A combine gathers and processes a cereal crop in the Ukraine. The country has extremely rich soil and is one of the world's leading producers of cereals, such as wheat, and is the largest producer of sugar beets.

The Ukraine is the second largest of the former states of the Soviet Union, second only to the Russian Federation in land area and population. Most of the Ukraine consists of fertile plains, known as steppes, and plateaus. Much of the northern part of the country is covered in dense forests. Mountains are found to the west and in the Crimean Peninsula. The Ukraine has a long shoreline with the Black Sea and also borders the Sea of Azov, which measures around 14,646 sq. mi. The Ukraine has a continental climate with warm summers and cold winters, especially in the east. The Crimean coastline, however, has a Mediterranean climate with hotter summers. The levels of rainfall vary greatly depending on the region, with more rain in the north and west of the country and heavy snowfalls in the country's mountainous areas.

RICH IN MINERALS

An estimated five percent of the entire world's mineral reserves are found within the Ukraine. The country has the world's largest reserves of manganese and titanium and the third-largest iron ore reserves. The country has giant coal reserves, the largest of which are situated to the east around the city of Donetsk.

RUSSIA

The world's largest nation, the Russian Federation bestrides two continents and 11 time zones. Its people are undergoing great changes to their way of life.

Area: 6,592,800 sq. mi.
Population: 144,979,543
Capital: Moscow (8,316,000)
Major languages spoken: Russian, Tatar, Ukrainian, Chuvash, Bashkir, Chechen, Mordovinian
Main religions: nonreligious (over 70%), Russian Orthodox, Islam
Currency: Russian ruble
Main exports: fuels and lubricants, ferrous and nonferrous metals, machinery and transportation equipment, chemicals, precious metals, timber and forestry products
Type of government: federal republic

Russia is a gigantic nation extending almost 6,200 mi. west to east and more than 2,480 mi. north to south at its greatest extent. Vast plains cover much of Russia's territory, while mountain ranges are found mainly in the eastern and southern regions. The Ural Mountains, running north to south, divide western, European Russia from eastern, Asian Russia. Much of Russia experiences a continental climate, although there is great variation both in climate and vegetation in such a large country, with large temperate regions, giant forests, and vast tracts of icy wastes to the north. The country has large areas of fertile farmlands and a great wealth of mineral resources. It is one of the world's leading producers of fossil fuels and a wide range of metals. The largest and most powerful republic of the former Soviet Union, Russia has had to deal with a number of political and economic problems since its independence in 1991.

▲ With an area of 87,600 ft., the giant Red Square is the focal point of the city of Moscow. On its west side lies the tomb of the communist leader Lenin, in front of which a changing-of-the-guard ceremony is occurring.

WESTERN RUSSIA

The most economically powerful part of the Russian Federation, western Russia is the home of the country's largest cities and most of its productive farmland.

Western Russia borders Kazakhstan, Georgia, and Azerbaijan to the south and has coastlines with both the Caspian and Black seas. To the west the country borders Ukraine, Belarus, Latvia, Lithuania, and Finland and, to the far north, Norway. Its territory includes the enclave of Kalingrad, which is separated from the rest of Russia by Lithuania and Latvia. Western Russia is mostly part of the Great European Plain, which increases in width eastward.

▲ The ornate marble halls of a Moscow underground railroad station. The Moscow subway was built in the 1930s and carries more than six million passengers every day.

THE KOLA PENINSULA AND BARENTS SEA

The highest elevations of western Russia are found in the Caucasus in the southwest and in the Kola Peninsula, which faces the Barents Sea to the east. The Barents Sea is a shallow arm of the Arctic Ocean and is subject to freezing during the winter. However, warm waters from the Gulf Stream keep a coastal shipping lane open throughout the year. Western Russia's two largest islands, which form the archipelago called Novaya Zemlya, are found in the Barents Sea. Perched on the Kola Peninsula is the strategically important port of Murmansk. A major Russian naval base, the city also has fishing, shipbuilding, and marine research facilities.

THE URAL MOUNTAINS

The Great European Plain extends east until it reaches the Ural Mountains. Formed by continental drift that forced Siberia and Europe together, the Urals are around 250 million years old. Erosion has worn these mountains down so that they now have an average elevation of 1,968 ft. The Urals are, however, rich in important minerals, including coal, iron ore, platinum, lead, chromium, and copper. West of the southern Urals several industrial cities, including Perm and Ufa, have sprung up owing to the extraction and processing of these minerals and the development of manufacturing industries.

THE FERTILE TRIANGLE

The large majority of Russia's farmland lies in western Russia in what is called the "fertile triangle." The fertile triangle extends from the Black Sea to the Baltic Sea along Russia's western borders and stretches from the area of the city of St. Petersburg southeast to the southern Ural Mountains. In the fertile triangle large

▼ The Kremlin was founded as a fortress within the city of Moscow in 1156. Rebuilt on several occasions, it is now used as the central seat of the Russian government.

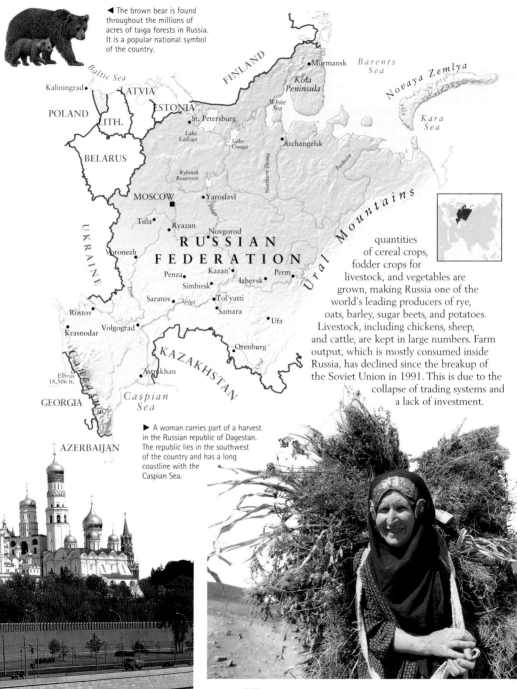

◄ The brown bear is found throughout the millions of acres of taiga forests in Russia. It is a popular national symbol of the country.

Baltic Sea

Kaliningrad •

POLAND

LATVIA
LITH.
ESTONIA

BELARUS

FINLAND

• Murmansk

Kola
Peninsula

Barents Sea

Novaya Zemlya

White
Sea

St. Petersburg •

Lake
Ladoga

Lake
Onega

• Archangelsk

Kara Sea

Northern Dvina

Pechora

Rybinsk
Reservoir

MOSCOW ■

• Yaroslavl

Tula •

• Ryazan

Novgorod

Volga

R U S S I A N
F E D E R A T I O N

Voronezh •

Penza •

Kazan' •

Perm •

Simbirsk •

Izhevsk •

Ural Mountains

Saratov •

Volga

Tol'yatti •

Samara •

• Ufa

Rostov •

Volgograd •

Krasnodar •

Don

Orenburg •

KAZAKHSTAN

Ural

Elbrus
18,506 ft.

Astrakhan •

Caucasus

GEORGIA

Caspian Sea

AZERBAIJAN

UKRAINE

quantities of cereal crops, fodder crops for livestock, and vegetables are grown, making Russia one of the world's leading producers of rye, oats, barley, sugar beets, and potatoes. Livestock, including chickens, sheep, and cattle, are kept in large numbers. Farm output, which is mostly consumed inside Russia, has declined since the breakup of the Soviet Union in 1991. This is due to the collapse of trading systems and a lack of investment.

► A woman carries part of a harvest in the Russian republic of Dagestan. The republic lies in the southwest of the country and has a long coastline with the Caspian Sea.

141

▲ A large area of apartment buildings offers accommodation for some of Moscow's eight million inhabitants. Apart from being Russia's largest and most politically dominant city, Moscow is also the spiritual center of the Russian Orthodox church.

TWIN CITIES OF POWER

Russia has a long history of settlement and has been a powerful force in Europe and Asia for hundreds of years. Two cities have been its capital and center during its history—Moscow and St. Petersburg. The first Russian leader to use the title of emperor was Peter the Great, who founded the city of St. Petersburg in the early 1700s. The city became the home of the czars—the Russian royal family—from 1713 onward. Its position connected to the Baltic Sea by the Gulf of Finland enabled St. Petersburg to rise as a trading power and to become a major cultural center of eastern Europe. Today St. Petersburg is Russia's second-largest city and the home of many large industries, especially engineering, chemicals, and shipbuilding, as well as being its largest seaport. A system of rivers and artificial inland waterways links St. Petersburg in the south to the Caspian Sea and also to the White Sea and Volga river.

Moscow was founded as a city in 1138 and was the capital of Russia prior to the establishment of St. Petersburg. It became the capital again in 1918 after communist forces toppled the czar and came to power. For 70 years Moscow was the capital city of the former Soviet Union. During this period its industry boomed—it produced around one sixth of the entire Soviet Union's industrial output. Moscow has sprawled into a giant city and is the home of both the leader of the country, the president, and the highest legislative body, the Federal Assembly.

More than three fourths of Russia's population live in Moscow, St. Petersburg, and other urban areas found in western Russia.

▼ Novgorod is a major transportation terminus and industrial center, producing cars, airplanes, and electrical goods. It lies on the Volga river. The Volga is navigable along almost all of its 2,189 mi. length and is the longest river in Europe.

EASTERN RUSSIA

Russia east of the Ural Mountains is a sparsely populated land of mountains, rivers, and icy wastelands where huge resources remain largely untapped.

▲ A train on the Trans-Siberian railroad passes by Lake Baikal. The lake holds 85 percent of all of Russia's lake water and around one fifth of the entire world's lake water. The Trans-Siberian railroad runs a long distance of 5,764 mi. from Moscow to Vladivostok on eastern Russia's Pacific coast. In the late 1990s the entire trip took six days.

East of the Ural Mountains, Russia stretches more than 3,000 mi. eastward to form a long coastline with the Pacific Ocean. Eastern Russia borders three nations to the south: Kazakhstan, Mongolia, and China. Most of the Russian territory near Mongolia and China is part of a series of mountain ranges, including the Yablonovy and Stavonoy ranges.

Geographically, eastern Russia is often divided into four broad regions: the southern mountain ranges mentioned above, the West Siberian Plain, the Central Siberian Plateau, and the Russian Far East. Each of these regions is vast, has large tracts of barely inhabited territory, and has much variation in rock formations, landscape, and vegetation.

THE SIBERIAN PLAIN

To the east of the Urals is the gigantic West Siberian Plain. This area stretches around 1,178 mi. from west to east and around 1,488 mi. from north to south. It covers an area of more than 975,000 sq. mi. Over half of the plain lies at elevations below 328 ft., and only in the south does the land rise above 820 ft. Much of the plain is poorly drained and consists of some of the world's largest swamps and floodplains. Important cities include Omsk and Chelyabinsk, which is located near the Urals in a rich coal-mining region. The long Yenisey river flows broadly south to north, a distance of 2,195 mi., where it completes its journey, discharging more than five million gallons of water per second. Together with its tributary, the Angara, the two rivers flow 3,435 mi. The valley it has formed acts as a rough dividing line between the West Siberian Plain and the Central Siberian Plateau.

Far East. Along with the Caucasus in the southwest of Russia, Kamchatka is one of Russia's main areas of earthquake activity. The volcanic chain continues from the southern tip of Kamchatka through the Kuril Islands. This island chain extends for approximately 744 mi., ending close to Hokkaido—the northern island of Japan. The islands contain 100 volcanoes, of which around one third are either dormant or active. Some of the southernmost Kuril Islands have their ownership disputed by Japan. Located on the far south of the Far Eastern Russian mainland, the city of Vladivostok is the largest in the region. Founded as a military naval outpost in 1860, Vladivostok now has a population in excess of 620,000. It is an important port and is a base for fishing and whaling fleets.

▲ Eastern Russia has large untapped oil reserves, but oil exploitation of much of the region is beset with problems, including transportation and the hostile climate.

▼ A camp of Koryak nomads is pitched amidst the icy tundra of northeast Russia. The Koryak continue traditional ways of living, mainly herding reindeer and hunting for furs. Koryak people who live on the coast fish, especially for crabs.

THE CENTRAL SIBERIAN PLATEAU AND FAR EASTERN RUSSIA

The Central Siberian Plateau is, in fact, several plateaus lying between 984–2,296 ft. in elevation. Mountains border the plateaus to the south and much of the east. The region is rich in mainly untapped mineral resources.

Far Eastern Russia has a complex geography consisting of many mountain ranges formed in different ways. A major feature of the region is the Kamchatka Peninsula, which juts southward into the Sea of Okhotsk, itself an arm of the Pacific Ocean. The peninsula has many volcanic peaks, some of which are still active. The highest is the 15,584-ft.-high Kliuchevskoi volcano, the highest point in the Russian

TUNDRA AND TAIGA

Eastern Russia's main zones of vegetation vary with latitude and run from north to south. To the south are steppes, plains of grassland that form eastern Russia's best farmland. The northernmost reaches of Russia, stretching the entire width of the country, consist of tundra. These are largely icy and treeless plains with very cold winters and limited plant life. South of the tundra are large belts of forests called taiga. These are the world's largest forest regions and consist of coniferous trees such as Siberian cedar, fir, pine, and larch.

RIVERS AND LAKES

Russia is crossed by more than 100,000
rivers; most of the longest are found in
the east. The Ob-Irtysh river system, for
example, flows a distance of 3,354 mi.
from western China north through Siberia
before emptying into the Arctic Ocean.
Around 84 percent of Russia's surface
water is located east of the Urals in its
rivers and lakes. The largest lake, Lake
Baikal, is found in central south Siberia.
Measuring 384 mi. and varying between
9–50 mi. in width, the lake reaches
a depth of 5,369 ft., making it the
world's deepest freshwater lake.

RUSSIA'S PEOPLE

Russia's population is a striking
multicultural mix in both the eastern
and western portions of the country.
When it was the dominant part of the
Soviet Union throughout much of the
1900s, ethnic Russians made up around
50 percent of its population. Many
republics of the Soviet Union containing
other ethnic groups started to press for
independence during the 1980s. Reforms,
such as glasnost (openness) and perestroika
(restructuring), were introduced by the
Soviet Union's leader, Mikhail Gorbachev.
They were attempts to modernize the way
the country was run and to give some of
these republics more control. However,
by December 1991 the Soviet Union split
into 15 independent republics, of which
the Russian Federation is the largest. Ethnic
Russians now comprise 82 percent of the
population, but there are large minority
groups, including more than five million
Tatars—Islamic peoples who descended
from the Mongols who invaded Russia
over 750 years ago. In total, over 120
different nationalities and ethnic groups
are found within the country's borders.
Russia's people have faced many changes
in the past. They are currently witnessing
further, enormous, and often difficult
changes in the way their country and
businesses are run. Health and other
social services are in crisis, and crime
is rising. Most Russians are having to deal
with a drop in their standard of living.

▲ A woman watches a
helicopter run by the state
airline, Aeroflot, depart
from a landing site near
her isolated village in the
far east of Russia. In many
isolated parts of eastern
Russia air transportation
is the only way to travel
outside the local area.

THE CAUCASUS AND ASIA MINOR

A land bridge between Europe and Asia since prehistoric times, the region that includes the Caucasus and Asia Minor has a long and complex history. Wave after wave of armies, traders, and settlers have passed through the region, which is bounded by three different seas: the Mediterranean Sea, the Black Sea, and the Caspian Sea. As a result, there is a large number of different ethnic groups, languages, and cultures found in the region. The area's largest and most populous nation is Turkey, which straddles the traditional boundaries that separate Asia from Europe. East of Turkey lie three countries—Georgia, Armenia, and Azerbaijan—which sit between the Black Sea and the Caspian Sea. These three nations, all part of the former Soviet Union, are sometimes collectively known as the pair of mountain ranges that dominate their territory, the Caucasus. The land of the Caucasus nations is rugged yet fertile in places. Many of the mountain slopes are covered in coniferous trees, while a large number of rivers cross the land and empty into the Black Sea, the Caspian Sea, or the Sea of Asov to the north. Large mineral deposits, including oil, natural gas, and various metal ores, are found throughout the region.

▲ The enormous extinct volcano of Mount Ararat straddles the border between Turkey and Armenia and has a diameter of approximately 25 mi. at its base. The mountain has two peaks, the higher of which lies in Turkey and reaches an elevation of 16,850 ft.

GEORGIA

A mountainous country bordering
the Black Sea, Georgia was a part of
the former Soviet Union until 1991.

Area: 26,900 sq. mi.
Population: 4,960,951
Capital: Tbilisi (1,406,000)
Main languages spoken:
Georgian, Russian
Main religions: Georgian
Orthodox, Islam, Russian
Orthodox
Currency: lari
Main exports: food
products, ferrous metals,
textiles, chemicals
Type of government:
republic

Georgia borders
Turkey, Armenia,
and Azerbaijan to the
south and the Russian
Federation to the north.
The Caucasus Mountains
define the country's northern border
and are home to its highest point, Mount
Shkhara. The southern part of Georgia is
crossed by the Lesser Caucasus Mountains.
Sandwiched between the two mountain
ranges are lower-lying lands, including
the valley of the country's major river,
the Kura. Lower-lying areas also exist
in the east and the west of the country.
To the west the region close to the Black
Sea was formerly swamps and wetlands,
but much land has been reclaimed. This
region now forms the most productive
farmlands of Georgia. The warm, humid
climate in that area allows citrus fruits, tea,
grapes, and tobacco to be grown. Farther
inland less rain falls,
and the climate is
continental with
cold winters.
Glaciers and snow
cover the upper
reaches of most
of the Caucasus
Mountains. Large
forests of birch,
beech, and oak
grow over the
lower mountain
slopes. Almost
two fifths of the
country is forested.

▼ A man stands close
to one of the medieval
towers found in Georgia.
Most of the around 200
surviving towers date
back to the 1100s, but
a few are more than
one thousand
years older.

A CROSSROAD

Despite its rugged terrain, trade routes
through Georgia have been established
for thousands of years. The country's status
as a crossroad resulted in its highly diverse
population. Ethnic Georgians comprise
around 70 percent of the population, but
there are also around 100 different ethnic
groups in the country. Tensions between
groups, especially in the Abkhazia region
in the northwest of the country, which
sought independence from Georgia, led
to conflict in the 1990s and weakened
an economy trying to develop to compete
in the world market. Most Georgian
people live in poverty, although improving
transportation links, tourism promotion,
and exploiting
the country's
largely untapped
oil reserves
bring hope of
improvement
in the quality
of their life.

ARMENIA

Once the smallest republic of the former Soviet
Union, Armenia is a landlocked, mountainous
country with an average elevation of around 5,900 ft.

Area: 11,500 sq. mi.
Population: 3,330,099
Capital: Yerevan
(1,420,000)
Main language spoken:
Armenian
Main religion: Armenian
Orthodox
Currency: dram
Principal exports: jewelry,
various machinery and
equipment, minerals,
textiles
Type of government:
republic

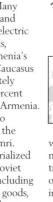

▼ Armenian peasants dig
in potato fields in northern
Armenia. Potatoes, along
with wheat, tobacco,
and other vegetables,
are the main crops
grown in the country.

Armenia is one of the most rugged
countries in all of Eurasia, with large
mountains and steep-sided valleys. Many
smaller rivers and streams cross the land
and provide the country with hydroelectric
power. There are also many waterfalls,
river rapids, and mountain lakes. Armenia's
largest lake, Lake Sevan, lies in the Caucasus
Mountains and measures approximately
530 sq. mi. It holds more than 85 percent
of all of the standing water found in Armenia.
Parts of the country are susceptible to
earthquakes; in 1988 one devastated the
country's second-largest city of Gyumri.
Armenia was one of the most industrialized
and wealthiest states in the former Soviet
Union, with a variety of industries, including
machine building, chemicals, canned goods,
and leather products. Since independence
in 1991 Armenia has
been in conflict with
Azerbaijan over
Nagorno Karabakh,
an area of Azerbaijan

with a largely Armenian
population. The cost of
war included fuel shortages that damaged
many of the country's industries. Armenia's
transportation and communications links are
old and in need of repair and modernization
in many places. Its capital city, Yerevan, is
one of the oldest cities still in existence,
with archaeological evidence of settlement
for more than 5,000 years. Ethnic Armenians
make up more than 90 percent of the
country's population. There are more
people of Armenian
descent living
overseas.

AZERBAIJAN

A mountainous and oil-rich country, Azerbaijan has been beset by economic difficulties and territorial disputes.

Area: 33,400 sq. mi.
Population: 7,798,497
Capital: Baki (1,964,000)
Main languages spoken: Azeri, Russian, Armenian
Main religions: Islam, Orthodox
Currency: manat
Principal exports: petroleum and petroleum products, cotton, machinery, food products
Type of government: republic

Azerbaijan is ringed by mountains on almost all sides, except to the east where it borders the Caspian Sea. To the north lie the Russian Federation and Georgia, Iran lies to the south, and Armenia lies to the west. Azerbaijan and Armenia's border is complex, with enclaves of both nations surrounded by the lands of the other and some territory disputed. The largest disputed area, Nagorno Karabakh, was the subject of violent conflict during the 1990s. The Greater and Lesser Caucasus mountain ranges run through Azerbaijan, and the fast-flowing rivers that flow down the mountain slopes are not only harnessed to generate electricity, but they are also diverted and used for water reservoirs and irrigation systems. Parts of Azerbaijan, particularly the peaks of the Caucasus Mountains and the extreme southeast of the country, receive heavy rainfall, but much of the remainder of the country is warm and dry, receiving less than 12 in. of rain per year. Irrigation enables the farmers to grow cereal crops, tobacco, grapes, and cotton. Agriculture remains the biggest employer in the country. Unlike its Caucasus neighbors, the people of Azerbaijan are mostly Muslims. They are descended from people who conquered the territory more than 900 years ago. The country not only has large natural gas reserves but also big deposits of oil.

▲ Azerbaijan fishermen bring in their catch from the Caspian Sea. In 2001 8,488 tons of fish were caught in the Caspian.

▼ One century ago Azerbaijan was the world's leading producer of oil, but the industry declined as oil was discovered in many other places in the world.

TURKEY

A large country with extensive mountains and long coastlines, Turkey straddles the point where southern Europe and Asia meet and has a long history.

Area: 297,600 sq. mi.
Population: 67,308,928
Capital: Ankara
(3,208,000)
Main languages spoken:
Turkish, Kurdish, Arabic
Main religion: Islam
Currency: Turkish lira
Main exports: textiles
and clothing, iron and
steel, electrical and
electronic machinery, fruit
Type of government:
republic

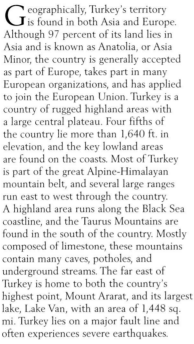

Geographically, Turkey's territory is found in both Asia and Europe. Although 97 percent of its land lies in Asia and is known as Anatolia, or Asia Minor, the country is generally accepted as part of Europe, takes part in many European organizations, and has applied to join the European Union. Turkey is a country of rugged highland areas with a large central plateau. Four fifths of the country lie more than 1,640 ft. in elevation, and the key lowland areas are found on the coasts. Most of Turkey is part of the great Alpine-Himalayan mountain belt, and several large ranges run east to west through the country. A highland area runs along the Black Sea coastline, and the Taurus Mountains are found in the south of the country. Mostly composed of limestone, these mountains contain many caves, potholes, and underground streams. The far east of Turkey is home to both the country's highest point, Mount Ararat, and its largest lake, Lake Van, with an area of 1,448 sq. mi. Turkey lies on a major fault line and often experiences severe earthquakes.

SURROUNDED BY SEAS

Almost all of Turkey's northern border is a 989-mi.-long coastline with the Black Sea. To the south and the west of Turkey are the Mediterranean and Aegean seas. Its Aegean coastline is heavily indented and contains many of the country's 159 islands. To the northwest of the country lies the Sea of Marmara, which is connected to both the Black Sea and the Aegean Sea through two narrow straits. The Sea of Marmara separates the European part of Turkey from the Asian part. The sea has an area of 4,345 sq. mi.

tobacco, fruits, and nuts. Almost half of the workforce are engaged in farming, and Turkey is self-sufficient in many basic foods. Turkey is also relatively rich in mineral deposits, including coal, oil, and a number of metals. Thirty-eight percent of the country's electricity is generated by hydroelectric power, particularly from fast-flowing rivers such as the Tigris.

▲ Turkish men enjoy their tea drinking in the Youth Park in the city of Ankara. The country's second-largest city, Ankara became its capital when Turkey was formed in 1923.

WHERE WEST MEETS EAST

Turkey's strategic location, at the point where the three continents of Africa, Asia, and Europe are closest, has meant that the region has been traveled and settled since ancient times. Its land has seen the birth of many civilizations, including the ancient Hittites, Persians, Romans, and Arabs. Turks today are descended from these and other peoples and make up the majority of the population, with the largest minority being Kurdish peoples.

▼ The stepped terraces of Pammukale in southwest Turkey attract many visitors who bathe in their hot waters. The limestone terraces have been formed over thousands of years from calcium-rich springs.

CLIMATE AND COUNTRY

Turkey has a range of climates based largely on altitude and closeness to the sea. The land bordering the Black Sea has hot summers and mild winters with high humidity and relatively heavy rainfall. In the Mediterranean and Aegean regions the climate is equally warm but drier, with most rainfall in the winter. Farther inland the country experiences a dry, continental climate. The range of climates allows a variety of crops to be grown, including cereals, cotton,

CYPRUS

The third-largest island in the Mediterranean, Cyprus is situated 50 mi. south of the Turkish coast. The country is currently divided into Greek and Turkish zones.

Area: 3,600 sq. mi., of which 1,308 sq. mi. are in the Turkish-controlled zone
Population: 767,314, including Turkish settlers in the north
Capital: Nicosia (199,000)
Main languages spoken: Greek, Turkish, English
Main religions: Greek Orthodox, Islam
Currency: Cyprian pound; Turkish lira is used in the Turkish Cypriot area
Main exports: Reexported cigarettes and electronic equipment, ship supplies, clothing, potatoes
Type of government: republic

▼ This orchard is located in the Troodos mountains in the southwest of Cyprus. The island's warm climate allows a large range of fruits to be grown.

Cyprus consists of a central plain with mountains to the south and north of the island. The largest mountain chain, the Troodos mountains, covers much of the southwest of the island. Much of Cyprus's forests have been cleared, and scrub grass and bushes are the most common vegetation. The island has no permanent rivers. Pasturelands used to graze sheep, goats, and pigs cover one tenth of the land area. The main crops grown include wheat, potatoes, tobacco, and grapes, which are used in Cyprus's wine-making industry. The island enjoys a warm Mediterranean climate with an average annual temperature of 69°F. Average annual rainfall is less than 20 in., although parts of the Troodos mountains can receive 42 in.

A DIVIDED ISLAND

Cyprus has been a colony of a number of nations, including Greece, Egypt, and the Ottoman Empire. Greek Cypriots make up around 78 percent of the population, with almost

all of the remainder of Turkish descent. Cyprus became independent from the United Kingdom in 1960, but in 1974 Turkey invaded the island and gained control of its northern one third. It later established the Turkish Republic of Northern Cyprus, but this has not been recognized by the rest of the world. Cyprus has remained divided, with a permanent United Nations peacekeeping force based there. Although the Turkish territory contained most of Cyprus's industrial centers, it is the south of the island that has improved its economy, particularly through tourism, with around 2.7 million visitors arriving in 2000.

ASIA

ASIA

Covering an area of 17.4 million sq. mi., Asia is the world's largest continent. It is geologically active, with many of the world's most active volcanoes within its territory, particularly to the east, where the continent faces the Pacific Ocean. Asia is also home to many of the planet's physical extremes, including the lowest point, the Dead Sea in Jordan, and the highest point, Mount Everest in the Himalayas. Central Asia is considerably more mountainous than other continents with the Himalayas just one of many ranges. To the south the most notable features are several major peninsulas: the Arabian Peninsula to the west, the Indian subcontinent and the Indochina peninsula, which extends into the South China Sea, and the large island archipelagos found in Southeast Asia. Every form of climate and vegetation zone is present in this continent, from icy tundra and large arid deserts to tropical rain forests and highly fertile plains and river valleys. Around 16 percent of Asia is covered in forests, with the largest found in Siberia, China, and Southeast Asia. Although parts of Tibet, Siberia, and a region of Saudi Arabia are virtually unpopulated, the continent is also home to the world's two most populous countries—China and India. Approximately one third of the entire world population is found within their borders. Although the people in Asia's most developed nations, such as Japan, enjoy a high standard of living, many are desperately poor.

▲ Bicycles and beasts of burden constitute most of the traffic in this busy street in the northern Indian city of Jaipur.

▼ Nomadic people herd horses in the isolated countryside of Mongolia. Nomadic people traveling with herds of livestock comprise just over 40 percent of Mongolia's population.

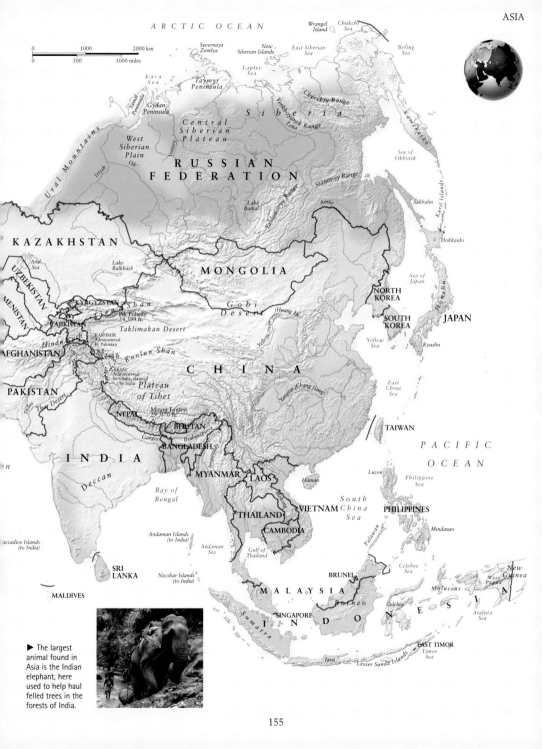

ARCTIC OCEAN

Wrangel Island
Chukchi Sea

Severnaya Zemlya
New Siberian Islands
East Siberian Sea
Bering Sea

Kara Sea
Taymyr Peninsula
Laptev Sea
Cherskiy Range

Yamal Peninsula
Gydan Peninsula

West Siberian Plain

Central Siberian Plateau
S i b e r i a
Verkhoyansk Range
Lena
Kamchatka

Ural Mountains
Irtysh
Ob'
Yenisey

R U S S I A N
F E D E R A T I O N
Stanovoy Range
Amur
Sea of Okhotsk

Lake Baikal
Yablonovyy Range
Sakhalin
Kuril Islands

KAZAKHSTAN
Hokkaido

Aral Sea
Lake Balkhash
M O N G O L I A
Sea of Japan
Honshu

UZBEKISTAN
NORTH KOREA

TURKMENISTAN
KYRGYZSTAN
Tien Shan
Pik Pobedy 24,399 ft.
Gobi Desert
SOUTH KOREA
JAPAN

TAJIKISTAN
Taklimakan Desert
Huang He
Yellow River
Yellow Sea
Kyushu

AFGHANISTAN
Hindu Kush
KASHMIR Administered by Pakistan
K2 28,251 ft.
Kunlun Shan
C H I N A
Yangtze (Chang Jiang)
East China Sea

PAKISTAN
AKSAI CHIN Administered by China, claimed by India
Plateau of Tibet

Indus
Thar Desert
Mount Everest 29,070 ft.
NEPAL
BHUTAN
Brahmaputra
TAIWAN

Ganges
BANGLADESH
Irrawaddy
PACIFIC OCEAN

I N D I A
Deccan
MYANMAR
LAOS
Hainan
Luzon
Philippine Sea

Bay of Bengal
Mekong
South China Sea
PHILIPPINES

THAILAND
VIETNAM
Mindanao

Andaman Islands (to India)
CAMBODIA

Laccadive Islands (to India)
Andaman Sea
Andaman Islands

SRI LANKA
Nicobar Islands (to India)
Gulf of Thailand
BRUNEI
Celebes Sea
West Papua
New Guinea

MALDIVES
MALAYSIA
Borneo
Moluccas
Celebes
Arafura Sea

Sumatra
SINGAPORE
I N D O N E S I A

Java
EAST TIMOR
Timor Sea
Lesser Sunda Islands

0   1000   2000 km
0   500   1000 miles

▶ The largest animal found in Asia is the Indian elephant, here used to help haul felled trees in the forests of India.

SYRIA

A large Arab nation, Syria borders Turkey, Iraq, Lebanon, Jordan, and Israel. Israel has occupied Syrian territory in the Golan Heights since 1967.

Area: 71,000 sq. mi., including areas of the Golan Heights occupied by Israel
Population: 17,155,814
Capital: Damascus (2,195,000)
Main languages spoken: Arabic, Kurdish, Armenian
Main religions: Sunni Islam, other Islam, Christian
Currency: Syrian pound
Main exports: crude petroleum and petroleum products, vegetables and fruit, cotton, textiles and fabrics
Type of government: republic (under military regime)

Syria consists of three main geographical regions. The most westerly is a coastal plain that contains the country's best farmland and is home to the majority of its population. Syria's Mediterranean coastline extends around 112 mi. between the borders of Turkey and Lebanon and is the location of the two major ports of Tartus and Al Ladhiqiyah (Latakia). Dividing much of the coastal plain from the interior are mountain ranges and several fertile basins in which large cities have developed. East of the mountains lie plateaus and a great expanse of rock and gravel desert. The Syrian Desert makes up over half of the country and extends into northern Saudi Arabia, Jordan, and western Iraq. The desert is bounded to the north by a region of fertile land through which the Euphrates river flows. A dam built on the river generates almost 35 percent of the country's electricity.

AGRICULTURE
Syria was a predominantly agricultural nation until the early 1960s, when large-scale state industries were developed. Agriculture still employs 40 percent of the workforce, with around 18,779 sq. mi. of cropland in which barley, wheat, olives, tobacco, fruit, and vegetables

▲ A textile printer at work in a souk in the city of Aleppo. With a population of 2,229,000, Aleppo is Syria's second-largest city .

are grown. The most important cash crop is cotton. Almost all crop farming depends on irrigation systems since, even in the wettest regions, most rain falls in the winter. Large parts of the country north of the Syrian Desert are not cultivated but are used as pastures for Syria's 14.5 million sheep and 1.1 million goats.

POWER AND INDUSTRY
The areas in and around the Syrian cities of Damascus, Aleppo, and Homs have become the chief industrial centers. In these regions oil and tobacco are processed, chemicals are produced, cotton-based textiles are woven, and a wide range of handicrafts, including

▼ Huge olive groves span low hills in Syria. In 2001 Syria produced around 26 percent of the world's olive oil.

silk, leather, and glass goods,
are made. The development of Syria's
oil industry has made it, since 1974, the
country's largest export earner. In 2001 it
accounted for 68 percent of the country's
exports. A series of oil pipelines crosses
Syria, linking it to Iraq, Jordan, and
the Mediterranean coast.

ARAB PEOPLE
Syria has been settled continuously for
many thousands of years by different
civilizations, including the Egyptians,
Hittites, Babylonians, and Persians.
Although Syria was part of the Ottoman
Empire from the 1500s until 1918, its
modern population is largely descended
from Arab people who conquered the
country in the 600s and ruled for 800
years. Over 90 percent
of the population are of
Arab descent, with the
largest minorities being
Kurds, who are found
near the Turkish border,
and Armenians. Syria's
capital, Damascus,
is one of the world's
oldest surviving cities and claims to
be the oldest continuously inhabited
capital city in the world. Situated in the
southwestern corner of the country,
Damascus is located at the border
of a fertile plain and at the foot
of mountains that divide
Syria from Lebanon.

▲ Lively markets, known
as souks, are a feature of
towns in Syria and other
Arab nations. The large,
bustling Souk al-Hamidiye
is found in Damascus.

ISRAEL

Established as a homeland for Jewish people in 1948, Israel stands apart from the rest of the Middle East, with which it has been in conflict since its formation.

Area: 7,800 sq. mi., excluding areas annexed by Israel (East Jerusalem and the Golan Heights)
Population: 6,029,000, including Golan Heights and East Jerusalem
Capital: Jerusalem (661,000); Jerusalem is not recognized as the capital of Israel by the international community
Main languages spoken: Hebrew, Arabic, English
Main religions: Judaism, Islam
Currency: new shekel
Main exports: machinery and transportation equipment, cut diamonds, chemicals, clothing, food and beverages
Type of government: republic

▼ A gardener plants a tree at a kibbutz. Some farms in Israel are organized as *kibbutzim*, settlements and communities in which people share their income and property.

Israel is located at the eastern end of the Mediterranean Sea and is bordered by Egypt, Lebanon, Syria, Jordan, and the occupied territories of Gaza and the West Bank. Its most southerly point is a short Red Sea coastline, which has been developed as a tourist center. The country has a variety of landscapes, including hills that run from the north into its center and a large depression, part of the Great Rift Valley, along its most eastern lands. Israel's coastal plain runs parallel to the Mediterranean Sea and is bordered by stretches of fertile farmland extending up to 25 mi. inland. This plain contains over half of Israel's population, most of its industry, and much of its agriculture. To the south lies the dry and rugged Negev Desert.

ISRAEL'S ECONOMY AND PEOPLE

Although agriculture has been developed using advanced techniques and irrigation, the country's economy is dominated by service, defense, and manufacturing industries. Israel is a major world center for the cutting and polishing of gems and has large computing, machine making, and chemical industries. Tourism, although declining since the late 1990s, has been important, with visitors attracted by the warm climate and the religious history of a land that holds importance for three of the world's major religions: Islam, Christianity, and Judaism. In the 1990s Israel's economy expanded, partly owing to the mass immigration of large numbers of highly skilled Jews from the former Soviet Union. They joined

a highly mixed population consisting of approximately 80 percent Jews and 20 percent Arabs. An open immigration policy to Jewish people around the world has resulted in Jews from over 100 countries settling in Israel.

AID, TRADE, AND CONFLICT

The U.S. maintains a strong relationship with Israel. It is its largest trading partner, and it donates more aid to Israel than any other nation. Israel trades heavily with a number of European countries but very little with its immediate Arab neighbors. The country has been in political and sometimes military conflict with these neighbors over

its territory and ultimate existence. A series of wars since Israel's formation saw Israel occupy parts of the neighboring countries. The Gaza Strip on the Mediterranean coast was once part of Egypt. The West Bank and East Jerusalem were once part of Jordan, while Golan Heights was previously Syrian territory. Israel's strained relationship with its Arab neighbors and the violence between Jews and Palestinians mean that over one fourth of the national budget is spent on defense. The major issue remains the fate of the Palestinian people, who were expelled from their territory when Israel was formed in 1948. They seek their own homeland in the West Bank and Gaza.

▲ A dry riverbed in the hostile Negev Desert. Covering over half of Israel's territory, the Negev holds less than seven percent of the country's population. Hot and dry, the landscape becomes more rugged and rises in elevation to the south.

▼ Jerusalem is Israel's third-largest city. In 1950 Israel proclaimed Jerusalem as its capital, although the United Nations does not recognize this, and almost all countries maintain their embassies in the coastal city of Tel Aviv.

LEBANON

Occupying a narrow strip of land along the eastern coast of the Mediterranean Sea, Lebanon is a nation that is rebuilding after a prolonged civil war.

Area: 3,900 sq. mi.
Population: 3,667,780
Capital: Beirut (2,115,000)
Main languages spoken: Arabic, French, English, Armenian
Main religions: Islam, Christian
Currency: Lebanese pound
Main exports: reexports, paper products, food and live animals, machinery and transportation equipment
Type of government: republic

Lebanon is a small country bordered to the south by Israel and on its north and eastern sides by Syria. The country consists of a coastal plain that rises to a pair of mountain ranges in the east. Between these mountain ranges lies a large, fertile valley, the Bekaa. Lebanon has two main climatic zones. Its coast with the Mediterranean experiences warm, dry summers and rainy, yet mild, winters. Inland, in the Bekaa valley, the summer months are hot and dry. The Litani river runs through the valley and is harnessed to provide hydroelectricity, as well as irrigation for both the southern part of the valley and, via a mountain tunnel, water for part of the coastal plain. Compared to many countries in the region, Lebanon receives relatively high rainfall. Farming is a key occupation both in the coastal plain and in the Bekaa, with crops including cereals, vegetables, and a large range of fruits.

CIVIL WAR AND RECONSTRUCTION

The site of ancient Phoenician cities built over 3,000 years ago, Lebanon was a prosperous nation and a commercial and trading center. Beirut, its capital city, attracted many tourists. The country's complex ethnic background features many different Christian and Muslim groups. Tensions between religious groups were responsible for a lengthy civil war that started in 1975 and devastated much of the country. Stability in the 1990s has allowed foreign aid and government spending to rebuild the country.

▲ The majestic cedars of Lebanon, some of which are 1,500 years old, are a national symbol. Much of Lebanon was once covered in huge forests, but these now occupy less than eight percent of its land.

▶ New hotels and apartment buildings, viewed from a beach café, show how Beirut is redeveloping and attracting large numbers of tourists after many years of devastating conflicts.

JORDAN

Lying between Saudi Arabia, Israel, Syria, and Iraq, the almost landlocked, small Arab kingdom of Jordan became fully independent in 1946.

Area: 35,300 sq. mi.
Population: 5,307,470
Capital: Amman (1,181,000)
Main languages spoken: Arabic, English
Main religions: Sunni Islam, Christian
Currency: Jordanian dinar
Main exports: chemicals and chemical products, reexported petroleum, phosphate fertilizers, potash, fruit, vegetables, and nuts
Type of government: constitutional monarchy

Jordan has three distinct geographical regions: the Jordan Valley to the west, an eastern desert region, and, between them, an area of highlands and plateaus. Western Jordan has a Mediterranean climate with hot, dry summers, cool, wet winters, and two short transitional seasons. The remaining three fourths of the country have a largely desert climate with less than ten inches of rainfall per year. Water shortages are a major problem in Jordan, which also lacks large oil and other major mineral reserves—with the exception of phosphates, which, along with with fertilizer and potash, are the country's major exports. Less than five percent of its land is capable of supporting crops, which include tomatoes, fruits, wheat, and olives. Sheep are the country's most important livestock, with an estimated 1.6 million in 2002. Jordan lost around one fifth of its industrial production and much of its best farmland following the Israeli occupation of the West Bank in 1967. Around three fourths of its people, many of them displaced Palestinians, live in cities, including Amman, the capital.

THE JORDAN VALLEY

Part of the Great Rift Valley of Africa, the Jordan Valley extends down the entire western flank of the country. The valley contains the Jordan river, which is heavily exploited to irrigate the surrounding land and provide water for the local population. This river flows into the Dead Sea, which, at 1,338 ft. below sea level, is the lowest point on the surface of Earth.

▲ Tourism is a major source of revenue for Jordan, and many visitors flock to see the ruins of the ancient city of Petra. Petra's stunning buildings, including this tomb known as the Treasury of the Pharaohs, are carved out of red sandstone cliffs.

▶ Lying on the Gulf of Aqaba, an arm of the Red Sea, the city of Aqaba is Jordan's only port. It is also used as a base for divers who visit the rich coral reef farther south in the gulf.

IRAQ

Iraq is a nation of mountains, deserts, and fertile plains. It has been in conflict with the international community for over one decade.

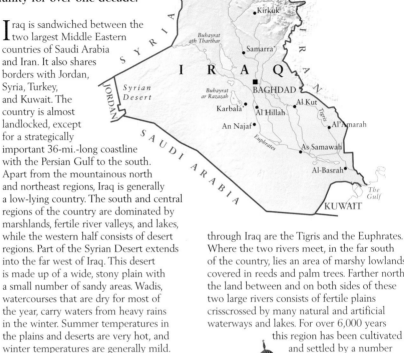

Area: 167,600 sq mi.
Population: 24,001,816
Capital: Baghdad
(4,958,000)
Main languages spoken:
Arabic, Kurdish
Main religions: Shi'a
Islam, Sunni Islam
Currency: Iraqi dinar
Main exports: crude
petroleum and petroleum
products
Type of government:
republic

Iraq is sandwiched between the two largest Middle Eastern countries of Saudi Arabia and Iran. It also shares borders with Jordan, Syria, Turkey, and Kuwait. The country is almost landlocked, except for a strategically important 36-mi.-long coastline with the Persian Gulf to the south. Apart from the mountainous north and northeast regions, Iraq is generally a low-lying country. The south and central regions of the country are dominated by marshlands, fertile river valleys, and lakes, while the western half consists of desert regions. Part of the Syrian Desert extends into the far west of Iraq. This desert is made up of a wide, stony plain with a small number of sandy areas. Wadis, watercourses that are dry for most of the year, carry waters from heavy rains in the winter. Summer temperatures in the plains and deserts are very hot, and winter temperatures are generally mild. These regions receive little rainfall. The northeast is cooler and wetter, especially in the mountains.

LAND BETWEEN THE RIVERS

Iraq covers a region known in ancient times as Mesopotamia, a Greek word meaning "land between the rivers." The two major rivers that flow through Iraq are the Tigris and the Euphrates. Where the two rivers meet, in the far south of the country, lies an area of marshy lowlands covered in reeds and palm trees. Farther north the land between and on both sides of these two large rivers consists of fertile plains crisscrossed by many natural and artificial waterways and lakes. For over 6,000 years this region has been cultivated and settled by a number of ancient civilizations, including the Sumerians, Babylonians, and

▲ An image of Saddam Hussein, Iraq's leader from 1979 until the U.S.-led invasion of Iraq in 2003, adorns a Baghdad street.

▶ Situated in a suburb of Iraq's capital, Baghdad, the Kadhimain mosque was built in 1515 and is decorated with gold minarets and ornate designs.

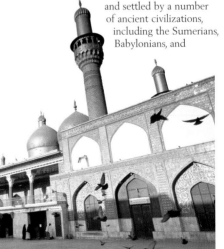

Assyrians. Today this region is where most Iraqis live. Many are engaged in agriculture, either raising livestock or growing cereal crops and a large range of fruits. Before the 1991 Gulf War Iraq produced 80 percent of the world's dates.

OIL AND WAR

Oil was first discovered in Iraq in 1927, and since that time the country has become one of the world's leading oil producers. Before 1990 the country rose to become the world's third leading oil producer. Iraq also has one of the world's largest reserves of sulfur, an element widely used in industry. Much of the oil revenue was channeled into building a large military force. Iraq invaded Iran in 1980, and by the time a cease-fire was struck in 1988 over 300,000 Iraqis had lost their lives. Two years later the country occupied the small, oil-rich state of Kuwait. In 1991 a coalition of nations led by the U.S. pushed Iraq's forces out of Kuwait. Following United Nations sanctions after the Gulf War Iraq was only able to use its enormous oil reserves for domestic use until 1996, when limited and supervised exports were allowed. As a result, the country's gross national product (GNP) was cut in half. Damage inflicted on the country during the Gulf War and the subsequent embargoes on trade have disrupted both agriculture and industry. As a result, widespread poverty and hardship have been created, especially among the poorer sections of Iraqi society. Iraq, under the strict leadership of Saddam Hussein, remained isolated and at odds with much of the rest of the world. In March 2003 an international coalition force led by the U.S. invaded Iraq. Within four weeks the coalition force had captured much of the country and toppled Saddam Hussein from power, paving the way for an elected Iraqi government. The future of Iraq remains uncertain as the country beings rebuilding.

▼ Poor treatment of the Kurdish minority by the Iraqi government has generated thousands of refugees. Here a Kurd from Iraq sits in a refugee camp inside the Turkish border.

▼ A group of Iraqi Arab women walk in front of a bomb-damaged building in the capital city of Baghdad. Iraqis are predominantly Arab people, with Kurds the one large minority.

IRAN

The most populous and second-largest nation in the Middle East, the Islamic Republic of Iran is a rugged country with huge fossil fuel deposits.

Area: 631,700 sq. mi.
Population: 66,622,704
Capital: Tehran
(7,038,000)
Main languages spoken:
Farsi (Persian), Turkic,
Kurdish, Luri
Main religions: Shi'a
Islam, Sunni Islam
Currency: rial
Main exports: petroleum
and natural gas, carpets,
pistachios, iron and steel
Type of government:
Islamic republic

Iran is bordered by seven nations and has coastlines with three large seas: the Gulf of Oman, the Persian Gulf, and the Caspian Sea. The country's main geographical features are several large mountain ranges and a giant plateau. Lying in the center of the country, the Iranian Plateau extends eastward into central Asia. Around 4,000 ft. in elevation, the plateau is hot, dry, and contains two large deserts in the northeast and east— the Dasht-e Kavir (70,200 sq. ft.) and the Dasht-e Lut (over 64,740 sq. ft.)— which occupy most of the northeast and east of the central plain. There are a large number of climatic regions throughout Iran. Yet, although the northern mountains bordering the Caspian Sea receive heavy rainfall, Iran is a country in which precipitation is relatively scarce and is dependent on the seasons.

▲ One of hundreds of carpet workshops found in the central Iranian city of Esfahan. The city is a center of textile mills that process cotton, silk, and woolen cloth for manufacturing clothing and carpets.

IRANIAN MOUNTAINS

Iran's longest mountain range—the Zagros —stretches from the northwest of the country close to the border with Armenia southward and southeastward along the Persian Gulf, where it ends near the Strait of Hormuz, which link the Persian Gulf and the Gulf of Oman. Its terrain includes

many peaks over 9,840 ft., while many of its deep valleys are fertile and are farmed. The Elburz mountain range runs along the southern shore of the Caspian Sea. The highest of its volcanic peaks is Qolleh-ye Damavand (18,381 ft.), Iran's highest point. The northern slopes of the Elburz Mountains are densely covered with deciduous trees, forming the largest area of vegetation in Iran. Many of Iran's seasonal rivers start in these mountains and flow north into the Caspian Sea. The country's capital city, Tehran, is located on the southern slopes of the Elburz Mountains at a height of around 3,510 ft.

AN OIL ECONOMY

Iran's economy is closely tied to its natural resources; 85 percent of its export revenues are derived from oil and gas. Iran contains around eight percent of the known global oil reserves and almost one fifth of the world's total reserves of natural gas. Under modernizing programs introduced by Shah Mohammad Reza Pahlavi—the country's monarch from 1953 to 1979—Iran developed oil-processing and transportation industries at a number of large ports on its Persian Gulf coast, including Bandar-e' Abbas and Abadan. Industries, such as chemicals, textiles, machinery, and cement production, were also developed.

REVOLUTION AND WAR

The Iranian people are deeply religious, and all aspects of life are heavily influenced by the Islamic faith. In 1979 the shah was overthrown in a revolution, and Iran was declared an Islamic republic. Iran outlawed many Western influences and enforced a strict code of Islamic law. In 1980 the country was invaded by Iraq, and in the ensuing eight-year-long war over 400,000 Iranians died. The country's support for strong Islamic rule elsewhere has brought it into conflict with some of its Middle Eastern neighbors, as well as Western nations.

▲ A petroleum refinery found in the city of Abadan. Located at the northernmost end of the Persian Gulf, Abadan is a major center of oil processing and transportation.

▼ Iranian farmworkers prepare to gather harvested crops. Agriculture contributes one fifth of GDP, with important crops including wheat, barley, rice, sugar beets, tobacco, and wool.

SAUDI ARABIA

The desert kingdom of Saudi Arabia covers much of the Arabian Peninsula and is the largest and wealthiest oil-producing nation in the Middle East.

Area: 830,000 sq. mi.
Population: 25,513,330
Capital: Riyadh (4,761,000)
Main language spoken: Arabic
Main religion: Sunni Islam
Currency: riyal
Main exports: petroleum, petrochemicals, natural gas
Type of government: monarchy with council of ministers

Saudi Arabia borders seven countries and is connected to an eighth, Bahrain, by a highway. The country is about one fourth of the size of the U.S. and has 1,637 mi. of coastline, approximately 1,091 mi. with the Red Sea to the west and the remainder with the Persian Gulf. A narrow coastal plain between 9–40 mi. in width extends along the Red Sea coast, and a range of mountains runs farther inland and parallel to this plain. These mountains increase in height as they extend southward, reaching the country's highest point on the slopes of Jabal Sawda (10,276 ft.). A large plateau stretches out to the northeast of Saudi Arabia, reaching a maximum height of 5,904 ft. and dropping in altitude as it slopes down toward the Gulf in the east. To the south and southeast Saudi Arabia contains the world's largest continuous sand desert, the Ar Rub' Al-Khali, or Empty Quarter. In parts of this hostile environment rain has not fallen for years.

▲ Excess gas is burned off at an oil well in Saudi Arabia. Oil and natural gas are transported around the country to refineries and ports via over 10,540 mi. of pipelines.

WATER AND AGRICULTURE

Saudi Arabia's climate is generally hot and dry. Temperatures can reach 122°F on summer days, although nights are cool, and frosts occur in the winter. Rainfall is generally low; the capital city, Riyadh, receives an average of 34 in. per year, although the Asir mountains tend to receive three to four times as much. Saudi Arabia's generally dry climate means that the country has no permanent rivers or large lakes. Agriculture has traditionally been restricted to livestock herded by nomadic Bedouin Arabs, with crops only grown in the mountainous Asir region in the southwest

of the country and in the oases that dot the desert landscape north of the Empty Quarter. Huge desalination projects, where the seawater is processed, the salt removed, and freshwater created, have helped generate millions of gallons of water. Desalination, along with recent irrigation projects, has helped reclaim many square miles of desert and turn it into fertile land. As a result, Saudi Arabia's farming sector is growing. The country's leading crops are wheat, barley, dates, dairy products, and a range of fruits. Sheep, goats, and camels are the most commonly raised livestock.

WORLD'S BIGGEST OIL PRODUCER

Oil was first discovered in Saudi Arabia in 1936, and in 2002 an estimated 10.5 million barrels per day were produced. The country has the world's largest oil and natural gas reserves and an estimated one fourth of the entire world's oil deposits. As a result, oil revenues not only dominate the country's economy, making up over 90 percent of exports, but they also give the country great importance in the global economy. Its oil region lies primarily in the east along the Gulf. The enormous revenue from oil has been used to build modern cities, develop infrastructure, ports, hospitals, and schools, and bring electricity to towns. It has also been used to develop other industries such as chemicals, metalworking, and medicines.

INDEPENDENCE AND GOVERNMENT

Although the region has a long history and has been settled for thousands of years, the actual kingdom of Saudi Arabia is a fairly young nation. It emerged in the early 1900s as Abd al-Aziz ibn Saud (1882–1953) conquered successive territories in the Arabian Peninsula, beginning with Riyadh in 1901 and ending largely in 1920 with the incorporation of the region of Asir. The year 1932 saw the formation of the kingdom of Saudi Arabia by Abd al-Aziz ibn Saud. Descendants of the Saud family continue to run the country, with absolute power invested in the monarch. In 1993 the current monarch, King Fahd ibn Abdul Aziz, introduced political reforms, creating a Consultative Council of 60 members who advise the king. A bill of rights was also established, and power was given to the local governments of the 13 provinces into which Saudi Arabia is divided. However, Saudi Arabia still remains a nation dominated by one family who makes all key political appointments. There are no political parties, and strong media censorship is imposed. Satellite television, for example, was banned in 1994, while there are strict rules regarding the Internet and religion.

▼ Two Saudis engage in falconry, the training of falcons or hawks to capture wild animals or other birds. Falconry is now a sport enjoyed by wealthy Saudis. It is carefully regulated in order to protect the endangered species on which falcons prey.

▼ A Bedouin camel train winds its way across the Saudi Arabian desert. Many Bedouins are no longer nomadic and now work in the oil industry or have settled in cities.

▲ Saudi stock traders monitor prices of companies' shares in their business suite in the city of Riyadh. The Tadawul, the Saudi stock market, is now the largest in the Arab world.

▼ Pilgrims at the Great Mosque in Mecca surround the Kaaba, the holiest place on Earth to Muslims.

A REGIONAL SUPERPOWER

As the wealthiest of the Middle East nations Saudi Arabia has strong ties and great influence with both its Arab neighbors and the Western world. This power has increased as the country has grown richer and has made more contributions to military and economic operations in the Middle East. It has also funded a number of aid and investment projects in the Gulf and Middle East region and frequently contracts U.S., Japanese, French, and British companies for defense and civil engineering projects. Many Saudis are sent overseas to Europe and North America to complete their higher education.

THE BIRTHPLACE OF ISLAM

The world's second-largest religion has its origins within Saudi Arabia. The founder of Islam, the prophet Muhammad (c. A.D. 570–632), was born in the city of Mecca, around 43 mi. inland from the Red Sea port of Jeddah. The Islamic calendar began in A.D. 622, the year of the hegira, or Muhammad's flight from Mecca. He returned to capture the city in A.D. 630, and it is now the holiest city in the Islamic world. Every Muslim strives to make the religious pilgrimage, known as a hajj, to Mecca once in their lifetime, and millions of Muslims visit Mecca every year. There they attend the Great Mosque, or Al-Haram, a religious place of worship large enough to hold 300,000 people. In the center of the Great Mosque's courtyard lies the Kaaba, a small building in which the Black Stone of Mecca is housed. It is the holiest shrine in the entire Islamic world. Medina, 211 mi. north of Mecca, is also a holy city and houses Muhammad's remains in a tomb. Saudi Arabia is run as a strict Muslim state in which Islamic law, *sharia*, is paramount. Women have no role in public life, are prevented from taking jobs in many fields, apart from teaching and health care, and cannot obtain driving licenses. Strict Islamic punishments for certain crimes are enforced, generating criticism from international human rights groups.

KUWAIT

Dwarfed by its neighbors, Saudi Arabia, Iraq, and
Iran, Kuwait is an intensely oil-rich nation that is still
recovering from the effects of the 1990 Iraqi invasion.

Area: 6,900 sq. mi.
Population: 2,111,561
Capital: Kuwait City
(888,000)
Major language spoken:
Arabic
Major religion: Islam
Currency: dinar
Main exports: petroleum
and petroleum products
(account for 94 percent
of exports)
Type of government:
econstitutional monarchy

Kuwait is located on the northernmost
end of the Gulf. Its territory includes
a number of islands in the Gulf, most
of which are uninhabited. The country's
landscape is flat and almost featureless.
It consists largely of a rolling sandy
plateau that rises in the west to an
elevation of 948 ft. near the country's
borders with Saudi Arabia and Iraq.
Average annual rainfall is around five
inches, there is little surface water,
and the country relies on advanced
desalination projects for most water.
Fertile soil is minimal. The one major
exception is the oasis at Al Jahrah, 31 mi.
west of Kuwait City. The remaining few
areas of natural vegetation occur in salt
marshes in the northeast and along parts
of the coast. Green areas in Kuwait's large
towns and cities have been created using
imported soil. Fishing is the country's
only major food-related industry, with
shrimp the most
profitable catch.

OIL, INVASION,
AND REBUILDING

Beneath Kuwait's barren,
featureless land lie enormous oil and
smaller, but still significant, natural gas
deposits. Kuwait has an estimated ten
percent of the world's proven reserves
of crude oil and, in 2002, produced
approximately 2.2 million barrels per day.
This is a recovery from a major slump that
followed the invasion of the country by Iraq
in 1990. The Iraqi invasion and subsequent
war, in which an international coalition
forced Iraqi troops to withdraw, proved to
be both an economic and ecological disaster.
In 2003 Kuwait became a base for large
numbers of international coalition forces
that invaded Iraq.

▼ An oil worker in
Kuwait works on one
of the country's many
modern oil rigs. Kuwait's
oil industry employs
thousands of foreign
workers, mainly from
southern Asia and
other Arab nations.

BAHRAIN

Lying in the Persian Gulf between Qatar and Saudi Arabia, the small kingdom of Bahrain consists of one large and a number of smaller islands.

BAHRAIN

Area: 239 sq. mi.
Population: 656,397
Capital: Manamah (150,000)
Main languages spoken: Arabic, English, Farsi, Urdu
Main religions: Shi'a Islam, Sunni Islam
Currency: Bahraini dinar
Main exports: petroleum and petroleum products, basic manufactures
Type of government: traditional monarchy

Bahrain island, the nation's main land area, has a rocky center and is linked to the Saudi Arabian mainland by a large highway. The island's climate is hot and extremely dry, with no more than four inches of rainfall annually. Imported soil, irrigation, and drainage programs have helped Bahrain grow some fruit and vegetables. Bahrain was the first Gulf state to start producing oil in commercial quantities, but the nation's reserves are heavily depleted and may run out in the next 10–20 years. Investment in other industries, including aluminum production, chemicals, and plastics, has occurred, while many educated Bahrainis work in flourishing service industries such as insurance and banking. The country, run by the powerful al-Khalifa family, owns one fourth of the region's Gulf Air airline. Bahrain came under the protection of the United Kingdom in the 1800s and declared independence in 1971. English is still widely spoken by both the Arab population and the large communities of foreign workers.

▶ Part of the large business district in Bahrain's capital city, Manamah. The city is connected to the nearby island of Al Muharraq, on which the country's airport is located.

QATAR

The emirate of Qatar occupies a peninsula jutting out into the Persian Gulf. It is a flat, dry desert land with particularly high reserves of natural gas.

Area: 4,200 sq. mi.
Population: 793,341
Capital: Doha (285,000)
Main languages spoken: Arabic, English
Main religion: Sunni Islam
Currency: Qatari riyal
Main exports: petroleum and natural gas, chemicals
Type of government: traditional monarchy

Qatar shares land borders with the United Arab Emirates and Saudi Arabia. Much of Qatar consists of rolling deserts, with some low hills to the west facing the coast. Rainfall is very low, less than four inches per year, and tends to fall only in heavy storms during the winter. Some freshwater is tapped from underground sources, but Qatar relies on desalination plants, which process seawater into freshwater. Not much land is suitable for farming, but irrigation programs do allow melons, tomatoes, and eggplants to be cultivated. Fishing off the peninsula coast is important, with around 5,000 tons caught per year. Qatar has one of the smaller reserves of oil in the Middle East but has the world's third-largest natural gas deposits.

A NATIVE MINORITY
Only one in five of the country's population was born in Qatar. Since oil production began large numbers of foreign workers have been employed in Qatar, especially people from Iran, Pakistan, and India. The native people are descendants of nomadic Bedouin Arabs. Now over 80 percent of native Qataris live in cities, and many small villages and settlements lie abandoned. Ruled by the ath-Thani family, Qatar has grown very wealthy from its oil and natural gas reserves. The country's population has a high standard of living, with no income tax and free health and education services.

UNITED ARAB EMIRATES

A federation of seven states, or emirates, the United
Arab Emirates lies on the Gulf and is a dry desert
land that is prosperous from gas and oil revenues.

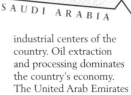

Area: 32,300 sq. mi.
Population: 2,445,000
Capital: Abu Dhabi
(471,000)
Main languages: Arabic,
Persian, English, Hindi,
Urdu
Main religions: Islam,
Christian, Hinduism
Currency: dirham
Main exports: crude and
refined petroleum, natural
gas, manufactures, dates
Type of government:
constitutional monarchy

The United Arab Emirates
is a land of mainly low-
lying deserts and salt flats with
an average elevation of under 492 ft.
To the east the land rises sharply to
a height of 5,000 ft. along the border
with Oman. The country has a long
coastline with the Persian Gulf and a short
coast facing the Gulf of Oman. The waters
in the Gulf of Oman are much deeper and
richer in nutrients and support a vibrant
fishing industry. In 2001 115,000 tons of
fish were caught. The country is extremely
dry, with as little as two inches of rainfall
per year, rising to six inches per year in
the mountainous areas. Agriculture is
only possible via irrigation.

In 1971 the United Arab Emirates
formed as a federation comprising the seven
emirates of Abu Dhabi, Dubai, Sharjah,
Ajman, Umm al-Qaiwain, Ras al-Khaimah,
and Fujairah. Formerly known as the Trucial
States, the federation was formed after
British forces left the region. Abu Dhabi was
the largest of the former states in land area
and is home to the country's
political capital city of the
same name. Along with
the sizable city of Dubai,
these are the two main

industrial centers of the
country. Oil extraction
and processing dominates
the country's economy.
The United Arab Emirates
has approximately nine percent of the
world's proven reserves of oil and produces
around 2.5 million barrels per day. The
world's largest artificial port, 19 mi. south
of the city of Dubai, has become a major
transportation terminus for the Gulf nations.
The United Arab Emirates has used some of
its oil revenue to develop other industries,
including finance, metal production, and
tourism, as well as providing high-quality
transportation links and other services for its
people. The citizens of the U.A.E. have
the highest income per capita
in the entire Arab world
and pay no income tax.

▲ The United Arab
Emirates is largely self-
sufficient in many fruits,
including dates, here being
harvested from palm trees.

▶ The New Souk market
building (right) sits in front
of a Muslim mosque in the
city of Sharjah. The city's
population has increased
20 times over since
1968 as foreign workers,
predominantly male, have
arrived to work in the
oil and other industries.
Today over two thirds
of the entire country's
population are male.

OMAN

Located strategically at the entrance to the Persian Gulf, Oman has large oil reserves but is one of the least developed of the Gulf states.

Area: 82,000 sq. mi.,
Population: 2,713,462
Capital: Muscat (540,000)
Main language spoken:
Arabic
Main religion: Ibadhi Islam
Currency: Omani rial
Main exports: petroleum (accounts for over 80 percent of exports), reexports
Type of government: absolute monarchy

▼ This rugged mountain landscape is found in the Musandam Peninsula, an enclave of Oman separated from the rest of the country by territory belonging to the United Arab Emirates.

The terrain of Oman is dominated by a vast desert plain that covers over three fourths of the country. In the north lie mountains that rise to heights of over 9,840 ft. The narrow coastal plain, which is fertile in places, is separated from the desert interior by a range of hills that runs southwest parallel to the Arabian Sea. The country has a 1,297-mi.-long coastline with both the Gulf of Oman and the Arabian Sea. The coastline has a variety of terrain, including deep fjords, long, sandy beaches, mangrove lagoons, coral reefs, and rocky islets. There are no major rivers or lakes in Oman, and with a warm, dry climate with less than 4.4 in. of rainfall per year, there is little agriculture. Oman is reliant on irrigation and concentrates on export crops such as limes and dates. Fishing is important, especially to Omani people living in small coastal settlements. Oman is ruled by a sultan who appoints a cabinet and council of regional representatives. The country has no political parties or law-making assembly. Oil dominates the economy and was first discovered in Oman in 1964.

The country started large-scale oil production in 1967. From 1970 onward Oman has undergone a rapid transformation. Previously there were few schools, few communications links, and only 6.2 mi. of paved roads. Using oil revenues, Oman, under the leadership of Sultan Qaboos, has developed a modern infrastructure and public services. This process is still continuing. For example, 100 new schools have been built since 1996, and the country's literacy rate has risen rapidly to almost 80 percent.

YEMEN

A union of two former nations, Yemen is the newest country in the Middle East. It occupies the rugged and arid southwestern corner of the Arabian Peninsula.

Area: 203,800 sq. mi.
Population: 18,701,257
Capital: Sana (1,410,000)
Main language spoken: Arabic
Main religion: Islam
Currency: Yemeni rial
Main exports: petroleum (over 90 percent of exports), food and live animals, crude minerals
Type of government: republic

▼ A goatherder tends his flock in front of a hill topped with an old fortress in Al-Mahwit province, the smallest of Yemen's 18 administrative divisions.

Yemen shares land borders with Oman to the east and Saudi Arabia to the north, both of which were finally agreed in 1992–2000 following disputes. Yemen's territory also includes a small number of islands, the largest of which is Socotra, with an area of 1,396 sq. mi. The country has coastlines with both the Red Sea and the Gulf of Aden, which flows out into the Indian Ocean. Yemen's location has been strategically important since ancient times, with Aden a major port for over 2,000 years. The country's landscape is varied and consists of a semidesert plain facing the Red Sea that then rises to form mountains and plateaus that are cut by deep valleys. East of the central region the landscape is rugged deserts and mountains. Rainfall varies depending on location, with the southern coast receiving less than four inches per year, while up to 30 in. falls in the western mountain region. The wettest area of Yemen is also the most highly populated, with

▲ A Yemeni market worker trades and sells qat. The leaves of this evergreen shrub have a mild stimulating effect when chewed, a popular practice in Yemen.

Sana, the largest city and capital, and other major towns such as Ibb and Ta'izz.

The vast majority of Yemenis are Muslim Arabs, and the population is one of the most rural of all Arab nations. More than half of the workforce are engaged in agriculture, often farming small plots of land. Ancient terraces cut into the mountainsides provide extra farmland. Wheat, millet, and other cereal crops are vital staple foods, along with citrus fruits, tomatoes, and some vegetables. The main cash crops for export are coffee and cotton. Mocha coffee has been exported from Yemen for 1,200 years. Today oil is the dominant export, accounting for the majority of the country's export revenue. Yemen was formed in 1990 when the Yemen Arab Republic (North Yemen) and the People's Democratic Republic of Yemen (South Yemen) unified. The newly formed nation supported Iraq during the 1991 Gulf War, and reprisals followed, with Saudi Arabia and Kuwait expelling many Yemeni migrant workers. This has had a severe effect on the economy, with over 30 percent unemployment. A civil war between northern and southern forces broke out in 1994, but since that time an uneasy peace has held.

KAZAKHSTAN

The biggest of the central Asian states and the ninth-largest country in the world, Kazakhstan is a land of deserts and plains with vast mineral reserves.

Area: 1,049,200 sq. mi.
Population: 16,741,519
Capital: Astana (328,000)
Main languages spoken: Kazakh, Russian
Main religions: Islam, Russian Orthodox
Currency: tenge
Main exports: oil and natural gas, rolled ferrous metals, refined copper, cereals, coal
Type of government: republic

Much of Kazakhstan's vast area consists of grassy plains, known as steppes, that cover the north and some of the central regions of the country. The south and south-central regions of the country are covered by deserts, while to the extreme east and south the land rises to form several high mountain ranges. This area features the country's highest point, Mount Khan Tangiri (22,943 ft.). In contrast, the western part of the country, which borders the Caspian Sea, has a low point of 92 ft. below sea level. Kazakhstan has a continental climate with great extremes of temperature and rainfall. The mountains to the east, for example, can receive an annual average rainfall of 60 in. Most of the country receives between 8–16 in. per year, while parts of the central desert region receive no more than four inches. Much farming relies on irrigation from the country's rivers and lakes. The largest lake entirely in Kazakhstan is Lake Balkhash, which has an area of 6,786 sq. mi. Russians form 29 percent of the nation's population, and there are large minorities of Ukranians, Tatars, and Uzbeks. The Kazahks are the biggest ethnic

▲ Founded in 1824 as a fortress settlement, Kazakhstan's capital city of Astana has been known as Akmolinsk, Tselinograd, and Aqmola in the past. Its status is a duty-free tax zone to encourage foreign investment.

group in the country, making up almost half of the population. Historically most Kazahks lived a nomadic life, but during the 1900s many were forced to settle in one place. Mining is the largest industry, while agriculture remains important. Kazakhstan has enormous reserves of many minerals, including lead, zinc, chromium, and tungsten, as well as coal, iron ore, and nickel. Large oil and natural gas deposits are found in the Caspian Sea, and the country has formed partnerships with foreign companies in order to exploit these reserves.

▲ A *Soyuz-Fregat* rocket launch occurring at the Baikonur Cosmodrome. The site of the former Soviet Union's space program, it lies approximately 124 mi. northwest of the city of Qyzylorda.

UZBEKISTAN

Uzbekistan is the most populous country in central Asia.
It has huge mineral resources, but its infrastructure
is limited, and many of its people are poor.

Area: 172,700 sq. mi.
Population: 25,563,441
Capital: Tashkent
(2,157,000)
Main languages spoken:
Uzbek, Russian
Main religions: Islam,
Eastern Orthodox
Currency: som
Main exports: light
industrial products,
petroleum and natural
gas, machine-building
equipment, food
Type of government:
republic

Uzebkistan is one of only two
countries in the world that
are doubly landlocked—
surrounded by other
landlocked countries
(Liechtenstein is the
other). Approximately
one third of the
country's territory
consists of
mountains and
foothills to the east
and southeast, where they
merge with the mountain ranges
of neighboring Kyrgyzstan and Tajikistan.
Most of the remainder consists of dry
desert plains. Uzbekistan's continental
climate is characterized by low rainfall
levels of between 8–16 in. per year across
the country. Farming tends to rely on
irrigation and occurs mainly to the east and
in the fertile river valley of the Amu Darya,
which feeds the Aral Sea. Overuse of river
and lake water for irrigation has caused
severe ecological problems. Cotton is the
most important crop, followed by tobacco,
fruit, and vegetables, but the country
produces only one third of the cereals
it requires and has to import the rest.
Uzbek people comprise 80 percent of the
population, with Russians making up five
percent, Tajiks three percent, Kazakhs four
percent, and Tatars two
percent. The country's
population is concentrated
in the south and east of the
country. Many live in towns and cities
that date back many centuries. Samarqand
is one of the oldest cities in central Asia.
Tashkent is the country's capital and is the
center of Uzbekistan's manufacturing and
heavy industry, which includes car and
aircraft production, farm machinery, and
jewelry, using gold from several large
mines in the Kizilkum desert.

▲ Uzbekistan is one
of the world's leading
producers of cotton.

▼ Since 1960 the Aral
Sea has shrunk in area by
approximately 40 percent
owing to overuse of the
rivers that have fed it
for thousands of years.
In addition to the stranded
boats, the salt and sand
left behind have made
the surrounding land
unsuitable for agriculture.

TURKMENISTAN

The least populous central Asian country, Turkmenistan is an isolated, largely desert nation with large natural gas reserves.

Area: 188,500 sq. mi.
Population: 4,688,963
Capital: Ashgabat (558,000)
Main languages spoken: Turkmen, Russian, Uzbek
Main religions: Islam, Eastern Orthodox
Currency: manat
Main exports: natural gas and oil products (almost 70 percent of exports), cotton, textiles
Type of government: republic

Four fifths of the land of Turkmenistan consist of the large, flat Karakum desert, famous for its black sands, which experiences maximum temperatures in excess of 122°F. Turkmenistan has a very dry climate with extremes of temperature; in the winter temperatures can fall below -22°F. The country's principal river, the Amu Darya, flows through the eastern part of the country. Near the country's border with Afghanistan some of its waters are diverted along a 682-mi.-long irrigation canal westward to Ashgabat. The Karakum Canal is the world's largest irrigation canal and brings water to farmlands along its route, enabling cotton, wheat, silk, and fruit, among other crops, to be grown. Many people in the country suffer from health problems, due to the scarcity of clean water. Turkmenistan's largest city, Ashgabat, was completely destroyed by an earthquake in 1948 but has since been rebuilt and is the country's capital. It is well-known as the center of the country's cotton and textiles industries. However, these are second as export earners to oil and natural gas production.

TAJIKISTAN

The smallest and poorest central Asian nation, Tajikistan is also the most mountainous. Over half of the country lies above 9,840 ft.

Area: 55,300 sq. mi.
Population: 6,719,567
Capital: Dushanbe (552,000)
Main languages spoken: Tajik, Uzbek, Russian
Main religions: Sunni Islam, Shi'a Islam
Currency: Tajik rouble
Main exports: aluminum (over half of exports), electricity, cotton fibers, fruit, vegetable oil
Type of government: republic

Mountains cover more than 90 percent of Tajikistan, with the highest peaks found in the Pamirs in the southeast of the country. Mountain glaciers feed many streams, which allows the country to generate surplus electricity in order to support both its own aluminum industry and to export to neighboring nations. Only six percent of the country is farmed. Irrigation allows parts of the country's lowlands to be used to grow a range of crops, including cotton, fruit, and mulberry trees. Tajikistan has substantial reserves of a number of minerals, including mercury, silver, gold, and over one tenth of the world's proven reserves of uranium. However, the mountainous terrain makes mining and transportation extremely difficult. The country is named after the Tajik people, who are descended from Iranians and comprise over 64 percent of the country's population. The Uzbeks are the largest minority group, comprising 25 percent. Most of the country's people are followers of the Islamic religion. A civil war following independence in 1991 and the emigration of highly skilled Russian workers are key causes of a decline in the country's industries. Over 80 percent of the population live in poverty, with poor health-care facilities.

KYRGYZSTAN

A mountainous republic, Kyrgyzstan is the most rural central Asian nation. The country's economy relies on mining its extensive mineral deposits.

Area: 76,600 sq. mi.
Population: 4,822,166
Capital: Bishkek (736,000)
Main languages spoken: Kyrgyz, Russian
Main religions: Islam, Russian Orthodox
Currency: som
Main exports: food products, light manufactures, metals, machinery
Type of government: republic

◀ A yurt formed from a frame of wooden poles covered in cloth acts as a portable summer home for nomadic livestock herders in Kyrgyzstan.

Kyrgyzstan's landscape is dominated by mountains that extend through much of the country and into neighboring China. The highest peaks in these snow- and ice-covered mountains rise to over 22,960 ft. in elevation. Overlooked by the Tien Shan mountains in the east of the country lies Ozero Issyk-Kul', one of the world's largest mountain lakes and the fourth deepest in the world. The country experiences a continental climate, with average daily temperatures in the valleys reaching 81°F in July and 25°F in January. Large reserves of many minerals, including gold, coal, iron, zinc, mercury, and natural gas, are found within its mountainous terrain. Despite less than seven percent of the land being suitable for farming, agriculture employs larger numbers of people than any other sector. The raising of sheep and the herding of cattle, goats, and horses, all for their meat and milk, are widespread and help make the country self-sufficient in basic foodstuffs.

AFGHANISTAN

A mountainous nation, Afghanistan has been torn apart by conflict over the past 25 years. Most of its people live in poverty.

Area: 250,000 sq. mi.
Population: 27,755,775
Capital: Kabul (2,734,000)
Main languages spoken: Pashtu, Dari (Persian), Turkic
Main religions: Sunni Islam, Shi'a Islam
Currency: afghani
Main exports: dried fruit and nuts, carpets and rugs, wool and hides, cotton
Type of government: republic

▼ Afghanistan's forbidding mountainous landscape has hampered transportation and trade and leaves many small settlements isolated.

Almost three fourths of Afghanistan are covered in mountains and highland areas. Principal among its mountains is the Hindu Kush range, which extends around 496 mi. through central Afghanistan and into Pakistan and Tajikistan. The highest peaks there rise to over 22,960 ft., and the average altitude of the region is approximately 14,104 ft. The Hindu Kush forms a natural and imposing barrier between the country's northern plains, its major farmlands, and the rest of the country.

South and southwest of the Hindu Kush lies a flat plateau with an average height of approximately 3,280 ft. Most of this plateau is covered in deserts. The soil there supports little life, except for the immediate lands around the rivers that run through the region. Chief among these is the Helmand river, Afghanistan's longest, which

begins its life approximately 50 mi. south of Kabul and flows through the Dasht-i-Margo desert into Iran. Afghanistan's climate varies with elevation, but generally the country experiences cold winters and hot summers, in which temperatures in the southern deserts can exceed 113°F. All of the country receives low levels of rainfall; the average annual precipitation is around 12 in. Droughts sometimes cause serious problems for the country's farmers.

AFGHAN PEOPLE

Afghanistan has a long history going back over 5,000 years, and its people come from a range of origins—the main groups are: Pashtuns, Tajiks, Hazaras, and Uzbeks. Over 30 languages are spoken, and many Afghans speak their own local language, as well as one of the two official languages. Ninety-nine percent of the population are Muslims. Most Afghans are rural people who depend on farming to live. The flat northern plains and foothills are where the majority of crops, including corn, rice, wheat, cotton, and nuts, are grown. Many Afghans raise sheep and goats that provide milk, as well as wool for making rugs—one of the key crafts of the country. Several million Afghans still live nomadic lives tending small herds of livestock.

A SUCCESSION OF WARS

Afghanistan's strategic position between central Asia and the Indian subcontinent has seen it invaded and fought over a number of times in its past. In 1979 the Soviet Union invaded the country to support an unpopular government, and a lengthy war was fought between Soviet and government forces and the mujahideen—rural tribesmen supported by the United States and Pakistan—that continued for ten years. Further conflicts between different Afghan groups occurred before a strict Islamic group, the Taliban, came to power in 1996. The Taliban was deposed by the United States and its allies in 2001. These conflicts have left behind a devastated nation, with many towns in ruins and land mines killing or maiming 80 people every month. In the past Afghans were self-sufficient in wheat and other basic foodstuffs, but one third of its farmland has since been destroyed, and many people are reliant on food aid. Less than ten percent of the population has access to clean water, and around one fourth of Afghan children die before they reach five years of age.

▲ A school for female students in Kandahar, which opened in January 2002. Afghan women have a literacy level of 21 percent—the lowest level in the world.

PAKISTAN

The Islamic Republic of Pakistan borders Afghanistan, Iran, and India. It is a country of dramatic and contrasting scenery, people, and cultures.

Area: 300,700 sq. mi. excluding 33,649 sq. mi. of the Pakistani-held areas of Kashmir and the disputed Northern Areas (Gilgit, Baltistan, and Diamir)
Population: 147,663,429
Capital: Islamabad (636,000)
Main languages spoken: Urdu, English, Punjabi, Sindhi, Pashtu
Main religions: Sunni Islam, Shi'a Islam
Currency: Pakistani rupee
Main exports: textiles, clothing, rice, leather goods, fish, cotton
Type of government: republic

▲ A bustling street in the city of Faisalabad in northeast Pakistan. Faisalabad is a major transportation terminus and industrial center with engineering works, cotton, sugar, and flour mills, and large textile factories.

The landscape of Pakistan is partly divided by the Indus river system, which enters the country in the northeast and flows southward before emptying into the Arabian Sea. The Indus Plain, found mostly along the eastern side of the river, varies in width between 50–205 mi. and is the most densely populated and farmed region of Pakistan. A series of mountain ranges, including the Toba Kakar Range, dominate the northern regions of the country, and Pakistan is crossed by part of the Thar Desert in the southeast. The country's climate varies greatly according to elevation and region, but most of Pakistan suffers from scarce rainfall, with droughts common.

FARMING AND INDUSTRY
Around 44 percent of the working population are involved in agriculture. Pakistan produces many crops, is self-sufficient in cereals, and is one of the world's leading producers of cotton, which provides the raw material for a giant textiles industry. However, farming faces a number of environmental challenges, including saltwater logging of the soil, droughts, and floods. Although around 60 percent of Pakistanis live in rural areas, the country has a number of large cities. Lahore is a major distribution and trading center for the surrounding heavily industrialized areas. Hyderabad is a center of heavy industry, while Karachi, lying on the coast, is Pakistan's chief port and the most populous city of all. Manufacturing, services, and mining a range of minerals are all major employers in the country.

INDEPENDENCE AND POLITICS
The lands that now comprise Pakistan have been invaded and controlled by many different peoples, including Persians, Huns, Turks, and Arabs. European traders started to visit the area in the 1500s, and by the mid-1700s the region, including the territory of both India and Pakistan, was under British rule. Demands for independence grew until 1947, when the region was partitioned into India, containing mainly Hindus, and

a separate Muslim nation of East and West Pakistan. Separated by 992 mi. of land, cultural and political differences grew between the two Pakistans, leading to war in 1971, with East Pakistan becoming the independent nation of Bangladesh. Pakistan has experienced much political instability, with military coups, political assassinations, and rule by the army for many years. A serious dispute over the region of Jammu and Kashmir on the northern border between India and Pakistan has existed since 1947.

PAKISTAN'S PEOPLE

The people of Pakistan are a racial mixture of various groups who have moved to and settled in the region over thousands of years. The five largest ethnic groups are: Punjabis, Pashtuns, Sindhis, Balochis, and Muhajirs. Punjabis comprise approximately 48 percent of Pakistan's population, and their language is widely spoken. Sindhis are the second-largest group, making up around 12 percent of the population. When Pakistan was separated from the Hindu state of India in 1947, millions of Muslims left India to settle in Pakistan. These people and their descendants are the Muhajirs, who tend to speak Urdu. Ninety-seven percent of Pakistanis are Muslim. While a wealthy elite, mainly Punjabis, live in considerable luxury, a large proportion of Pakistan's population barely survives. The country has one of the lowest access rates to doctors, hospitals, and essential medicines in the world. Malaria, tuberculosis, and other diseases are common, and food and water shortages are widespread.

▲ Sugarcane being harvested in the province of Sind in southeast Pakistan. In 2000 Pakistan produced around 46.2 million tons of sugarcane.

▼ Distinctive trucks wait for the road ahead to clear on the mountainous Karakoram Highway. This road took the efforts of over 24,000 workers to complete.

INDIA

Home to over one billion people, India is a vast and diverse country with much variety and richness in culture. India is also the world's largest democracy.

Area: 1,148,000 sq. mi.
Population: 1,045,845,226
Capital: New Delhi (12,987,000)
Main languages spoken: Hindi, English, 14 regional official languages
Main religions: Hinduism, Islam
Currency: Indian rupee
Main exports: agricultural products, cut and polished diamonds and jewelry, clothing, machinery and transportation equipment, metals with iron and steel, cotton
Type of government: federal republic

India is the seventh-biggest country in the world and the second most populous. It shares borders with six countries, mostly to the north and including Myanmar, Nepal, and Bhutan. India surrounds the country of Bangladesh on three sides and is involved in long-running disputes over territory with its two other neighbors, Pakistan to the northwest and China to the north. Its landscape is incredibly varied, with dry desert regions, lush, wet highlands, vast plains, and plateaus. The country is also home to a large part of the world's youngest and highest mountains—the Himalayas. The Himalayas and their foothills form a massive geological barrier across almost all of northern India, extending a distance of over 1,426 mi. They were formed and continue to rise owing to the immense forces that are pushing the Indian subcontinent northward toward China. Extending south from the highlands region, much of India consists of a giant peninsula jutting out into the Indian Ocean. The Arabian Sea lies to the west of India, and to the east lies the Bay of Bengal.

THE NORTHERN PLAINS

Lying south of the Himalayas is a huge belt of flat land known as the Northern Plains. Much of this land surface has been formed by rivers, including the Ganges and Brahmaputra, depositing sediment on great floodplains and deltas and creating extremely rich and fertile soils. Many of India's rivers start their life in the Himalayas, among them the Ganges.

▼ Situated in Kashmir in northwest India, Lake Dal is known for its beautiful location, lotus flowers, and its striking lake dwellers, who live in wooden houseboats and tend floating gardens.

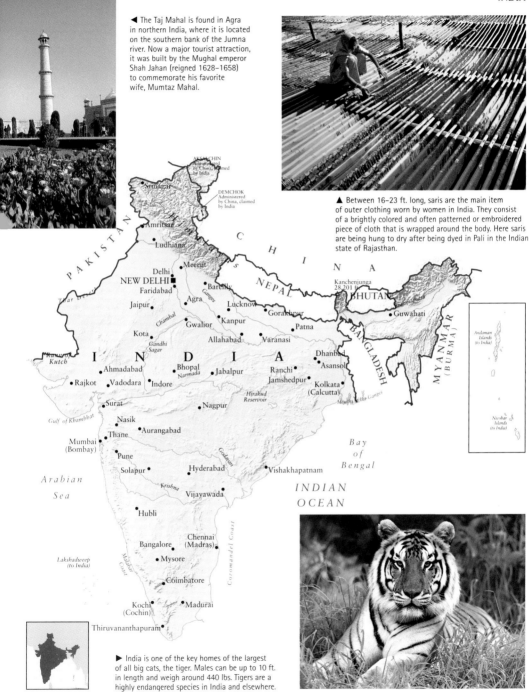

◀ The Taj Mahal is found in Agra in northern India, where it is located on the southern bank of the Jumna river. Now a major tourist attraction, it was built by the Mughal emperor Shah Jahan (reigned 1628–1658) to commemorate his favorite wife, Mumtaz Mahal.

▲ Between 16–23 ft. long, saris are the main item of outer clothing worn by women in India. They consist of a brightly colored and often patterned or embroidered piece of cloth that is wrapped around the body. Here saris are being hung to dry after being dyed in Pali in the Indian state of Rajasthan.

▶ India is one of the key homes of the largest of all big cats, the tiger. Males can be up to 10 ft. in length and weigh around 440 lbs. Tigers are a highly endangered species in India and elsewhere.

183

▲ Pilgrims flock to the Har Mandir Sahib, or Golden Temple, in Amritsar, the most sacred shrine to followers of the Sikh religion. Originally built in 1604 and rebuilt in the 1800s, the Golden Temple sits on a small island surrounded by the Pool of the Nectar of Immortality, called Amrita Sar, from which the city gets its name.

AN ENORMOUS POPULATION

With around two percent of the world's land area, India supports around 15 percent of the world's population. Although it is still a predominantly rural country, India has an urban population of over 250 million and two of the top-ten largest metropolitan areas in the world: Mumbai (Bombay) with 16.1 million people and Kolkata (Calcutta) with 13.1 million people. Extremes of wealth and poverty are often seen side by side. India's wealthy middle classes number over 150 million, yet under four percent of Indian households have an annual income of more than $2,500. The United Nations estimates that 25 percent of the population live below the poverty line, many in city slums or without homes.

LANGUAGE, RELIGION, AND CASTE

The country has been settled since prehistoric times, and waves of different invaders and settlers have been absorbed, giving the country a rich culture. This is reflected in the two official, 14 recognized, and several hundred more languages spoken in the country, of which Hindi is the most widely used. Although 81 percent of the people are Hindu, India is also home to one of the world's largest Muslim populations, numbering over 120 million. The varied religions found in India include over

20 million Christians, around 20 million Sikhs, as well as Buddhists, Parsis, and Jains. A complex caste system exists in India in which people are placed in one of around 3,000 social class positions that limit where they can work, who they can interact with, and who they can marry. Despite government reforms, the caste system remains an important factor in Indian life.

THE WORLD'S LARGEST DEMOCRACY

India gained independence from British rule in 1947 and established its present constitution in 1949. The country is a multiparty democracy with an electorate

◀ Farmers plow rice paddy fields in the southeastern Indian state of Tamil Nadu. India has more land devoted to growing rice than any other country in the world. India became self-sufficient in rice production in the late 1970s and is now the world's second-largest rice exporter.

of 619.5 million, making it the largest in the world. India has a federal form of government with 28 states, each with a large amount of control over their own affairs, and seven union territories with less control. Each state is headed by a governor who is appointed for a five-year term by the country's head of state, the president. The prime minister is the holder of most political power in India. He and his Council of Ministers are responsible to the parliament, which is based in New Delhi. India's parliament consists of two chambers, the Rajya Sabha (Council of States) and the Lok Sabha (House of the People).

JAMMU AND KASHMIR

Jammu and Kashmir is a region on the northern borders of India and Pakistan. Famous for its natural beauty, the region is home to K2 (or Mount Godwin Austen), at 28,244 ft. the world's second-highest mountain, and around 12 million people. Both India and Pakistan claim the region as a part of their own territory. After several armed conflicts the area was separated, with the eastern region, including the valley of Kashmir, Jammu, and Ladakh, administered by India. The potential for conflict to flare up into full-scale war remains, with both countries having tested nuclear devices in the 1990s. Partly as a result of the ongoing problems over Jammu and Kashmir, defense spending is high. India keeps one of the world's largest military forces, made up of 1.3 million personnel.

▲ A crowded train operates on part of India's enormous railroad system. Approximately 22,754 mi. of tracks link the country and carry millions of passengers and millions of tons of cargo.

▼ Simla lies on the southern slopes of the Himalayas and was the summer capital of British India between 1865 and 1939. In 1971 a meeting of Indian and Pakistani leaders formed the Simla Agreement, dividing Jammu and Kashmir.

BANGLADESH

Lying on the Bay of Bengal and bordered by
India and Myanmar, Bangladesh was formerly West
Pakistan before it gained its independence in 1971.

Area: 51,700 sq. mi.
Population: 133,376,684
Capital: Dhaka
(13,781,000)
Main languages spoken:
Bengali, Bihari
Main religions: Islam,
Hinduism
Currency: taka
Main exports: clothing,
jute manufactures, fish
and shrimp, hides
and leather
Type of government:
parliamentary democracy

Much of the land of Bangladesh
is a low-lying floodplain
formed by two large rivers, the
Ganges and the Brahmaputra.
These and other rivers carry
meltwaters from the Himalaya
mountains southward to empty
into the Bay of Bengal. Few places
in the world are more susceptible to
floods than Bangladesh. Some parts
of the country can receive over 2,000 in.
of rainfall annually, and approximately
two thirds of the land are flooded for part
of the year. The floods often result in great
loss of life and crops and property damage.
The coastal regions of Bangladesh are also
prone to cyclones. These intense storms
can generate 23-ft.-high waves and wind
speeds of over 150 mph. The rich soils
created by sediment left by rivers in the
delta region and a long growing season
create fertile farming conditions.

Bangladesh is the world's leading producer
of jute, a natural fiber particularly used
in making rope, string, baskets, and rough
forms of paper. Sugarcane and tea are other
important crops grown for export. However,
most of the agriculture in the country is on
a small scale, and many Bangladeshi farmers
struggle to grow enough food to feed their
families. Rice is the most important crop,

along with pulses, such as lentils, and
a range of vegetables. Over 1.1 million
tons of fish, mainly freshwater varieties, are
caught each year. The water that damages
Bangladesh's land and threatens its people
is also harnessed to irrigate farmlands in
the dry season and to generate electricity.
In the past Bangladesh's mineral reserves
were untapped. However, recent discoveries
of large natural gas reserves are now being
exploited, with pipelines carrying the gas
to the major industrial center of Dhaka
and the major port of Chittagong.

▼ A traffic jam of
pedestrians and bicycle
rickshas occupies a crowded
street in Dhaka, the capital of
Bangladesh. However, around
80 percent of Bangladeshis
live in small rural villages.

NEPAL

Home to Mount Everest and many other Himalayan peaks, the kingdom of Nepal has developed a financially important tourist industry.

Mount Everest
29,070 ft.

Area: 52,800 sq. mi.
Population: 25,873,917
Capital: Kathmandu (755,000)
Main languages spoken: Nepali, many dialects
Main religions: Hinduism, Buddhism
Currency: Nepalese rupee
Main exports: basic manufactures, textiles and clothing, food
Type of government: constitutional monarchy

▶ Offerings are left at the Swayambunath temple, a Buddhist temple near the capital city of Kathmandu. Only eight percent of the Nepalese population are Buddhists. Eighty-six percent are Hindus.

Four fifths of Nepal are covered in mountains, with eight of the world's ten-highest peaks within its borders. To the south of the country the land is lower-lying and forms an area of plains and marshlands that runs across the border with India. This region contains both hardwood and bamboo forests, which provide homes for tigers, leopards, and some elephants. Most of Nepal's population live in these southern plains or in the large central valley, in which the country's largest city, Kathmandu, is found. Farming dominates the economy, with most Nepalese engaged in growing crops and raising livestock such as goats and buffalo. Nepal's landlocked and mountainous location has made large-scale industry hard to develop. Carpets and textiles are the main manufacturing industries. Nepal once attracted 500,000 tourists each year to its mountains and

historic and religious sites, but recent numbers have fallen owing to instability and attacks by rebel groups. Nepal is a poor country in which over one third of its population is undernourished.

BHUTAN

A mountainous landlocked kingdom surrounded by China and India, Bhutan remains one of the most isolated and unknown of all nations.

Area: 118,100 sq. mi.
Population: 2,094,176
Capital: Thimphu (32,000)
Main languages spoken: Dzongkha (Bhutanese), Nepalese
Main religions: Lamaistic Buddhism, Hinduism
Currency: ngultrum
Main exports: electricity, cement, timber, fruit and vegetables
Type of government: monarchy

The northern part of Bhutan is located in the Great Himalayas, with mountain peaks rising to elevations of over 23,944 ft. In the center of the country are the lower-lying Lesser Himalayas. Between many of these mountain peaks are wide, fertile valleys. The only portion of Bhutan that is not mountainous is the Duars Plain, which is a narrow strip along the southern border covered largely in dense forests. The people of Bhutan are among the most rural in the world. Only seven percent are estimated to live in towns, and around 93 percent are dependent on farming. Sheep and cattle are raised, while yaks, used for transportation, meat, and wool, are herded

on colder mountain slopes. Only 42 percent of the country's adults are able to read and write, and the country's industries and infrastructure remain underdeveloped. India is Bhutan's key trading partner, accounting for 77 percent of imports and 94 percent of exports. Bhutan is a strongly traditional Buddhist society. Until 1999 TV was banned, and tourism still remains restricted.

SRI LANKA

A British colony until 1948, Sri Lanka is a pear-shaped island lying just off the coast of India. However, since 1983 its people have experienced a violent civil war.

Area: 25,000 sq. mi.
Population: 19,576,783
Capitals: Colombo, the administrative capital, and Sri Jayewardenpura, the legislative capital (combined population 1,260,000)
Main languages spoken: Sinhala, Tamil, English
Main religions: Buddhism, Hinduism, Christian, Islam
Currency: Sri Lankan rupee
Main exports: textiles, clothing, tea, diamonds, coconut products
Type of government: republic

▼ Much of Sri Lanka's tea is grown on large plantations in the central highlands, where cooler temperatures allow the tea plants to grow slowly and with more flavor. In 2000 283,760 tons of tea were grown.

Sri Lanka's main geographic feature is an extensive area of rugged highlands in the central and southern parts of the island. These include peaks rising up over 4,920 ft., steep river gorges, and large plateaus. North of the highlands the land consists of more gently rolling plains crisscrossed by a number of rivers. Lying close to the equator, the island has an essentially tropical climate, while the central highlands are cooler and temperate. Sri Lanka has an average of 48 in. of rainfall per year, but parts of the southwest of the country can receive between two and three times more. This wet zone is also the most densely populated part of the country. Sri Lanka has no fossil fuel reserves, relying instead on hydroelectricity to supply 68 percent of its electricity needs. It does have reserves of iron ore and graphite and is a major source of a number of semiprecious and precious gemstones. Around 36 percent of the population work in agriculture. The most common crop is rice, which is grown primarily as a local food source. Almost three million tons of rice were produced in 2001, yet the country has to import more rice and many other foodstuffs.

Only 12 percent of Sri Lanka's farmland is used to grow tea, but the country is the world's largest tea exporter.

SINHALESE AND TAMIL PEOPLES

Sri Lanka's population consists largely of two peoples: the Sinhalese, who are mainly Buddhist and comprise around 74 percent of the population, and the Tamils, most of whom are Hindus, who make up around 18 percent. Both peoples have inhabited Sri Lanka for over 1,400 years. Tensions between them spilled over into violent civil war from 1983 onward. Many Tamils, especially in the north and east of Sri Lanka, want an independent state. Conflict between government forces and the Tamil rebel group, called the Liberation Tigers of Tamil Eelam (Tamil Tigers), has seen over 60,000 deaths and large military forces, which have been a major drain on the Sri Lankan economy. In 2002–2003 cease-fire talks promised more autonomy for the Tamils.

INDIAN OCEAN ISLANDS

The third-largest of the oceans, the Indian Ocean extends from the eastern coast of Africa east to the Australian coast. A number of islands are contained in its waters; most are considered geographically to be part of the continent of Africa, although they have been settled by people of both African and Asian descent. The exception is the Maldives island group, which is considered part of Asia. Apart from Madagascar, which has an area larger than the European country of France, the remaining islands tend to be relatively small. Lush vegetation is found on many islands, yet the terrain often allows only small areas of land to be farmed. Tourism, encouraged by the palm-fringed beaches of the islands, is the biggest-growing industry.

MALDIVES

A chain of over 1,200 coral islands, of which around 200 are inhabited, the Maldives lies southwest of India. Fishing dominates the economy of these isles.

Area: 116 sq. mi.
Population: 320,165
Capital: Male (84,000)
Main language spoken: Dihevi
Main religion: Sunni Islam
Currency: rufiya
Main exports: fish, clothing, textiles
Government: republic

The Maldives consists of a 471-mi.-long series of island groups in the Indian Ocean. All of the islands are low-lying, with none over 6.5 ft. in height, and many are under threat from rising sea levels owing to global warming. Many have sandy beaches fringed with lush palm trees and other vegetation. The islands lie in the tropical zone and have a hot climate, with an average temperature of 80°F. Moist, seasonal winds, known as monsoons, blow across the islands, bringing an annual average of 61 in. of rain, mainly between May and August. The two major naturally growing food resources on the islands are coconut palms and breadfruit trees. However, the islands' most important resource is its rich marine life. Over 107,000 tons of fish, especially tuna, were caught in 2002. Along with a growing tourism industry, fishing accounts for the greater part of the Maldives' exports.

MALE

M A L D I V E S

▼ A typical small, low-lying island in the Maldives.

MADAGASCAR

The fourth-largest island in the world, Madagascar lies in the Indian Ocean. It is a poor country and is best known for its many unique plant and animal species.

Area: 224,500 sq. mi.
Population: 16,473,477
Capital: Antananarivo (1,689,000)
Main languages spoken: Malagasy, French
Main religions: indigenous beliefs, Christian, Islam
Currency: Malagasy franc
Main exports: coffee, vanilla, shrimp, cotton, cloves
Type of government: republic

Madagascar was once part of the African continent, from which it split approximately 50 million years ago. Its current position is around 250 mi. east of Africa, separated by the Mozambique Channel. Highlands run north to south through the island and drop sharply to the east. To the west they descend more gently to a coastal plain. Almost all of Madagascar was once covered in forests, but much of the land has now been cleared. Areas of the island are covered in a rich, red soil that is suitable for farming. Isolated from mainland Africa, over three fourths of the island's species of plants and animals are not found anywhere else in the world. Large amounts of foreign aid have been targeted to protect many of these species and their habitats, which are under threat from deforestation and soil erosion.

MADAGASCAR'S PEOPLE

The island's people are of a range of origins, with the largest groups descendants of Indonesian peoples believed to have settled on the island over 1,000 years ago. Today most Madagascans are engaged either in agriculture or in industries that process livestock and crops into products, including foods, sisal rope, sugar, and textiles. The main staple food is rice, while cassava, beans, taro, and bananas are widely grown. Over 10 million cattle exist on the island, many of which are a type of humped cattle called zebu. Madagascar is one of the poorest countries in the world. It struggles to import enough food to help feed its population, which is growing at a rate of three percent every year. Health and education services are also underdeveloped, although there have been recent successes in reducing the levels of diseases such as malaria.

▶ Lemurs are a member of the primate family that includes monkeys, apes, and humans. They are only found naturally in the wild on Madagascar. Forty distinct species of lemurs have been cataloged.

COMOROS

An island archipelago lying between the eastern coast of Africa and Madagascar, Comoros is a poor nation; its population is reliant on fishing and farming.

Area: 773 sq. mi.
Population: 614,382
Capital: Moroni (49,000)
Main languages spoken: Arabic, Comorian, French
Main religions: Sunni Islam, Roman Catholic
Currency: Comorian franc
Main exports: vanilla, ylang-ylang, cloves
Type of government: republic

Volcanic action has created the three major islands and the small number of islets that comprise Comoros. Mayotte, a neighboring island to the east, remained a dependency of France after Comoros became independent in 1974. Njazidja is the largest and youngest island in the archipelago. Its highest point, Le Kartala, is an active volcano. The islands have over one dozen bird species and several animals not found anywhere else in the world. These include Livingstone's flying fox, a giant fruit bat with a wing span of over three feet. Most Comorians fish or farm small areas of land, growing cassava, rice, and sweet potatoes for food and coffee, vanilla, and other crops for export. Despite three fourths of the workforce being engaged in farming or fishing, over half of all food is imported.

SEYCHELLES

Consisting of 105 islands lying 992 mi. from the east coast of Africa, the Seychelles was formerly a British colony before achieving independence in 1976.

Area: 176 sq. mi.
Population: 80,098
Capital: Victoria (25,000)
Main languages spoken: English, French, Creole
Main religions: Roman Catholic, Anglican
Currency: Seychelles rupee
Main exports: canned tuna, reexported petroleum products, other fish and fish products, shrimp
Type of government: republic

▼ Tourists attracted to unspoiled scenery and beaches in the Seychelles help fuel the tourism industry, which employs over 30 percent of the islands' workforce.

The Seychelles consists of two different types of island formations. The Mahé group is mainly granite, while the remaining islands are largely formed from coral. The granite islands rise to heights of over 1,968 ft., and many contain small streams. In contrast, the coral-based islands rarely rise above 30 ft. and tend to have no freshwater. Forty-six of the islands are inhabited, but 98 percent of the population live on the four main islands: Mahé, Praslin, Silhouette, and Felicité. Mahé is the largest and most populous of the Seychelles. The islands have a tropical climate, with heavy rainfall in the highest areas. Many are covered in thick, lush vegetation, and in places where land has been cleared for farming crops, such as tea, cinnamon, tobacco, bananas, and sweet potatoes, are cultivated. Many tropical fruits also grow on the islands, including avocados, mangoes, papayas, and pineapples. The Seychelles has no mineral resources, but the islands' two greatest natural resources are the fish-rich seas and the white, sandy beaches. The beaches, abundant wildlife, and warm climate have enabled the Seychelles to attract over 125,000 tourists every year. As a result, the islanders have a relatively high standard of living.

RÉUNION

A French overseas dependency, Réunion is an island in the Indian Ocean. Its inhabitants rely on growing sugarcane, tourism, and financial aid from France.

Area: 970 sq. mi.
Population: 743,981
Capital: St.-Denis (158,000)
Main languages spoken: French, Creole
Main religion: Roman Catholic
Currency: euro
Main exports: sugar, machinery, lobsters
Type of government: dependency of France

Réunion is the largest of the Mascarene Islands, which lie in the western Indian Ocean. The island is located around 112 mi. southwest of Mauritius and around 422 mi. east of Madagascar. Volcanic in origin, most of Réunion's landscape consists of mountains that rise to their highest point of 10,066 ft. at Piton de Neiges in the center of the island. The climate is tropical, although cooler at higher altitudes, and there is much variation in rainfall. On the south and eastern sides rainfall is extremely heavy and can exceed 160 in. per year, while on the north and western sides rainfall can be lower than 40 in. per year. The island sometimes suffers from powerful tropical storms. The island was uninhabited when it was discovered by Portuguese explorers in the 1500s. In 1643 it was claimed by France, who named it Bourbon and imported slaves from Africa to work on sugar plantations. Renamed Réunion in 1793, the island became an overseas dependency of France in 1946. Réunion's economy has relied on agriculture for many years, particularly sugarcane, which has been the island's major crop for over one century. Other export products include rum, vanilla, and essences used in perfumes. The island's inhabitants are of mainly mixed African, Asian, and French descent.

MAURITIUS

Mauritius is an island republic in the Indian Ocean. Once a colony of the Netherlands, France, and then Great Britain, it achieved independence in 1968.

Area: 714 sq. mi.
Population: 1,200,206
Capital: Port Louis (176,000)
Main languages spoken: Indo-Mauritian, Creole
Main religions: Hinduism, Christian, Islam
Currency: Mauritian rupee
Main exports: clothing, sugar, yarn, pearls
Type of government: republic

Mauritius lies approximately 500 mi. east of the large island of Madagascar and consists of one large, dominant island with the name Mauritius and a number of smaller islands. Formed by volcanic activity, Mauritius has a mountainous southern region, a central plateau, and a lower-lying plain in the north. Traditionally reliant on sugarcane growing and processing, Mauritius has broadened its range of industries. Its white-sand beaches and coral reefs, together with its tropical climate, have attracted many foreign tourists. It has developed hydroelectric power to provide energy for industries such as clothes making and electronic goods. Sixty-eight percent of the population are Indo-Mauritians, mostly descendants of Indian laborers brought to the island in the 1800s. People of mixed descent, known as creoles, comprise 27 percent, while there are also significant minorities of Europeans and Chinese.

▶ Sugarcane plantations cover half the cultivated land and make up 30 percent of the country's export earnings.

TAIWAN

Officially known as the Republic of China, this large island lies 100 mi. off the coast of mainland China. Taiwan is in dispute with China over its independence.

Area: 12,500 sq. mi., including Quemoy and Matsu islands
Population: 22,538,009
Capital: Taipei (2,595,699)
Main languages spoken: Mandarin, Taiwanese
Main religions: Buddhism, Taoism, Confucianism, Christian
Currency: new Taiwan dollar
Main exports: nonelectrical machinery, electrical machinery, plastic articles, textiles, synthetic fibers, chemicals
Type of government: democracy

▼ A food stall in a night market in Taiwan's largest city, the capital, T'aipei. Since World World II Taiwan has undergone rapid urbanization.

Taiwan consists of Taiwan island and a number of smaller islands, including Pescadores. More than 60 percent is mountainous, with over 150 peaks above 9,840 ft. Many of the mountain slopes are covered in forests. Most Taiwanese live along the broad and fertile coastal plains to the west and south. Taiwan has heavy annual rainfall, with a tropical climate in the south and a subtropical climate in the higher elevations in the north. Agriculture contributes to less than two percent of Taiwan's income, with the major crops being rice, corn, pineapples, and bananas. The Taiwanese fishing industry is important and exports mainly to Japan.

ECONOMIC SUCCESS

Taiwan has relatively few mineral resources and is not an oil producer but has become an economic success. Land reforms in the 1950s gave many farm workers control of land, while former land owners were encouraged to set up businesses.

Taiwan is a strong industrial nation, with four fifths of its industry devoted to manufacturing a wide range of products, particularly electrical and electronic goods, textiles, plastics, and motor vehicles. Since the early 1990s Taiwan has been one of the world's top-five producers of computer hardware. The Taiwanese people have one of the highest standards of living in Asia.

TAIWAN AND CHINA

Formerly called Formosa, Taiwan became part of the Chinese empire in 1624 and for half a century (1895–1945) was ruled by the Japanese. In the late 1940s the communist takeover of China saw almost two million people flee to Taiwan. The former leader of China, Chiang Kai-shek, refused to recognize the Communist Party government and established his own administration on the island. Mainland China still considers Taiwan to be one of its provinces, and in 1971 Taiwan lost its seat in the UN. Today only a small number of countries recognize Taiwan as an independent nation, and the country's relationship with China dominates politics. With one of the world's top-ten largest armies, a large proportion of the government's expenditure goes to defense.

CHINA

The home of advanced civilizations stretching back over 5,000 years, the People's Republic of China is the world's most populous and fourth-largest country.

Area: 3,600,900 sq. mi.
Population: 1,284,303,705
Capital: Beijing (10,836,000)
Main languages spoken: Mandarin, Yue, Wu, Hakka, Xiang, Gan, Minbei, Minnan, Cantonese
Main religions: officially atheist; Buddhism, Taoism, Islam, Christian
Currencies: renminbi (yuan), Hong Kong dollar (legal only in Hong Kong), and pataca (legal only in Macau)
Main exports: machinery and equipment, textiles and clothing, footwear, toys and sports goods, minerals and metal products, electrical goods and office equipment
Type of government: Communist-Party-led state

▼ The waterfront of Hong Kong with its many high-rise offices and apartment buildings reflects the former British colony's status as one of the world's leading trade, banking, and finance centers. In 1997 control of Hong Kong was handed back to China.

China has a 8,990-mi.-long Pacific coastline and land borders of around 13,640 mi. with a total of 14 other nations. With enormous variation in climate and landscape, China can be broadly divided into three key regions: the southwest, the east and the north, and the northwest. The southwest is a cold, mountainous area containing the world's highest plateau, the Plateau of Tibet. Much of this region consists of frozen wastelands, marshlands, and salt lakes and is sparsely inhabited. The eastern region of China is where the majority of the country's huge population reside. Much of eastern China is at elevations below 1,312 ft., although highland regions do exist. Many rivers crisscross its land, which, over time, has created large floodplains and deltas that are fertile farming areas. The largest of China's rivers—and the longest in Asia—is the Chang Jiang, or Yangtze river; 700 tributaries flow into the Chang Jiang as it completes its 3,900-mi.-long journey, flowing essentially eastward from the Kunlun Shan mountains through central China before emptying into the Pacific just north of Shanghai. The northwestern regions of China are largely highlands marked by large desert basins and some mountains. East of these areas the giant Gobi Desert extends through northern central China. Deserts cover around 27 percent of China and are increasing at an annual rate of 605 sq. mi. owing to deforestation and over use of dry soils on farms near desert areas. Winds from the north generate giant sandstorms that envelop towns and cities, hamper transportation, and damage farmland. A 70-year project called the Great Green Wall seeks to plant millions of trees along the southern borders of the Gobi to help bar the further spread of deserts.

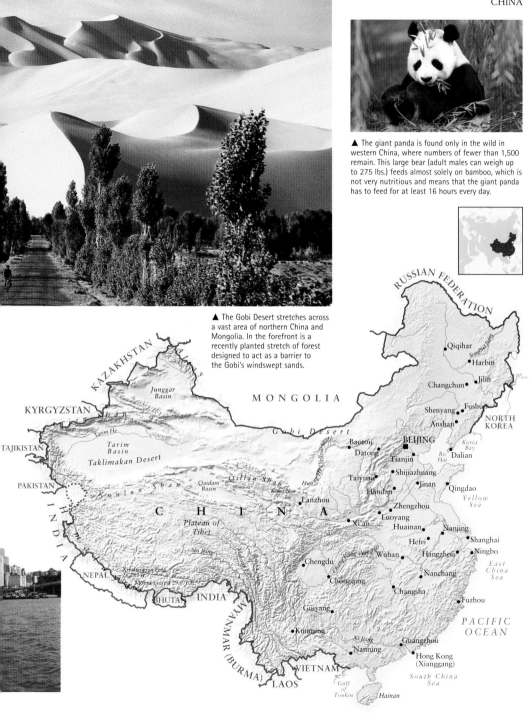

▲ The giant panda is found only in the wild in western China, where numbers of fewer than 1,500 remain. This large bear (adult males can weigh up to 275 lbs.) feeds almost solely on bamboo, which is not very nutritious and means that the giant panda has to feed for at least 16 hours every day.

▲ The Gobi Desert stretches across a vast area of northern China and Mongolia. In the forefront is a recently planted stretch of forest designed to act as a barrier to the Gobi's windswept sands.

COMMUNIST CHINA

The Chinese Communist Party (CCP) was formed in 1921 and came to power in 1949 after a bitter struggle with nationalist forces over two decades. This struggle culminated in a civil war (1945–1949) in which an estimated 12 million people died. The CCP, under its leader, Mao Zedong, embarked on a huge series of reforms to change China's economy and society. Some have been successful such as improving education, healthcare, and developing new infrastructure and industries.

ONE FIFTH OF ALL PEOPLE

In 1949 there were an estimated 500 million people in China. Fifty years later that figure had more than doubled to over 1.2 billion. Managing and feeding almost one fifth of the world's people is a massive task, and China has sometimes embarked upon methods that are criticized by the outside world. For example, to curb the high birth rate China introduced very strict one-child-per-family policies in the 1970s, but still over 11 million Chinese babies are born every year. The continued rise in China's population is due mainly to the increase in life expectancy. Since 1950 better healthcare and the eradication of some diseases have resulted in life expectancy more than doubling to just over 70 years. Approximately two thirds of China's population is rural. However, city sizes are still increasing. China has more large cities than any other nation, with 36 having a population of over one million.

▲ Over six million people live in the small but heavily built-up Special Autonomous Region of Hong Kong. It is one of the world's most densely populated areas.

▼ Since it was built in the 1600s the breathtaking Potala Palace has been the traditional home of Tibet's spiritual leader, the Dalai Lama, who now lives in exile.

◀ Construction work continues on the Three Gorges Dam across the Chang Jiang river. This enormous 1.2-mi.-wide dam is a part of the world's biggest hydroelectric power program, scheduled to open in 2009. It is being built to generate enormous quantities of electricity and to allow large ships to sail into China's interior. Environmentalists are concerned at the vast area of the river valley, which will be flooded, displacing over 1.5 million people.

PEOPLE AND RELIGION

China has over 55 different ethnic groups, but an estimated 93 percent are of Han Chinese origin. The largest minority, the Zhuang, number over 15.5 million. There are also approximately 8.6 million Hui and 7.2 million Uyghur peoples. Many of the largest populations of ethnic minorities are found in the border areas of China. Just over half of Chinese people consider themselves non religious, while one fifth practice one of many forms of traditional folk religions. In addition, millions of Chinese people follow Buddhism, Islam, Taoism, and various forms of Christianity.

AUTONOMOUS REGIONS

China has a number of autonomous regions in which a degree of local rule has been granted. Inner Mongolia, Guangxi Zhuang, and Xinjang Uyghur are three of the largest of these regions. The best-known autonomous region of China is Tibet, which China invaded in 1950–1951. The former British colony of Hong Kong is now a Special Autonomous Region with some control over its own affairs.

▼ Chinese women work on an assembly line building electronics equipment. Electronics and electrical goods manufacturing are fast-growing industries in China. Around 36 million TV sets were produced in China in 2002.

197

MONGOLIA

A large, remote country of mountains, plains, and deserts, Mongolia was once the center of a powerful empire. Today this isolated nation is one of the poorest in Asia.

Area: 604.200 sq. mi.
Population: 2,694,432
Capital: Ulan Bator (781,000)
Main language spoken: Khalkha Mongol
Main religion: Tibetan Buddhism
Currency: tugrik
Main exports: mineral products (particularly copper), live animals, textiles (cashmere and wool), animal products (including hides)
Type of government: republic

Mongolia is surrounded by the Russian Federation to the north and China to the south. Much of its land consists of a plateau lying between 2,952–4,920 ft. in elevation. This plateau is broken up by mountain ranges, especially to the west, where the Altai mountains rise to heights of above 13,120 ft. Large, grass-covered prairies exist in the northeast and northwest of the country, supporting flocks of sheep and herds of goats, cattle, and horses. Central and southeastern Mongolia are covered by the hostile Gobi Desert. This giant desert measures over 992 mi. west to east and over 589 mi. north to south. Its surface consists largely of rock and gravel. To the southeast the Gobi is extremely arid and supports minimal life. Elsewhere in the Gobi tough grass, scrubs, and thornbushes provide meager vegetation for the herds and groups of Mongolia's nomadic desert dwellers. Water comes from the occasional shallow lake and watering holes.

CLIMATE, RESOURCES, AND PEOPLE

Mongolia's climate is harsh, with great extremes in which the temperature can vary as much as 86°F in a single day. The summers tend to be short, cool to mild with low rainfall, and have many clear days. The winters are long and bitterly cold with temperatures ranging between -5°F and -22°F. Especially severe winters,

▶ This Mongolian farmer cuts and harvests hay using Bactrian camels to pull his simple plow. Over 350,000 camels are raised in the country, mainly as beasts of burden.

◀ A young child fetches water from a frozen river near the Mongolian capital city of Ulan Bator.

called Zud, can devastate the livestock on which many Mongolians depend. Agriculture and the processing of agricultural products into foods, cloth, and leather goods are a vital part of the Mongolian economy. Mongolia is also rich in a number of minerals, including iron ore, coal, copper, lead, and tungsten. The country's harsh climate and isolated location have so far prevented much of its mineral resources from being exploited.

From 1206 onward Mongolia was the center of the great Mongol empire, which extended throughout much of Asia and was feared for its fierce horse-riding warriors. Today the people live in one of the most undeveloped nations in Asia. Transportation links are sparse and often in disrepair. The country has just 992 mi. of paved roads, no highways, and limited water and rail links. Many Mongolians have given up their rural way of life and have moved to towns. An estimated 36 percent live below the poverty line.

▼ Nomadic Mongolian herders eat a meal inside their large, portable, tentlike home—a yurt.

NORTH KOREA

North Korea is run by a communist government
that has kept this mountainous country isolated
since the Korean Peninsula was partitioned in 1948.

Area: 46,500 sq. mi.
Population: 22,224,195
Capital: Pyongyang
(3,197,000)
Main language spoken:
Korean
Main religions:
nonreligious majority;
Buddhism, Confucianism,
Chondogyo
Currency: won
Main exports: minerals,
metallurgical products,
armaments, agricultural
products
Type of government:
communist state

▼ A political festival in
progress in a stadium in
North Korea's capital city
of Pyongyang. Only people
who are loyal to the strict
communist regime are
allowed to live in the city.

The Democratic People's Republic
of Korea occupies the northern half
of the Korean Peninsula. Four fifths of
its land are mountainous, with many
slopes covered with forests of
coniferous trees. The mountains
rise in elevation to the north,
where Pektu-san (9,000 ft.), the
country's highest peak, is located.
Most of the east coast of the
country is steep and rugged with
few islands. To the west the slopes
are more gentle and end in plains
and a network of river estuaries.
The country's lowlands, comprising
one fifth of the land, are found mainly
in the west and are where most of its
people live. Farming is also concentrated
there, and the country's major crops are
rice, corn and other cereals, potatoes,
and other vegetables. North Korea has
a continental climate with hot summers
and cold winters. The climate is influenced
by both the cold winds from Siberia and
the monsoon winds from east Asia. During
the summer months the monsoons bring
much of the country's rainfall.

AN ISOLATED COMMUNIST NATION

Since its formation North Korea has been
run by a strict communist government,
with the military exerting a powerful
influence. The state owns almost all farms
and industries and distributes the wealth
among its people. In practice loyal members
of the Korean Workers Party (KWP), the
only political party allowed by law, benefit
more than others. The country's media is
largely state-controlled, and opponents
of the government are often dealt with

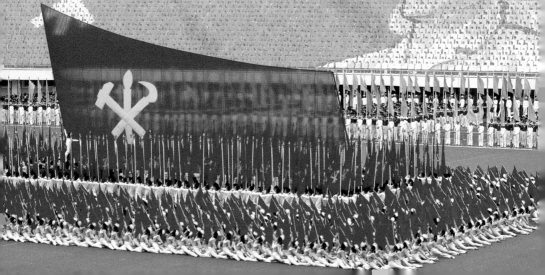

◀ Opened in 1984, the Mansudae Assembly Hall in Pyongyang is one of the major governmental buildings of North Korea. It is used to hold sessions of the Supreme People's Assembly.

harshly. While other communist nations have changed greatly, North Korea has remained apart and largely isolated. Trade and communications with the rest of the world are limited. This closed nation has recently opened its borders to aid and limited foreign investment as its economy has declined. Important industries in North Korea include the mining of coal, iron ore, tungsten, zinc, and other metals and heavy and engineering industries producing refined metals, machinery, and chemicals. The country produces almost two thirds of its electricity from hydroelectric power, but shortages are common. From 1995 to 1999 successive droughts and floods damaged vast tracts of farmland and brought a famine to North Korea in which as many as two million people died. Chronic food shortages remain.

NORTH AND SOUTH RELATIONS

The Korean Peninsula had a long history of settlement and civilization before coming under, first, Chinese and, by 1910, Japanese control. In 1948 the peninsula was partitioned into two separate nations. Two years later North Korea launched an invasion of South Korea in an attempt to unify Korea under a single communist government. The Korean War (1950–1953) was a bitter conflict in which North Korea was supported by

China, and South Korea was supported by a coalition of forces, mainly from the U.S. By the end of the war over one million Koreans and many thousands of foreign troops had died. Relations between the two nations have remained difficult, with many incidents since this time. Despite a summit meeting between the two countries' leaders in 2000, the first time they had ever met directly, there remains considerable tension between North and South. At the end of 2002 North Korea started to reactivate part of its nuclear program, leading to fears that it will embark on creating nuclear weapons.

▼ A class for North Korean schoolchildren is held outside. North Korean education starts with preschool. Education emphasizes science and technology, and English is compulsory as a second language for students above the age of 14.

SOUTH KOREA

Occupying the southern half of the Korean
Peninsula, South Korea industrialized rapidly
and is now one of Asia's most powerful nations.

Area: 37,900 sq. mi.
Population: 48,324,000
Capital: Seoul (9,862,000)
Main language spoken:
Korean
Main religions: Christian,
Buddhism
Currency: won
Main exports: electronic
products, machinery and
transportation equipment
(including motor vehicles),
steel, ships, textiles,
clothing and footwear
Type of government:
republic, with power
centralized in a strong
executive

Over two thirds of South Korea
are mountainous, with the largest
lowland areas to the west and the south.
South Korea's western coastline is indented,
and most of the country's 3,000 islands lie
off this coast in the Yellow Sea. The largest
of Korea's islands is Cheju, south of the
mainland. With a subtropical climate,
many fruits are grown there, and the island
attracts tourists to its spectacular scenery.
Ullung, the largest island off the eastern
coast, serves as a major fishery base. In
2002 a total of 2.7 million tons of fish
were caught by South Korean vessels.
The country's only land border is with
North Korea to the north. It features the
demilitarized zone, or DMZ, a 12.5-mi.-wide
strip of land that runs from the west coast to
the east coast of the peninsula. Thousands of
troops from the forces of the two countries
are stationed on both sides of
the DMZ. Tensions remain
high between the two nations.

▼ Sungnyemun, or the
South Gate, was originally
a grand entrance to the
capital city of Seoul and is
the oldest wooden structure
in the city. Seoul was also
the capital of Korea from
the late 1300s until 1948.

THE KOREAN PEOPLE

The population of the Korean Peninsula is unique in Southeast Asia in that it is made up almost entirely of one single ethnic group that has lived in the region for over 2,000 years. Between 1950-1990 the country's population more than doubled. Large numbers of people, particularly the young, moved to South Korea's cities, and now around 80 percent of the population are urban. Farming is still important in rural areas, with rice, potatoes, and cereals the biggest crops. The country's high population density has created environmental pressures, with serious air pollution in some cities.

AN ECONOMIC MIRACLE

South Korea had a largely agricultural and underdeveloped economy before the 1960s. From 1962 onward a series of five-year plans sought to build up the country's manufacturing industries, assisted by investment from foreign companies and aid, particularly from Japan and the U.S. South Korea's economy boomed as a result, growing by around nine percent every year between 1970 and the early 1990s. The country has become a giant in manufacturing areas such as shipbuilding, motor vehicle manufacturing, high-tech electronics, and computers. Much of the industry is run by enormous enterprises—known as *chaebol*, or conglomerates—such as Samsung or Hyundai. Most of its major industrial centers are located on or near the coastline, allowing ships to import many fuels and raw materials and to transport manufactured goods all over the world. The country's biggest port is Pusan, which is also South Korea's second-largest city after Seoul. South Korea has relatively few mineral resources, apart from raw materials used in the cement, glass, and ceramics industries. It is not an oil producer but refines crude oil imported from other nations. Around 38 percent of its electricity is generated using nuclear power.

▲ Cranes in Hyundai Heavy Industries' giant ship-building yard in the city of Ulsan. The world's largest shipbuilders, Hyundai Heavy Industry accounts for around 15 percent of the global shipbuilding market. South Korea is the world's 12th-largest trading nation.

▼ South Korean border guards in the heart of the demilitarized zone (DMZ), a heavily armed border zone separating North and South Korea.

JAPAN

The island nation of Japan lies on the western edge of the Pacific Ocean. A land of ancient and rich culture, the country has become a world economic superpower.

Area: 152,400 sq. mi.
Population: 126,974,628
Capital: Tokyo (26,546,000)
Main language spoken: Japanese
Main religions: Buddhism, Shintoism
Currency: yen
Main exports: motor vehicles, electrical and electronic equipment (particularly semiconductors and computers), office machinery, chemicals, scientific and optical equipment, iron and steel products
Type of government: parliamentary democracy

Japan is an island archipelago that extends over 1,798 mi. in a roughly north-south direction. It is separated from mainland Asia to the west by the Sea of Japan. The country's territory includes more than 1,000 smaller islands and four main islands, which are from north to south: Hokkaido, the most rural, Honshu, the largest, Shikoku, and Kyushu. South of Kyushu the Ryuku island chain, including Okinawa island, arcs in a southerly direction toward Taiwan. Japan's four main islands are located close enough for them all to be linked by tunnels, bridges, or highways. Together they comprise almost 98 percent of Japan's landmass and are where the large majority of Japanese live.

Japan's climate is varied in part owing to the fact that its land covers around 17 degrees of latitude. Winds from Siberia and cold ocean waters influence the climate of Hokkaido and northern Honshu, where the summers are short and the winters are long and severe, with plenty of snowfall.

Hokkaido's largest city, Sapporo, is a renowned winter sports center. Southern Honshu, Shikoku, and Kyushu enjoy longer, warmer, and more humid summers and milder winters partly created by warmer Pacific winds and the warm, fast-moving Kuroshio ocean current, which travels northeast from the Philippines. Typhoons can strike between June and October. The heavy rains and fierce winds can damage houses and crops. The Ryuku islands experience a subtropical climate. Precipitation also varies greatly, with Hokkaido the driest region, averaging just over 40 in. per year. In contrast, central Honshu's mountains can receive 152 in. per year.

JAPANESE FLORA AND FAUNA

Japan has rich plant life, with over 17,000 species. Forests cover over 60 percent of the land, particularly coniferous forests, although large parts of Honshu are covered in deciduous trees. Larger land animals include bears, wild boars, deer, and one species of monkey, the Japanese macaque. Over 400 species of birds exist.

VOLCANOES AND EARTHQUAKES

Japan is located on the meeting point of three of Earth's tectonic plates, and its landscape has been shaped by plate movement for millions of years. Japan's terrain is largely mountainous, with coastal plains on which almost all of the country's cities are located. More than 200 volcanoes exist, of which 77 are considered active. Examples of the volatility of Earth's crust below can be seen both in the numerous hot springs and occasional tsunamis, which tend to strike the country's eastern coast. An estimated 800–1,000 earthquakes strike Japan every year.

▲ A bullet train on the Shinkansen high-speed railroad line passes by a rice paddy—a typical Japanese scene of the traditional alongside the modern. The Shinkansen trains offer some of the most rapid land transportation in the world, reaching speeds in excess of 160 mph.

▼ Hikone Castle, one of the best preserved in Japan, lies on the eastern shore of Lake Biwa, around 33 mi. northeast of Kyoto. Construction of the castle began in 1603, and the city of the same name developed around it.

◄ A national symbol of Japan, the spectacular volcanic cone of Mount Fuji (Fuji san) lies approximately 62 mi. west of Tokyo. With a height of 12,385 ft., it is Japan's highest point. Although it has not erupted since 1707, Mount Fuji is not considered extinct and could erupt again in the future.

Map labels

Sea of Okhotsk
Taisetsu 7,511 ft.
Sapporo
Hokkaido
Uchiura wan
Tsugaru Kaikyo
Sado
Sendai
Sendai wan
Sea of Japan
Toyama wan
JAPAN
Yariga 10,450 ft.
Oki Shoto
Wakasa wan
TOKYO
Kawasaki • Chiba
Kyoto
Kobe
Nagoya
Fujisan 12,385 ft.
Yokohama
Tsushima
Yamaguchi
Hiroshima
Osaka
Ise wan
Izu-shoto
Fukuoka • Kitakyushu
Ki suido
PACIFIC OCEAN
Nagasaki
Kumamoto
Shikoku
Amami-O-shima
Kagoshima
Tokuno-shima
Kyushu
Yaku-shima
Tanega-shima
Kume-jima
Okinawa-jima
East China Sea
Miyako-jima
Philippine Sea
Tokara Retto
Irıomote-jima
Ishigaki-jima
Amami Oshima

▲ A Japanese rocket is assembled at a Mitsubishi Heavy Industries factory. Japan is one of the small and exclusive group of nations that has launched space vehicles. Its first satellite was launched in 1970, and the Nozomi space probe is expected to reach Mars in 2004.

AGRICULTURE AND FISHING

Although only around 13 percent of the country is suitable for cultivation, advanced, intensive farming and irrigation methods and government support have enabled Japan to be self-sufficient in its key staple foodstuff, rice. More than 40 percent of the cultivated land is devoted to rice production, but other crops are grown, including potatoes, sugar beets, onions, cucumbers, and mandarin oranges. Fish and seafood are a major part of the Japanese diet, and the country's fishing fleet is one of the biggest in the world. Japan has also developed aquaculture, or fish-farming techniques.

PEOPLE AND CITIES

Japan's rugged landscape means that little more than one fifth of its area is habitable, yet the country is the ninth most populous in the world. People tend to live in densely populated towns and cities, especially on Honshu, which accounts for four fifths of the population. The capital, Tokyo, in which 26.5 million people live,

is the world's largest metropolitan area. Ninety-nine percent of Japanese share the same ethnic and cultural background. Small minorities of Koreans, a native people of northern Japan called the Ainu, and small handfuls of foreign workers also exist. Japan has a rapidly aging population. By 2000 17 percent of its people were aged over 65.

A RICH AND UNIQUE CULTURE

Most Japanese practice Buddhism as a religion but also follow some traditions of the Shinto religion. For long periods of history Japan has remained

▼ A busy street scene at the heart of the world's largest metropolis, Tokyo. The city was known by the name of Edo until 1869, when it became the capital of Japan.

isolated from the rest of the world, absorbing influences from afar. This, along with its cramped living conditions, has given rise to a complex series of manners and behavior. Respect for elders, superiors, and companies is strong, and many ceremonies and traditions exist that are unique to the country. Japan's art, literature, music, and drama are world renowned, and the Japanese are among the world's most avid readers—70 million newspapers are sold every day, and around 1.5 billion books are sold every year.

A DYNAMIC ECONOMY

Japan first industrialized in the late 1800s, retaining its own culture but borrowing industrial ideas from the West. At around the same time it started to expand its empire, fighting wars with China and Russia and capturing much territory in east Asia. In World War II Japan was aligned with Germany and suffered a devastating defeat, surrendering after atomic bombs were dropped on Hiroshima and Nagasaki. Japan rebuilt its economy, embracing new technology. Forced to disband its costly military forces and helped by foreign aid, the Japanese economy boomed until the 1990s. By that time it had become the second-wealthiest and technologically most advanced economy in the world. Japan owns more than half of the world's industrial robots and has heavily invested

in higher education and research. It is one of the world's leading producers of many goods, as well as chemicals, textiles, and steel. Japan's government works closely with industry, many workers are employed for life, and many Japanese companies trade with each other in relationships called *keiretsu*, which makes it difficult for foreign companies to sell into Japan. In the past Japan has been ruled by clans, emperors, and rival feudal lords called shoguns. Japan still has an emperor, but his position is mainly ceremonial, and power lies with the prime minister and the parliamentary ruling party, the Diet.

▲ Ritsurin Park is one of the largest and most beautiful of Japan's many traditional gardens. It was built during the Edo Period (1603–1868) and covers an area of 936,000 sq. ft.

▼ The traditional Japanese thatched roofed housing, known as *Gassho-zukuri*, has made Shirakawa village a UNESCO World Heritage site and a popular destination for tourists from Japan and overseas.

THAILAND

One of the most peaceful and stable Southeast Asian nations, Thailand is a rapidly industrializing country with a large tourist industry.

Area: 197,600 sq. mi.
Population: 62,354,402
Capital: Bangkok (7,527,000)
Main languages spoken: Thai, Chinese
Main religion: Buddhism
Currency: baht
Main exports: electrical machinery (particularly computers and transistors), nonelectrical machinery, seafood and live fish, clothing, rice, plastics
Type of government: constitutional monarchy

▼ Wat Phra Si Sanphet is a beautiful Buddhist monastery found in Ayutthaya, the ancient capital of Thailand.

A series of mountain ranges cross Thailand and are at their highest and most extensive in the north. The Khorat Plateau, to the northeast, comprises over one fourth of the country's land area. This flat, relatively barren land is the poorest region of the country. The fertile central plains are the most densely populated part of Thailand. This region includes the Bangkok metropolitan area and is known as "Thailand's Rice Bowl." The country produced over 24 million tons of rice in 2002 and is one of the world's top-three exporters of rice. South of the central plains is the part of Thailand that occupies the Malay Peninsula and includes a number of beautiful islands and beaches. Tin mining, rubber cultivation, and fishing are also practiced in this region. Thailand's annual fish and shellfish catch in 2001

was 3.49 million tons. The country experiences a warm and wet tropical climate, with the peninsula in the south receiving almost twice the amount of the rainfall of central and northern areas. Thailand is rich in natural resources. Among the known mineral deposits are tin, coal, gold, lead, zinc, and precious gemstones. Oil production is minimal, but Thailand exploits its natural gas reserves. Around 28 percent of the country is forested with large, valuable hardwood forests, especially in the north and coastal areas. Many species of animals, including elephants, leopards, tigers, crocodiles, gibbons, and 50 species of snakes, inhabit the jungles and forests.

INDUSTRIALIZATION AND MIGRATION

Thailand has industrialized greatly since the 1970s and 1980s, with electronics and textiles the key industries, while the service sector is dominated by tourism, with over nine million tourists every year. The gap in the standard of living between people in urban and rural areas has widened dramatically, leading to a large migration

◄ Thailand's capital city, Bangkok, has exploded in population numbers and size in the past 40 years. The MBK shopping and entertainments center in the heart of Bangkok is just one of many modern developments in the city.

of the population into Thailand's towns and cities. Bangkok, in particular, is straining under the huge increase in population, with some of the worst traffic congestion and pollution anywhere in the world. The first stage of Bangkok's mass transit system was opened in 1999, and there are initiatives to relocate industries away from Bangkok.

THE KING AND HIS PEOPLE

Seventy-five percent of the people of Thailand are Thai, a people believed to have originated in southwest China and moved to Southeast Asia around 2,000 years ago. The Chinese are the largest minority group,

making up around 14 percent of the population, and there are smaller numbers of Malay Muslims, Cambodians, and Vietnamese. The hills of the far north and northeast are home to approximately 650,000 tribespeople with their own culture and languages. Unlike many Southeast Asian nations, there is relatively little tension between ethnic groups. Buddhism, a religion practiced by 95 percent of Thais, is a powerful force for peace. In 1932 a new constitution moved much political power from the monarch to the people. However, the country's King Bhumibol Adulyadej has remained as monarch since 1946 and wields great influence. He is the world's longest-serving head of state.

▼ A floating restaurant on the banks of the Mae Nam Khwae Noi river, known in English as the Kwai river. The river rises on the border with Myanmar west of Nakhon Sawan. It is known outside of the country for the bridge built across it by Allied prisoners of war during World War II.

MYANMAR (BURMA)

Beset by political troubles, Myanmar is an agricultural nation with large tracts of hardwood forests. It is one of the least known of all Southeast Asian countries.

Area: 254,000 sq. mi.
Population: 42,238,224
Capital: Rangoon (4,504,000)
Main languages spoken: Burmese, Shan, Karen, Rakhine
Main religion: Buddhism
Currency: kyat
Main exports: clothing (over half of all exports), food, live animals, wood and wood products, precious stones
Type of government: military

Myanmar is bordered by Bangladesh, India, China, and Thailand. It is a highly mountainous country with giant and largely impassable mountain ranges running in a horseshoe shape along its western, northern, and eastern sides. Lower mountains are also found in more central areas. The mountains reach their highest in the northern range, where the peak of Hkakado Razi reaches 19,289 ft., making it the highest point in Southeast Asia. Enclosed within the horseshoe of mountain ranges are the country's lowland areas, comprised mainly of valleys and deltas of the Chindwin and Irrawaddy rivers. The rich, fertile soils and the monsoon climate in this region make

it the center of the country's agriculture, employing the majority of Myanmar's people, principally growing rice, pulses, corn, and sugarcane. Myanmar extends south, occupying a narrow western strip of the Malay Peninsula. Its coastline tends to be rocky with some good natural harbors. The Irrawaddy is the country's principal river. It originates in the Chinese region of Tibet and flows north to south through almost the entire length of Myanmar. Navigable for over 868 mi., it is an important transportation route, especially for the movement of timber.

◀ Myanmar laborers cut and transport bamboo for a government project. Bamboo is used as an important building material for houses, especially in the countryside.

▼ One of over 2,000 Buddhist pagodas found in the village of Pagan. An historic center of Myanmar in the past, Pagan was founded in 849 on the banks of the Irrawaddy river and lies around 310 mi. north of Rangoon.

OVER EXPLOITATION OF RESOURCES

Almost half of Myanmar is forested, and the supplies of teak and other hardwoods are among the country's most valuable resources, though at severe risk from over exploitation. Along the coasts there are tidal mangrove forests and, in the mountainous north, pine forests. The country has varied wildlife, including rare creatures such as red pandas, rhinoceroses, and tigers—the latter two species are sometimes killed to make medicinal products. A number of minerals are mined, including copper, lead, and silver, and also sapphire and ruby gemstones. Industry is limited, under state control, and mainly confined to processing farming and timber products.

A BUDDHIST STRONGHOLD

Myanmar was the first country in Southeast Asia where the words of the Buddha were spread, and today Buddhism is the religion of almost nine tenths of the population. Buddhism has a great influence on the everyday life of most of Myanmar's population, with Buddhist temples the center of most villages and small towns. Many Buddhists in Myanmar also believe in certain spirits of the forests, mountains, and trees, called Nats, for which they build houses and hold festivals. Small minorities of Christians, Muslims, and Hindus also exist in the country.

INEQUALITIES AND CONFLICTS

Burmans comprise about 68 percent of the population, with smaller numbers of many ethnic groups, including Shan, Karen, Kachin, Mon, and Chin peoples. Largely ruled by the military since independence, internal conflicts between the majority Burmans and these minority groups have been widespread and violent. Opposition is not tolerated, and human rights abuses are frequent.

▼ Over 100 different species of trees are commercially exploited in Myanmar's forests such as this one 31 mi. west of the city of Tanggyi. Teakwood is the single most important commodity.

VIETNAM

Vietnam is a country of great river deltas, mountain chains, and coastal plains. Its people endured long periods of war and oppression during the 1900s.

Area: 125,600 sq. mi.
Population: 81,098,416
Capital: Hanoi (3,822,000)
Main languages spoken: Vietnamese, French, Chinese, English
Main religions: Buddhism, Roman Catholic, Taosim, indigenous beliefs
Currency: dong
Main exports: crude petroleum, fish and fish products, coffee, rice, rubber
Type of government: communist

▼ Vietnamese fishermen use small, simple boats to navigate West Lake near the capital city of Hanoi. In 2001 approximately 1.4 million tons of fish, crab, and shrimp were caught, mainly from the South China Sea but also from inland rivers and streams. However, many freshwater and marine fishing grounds are now in danger of being overfished.

The Socialist Republic of Vietnam is a long, S-shaped country that borders China to the north and has a 1,984-mi.-long coastline. The northwest of the country is mountainous, with the country's highest point, the peak of Fan Si Pan, reaching an elevation of 10,309 ft. Almost two thirds of the country are dominated by highlands, with the crest of this mountain range forming most of Vietnam's long westerly border with Laos and, farther south, Cambodia. Much of the mountain slopes are forested or have been cleared to create plantations growing tea, rubber, and coffee. Vietnam is one of the world's five-largest exporters of coffee. To the east of the highlands the land forms a long coastal plain bordering the Gulf of Tonkin and the South China Sea. Fishing is important to many Vietnamese living on this plain.

Vietnam has a mainly tropical climate with warm-to-hot temperatures and heavy rainfall. Seasonal monsoon winds bring rains and occasional typhoons during the summer and fall. In the mountainous north the climate is subtropical with cooler temperatures.

CHINA

Fan Si Pan
10,309 ft.

HANOI
Hải Phòng
Nam Định
Gulf of Tonkin
Vinh

LAOS

Hue
Da Nâng

VIETNAM

Qui Nhơn
South China Sea

CAMBODIA

Da Lat
Nha Trang
Cam Ranh

Bien Hoa
Ho Chi Minh City
My Tho
Vung Tao
Rach Gia
Can Tho

Con Dao

Mui Bai Bung

TWO RIVER DELTAS

The narrow strip of land that links the north of the country to the south is vulnerable to typhoons, and a series of sea dikes protects many villages from the worst weather. Vietnam's large and fertile river deltas (the Red, or Song Hong, river in the north and the Mekong in the south) are where rice production and a large proportion of the country's population are concentrated. Agriculture is the mainstay of Vietnam's economy, and rice is the dominant crop. Despite a large migration to cities, the Vietnamese population is still one of the most rural in Southeast Asia, with fewer than one fourth living in urban areas.

20TH-CENTURY WARS

Vietnam was home to a number of ancient civilizations before being dominated by China for many centuries. The country came under French rule in the 1800s, but this ended in the French Indochina War (1946–1954). Vietnam was then partitioned into northern and southern halves as a temporary measure. Tension between the communist north and the largely anticommunist south mounted, and in 1964 a full-scale war erupted. The conflict involved hundreds of thousands of troops from the U.S. and other nations. The 1973 cease-fire saw the U.S. withdraw its troops, and in 1975 the South Vietnamese capital of Saigon fell to northern forces. Vietnam has since been run by a staunchly communist government.

REPAIR AND RENOVATION

Repairing the extensive damage done to much of the country during the Vietnam War has been a major undertaking. Over seven million tons of bombs were dropped during the conflict, towns and cities were devastated, and unexploded land mines are still a threat. Five percent of Vietnam's forests were destroyed, and almost 50 percent were damaged by chemical weapons, which stripped trees of their leaves. Since 1986 the country has pursued an economic policy called *doi moi*, meaning "renovation." Investment from foreign companies was sought, trade links with other nations have been engaged, private enterprise has been encouraged, and in 2000 the country's first stock exchange opened. Industry is largely concentrated in the north, while Vietnam produces around 300,000 barrels of oil per day. In the 1990s Vietnam started to encourage tourists from noncommunist nations, and in 2001 around 2.1 million tourists visited the country, attracted by its history, culture, and areas of natural beauty.

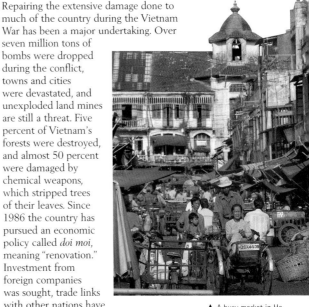

▲ A busy market in Ho Chi Minh City. The city was once the capital of South Vietnam. Known as Saigon before reunification, it is Vietnam's largest city, with a population of over four million, and is also a major shipping port.

CAMBODIA

Cambodia is a land of great history and natural beauty that has been beset by conflicts throughout the second half of the 1900s.

Area: 68,200 sq. mi.
Population: 12,775,321
Capital: Phnom Penh (1,109,000)
Main languages spoken: Khmer, French
Main religion: Theravada Buddhism
Currency: riel
Main exports: logs and timber, clothing, rubber, rice, fish
Type of government: constitutional monarchy

The center of Cambodia is a large, low-lying basin, the Tonle Sap, surrounded by a broad plain that is drained by the country's biggest river, the Mekong. To the southeast of the basin lies the Mekong delta, which extends into Vietnam before reaching the South China Sea. To the north and the southwest of the basin lie several mountain ranges, while highlands are in the northeast of Cambodia. These merge into the highlands in the center of the country that extend into Vietnam. In the center of the basin lies Southeast Asia's largest lake, also called Tonle Sap. This shallow lake varies enormously in size. At its smallest it measures around 1,053 sq. mi., with depths of between 3.3–9.8 ft. During the wet monsoon season, between June and November, the high waters of the Mekong feed into the lake, greatly increasing its size to around 4,017 sq. mi. and its depth to between 29.5–45.9 ft.

USING ITS NATURAL RESOURCES

Cambodia is poorly endowed with mineral reserves, but, in contrast, the country has relatively rich resources from the natural world. These include plentiful fish from its rivers and lakes, which are often fermented or salted to preserve them. The well-watered lowlands of Cambodia allow rice farming to dominate the country's agriculture. Almost 80 percent of all cultivated land is used for rice, with other crops including mangoes, bananas, and pineapples. Rubber, grown in the east of the country, is an important cash crop, along with corn, peppers, sesame, and cassava. A large proportion of the country is covered in forests, much of it tropical hardwoods such as teak and mahogany. However, deforestation is one of the most serious problems facing the country, with as much as half of its tree cover having disappeared in the past 35 years.

FROM KINGDOM TO KHMER ROUGE

Cambodia came under French rule in the 1800s. Regaining independence in 1954, the country underwent a period of stability before exploding into conflict from the late 1960s onward. Following the Vietnam War that enveloped the region a violent communist regime, called the Khmer Rouge, swept to power.

Between 1975-1979 as many as 1.5 million people were murdered, including most of the country's professional class of workers. The Khmer Rouge was ousted, and Cambodia is now a kingdom again. However, ongoing conflicts and changes of government have continued, with the result that Cambodia is one of Southeast Asia's poorest countries.

▲ Houses on stilts stand in the waters of Tonle Sap lake, where many Cambodians engage in carp raising and fishing. Fish is a major part of many Cambodians' diets.

▼ Constructed during the reign of King Suryavarman II, the 12th-century ruler of the Khmer kingdom, Angkor Wat is a gigantic Hindu temple built of stone and measuring 3,280 ft. in length.

LAOS

The most sparsely populated nation in Southeast Asia, Laos is an isolated, poor, and mountainous nation ruled by a communist government.

Area: 89,100 sq. mi.
Population: 5,777,180
Capital: Vientiane (663,000)
Main languages spoken: Lao Loum, Lao Theung, Lao Soung
Main religions: Buddhism, traditional beliefs
Currency: kip
Main exports: wood products, clothing, electricity, coffee, tin
Type of government: communist

▼ Laotian farmers tend vegetables grown in the rich soil of the banks of the Mekong river. Over half of the country's population live in the lowland areas of Laos, especially along the banks of the Mekong.

The Lao People's Democratic Republic shares borders with five nations: Vietnam, Thailand, Cambodia, Myanmar, and China. Around 70 percent of its land features mountains that run northwest to southeast and reach their highest elevation in the north of the country at Mount Bia, with an elevation of 9,246 ft. Approximately 55 percent of Laos is covered with forests of different types. In the north these are mostly tropical rain forests, while to the south tropical vegetation mixes with deciduous hardwood trees such as teak and rosewood. Large tracts of bamboo jungle can also be found in the south. Despite timber from these forests being one of Laos' principal exports, the forests help support a wide and varied range of wildlife, including tigers, leopards, panthers, and wild oxen called gaurs. Laos has a tropical monsoon climate with two distinct—wet and dry—seasons. The wet season runs from May to October, with rainfall almost every day and high humidity levels. During this period between 52–92 in. of rain falls in the central regions of the country. In the south rainfall can reach over 120 in.

THE MEKONG RIVER

Much of Laos' westerly border with Thailand and Myanmar is formed by the winding Mekong river, which extends over 1,116 mi. through Laos. Most of the country's major towns and cities are located on the Mekong, which can be navigated by boat south of the city of Louangphrabang. The people of Laos belong to over 65 different ethnic groups, with very diverse customs and lifestyles. The large majority of Laotians work the land, mainly growing rice, as well as sweet potatoes and corn. Raising livestock, including water buffalo and pigs, is important, as is the illegal growing and selling of opium poppies. The lands adjacent to the Mekong make up the most

extensive lowland area in Laos and are the site of much of the country's farming.

LANDLOCKED AND ISOLATED

Laos is the only landlocked country in Southeast Asia. Its rugged terrain of mountains and forests along most of its borders has hampered the country's industrial, transportation, and trading development with neighboring nations. Laos has no railroads, and roads are few in number and generally of poor quality. Most of the country's freight is transported by river, especially along the Mekong. Prior to 1994 foreign visitors to Laos arrived largely by air since there was no major road link to other countries. The Australian-funded Friendship Bridge was opened in 1994. It spans the Mekong river at Vientiane, the country's capital city, and links Laos to Thailand by road. Until very recently the country was as isolated politically as it is

geographically. After more than two decades of internal power struggles Laos became a one-party communist state in 1975 and restricted its foreign relations to a few communist nations, especially Vietnam. From 1986 the country started slowly to reintegrate with the world community, and its largest single trading partner today is Thailand. Laos is reliant on foreign aid and investment, while its industry remains undeveloped and its mineral resources unexploited. Around ten percent of babies die before reaching adulthood, and Laotians have a low average life expectancy of 54 years.

▲ Buddhist monks collect food in the morning from the local people for their one meal per day. Buddhism is the religion of around 60 percent of Laotians.

▼ A Khmu tribe family sits around the fire in their two-room house before dinner. The Khmu mainly live in small villages on mountain slopes near the Thailand-Laos border. They survive on subsistence agriculture, supplemented by fishing, hunting, and trading.

BRUNEI

Brunei is located on the northwest coast of the island of Borneo. Gaining independence in 1984, the country is rich in fossil fuel reserves.

Area: 2,000 sq. mi.
Population: 350,898
Capital: Bandar Seri Begawan (46,000)
Main languages spoken: Malay, English, Chinese
Main religion: Islam, Buddhism, Christian
Currency: Brunei dollar
Main exports: crude petroleum, natural gas, petroleum products
Type of government: independent sultanate

Brunei faces the South China Sea to the north and shares a border with Malaysia, dividing Brunei in half. The country consists of a narrow coastal plain lined largely with mangrove swamps, while the interior rises to form hill ranges covered mainly in rain forests. The country's highest point, Pagon (5,930 ft.), lies in the southeast of the country. Within Brunei's border are 33 islands that make up 1.4 percent of the country's total land area. Most of these islands are uninhabited and are important breeding grounds for certain endangered species of birds, flying foxes, and monkeys. Brunei has a tropical climate with rainfall averaging over 80 in. per year and a narrow temperature range averaging between 75°F–88°F. Most streams and rivers flow north to the coast. This includes the Belait river, the longest in the country, which runs close to the country's western border. A large proportion of Brunei, almost 80 percent, is covered in rain forests. This lush tree cover is filled with animal life, including Asian elephants, leopards, many species of monkeys, and numerous reptiles and birds.

▼ Oil exploitation in Brunei is mainly concentrated offshore. Brunei's oil fields produce approximately 194,000 barrels of oil per day.

OIL AND BRUNEI'S PEOPLE

By the 1500s Brunei was an independent sultanate, or kingdom, controlling almost the entire island of Borneo. Following a decline in influence it became a British protectorate in 1888. The indigenous people of Brunei now comprise just six percent of the population. People of Malay descent make up two thirds of Brunei's population, and there are large minorities of Chinese and Indians. Most of Brunei's nonindigenous and non-Malay population arrived when oil was found in 1929. The exploitation of the country's large oil and natural gas reserves completely dominates the economy of this small nation. Oil revenues have made the country's leader, Sultan Sir Muda Hassanal Bolkiah, one of the wealthiest people in the world. The people he rules have also benefited from the oil revenues with a generally high standard of living. There is no income tax, and there are high levels of medical care and education, as well as subsidized food and housing. However, political parties were banned in 1988, and all government workers are banned from political activity. Although Brunei's mixed population follows a number of religions, the country is more inclined to its state religion of Islam.

SINGAPORE

An island city-state, Singapore is one of the most prosperous and modernized Asian countries, with a standard of living equal to Western Europe.

Area: 241 sq. mi.
Population: 4,452,732
Capital: Singapore (4,108,000)
Main languages spoken: Chinese, Malay, Tamil, English
Main religions: Buddhism, Taoism, Islam, Christian, Hinduism
Currency: Singaporean dollar
Main exports: machinery and transportation equipment, consumer goods, chemicals, petroleum products
Type of government: republic

Singapore lies just off the southernmost tip of the Malay Peninsula, separated from Malaysia by a narrow body of water. The two countries are linked by a highway carrying road and rail links. The country consists of one major island, Singapore island, and a collection of 60 smaller islands. Singapore's land is mostly flat and low-lying with several small hills. A network of small streams runs through the main island, but Singapore remains reliant on neighboring Malaysia for some of its freshwater supplies. Lying close to the equator, the country has a tropical climate with an average annual temperature of 81°F and heavy rainfall, averaging over 97 in. per year, especially between November and March. Singapore was once covered completely in rain forests, but much of the land has been cleared and swamps and marshlands drained and reclaimed. Now only five percent of the land remains forested, much of this lying in protected reserves.

Singapore was barely settled before a British colonial administrator, Sir Stamford Raffles, founded Singapore City in 1819 as a trading post. Singapore grew as a port and naval base following the opening of the Suez Canal in 1869. The country is now one of the most densely populated nations in the world, with Chinese immigrants making up approximately 77 percent of the population and Malays (14 percent) and Indians (seven percent) the largest minorities. Although Singapore has to import all fuel and raw materials, the country has vibrant manufacturing industries, particularly electrical and electronic goods. The country also has large oil refining and chemicals industries.

▲ In 2001 146,265 vessels arrived at the port of Singapore, making it the busiest port in Southeast Asia.

▶ Singapore's high-rise financial district is the financial capital of the region. Over one fourth of the country's income is derived from financial and business services.

MALAYSIA

A multiethnic nation with rich natural resources, Malaysia has had one of Southeast Asia's fastest-growing economies in the past 30 years.

► Kek Lok Si Buddhist temple is situated at Ayer Itam on the island of Penang. The temple features gardens, shrines, a turtle pond, and the 98-ft.-high pagoda of Ten Thousand Buddhas.

Area: 126,900 sq. mi.
Population: 22,662,365
Capitals: Kuala Lumpur—legislative and diplomatic capital (1,141,000); Putrajaya—administrative capital (7,000)
Main languages spoken: Malay, English, Chinese dialects
Main religions: Islam, Hinduism, Buddhism, Christian
Currency: ringgit
Main exports: electronics, machinery, transportation equipment, petroleum and petroleum products, wood and wood products, rubber, textiles, chemicals
Type of government: federal parliamentary democracy with a constitutional monarchy

Malaysia is divided into two geographical areas separated by the South China Sea and lying around 400 mi. apart. Peninsula Malaysia occupies the southern portion of the Malay Peninsula, bordering Thailand to the north and close to the islands of Singapore to the south. It accounts for around 40 percent of the country's landmass and is divided by several central mountain chains, with poorly drained lowlands to the south, a narrow, forested belt to the east, and broader, fertile plains to the west. The western plains are the most densely populated and developed part of Malaysia. In contrast the two states of Sabah and Sarawak, which make up East Malaysia over 370 mi. away, are barely developed. Home to around 20 percent of the country's population, the land of East Malaysia consists of a coastal plain with many swamps, rising to densely forested hills and valleys before rising further to mountains. At 13,451 ft., Mount Kinabalu in Sabah is the country's highest peak.

TROPICAL CLIMATE AND WILDLIFE

Malaysia has a tropical climate with warm-to-hot temperatures and high humidity. The west coast of Peninsula Malaysia experiences a rainy season from September until to December, while the east coast, as well as East Malaysia, has its rainy season from October to February. The country has an extremely biodiverse environment in which around 8,000 different flowering plants exist.

THAILAND

George Town

Kota Baharu

M **A** **L** **A** **Y** **S** **I** **A**

Ipoh

Kuala Terengganu

Peninsula

Kuantan

Shah Alam KUALA LUMPUR

Kelang PUTRAJAYA

Seremban

Strait of Malacca

Johor Baharu

SINGAPORE

INDONESIA

South China Sea

Natuna Besar

Natuna Sea

Kuching

Kudat

Mount Kinabalu
13,451 ft.

Kota Kinabalu

Sabah

BRUNEI

Miri

Sarawak

Borneo

Sulu Sea

Sandakan

Tawau

Celebes Sea

INDONESIA

◀ A short distance from the coast of Sabah, the island of Pulau Sipadan is a coral seamount covered in dense jungles and surrounded by seas containing rich marine life.

▼ The 1,453-ft.-high Petronas Twin Towers in Kuala Lumpur are the world's tallest buildings. Completed in 1996, the towers are the headquarters of the national oil company of Malaysia.

East Malaysia has one of the largest and most varied bird populations in the world, and elephants, rhinoceroses, leopards, tigers, orangutans, and gibbons are among its larger animal species. Attracted by its wildlife, highland and rain-forest scenery, climate, and beaches along the peninsula coast, around ten million tourists visited Malaysia in 2001.

ABUNDANT NATURAL RESOURCES

Much of Malaysia's economic success is due to its rich natural resources. Oil deposits, particularly offshore of Sabah and Sarawak, are large, allowing Malaysia to produce over 800,000 barrels of oil per day. Sizable deposits of natural gas also exist, and metal ores, including tin, bauxite, copper, and gold, are mined. Much of Peninsula Malaysia's forests have been cleared for plantations, farmland, and settlements. The East Malaysia state of Sarawak still contains some of the largest and oldest original tropical forests on Earth. However, deforestation is the country's biggest environmental issue, with logging one of Malaysia's prime industries. The country is the world's largest exporter of tropical hardwood, logs, and timber, mostly from Sarawak. The World Bank estimates that trees are being felled at three times the rate they can be replaced.

SUBSISTENCE AND PLANTATION FARMING

Agriculture is a declining sector of the Malaysian economy, but it still employs approximately 18 percent of the workforce. A large number of agricultural workers farm their own small plots of land. Rice is the most common staple food, but the country is not self-sufficient and must import it. Vast plantations growing tea, tropical fruits, sugarcane, and especially cocoa and rubber dominate farming for export. Malaysia is one of the world's top-ten cocoa producers and was once the world's largest rubber producer. The country still ranks as one of the top-five largest producers of natural rubber. This is despite production declining owing to labor shortages, with workers increasingly becoming employed in the country's growing manufacturing industries. Many plantation owners are switching to other crops—palm oil in particular— that are possible to grow and harvest using machinery.

THIRTEEN STATES, MANY PEOPLE

Malaysia has been inhabited for over 30,000 years and is now a "melting pot" of different ethnic groups and cultures.

▲ These unusual, knifelike limestone pinnacles rise above the densely forested slopes of Gunung Mulu, Sarawak's largest national park.

▼ Malaysia is the world's largest producer of palm oil, used in the manufacture of soaps, ointments, margarine, and cooking oils. This plantation worker is loading palm fruit bunches into a container for transportation to a refinery.

▶ Logging is a huge industry in Malaysia, despite concerns about deforestation. To counter this there have been moves away from selling raw timber to manufacturing furniture. This now accounts for one fourth of all of Malaysia's exports from wood and wood products.

The Orang Asli are the original native people of Peninsula Malaysia, who now number just over 60,000. Larger numbers of indigenous people exist in East Malaysia. These include the Iban, Bidayuh, and Kadazan, the most numerous of some 30 different people, who together comprise approximately nine percent of Malaysia's total population. Approximately 48 percent of Malaysians are Malays, while 34 percent are of Chinese and eight percent of Indian origin. In addition, there are an estimated one million immigrants, mostly from the Philippines and Indonesia, working mainly in low-paid industries. Islam is the national religion of Malaysia, although religious freedom and toleration mean that almost all of the world's major religions are practiced in the country. Tensions between the traditionally wealthier Chinese and the Malay peoples have seen, since 1970, affirmative action in education, jobs, and business in favor of Malays.

A DEVELOPING SUCCESS STORY

In the early 1970s 70 percent of Malaysia's exports consisted of rubber and tin. In just 25 years the economic situation has completely changed so that over 75 percent of exports are now manufactured goods. The rapid growth of industry in Malaysia since the 1960s was, in part, due to the New Economic Policy (NEP), introduced in 1970 following large, violent

production of electrical and electronic equipment, motor vehicles, and chemicals. Today Malaysia is one of the world's leading exporters of high-tech components such as computer chips and disk drives. George Town and towns and cities around Kuala Lumpur are the key centers for the country's booming computer industry. Peninsula Malaysia is home to the large majority of the country's industry and has seen living standards rise for much of its population.

▲ Malaysia has become a major oil and natural gas producer, with its fields off the coast of Sarawak and Sabah yielding around 800,000 barrels per day.

ADVANCED DEVELOPMENT BY 2020

Although Malaysia is developing rapidly and is much wealthier than in the past, it still suffers economic and social problems. A major economic crisis in 1998 slowed growth dramatically, and there are shortages of skilled workers in some industries. Away from the cities and especially in East Malaysia many people's standard of living has not risen greatly, and a large number remain below the poverty line. Major government policies to complete Malaysia's transformation into an advanced nation by 2020 include greater technical education, improved health care, and the use of advanced technology. A new city has been developed, Putrajaya, to be the new administrative capital, 22 mi. south of Kuala Lumpur.

riots in the country. It aimed at changing the country's economic structure, where businesses had traditionally been owned by the Chinese population, and developing a range of new industries. Over one fourth of Malaysia's labor force are now employed in manufacturing, especially the processing of export commodities, such as rubber, tin, oil, wood, and metals, and the

▼ The Cameron Highlands in Perak province, on the western coast of Peninsula Malaysia, are the center of the country's tea plantations such as the Sungai Palas Estate.

INDONESIA

A gigantic island archipelago, Indonesia is a sprawling land of great natural and human diversity and is the fourth-most-populous nation in the world.

Area: 705,200 sq. mi.
Population: 232,073,071
Capital: Jakarta
(11,429,000)
Major languages spoken:
Bahasa Indonesia, English,
Dutch, Javanese
Main religions: Islam,
Protestant
Currency: Indonesian
rupiah
Main exports: crude
petroleum and natural gas,
electrical goods, plywood,
processed rubber, clothing
Type of government:
republic

Indonesia consists of over 13,660 islands that extend around one eighth of Earth's circumference. Sumatra is the most westerly of the larger islands and is separated from western Malaysia and Singapore by the Strait of Malacca. Papua, occupying the western part of the island of New Guinea, is Indonesia's most easterly territory. The vast majority of the population live on five islands: Java, Sumatra, Papua, Celebes, and Kalimantan—the Indonesian part of the island of Borneo. The country experiences a tropical climate with a small temperature range between the seasons owing to the islands' location close to the equator. Temperatures differ mainly with height, with only some highland areas of Papua receiving snowfall. Rainfall varies more, with the highest amount of rainfall occurring in the mountainous regions of Kalimantan, Sumatra, Celebes, and Papua, which receive in excess of 120 in. per year. Most lowland areas receive between 64–88 in.

▲ At 7,846 ft., Mount Bromo, on the eastern end of the island of Java, is one of 128 active volcanoes within Indonesia's territory. Much of Indonesia's land has been shaped by volcanic activity, with most islands featuring a mountainous interior. The ashes, lava, and mud flows from successive eruptions have helped create fertile soils in many places.

ASIA'S LARGEST TROPICAL RAIN FORESTS

A tropical climate, high rainfall, and fertile soils are largely responsible for the vast array of natural life throughout Indonesia. There are thousands of plant and animal species, although many are now under threat. Indonesia has the largest tracts of untouched rain forests in the world outside of the Amazon in South America. At the start of the 1900s over 82 percent of the country was covered in forests. Cutting down forests to clear land and for logging gradually increased throughout the 1900s as Indonesia developed large paper, timber, and wood pulp industries. Deforestation throughout the late 1990s was at a rate of around 7,800 sq. mi. per year, placing hundreds of species, such as the orangutan, under threat of extinction.

▼ Located on the northwest coast of Java, the city of Jakarta is the country's commercial and financial center. A sprawling urban area, much of which lies on a low, flat plain that is subject to swamping, Jakarta is southeast Asia's most populous urban area.

▲ A small river settlement in West Sumatra.

▼ Indonesian tea pickers at work. In 1998 Indonesia grew 166 million tons of tea, approximately six percent of the entire world market.

cassava, corn, soybeans, peanuts, and sweet potatoes. For such a populous nation livestock herds are relatively small, with around 15 million goats, 12 million cattle, and 10 million pigs. Chickens, however, are raised in large numbers; there were over one billion in Indonesia in 2002. Many Indonesians who farm smallholdings near rivers, lakes, or the coast also fish part-time. Large-scale sea fishing has increased with Japanese assistance.

INDONESIA'S RESOURCES
Much of Indonesia's farmland is devoted to growing cash crops on large plantations. Indonesia is one of the world's top-three rubber producers, the third-largest grower of coffee, and a leading producer of coconuts, tobacco, cacao, and a number of spices. Indonesia has large mineral reserves, with rich deposits of tin, copper, gold, bauxite, and nickel. In addition, Indonesia is the world's largest exporter of liquefied natural gas (LNG) and has relied on oil reserves to generate much export income.

RAPID INDUSTRIALIZATION
Although agriculture and the exporting of raw materials have dominated the economy, Indonesia has industrialized rapidly in the past 35 years. Larger industries process metals,

LIVING OFF THE LAND AND SEA
Since ancient times the people of Indonesia have made great use of their rich and diverse natural environment. Over 2,000 years ago Indonesian people in the coastal areas were already using irrigation systems to grow rice, while people in the interior tended to practice slash-and-burn agriculture, where forest areas were cleared and crops planted. Although less than 20 percent of Indonesia is cultivated, the country produces large amounts of many different crops. Other vital crops include

oil, wood, and wood products, and produce chemicals, cement, glass, rubber goods, machinery, and fertilizers. Indonesia has also become involved in high-technology fields such as electronics and aerospace. The country has a large textile industry, including batik, a technique for handprinting cloth. Despite the country's huge resources and growing industries, the Indonesian economy is fragile, with political instability, high unemployment, and large foreign debts. Progress has not occurred evenly, with Java and its neighboring islands the most economically developed but with great poverty elsewhere.

PEOPLE AND HISTORY
Indonesia came under Dutch control at the end of the 1600s. In 1945 Indonesia declared itself independent, an act recognized by the Netherlands in 1949 after a violent conflict. Indonesia is the most populous nation in Southeast Asia. Despite family-planning campaigns, the country's population is growing by around three million people every year. Overcrowding on the most populous islands resulted in transmigration, whereby over 3.5 million people were relocated in less populated parts of the country. This created some new jobs but also damaged the traditional cultures. Indonesia's people

come from around 300 different ethnic groups speaking over 250 distinct languages. The Javanese, the largest ethnic group in Indonesia, represent 45 percent of the population. Traders from India brought Hinduism and Buddhism to Indonesia almost 2,000 years ago, while Islam reached Sumatra in the 1200s. This religion spread throughout much of Indonesia, and there are now over 175 million Muslims, making it the world's largest Islamic country. Conflicts between different ethnic and religious groups have marred Indonesia since independence.

▲ Two of Kelimutu's three beautiful colored lakes. Kelimutu is a volcano located on the island of Flores, east of Java, and is in the middle of one of Indonesia's national parks.

▼ Members of the Organisasi Papua Merdeka (OPM) in their traditional dress on Papua. A collection of different tribal groups, the OPM has been fighting for Papua's independence from Indonesia since the 1960s.

EAST TIMOR

The first new nation of the 21st century, East Timor was finally recognized as an independent country in May 2002 after a long and violent struggle.

Area: 5,641 sq. mi.
Population: 825,000
Capital: Dili (140,000)
Main languages spoken: Portuguese, Tetum
Main religion: Roman Catholic
Currency: U.S. dollar
Main exports: timber (sandalwood), coffee, marble
Type of government: republic

▼ Two East Timorese farmworkers gather in a harvest. The people of East Timor are a diverse mixture of more than 15 ethnic groups, including some Indonesians and Chinese. Many are Roman Catholic, reflecting its long period as a Portuguese colony.

The island of Timor lies in the Malay Archipelago. East Timor occupies the eastern half of the island, the island of Pulau Kambing, and the enclave of Ambeno (also known as Oecusse). This lies on the northern coast of the remainder of Timor, which is part of Indonesia.

East Timor has a mostly mountainous landscape, with elevations rising inland to 9,718 ft. In the north the mountains rise almost immediately from the sea, while in the south there is a wide coastal plain that is broken up by river deltas and swampland. The country has a tropical climate with temperatures remaining high throughout the year but with great variations in rainfall. The southern side of the island tends to receive more rainfall, and the foothills are covered in bushes and trees, including eucalyptus. The northern side is more arid, and droughts can occur in the long dry season between May and November.

SUBSISTENCE AND CASH-CROP FARMING

The people of East Timor rely largely on farming, with corn the most important staple food, followed by rice, cassava, millet, and sweet potatoes. Buffalo, cattle, goats, and poultry are raised and traded. Outside the main settlements most trade occurs through bartering. A number of cash crops are grown, including coffee, coconuts, cloves, and sandalwood. The sandal oil extracted from the trees is used in soaps and perfumes. Australian-funded investigations have shown that offshore reserves of oil and natural gas exist.

BLOODSHED AND INDEPENDENCE

Portugal colonized the island in the 1500s, and East Timor remained a colony until 1975 when the Portuguese withdrew. Within ten days Indonesian forces invaded and declared East Timor part of Indonesia. Horrible human rights abuses occurred, and over 100,000 East Timorese died resisting the Indonesian occupation. In a referendum on East Timor's future in 1999 almost four fifths of the vote supported independence. East Timor was administered by the UN for almost three years after armed groups, supported by the Indonesian military, killed hundreds and destroyed much of the country's largest city, Dili. Much aid and investment has since poured into East Timor.

THE PHILIPPINES

The sprawling island nation of the Philippines occupies the northernmost part of the Malay Archipelago and lies in the western Pacific Ocean.

Area: 115,100 sq. mi.
Population: 84,525,639
Capital: Manila
(10,069,000)
Main languages spoken:
Pilipino, English
Main religions: Roman
Catholic, Protestant, Islam
Currency: Filipino peso
Main exports: electronic
equipment (particularly
computer components),
machinery and
transportation equipment,
clothing, coconut oil, wiring
Type of government:
republic

▼ The capital city
of Manila is at the heart
of a sprawling metropolis
that contains five individual
cities and houses more than
10.4 million people.

The Philippines consists of 7,107 islands, only a fraction of which are inhabited. Luzon to the north and Mindanao to the south are by far the largest and comprise two thirds of the country's total area. A further nine islands have land areas in excess of 975 sq. mi. Only two fifths of the islands are named, and only 350 of the islands have an area of more than 0.62 sq. mi. The islands are volcanic in origin and are the peaks of a partly submerged mountain chain. Their terrain is rugged, with the highest point on the island of Mindanao, where Mount Apo reaches 9,689 ft.

A DIVERSE LAND AND PEOPLE

The Philippines lies in the tropics and has a hot and humid year-round climate with an average annual temperature of 81°F and average rainfall of 81 in. per year. However, there is much variation in temperature and rainfall based on location and elevation. Around 45 percent of the country is under cultivation, and around one third remains forested, despite logging, much of it illegal, and slash-and-burn agriculture. There are over 10,000 species of trees, shrubs, and ferns, the most common of which are palms and bamboos. There are also more than 700 species of birds and many species of amphibians and reptiles. Rice and corn are the most common staple foods, but a wide range of crops are grown for both local consumption and export. Over 100 different ethnic groups live in the country, and a large range of languages and dialects are spoken. While Pilipino is the official language, English is widely used for commercial and governmental purposes. Over 80 percent of the population are Roman Catholics, while a large Muslim minority of around 15 percent are found particularly on the island of Mindanao.

▲ Many Filipino people, especially those who live on smaller islands, survive through fishing. In 2002 over 2.1 million tons of fish were caught off the Philippines.

▼ The San Guillermo Parish Church lies in the settlement of Bacolor, 37 mi. northwest of Manila. Founded in 1576, the church was severely damaged by a mudflow caused by an eruption of Mount Pinatubo in 1991.

NATURAL DISASTERS

As part of the Pacific's "Ring of Fire," the Philippines lies on some of the most geologically active parts of Earth's crust. The country regularly experiences earthquakes, including one in 1990 that struck the northern part of the island of Luzon, taking the lives of 1,600 people and leaving over 100,000 homeless. The islands also have an estimated 20 active volcanoes, including Mount Pinatubo on Luzon, which, after six centuries of lying dormant, erupted severely in 1991. The people of the Philippines also have to contend with floods, landslides, and relatively frequent typhoons (known as hurricanes in the Atlantic) that tend to occur during the wet season, particularly from September to December. In 2002 the United Nations Office for Civilian and Humanitarian Affairs (OCHA) released statistics showing that the Philippines was the most disaster-prone nation on Earth. Around 757 natural disasters struck the Philippines between 1900-2001.

AN HISTORIC TRADING CENTER

The Philippines came under Spanish colonial rule in 1521 when it was named Felipinas in honor of Spain's then ruler, Philip II. Lying in a strategic location between Asia and the "new world" of the Americas, the Philippines grew as a trading and transportation hub. Spain's colonial rule lasted until the U.S. gained possession following victories in the Spanish-American War of 1898 and the Philippine-American War (1899–1901). After occupation by Japan during World War II the Philippines became an independent republic in 1946. Ferdinand Marcos came to power in 1965, and he suppressed all political opposition. The Marcos regime was finally overturned in 1986, and despite bouts of corruption and political scandal since then, the Philippines is now an emerging democratic nation. The brutal years of the Marcos rule, as well as corruption and natural disasters since, have acted as a brake on the Philippines' economic growth. Manufacturing industries, such as textiles, electronics, chemicals, and machine parts, are growing, but there is great poverty and overcrowded slums in many cities.

AFRICA

AFRICA

The second-largest continent, Africa holds around
one fifth of Earth's total land area. It is bordered
by the Mediterranean and Red seas, as well as two oceans,
the Atlantic and the Indian. Off its Indian Ocean coastline
lies the world's fourth-largest island, Madagascar (see page
286). Africa's landscape is varied—from the world's largest
desert, the Sahara, in the north to lush tropical jungles and
rain forests in the middle of the continent. Africa is home
to an amazing variety of wildlife, including the world's
largest land animals such as the African elephant, the
rhinoceros, and the giraffe. Africa has a rich and diverse
human population consisting of more than 3,000 different
ethnic groups. In the past much of Africa was ruled as
colonies of major European powers such as Great Britain,
France, and Belgium. They divided the land with little
regard for ethnic boundaries and territories. Today Africans
live in many nations, most obtaining independence in
the last 50 years. Many of these countries are the
least developed in the world and have been
marred by ethnic conflicts, civil wars, and
natural disasters, including droughts,
famines, and diseases.

▲ These Nigerian women transport market goods by
foot to the town of Ikere-Ekiti in southwestern Nigeria.
The large majority of Africans live in rural areas and
depend on farming in order to make a living.

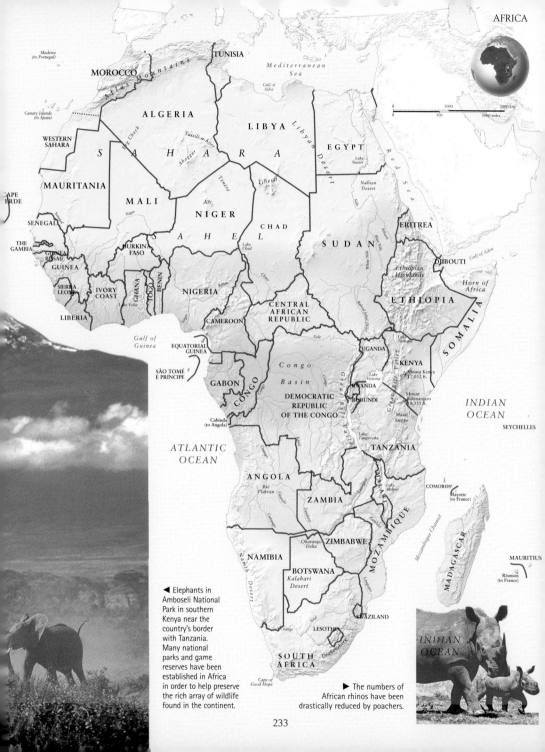

Madeira
(to Portugal)

MOROCCO

TUNISIA

Atlas Mountains

Mediterranean Sea

Gulf of Sidra

Canary Islands
(to Spain)

ALGERIA

LIBYA

EGYPT

Libyan Desert

Red Sea

WESTERN
SAHARA

S A H A R A

Tassili-n-Ajjer

Erg Chech

Ahaggar

Ténéré

Tibesti

Lake Nasser

Nubian Desert

Nile

CAPE
VERDE

MAURITANIA

MALI

Aïr

NIGER

CHAD

Lake Chad

SUDAN

ERITREA

Gulf of Aden

DJIBOUTI

SENEGAL

Senegal

S A H E L

Niger

Chari

Blue Nile

White Nile

Ethiopian Highlands

Horn of Africa

THE
GAMBIA

GUINEA-
BISSAU

GUINEA

BURKINA
FASO

Benue

NIGERIA

CENTRAL
AFRICAN
REPUBLIC

Bahr el Jebel (Nile)

ETHIOPIA

SOMALIA

SIERRA LEONE

IVORY
COAST

GHANA

TOGO

BENIN

Lake Volta

CAMEROON

Uele

Lake Turkana

LIBERIA

Niger

Gulf of Guinea

EQUATORIAL
GUINEA

Ogooué

Congo Basin

UGANDA

KENYA

Great Rift Valley

SÃO TOMÉ
E PRÍNCIPE

GABON

CONGO

DEMOCRATIC
REPUBLIC
OF THE CONGO

Congo

RWANDA

BURUNDI

Lake Victoria

▲ Mount Kenya
17,052 ft.

Mount
Kilimanjaro
19,335 ft.

Masai Steppe

INDIAN
OCEAN

SEYCHELLES

Lualaba

Lake Tanganyika

TANZANIA

ATLANTIC
OCEAN

Cabinda
(to Angola)

Kwango

Kasai

ANGOLA

Bié Plateau

Cuando

Cubango

ZAMBIA

Zambezi

Lake Malawi

Luangwa

MALAWI

Lake Malawi

COMOROS

Mayotte
(to France)

Mozambique Channel

MADAGASCAR

MAURITIUS

Réunion
(to France)

NAMIBIA

Namib Desert

Okavango Delta

ZIMBABWE

Limpopo

MOZAMBIQUE

BOTSWANA

Kalahari Desert

Cubango

SWAZILAND

◄ Elephants in Amboseli National Park in southern Kenya near the country's border with Tanzania. Many national parks and game reserves have been established in Africa in order to help preserve the rich array of wildlife found in the continent.

Orange

Vaal

LESOTHO

Drakensberg

SOUTH
AFRICA

Cape of
Good Hope

INDIAN OCEAN

► The numbers of African rhinos have been drastically reduced by poachers.

0   1000   2000 km
0   500   1000 miles

233

MOROCCO

The rugged and mountainous kingdom of Morocco faces Spain across the Straits of Gibraltar. It gained independence from France and Spain in 1956.

Area: 172,300 sq. mi., excluding the disputed Western Sahara territory, or 274,300 sq. mi. including the Western Sahara
Population: 31,167,783
Capital: Rabat (1,668,000)
Main languages spoken: Arabic, Berber dialects
Main religion: Islam
Currency: dirham
Main exports: phosphates, food and beverages (particularly fruit, wine, and vegetables), consumer goods
Type of government: constitutional monarchy

▼ The lively central square, Djemaa el Fna, of the city of Marrakech. Located inland on a fertile plain, the city was founded in the 1000s and is an important transportation and trade center.

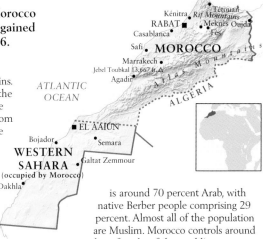

Morocco's land contains two large mountain chains. The Rif mountains run along the Mediterranean coast, while the higher Atlas Mountains run from southwest to northeast and are heavily forested in places. A large amount of snow and rainfall falls on these mountains, and this water flows through a network of streams. To the south and southeast lies part of the Sahara desert. Around 50 percent of the Moroccan workforce are engaged in farming and fishing. Cereals, sugarcane, sugar beets, dates, olives, and citrus fruits are key crops, while large herds of sheep and goats are raised. Fishing is important, with over 750,000 tons of fish caught every year. The country's location on both the Mediterranean and Atlantic coasts has seen a number of large ports develop, including Casablanca, the country's most populous city. Morocco's population is around 70 percent Arab, with native Berber people comprising 29 percent. Almost all of the population are Muslim. Morocco controls around three fourths of the world's reserves of phosphates, substances that are an important ingredient of fertilizers, metal-cleaning agents, toothpastes, and detergents. Morocco has some deposits of coal, iron ore, lead, and other metals, while oil was discovered in the northeastern desert area in 2000. Tourism has become an increasingly important industry and is vital to Morocco's economy. The country's warm climate, beaches, scenery, and ancient cities, such as Fès, Tangier, and Marrakech, attracted 4.1 million tourists in 2002.

ALGERIA

Algeria won independence from France in 1962 after a bitter struggle. Its land is dominated by the Sahara desert, and its economy is overshadowed by oil and natural gas.

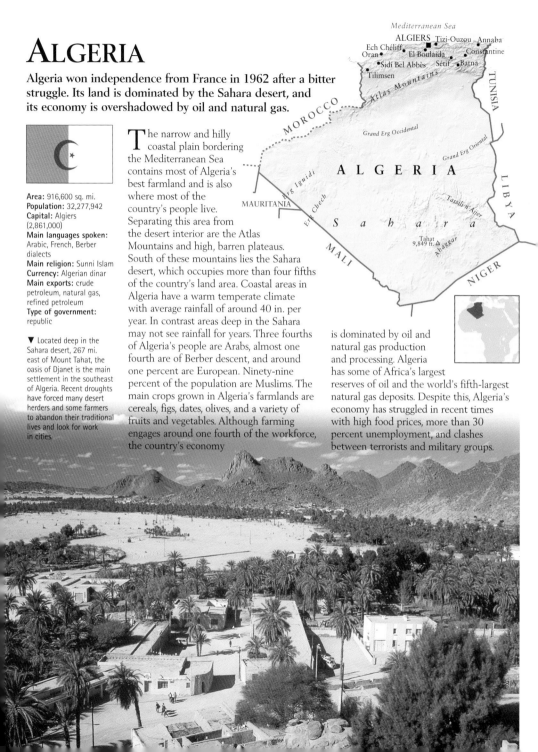

Area: 916,600 sq. mi.
Population: 32,277,942
Capital: Algiers (2,861,000)
Main languages spoken: Arabic, French, Berber dialects
Main religion: Sunni Islam
Currency: Algerian dinar
Main exports: crude petroleum, natural gas, refined petroleum
Type of government: republic

▼ Located deep in the Sahara desert, 267 mi. east of Mount Tahat, the oasis of Djanet is the main settlement in the southeast of Algeria. Recent droughts have forced many desert herders and some farmers to abandon their traditional lives and look for work in cities.

The narrow and hilly coastal plain bordering the Mediterranean Sea contains most of Algeria's best farmland and is also where most of the country's people live. Separating this area from the desert interior are the Atlas Mountains and high, barren plateaus. South of these mountains lies the Sahara desert, which occupies more than four fifths of the country's land area. Coastal areas in Algeria have a warm temperate climate with average rainfall of around 40 in. per year. In contrast areas deep in the Sahara may not see rainfall for years. Three fourths of Algeria's people are Arabs, almost one fourth are of Berber descent, and around one percent are European. Ninety-nine percent of the population are Muslims. The main crops grown in Algeria's farmlands are cereals, figs, dates, olives, and a variety of fruits and vegetables. Although farming engages around one fourth of the workforce, the country's economy is dominated by oil and natural gas production and processing. Algeria has some of Africa's largest reserves of oil and the world's fifth-largest natural gas deposits. Despite this, Algeria's economy has struggled in recent times with high food prices, more than 30 percent unemployment, and clashes between terrorists and military groups.

TUNISIA

The smallest nation in northwest Africa, Tunisia
is sandwiched between Algeria and Libya and has
a historically important Mediterranean coastline.

Area: 60,000 sq. mi.
Population: 9,815,644
Capital: Tunis (1,927,000)
Main languages spoken:
Arabic, French
Main religion: Sunni
Islam
Currency: Tunisian dinar
Main exports: clothing
and accessories,
machinery and electrical
apparatus, phosphates
Type of government:
republic

▼ A livestock market is
held each week in Douz,
68 mi. west of Gabès. Douz
is the largest of Tunisia's
desert oasis settlements
and has a population of
around 15,000. Every year
the town hosts the
International Festival of the
Sahara, which draws
performers and artists from
across northern Africa.

Mountainous and very green
in the north, Tunisia becomes
flatter and drier toward the south.
The Atlas Mountains extend into
the northern section of Tunisia,
forming two ranges that contain
the country's highest point, the
peak of Jebal Chambi, with
an elevation of 5,064 ft.
A mountainous plateau
extends northeast, sloping
down toward the coast. Toward
the south lies a region of salt lakes,
some of which are below sea level.
South of these lakes the land becomes
part of the Sahara desert, with isolated
watering holes and settlements. The
large lake of Shatt al Jarid lies in the
center of the country. In the north
is the country's most fertile farming
area. Compared to its neighbors, a
much greater proportion of Tunisia
can be farmed using irrigation.
However, periodic droughts have an
enormous effect on farm output. Cereals,
citrus fruits, olives, and vegetables are key
crops, while herds of sheep, goats, cattle,
and camels are raised. Tunisia has a mixed
economy in which farming, manufacturing,
mining, and tourism each play a role. Much
of the country's manufacturing industry has

been developed since independence
from France in 1956 and is based around
Tunis, its largest city. Steelmaking, food
processing, chemicals, and leather products
are among the leading manufacturing areas,
while phosphates, lead, and oil are the most
important mined products. Separated from
the island of Sicily by just 99 mi. of water,
Tunisia has had much contact with Europe
for over three centuries. The Phoenicians
established colonies in the country over
3,000 years ago. The city of Carthage, located
close to Tunis, became the center of a major
Mediterranean power until it was overthrown
by the Romans in 146 B.C. Ancient remains
from these civilizations, along with Tunisia's
many sandy beaches and warm climate,
attracted 5.1 million visitors in 2002.

LIBYA

Libya is a sparsely populated desert nation whose people have benefited from its large oil reserves.

Area: 679,400 sq. mi.
Population: 5,368,585
Capitals: Tripoli (1,776,000)—official and diplomatic capital; Surt (40,000)—legislative and administrative capital
Main language spoken: Arabic
Main religion: Sunni Islam
Currency: Libyan dinar
Main export: crude petroleum
Type of government: Islamic Arabic socialist "mass state"

▼ A desert oasis in the Sahara desert. Large amounts of water lie underneath the surface of the land in south and southeast Libya. The Great Manmade River Project, one of the largest engineering programs in the world, transports water from this region to the cities on the coast.

The Great Socialist People's Libyan Arab Jamahiriya borders Tunisia, Algeria, Niger, Chad, Sudan, and Egypt and has a long coastline with the Mediterranean Sea. Most of its people live in towns and cities situated on or close to the coast. Small, isolated settlements exist southward in the Sahara and in the northeastern arm of the desert. Less than one percent of the land is cultivated, with barley, tobacco, dates, figs, and grapes grown. Livestock, particularly sheep, goats, and poultry, is more important than crop growing. Until the discovery of oil in the 1950s Libya was a desperately poor nation reliant on aid and imports of food to enable its people to survive. Oil output today is around 1.5 million barrels per day, and crude oil makes up 99 percent of all of Libya's exports. Oil revenue has enabled the government to establish a welfare state in which education and health care are free, although under resourced and less common in rural areas. It has also enabled Libya to build up its military forces. Libya invaded part of its southern neighbor, Chad, in the 1970s, but its forces were driven out in 1987. Ruled since 1969 by a dictator, Colonel Mu'ammar Gadhafi, Libya's economy and people suffered as the result of United Nations' sanctions owing to the country's link with terrorism. These were lifted in 1999 as relations with Libya improved.

MEDITERRANEAN SEA

TUNISIA
Az Zawiyah
TRIPOLI
Al Khums
Misratah
Gulf of Sidra
Al Marj
Benghazi
Tubruq
SURT

ALGERIA

L I B Y A

Great Sand Sea

EGYPT

S a h a r a

NIGER
CHAD

△ Bikku Bitti 7,435 ft.

EGYPT

The birthplace of the great ancient Egyptian civilization, Egypt captivates and fascinates people to this day.

Area: 384,300 sq. mi.
Population: 70,712,345
Capital: Cairo (9,586,000)
Main language spoken: Arabic
Major religions: Sunni Islam, Coptic Christian
Currency: Egyptian pound
Main exports: petroleum and petroleum products, cotton yarn and textiles, basic manufactured goods, clothing
Type of government: republic

Egypt is roughly square in shape with long coastlines in the north and east. The Sinai Peninsula lies between the main body of Egypt and Israel and the Gaza territory to the northeast. It is separated from the rest of Egypt by the Gulf of Suez and the Suez Canal, the artificial waterway that links the Mediterranean to the Red Sea. The north of Sinai consists of sandy deserts, while the south is mountainous and contains the country's highest point, Jabal Katrina (8,623 ft.). Over 90 percent of Egypt's land is very dry desert that is split into two regions by the world's longest river, the Nile (930 mi. long). The Libyan Desert is a low-lying series of gravel and sand plateaus. There are no rivers or streams, and rain that does fall gathers in depressions, forming temporary salt lakes. A smaller desert to the east is more rugged and contains mountains and plateaus that end in cliffs facing the Red Sea.

THE EGYPTIAN PEOPLE

Ninety-eight percent of Egyptians are descendants of either the native ancient Egyptian population (Hamites) or of Arabs who conquered Egypt in A.D. 642 and settled in the region. Before the Arab invasion most Egyptians had been Christians, but the Arab settlers introduced the Islamic religion, and today over 90 percent of Egyptians are Muslims. Egypt's population is growing at a fast rate, with around 1.2 million babies born every year. This is putting great pressure on both Egypt's economy and the already densely populated habitable land. Large cities—such as Alexandria, its major seaport, and, the largest of all, Cairo—are being forced to grow rapidly in size.

▼ The ancient Egyptian pyramids near El Giza are among the most majestic monuments to this great civilization. For almost 3,000 years a largely unbroken line of pharaohs presided over an empire in which culture, arts, science, and technology all flourished.

SUDAN

The largest African nation, Sudan has distinctly different northern and southern halves. The peoples of these two regions have been in conflict for many years.

Area: 917,400 sq. mi.
Population: 37,090,298
Capital: Khartoum (2,853,000)
Major languages spoken: Arabic, Nubian, Ta Bedawie
Main religions: Sunni Islam, indigenous beliefs, Christian
Currency: Sudanese dinar
Main exports: cotton, sheep and lamb, sesame seeds, gum arabic, gold
Type of government: republic with strong military influence

▼ This Sudanese nomad tends his herd of cattle, some of the over 38 million head that exist in the country. Around two million Sudanese are nomads making a living through herding cattle, sheep and goats.

With the exception of small areas of highlands, Sudan is mostly a land of flat plains. The northern part of the country is split by the Nile river into the Libyan Desert to the west and the Nubian Desert to the east. The clay plains in the center of the country support dry savannas that change to giant swamplands and rain forests in the south. The lands around the two key tributaries of the Nile, the Blue and White Nile, are the most fertile farming areas of the country. Sudanese people come from more than 500 different tribes, clans, and groups. Around two-thirds live in rural areas and depend on agriculture, which is often hit by droughts, to survive. Cotton is the main cash crop, while a range of food crops, including wheat, millet, and sorghum, are grown. The people of northern Sudan are mainly of Arab origin and follow the Islamic religion. Some non-Arab peoples in the north have also become Muslims. The people of southern and central Sudan are predominantly black Africans who practice traditional African religions or are Christians. Conflict and civil war have blemished Sudan since independence in 1956, particularly through attempts by Muslims to impose their values on the southern population.

SOMALIA

Formed in 1960 from Italian and British Somaliland colonies, Somalia is drought and war-ridden and is one of the poorest nations in the world.

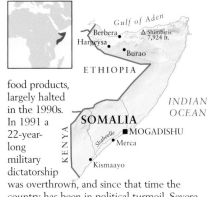

Area: 242,200 sq. mi.
Population: 7,753,310
Capital: Mogadishu (1,212,000)
Main languages spoken: Somali, Arabic
Main religion: Sunni Islam
Currency: Somali shilling
Main exports: sheep and goats, bananas, camels and cattle
Type of government: republic; no effective national government

Somalia's land generally consists of rugged plains and plateaus. Much of the country is very dry, receiving between 2–6 in. of rainfall per year. Bananas and other fruit, along with corn, sugarcane, and cotton, are grown in the southwest. More than half of the population are nomadic, wandering with herds of animals in search of grazing lands. Industry, limited to processing leather and food products, largely halted in the 1990s. In 1991 a 22-year-long military dictatorship was overthrown, and since that time the country has been in political turmoil. Severe droughts and famines, along with vicious tribal fighting, have added to the troubles of the already desperately poor people.

ETHIOPIA

Formerly called Abyssinia, Ethiopia is one of the world's oldest nations and one of the only parts of Africa that has never been a European colony.

Area: 403,200 sq. mi.
Population: 67,673,031
Capital: Addis Ababa (2,753,000)
Main languages spoken: Amharic, Tigrinya, Orominga
Main religions: Islam, Ethiopian Orthodox, animist
Currency: birr
Main exports: coffee (accounts for almost two thirds of exports), animal hides, pulses, petroleum products
Type of government: federal republic

Ethiopia is dominated by highland areas and is divided by the Great Rift Valley, which runs from north to south. Three fourths of its land is above 4,592 ft. in elevation. Lake Tana, which lies in the north of the country, is northeast Africa's largest lake. To the east lies a semidesert plain, and north of this plain is one of the hottest places on Earth, with temperatures reaching 122°F. Rainfall varies greatly, usually with elevation, but is often not enough to prevent devastating droughts. Over 80 percent of Ethiopians are rural and rely on farming to survive, with coffee the key cash crop and livestock herding vital for domestic food. Ethiopia is one of the least developed and poorest nations in the world. Frequent droughts, famines, and wars have all damaged the economy and created great suffering among the country's people.

▼ A cascading waterfall on the Blue Nile river as it runs through Ethiopia. The Blue Nile, known as Abay to Ethiopians, is a major tributary of the Nile.

ERITREA

One of the youngest African nations, Eritrea became independent from Ethiopia in 1993. The country has a 620-mi.-long coastline with the Red Sea.

Area: 46,800 sq. mi.
Population: 4,465,651
Capital: Asmera (503,000)
Main languages spoken: Tigrinya, Tigre, Kunama, Afar, Amhanc, Arabic
Main religions: Islam, Coptic Christian, Roman Catholic, Protestant
Currency: nakfa
Main exports: raw materials (including animal hides), food products, manufactures (including footwear and textiles)
Type of government: republic

Eritrea's land consists of a hot, dry coastal plain that rises to form areas of highland plateaus with an elevation of between 4,920–8,036 ft. Rainfall is higher in the highland areas but is still relatively low, and at times the country suffers from droughts. Handed to Ethiopia by the United Nations in 1952, Eritreans embarked upon a 30-year-long war of independence in which many hundreds of thousands of people died, and the forests and most of the country's infrastructure were destroyed. In the future oil deposits off the country's coast may prove significant, but in the meantime most people survive through subsistence farming. An estimated 70 percent of the people survive on food aid from international organizations.

DJIBOUTI

A small nation, Djibouti is a dry desert land that lies at the entrance to the Red Sea. Its capital, also called Djibouti, is a major regional port.

Area: 8,500 sq. mi.
Population: 472,810
Capital: Djibouti (542,000)
Main languages spoken: French, Arabic, Afar, Somali
Main religion: Sunni Islam
Currency: Djibouti franc
Main exports: reexports, live animals
Type of government: republic

Mountainous to the north, with low plains to the center and south, most of Djibouti's land is hot deserts broken up by occasional oases and salt lakes. Rainfall is highest in the mountains but even there rarely exceeds 13 in., while most of the country receives less than six inches per year. Raising livestock is the chief farming activity, and close to three fourths of the population live in or around the city of Djibouti. The country's economy is highly dependent on the port's strategic location at the junction of the Red Sea and the Gulf of Aden. Much of Djibouti's income is derived from port trade since it is the main outlet for landlocked Ethiopia's coffee crops and other produce. Djibouti became independent from France in 1977 and still relies on aid from that country. Unemployment is high, poverty is common, and tensions between the country's two main peoples, the Issa and the Afar, have resulted in occasional conflicts.

▶ Salt is extracted from Lake Assal in the center of Djibouti. At 515 ft. below sea level, the lake is the lowest point in Africa.

CAPE VERDE

Lying off the west coast of Africa, the island group of Cape Verde became independent from Portugal in 1975. Over half of the people live on the island of São Tiago.

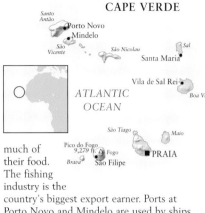

CAPE VERDE

Area: 1,600 sq. mi.
Population: 408,760
Capital: Praia (82,000)
Main languages spoken: Portuguese, Crioulo (Portuguese Creole)
Main religion: Roman Catholic
Currency: Cape Verdean escudo
Main exports: shoes, clothing, and textiles, fish and fish products, salt, bananas
Type of government: republic

The ten islands and five islets that comprise Cape Verde are of volcanic origin and contain one active volcano, Pico do Fogo, which, at 9,279 ft., is also the island's highest point. Rainfall (less than ten inches per year), vegetation, and wildlife are all fairly sparse on these rugged islands, most of which are mountainous. Farming is only possible in limited areas in valleys using irrigation, and the islands have to import much of their food. The fishing industry is the country's biggest export earner. Ports at Porto Novo and Mindelo are used by ships as refueling stops, also bringing in revenue. Aid, mainly from the European Union, has helped improve health care and education.

MAURITANIA

The largely desert nation of Mauritania received its independence from France in 1960 and since that time has increased its ties with the Arab world.

Area: 397,800 sq. mi.
Population: 2,828,858
Capital: Nouakchott (626,000)
Main languages spoken: Hasaniya, Arabic, Wolof, Pular, Soninke
Main religion: Islam
Currency: ouguiya (the world's only nondecimal currency)
Main exports: iron ore, fish and fish products
Type of government: Islamic republic

Like Mali, which it borders to the south and east, most of Mauritania lies within the Sahara desert. Only its southern lands and some areas of its Atlantic coast are capable of supporting varied vegetation. Farming is mainly confined to the valley along the border area with Senegal, where millet, pulses, and dates are among the crops grown. The rich fishing grounds off its coastline make fish and fish processing one of the country's major exports behind iron ore, which accounts for 60 percent of exports. The country also has some of the world's largest gypsum deposits. Fishing and mining account for over 99 percent of its earnings from exports. The majority of Mauritania's population are either Moors, a north African people, or of mixed Arab origin. Black Africans from many different ethnic groups make up around 30 percent. Ethnic tensions and occasional conflicts exist between the Moors, who are dominant in politics, and the black minority.

▶ Imraguen fishermen gather a catch of golden mullet at the Banc d'Arguin National Park off the coast of Mauritania. Imraguen fishermen have fished this area for thousands of years.

MALI

Once the center of a great Saharan trading empire, Mali is a landlocked, underdeveloped country in which droughts and famines have created widespread poverty.

Area: 471,000 sq. mi.
Population: 11,340,480
Capital: Bamako (1,161,000)
Main languages spoken: Bambara, French, many African languages
Main religions: Islam, indigenous beliefs
Currency: CFA franc
Main exports: cotton and cotton products, live animals, gold
Type of government: republic

▶ Droughts and political boundaries have forced many of the Saharan nomadic Tuareg peoples to settle in towns and cities.

Almost half of Mali's land is part of the Sahara desert, while semiarid sand areas cover much of the rest of the country. Mountains rise to the south, and hydroelectric dams on the Niger river provide 57 percent of Mali's electricity. Mali's fast-growing population is concentrated in the southern part of the country and is reliant on the Niger river for water for crop irrigation, as well as for the rich fish stocks it holds. Deforestation and desertification are rampant, and less than ten percent of the country's people have access to adequate sanitation. Most people are rural farmers and livestock herders. The key industries of the country are cotton growing and, increasingly, mining for gold and other minerals.

NIGER

Niger is a poor, desertlike country. The majority of its people live in a semifertile southern strip bordering Nigeria and, to the southwest, the Niger river.

Area: 489,100 sq. mi.
Population: 10,639,744
Capital: Niamey (821,000)
Main languages spoken: French, Hausa, Djerma
Main religions: Islam, traditional beliefs
Currency: CFA franc
Main exports: uranium, livestock, black-eyed peas
Type of government: republic

The northern two thirds of Niger are part of the Sahara desert, which is spreading southward as desertification continues. Ninety percent of the population work in agriculture, although less than four percent of the land can be cultivated. Herding livestock is a major occupation, while some people fish the Niger river and Lake Chad to the southeast. Niger was one of the world's leading producers of uranium, used in atomic energy, but demand has dropped, creating large debts.

Coal, phosphates, tin, and salt are also mined. Niger's population is ethnically diverse. The largest group is the Hausa, who make up more than half of the population, and the Djerma comprise around 23 percent. Other large minorities include the Tuareg, many of whom live a nomadic life in the north. The average life expectancy in Niger is just 42 years.

243

SENEGAL

The former French colony of Senegal lies on the bulge of western Africa, bounded by the Atlantic Ocean, Mauritania, Mali, Guinea, and Guinea-Bissau.

Area: 74,100 sq. mi.
Population: 10,589,571
Capital: Dakar (2,160,000)
Main languages spoken: French, Wolof, Pulaar, Diola, Mandingo
Main religion: Islam
Currency: CFA franc
Main exports: fish and crustaceans, chemicals, peanut oil, phosphates
Type of government: republic

▼ Senegalese women carry a harvest of millet in baskets perched on top of their heads. Millet is a staple grain used in stews and many Senegalese meals.

S enegal is a largely flat, sandy, and low-lying country with an average elevation below 656 ft. Higher land is only found in the extreme southeast, where mountains rise to elevations above 1,640 ft. Senegal has a hot, tropical climate with more rainfall toward the south. As a result of this, there are dry savannas in the north and considerably more lush areas of rain forests in the south. Four major rivers cross the country, including the large Sénégal river, which forms most of the country's border with Mauritania. The Sénégal floods every year and deposits fertile sediment over a large area on which a number of crops are grown. Almost 70 percent of the workforce are employed in farming. The country is encouraging the growth of crops like sugarcane, cotton, rice, and vegetables to reduce its reliance on the single

dominant crop of peanuts. The country's population consists of seven main ethnic groups, with the Wolof making up almost 45 percent. Compared to many neighboring countries, Senegal is fairly wealthy. It has well-developed transportation and communications systems and a relatively large industrial sector. Senegal's capital and largest city, Dakar, is located on the Cape Verde peninsula, which contains mainland Africa's most westerly point.

THE GAMBIA

Surrounded by Senegal on three sides, the Gambia is the smallest nation on the west African mainland and at no point measures more than 50 mi. wide.

Area: 3,900 sq. mi.
Population: 1,455,842
Capital: Banjul (418,000)
Main languages spoken: English, Madinka, Wolof, Fula
Main religion: Islam
Currency: dalasi
Main exports: reexports (mainly to Senegal), fish and fish products, groundnuts, processed food
Type of government: republic

▲ Formerly a naval port, the Gambia's capital city of Banjul is located on Banjul island. This road, Independence Drive, connects the city to the mainland.

The Gambia is dominated by the Gambia river, which runs east to west through the entire country and divides it in half. Most of its land is savanna grasslands, with some forested areas and swamplands close to the river and the coast. Rice and peanuts are the two largest crops. Gambia's industry is mainly limited to processing farm products. The country has a tropical climate with a short rainy season between June and October. Gambians come from many different ethnic groups, and around 90 percent are Muslims. Many rural Gambians are migrating to towns, where incomes are often three or four times higher than in rural areas. There they work in service industries, transportation, and tourism. The country's capital city, Banjul, is located on a deep natural harbor, one of the best on the entire west coast of Africa. Revenue from tourists, most of whom come from the U.K., Germany, and other European nations, is the fastest-growing part of the country's economy.

GUINEA-BISSAU

Guinea-Bissau, one of the poorest nations in west Africa, has been troubled by internal strife since its independence from Portugal in 1974.

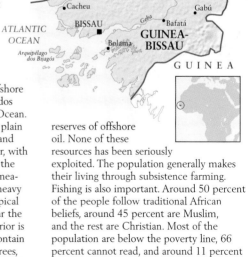

Area: 10,800 sq. mi.
Population: 1,345,479
Capital: Bissau (292,000)
Main languages spoken: Portuguese, Crioulo (Portuguese Creole), tribal languages
Main religions: indigenous beliefs, Islam
Currency: CFA franc
Main exports: cashews, timber, cotton, fish
Type of government: republic

Guinea-Bissau has a heavily indented coastline, and its territory includes more than 60 offshore islands, including the Arquipélago dos Bijagós, which lies in the Atlantic Ocean. The landscape consists of a coastal plain split by many river estuaries. The land rises to a low plateau in the interior, with highlands in the northeast close to the country's border with Guinea. Guinea-Bissau has a tropical climate with heavy rainfall. Mangrove swamps and tropical jungles cover much of the land near the coast. Much of the land in the interior is savannas. Guinea-Bissau's forests contain commercially valuable hardwood trees, and the country has mineral deposits of tin, bauxite, and copper, as well as possible reserves of offshore oil. None of these resources has been seriously exploited. The population generally makes their living through subsistence farming. Fishing is also important. Around 50 percent of the people follow traditional African beliefs, around 45 percent are Muslim, and the rest are Christian. Most of the population are below the poverty line, 66 percent cannot read, and around 11 percent of all babies die before reaching adulthood. The country is heavily reliant on foreign aid.

GUINEA

Independent since 1958, Guinea is a poor country and is reliant on foreign aid, despite being rich in mineral reserves.

Area: 94,900 sq. mi.
Population: 7,775,065
Capital: Conakry (1,272,000)
Main languages spoken: French, tribal languages
Main religions: Islam, Christian
Currency: Guinean franc
Main exports: bauxite, alumina, gold, coffee, diamonds, fish
Type of government: republic

Guinea consists of four regions: the wet coastal plain, the northwestern Fouta Djallon hill region, the northern dry lowlands, and the hilly, forested area of the southeast. Guinea is one of the wettest countries in west Africa, and its capital and largest city, Conakry, receives over 141 in. of rain per year. Many crops are grown, including rice, cassava, pineapples, and peanuts. Guinea has more than 30 percent of the world's reserves of bauxite ore, from which aluminum is smelted. Bauxite makes up over 75 percent of all exports. The country remains poor and underdeveloped, with large numbers of refugees fleeing from conflicts in neighboring countries.

SIERRA LEONE

Founded in 1787 for freed African slaves, Sierra Leone became independent in 1961. Scarred by war and political instability, the country is extremely poor.

Area: 27,700 sq. mi.
Population: 5,614,743
Capital: Freetown (837,000)
Main languages spoken: English, Mende, Temne, Krio (English Creole)
Main religions: Islam, traditional beliefs
Currency: leone
Main exports: diamonds, rutile/titanium ore, cocoa, coffee
Type of government: republic

Sierra Leone's land consists of a swampy coastal plain that rises to a plateau and mountains in the northeast. The capital, Freetown, is located on a rocky peninsula overlooking one of the world's largest natural harbors. Savanna grasslands are found in the northern interior, with dense rain forests in the south. Valuable tropical hardwoods, including teak and mahogany, as well as wildlife, including chimpanzees, monkeys, and numerous bird species, are under threat from heavy deforestation. In the 1990s an estimated three percent of Sierra Leone's forests were cut down each year. Two thirds of the country's workforce are involved in subsistence farming, with rice the largest staple crop. After a devastating civil war in the 1990s Sierra Leone now relies heavily on foreign aid. The country remains unstable and under threat of more conflicts. Its people, comprising more than 20 ethnic groups, are among the world's poorest, with just one doctor per 15,000 people.

► A group of Sierra Leonean women tie-dye cloth to make a traditional form of brightly patterned cloth called *gara*.

LIBERIA

Liberia was founded in 1847 by freed African slaves from the U.S. The majority of its population are engaged in subsistence farming.

Area: 37,200 sq. mi.
Population: 3,228,198
Capital: Monrovia (491,000)
Main languages spoken: English, tribal languages
Main religions: traditional beliefs, Islam, Christian
Currency: Liberian dollar (the U.S. dollar is also in circulation as legal tender)
Main exports: iron ore, rubber, timber, diamonds, gold
Type of government: republic

Liberia's land includes a rocky coastline with lagoons and sandbars and a coastal plain on which the majority of its population live. This plain rises to a series of plateaus and low mountains. With an elevation of 4,529 ft., Mount Wuteve, near the border with Guinea, is Liberia's highest peak. One fifth of the country is forested. Between 1990 and 1997 a bloody civil war destroyed most of Liberia's economy. Before the war giant rubber plantations and large-scale iron ore mines accounted for most of its exports. Since the conflict the country, which had previously retained close ties with the U.S., has struggled to maintain peace. Liberia has the world's largest registered fleet of ships, but almost all of the vessels are owned by foreign companies.

▼ Digging for diamonds—Liberia is one of the world's top-20 diamond producers.

TOGO

A long, narrow country with a mixture of coastal swamps, plateaus, and low mountains, Togo stretches from the Gulf of Guinea around 319 mi. into west Africa.

Area: 21,100 sq. mi.
Population: 5,285,501
Capital: Lomé (732,000)
Main languages spoken: Ewe, Mina, Dagomba, Kabye
Main religions: indigenous beliefs, Christian, Islam
Currency: CFA franc
Main exports: cotton, reexports, phosphates, coffee
Type of government: republic

Almost 65 percent of Togo's workforce are engaged in agriculture. Most of the country's food is grown on small farms, with staple crops such as cassava, yams, sorghum, corn, and plantains. Minerals, particularly phosphates, have become the country's leading export earner, and mining is the country's main industry. The capital city, Lomé, is also a major regional port. The people of Togo come from many ethnic groups. Tensions exist between the two largest groups—the Kabye in the north and the Ewe in the south. Fifty-one percent of the population practice traditional African religions, while 29 percent are Christians.

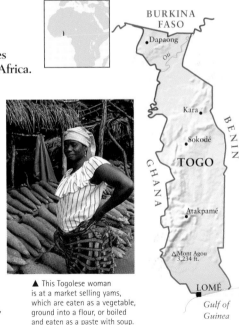

▲ This Togolese woman is at a market selling yams, which are eaten as a vegetable, ground into a flour, or boiled and eaten as a paste with soup.

IVORY COAST

The Republic of Côte d'Ivoire, or the Ivory Coast, is a large, square-shaped west African nation with a tropical climate and large areas of fertile land.

Area: 122,800 sq. mi.
Population: 16,804,784
Capitals: Yamoussoukro (245,000)—official capital; Abidjan (3,956,000)—diplomatic and administrative capital
Main languages spoken: French, Dioula
Main religions: Islam, indigenous beliefs, Christian
Currency: CFA franc
Main exports: cocoa, coffee, wood and wood products, petroleum products, fish products
Type of government: republic

▼ Yamoussoukro's Basilica of Our Lady of Peace was modeled after St. Peter's Basilica in Rome, Italy, and is one of the largest Catholic churches in the world. It took three years to build at a cost of over $300 million.

The Ivory Coast consists of an extensive plateau rising gradually from sea level to an elevation of almost 1,640 ft. The country's coast is not easily navigable since it is fringed with lagoons, sandbars, and swamps, with some cliffs and bays to the east. A canal, completed in 1950, links the country's major city, Abidjan, to the sea so that ocean-going ships can dock. The northern part of the country is largely savanna grasslands, with mountains to the northwest, while the center is dominated by heavy rain forests that support a rich array of wildlife. Most forest clearance has occurred in the central and south-central regions of the country.

Farming is the chief occupation of the Ivory Coast's workforce. While many people grow only enough to feed their families, much of the country's farming is conducted on a larger scale. The Ivory Coast is one of the world's top-five producers of cacao beans, used to make chocolate and cocoa. It is Africa's leading coffee producer and also grows cotton, palm oil, and rubber for export. Yamoussoukro, near the country's largest lake, Lac de Kossou, was declared the country's capital in 1983, but many government offices remain in Abidjan,

the country's major port, commercial center, and its most populous city. Compared to many of its west African neighbors, the Ivory Coast has had a stable political past. It became independent from France in 1960 and was ruled for 33 years by a single president, Félix Houphouet-Boigny. During the 1960s and 1970s the country's economy flourished with financial assistance from France. Expensive projects were undertaken, including the building of some of the world's largest churches and mosques. But in the 1980s the economy took a downturn. Today the Ivory Coast is struggling to repay giant foreign debts. Forty percent of its people are foreigners who were attracted to the country's former prosperity. Tensions between native and foreign-born people have led to much instability since 1999.

GHANA

Once the center of ancient empires, Ghana is one of the most developed countries in west Africa. Its economy is based mainly on agriculture and mining.

Area: 88,800 sq. mi.
Population: 20,244,154
Capital: Accra (1,925,000)
Main languages spoken: English, Akan, Moshi-Dagomba, Ewe, Ga
Main religions: indigenous beliefs, Islam, Christian
Currency: cedi
Main exports: gold, cocoa, food products, timber, electricity
Government: republic

▼ A traditional wooden boat, known as a pirogue, travels along the Volta river. The Volta river and lake system provide almost 10 percent of the country's annual fish catch of over 440,000 tons.

Ghana is a low-lying nation in west Africa. Half of its land lies below 93 ft., and its highest point, Mount Afadjato (2,886 ft.), is located in the eastern hills near the border with Togo. Much of the country's landscape is formed by the basin of the Volta rivers. The northern region is drained by the Black Volta and White Volta rivers, which join to form the Volta. This river is crossed by the Akosombo hydroelectric dam in the southeast of the country, which forms one of the world's largest artificial lakes, Lake Volta. Almost all of Ghana's electricity is generated via hydroelectric power. Ghana has a tropical climate, with daily temperatures tending to range between 70°F–90°F. There are two rainy seasons, from March to July and from September to October. Annual rainfall varies greatly throughout the country, ranging between 40 in. in the north to 82 in. in the southeast. In the north large areas are savannas, while a mixture of savannas and rain forests covers the center and south of the country. Much of the original vegetation has been cleared for farming and by the country's large timber industry. Ghana is one of Africa's leading timber exporters, and cocoa is its chief export crop. Ghana was a British colony until 1957 and was known as the Gold Coast. The country lives up to its former name, being the second-largest producer of gold in Africa, producing around 176,600 lbs. in 2002. It also has diamond, bauxite, and manganese mines. Ghanaians have suffered from political instability and corruption, with long periods of military rule.

NIGERIA

The most populous country in Africa, Nigeria is home to several hundred different ethnic groups. This large nation is rich in natural resources, especially oil.

Area: 351,700 sq. mi.
Population: 129,934,911
Capital: Abuja (420,000)
Main languages spoken: English, Hausa, Yoruba, Ibo
Main religions: Islam, Christian
Currency: naira
Main exports: crude petroleum (over 90 percent of exports), cocoa beans, rubber, textiles
Type of government: republic

Nigeria's coast consists of a number of long, sandy beaches broken up by mangrove swamps where rivers meet the sea. The Niger river, which enters the country in the northwest and flows through the western region of Nigeria, is the country's major river system. As the Niger heads toward the coast it fans out to form Africa's largest river delta, around 14,000 sq. mi. in area. High rainfall in the river valleys and along the coast enables a large range of crops to be grown. Along the river floodplains rice is a common crop. Along the coastal region, which extends up to 62 mi. inland, the land becomes hilly and largely covered in forests before rising to the Jos Plateau in the center of the country. North of this are savanna plains, which are the largest areas of farmland in the country. The savanna gets drier and becomes semidesert and desert in the far north.

AN OIL-DEPENDENT ECONOMY

Nigeria is rich in natural resources, including tin, iron ore, coal, limestone, zinc, and lead. Chief among its mineral reserves, however, are oil and natural gas. Nigeria is one of the world's leading crude oil producers, extracting approximately two million barrels per day. Oil accounts for over 90 percent of the

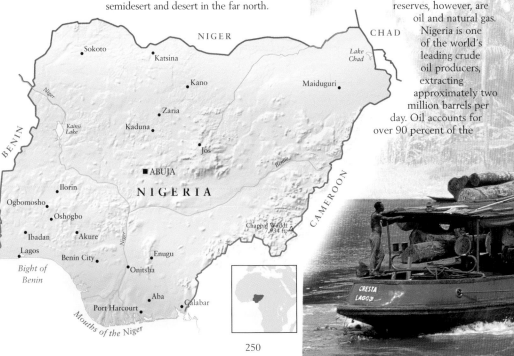

sorghum, millet, corn, yams, taro, and rice. The country's fast-growing population means that Nigeria has to import a large amount of its food.

MANY DIFFERENT PEOPLES

Nigeria has a long history, not just of settlement but also of empires and city-states—long before the region was colonized by European powers. Peoples such as the Hausa in the north, the Ibo (Igbo) in the southeast, and the Yoruba, based around the city of Ife in the southwest, had formed well-organized kingdoms centuries before European arrivals. The Hausa, Yoruba, and Ibo peoples make up over half of the country's population. The remainder belong to over 250 different ethnic groups that not only contribute to Nigeria's extremely rich culture and arts but also divide the country along both ethnic and language lines. In addition, there is a religious divide, with people in the north predominantly Muslim and those in the south mainly Christian or practicing traditional African beliefs. Keeping so many different peoples with different cultures and beliefs together in one single nation has proved difficult, especially since the divide between the Muslim north and the rest of the country is increasing. Since independence in 1960 Nigeria has had to contend with many conflicts within its borders, including a civil war (1967–1970) when the Ibo people tried to break away to form their own nation of Biafra. There have been more years of rule by military dictatorships than elected civilian governments, and the country maintains an uneasy peace to this day.

◄ Lagos is the most important city in Nigeria, with a fast-growing population rivaling Cairo, Egypt, for the title of Africa's largest city. The country's chief port, around half of the entire country's manufacturing industry is based in or around Lagos.

country's exports, but the wealth generated has only benefited very few because corruption is rampant. In addition, the reliance on a single commodity means that the economy is severely affected by changes in oil prices. In comparison to oil, Nigeria's natural gas and other mineral deposits are under exploited. Agriculture employs 70 percent of the country's workforce, and cocoa, rubber, and textiles are the chief exports. However, the large majority of farming is performed on small family farms growing staple foods, including

▼ A tugboat maneuvers a raft of logs along one of Nigeria's rivers. Logging is a major industry in Nigeria, with the majority of wood used by Nigerians as firewood.

BURKINA FASO

Burkina Faso is a landlocked country on the fringe of the Sahara. Severe droughts and desertification have increased the nation's difficulties.

Area: 274,122 km²
Population: 12,603,000
Capital: Ouagadougou (710,000)
Main languages spoken: Mossi, French, Fulani, Gurma
Main religions: Sunni Islam, traditional beliefs, Roman Catholic
Currency: CFA franc
Main exports: cotton, live animals, gold, hides and skins
Type of government: republic; limited democracy

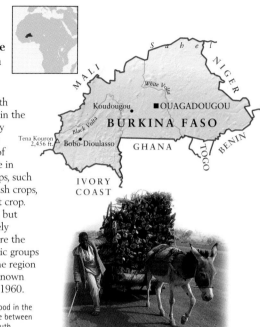

Most of Burkina Faso is flat, with some rolling hills and forests in the southwest. The north of the country is dry, and frequent droughts afflict most of the country. The majority of the population are farmers who live in the south and grow either food crops, such as rice, cereals, and vegetables, or cash crops, including cotton, the leading export crop. Goats, sheep, and cattle are herded, but livestock numbers have been severely decreased by droughts. The Mossi are the largest of Burkina Faso's many ethnic groups and were the traditional rulers of the region before it became a French colony, known as Upper Volta, between 1895 and 1960.

▶ A Burkinan man guides his cart carrying wood in the Sahel region. The Sahel is a dry transition zone between the Sahara and more lush grasslands in the south.

BENIN

Formerly known as Dahomey, Benin is a small west African nation that stretches north around 415 mi. from the Gulf of Guinea to the Niger river.

Area: 42,700 sq. mi.
Population: 6,787,625
Capitals: Porto-Novo (218,000)—official capital; Cotonou (750,000)—diplomatic and administrative capital
Main languages spoken: French, Fon, Yoruba
Main religions: indigenous beliefs, Islam, Christian
Currency: CFA franc
Main exports: cotton yarn, reexports of manufactures, petroleum
Type of government: republic

Benin's sandy, 75-mi.-long coastal strip is indented with lagoons and mangrove swamps. North of this region is a fertile plateau that contains large marshlands. The plateau gradually rises and is crossed in the center of the country by mountains. Benin's climate is tropical but with relatively low average rainfall, which is highest in the south. Desertification is a major problem in the northern region. The people are a mixture of different ethnic groups, with the Fon, the largest group, making up just under 40 percent. The people make their living mainly through subsistence farming. Rice, corn, cassava, millet, and yams are among the crops grown. In the north goat, sheep, and cattle herding is the major occupation. For more than six centuries the city of Abomey was the center of a prosperous kingdom before coming under French control. Independence was achieved in 1960, and in 1975 the country changed its name to Benin. The early years of independence saw a number of military coups, but multiparty elections were restored in the 1990s.

ZAMBIA

Zambia, formerly known as Northern Rhodesia, is one of Africa's most urbanized nations, with around 44 percent of people living in towns and cities.

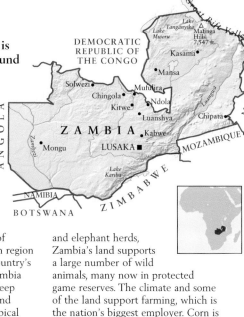

Area: 286,000 sq. mi.
Population: 9,959,037
Capital: Lusaka (982,000)
Main languages spoken: English, indigenous
Main religions: Christian, Hinduism, Islam
Currency: Zambian kwacha
Main exports: copper (over 70 percent of exports), cobalt
Type of government: republic

▼ The 420-ft.-high Kariba Dam on Zambia's border with Zimbabwe was completed in 1959. The 1,900-ft.-long dam is part of a giant hydroelectric power plant.

Zambia's northern border is divided by land belonging to the Democratic Republic of the Congo. The territory extends deep into the middle of Zambia, partly dividing the country into eastern and western sections. The eastern region is more sparsely populated. Running to the west and parallel to the Luangwa river are mountains that are the home of Zambia's highest hills. The western region of Zambia is where most of the country's population and industry reside. Zambia sits on a high plateau crossed by deep river valleys and occasional lakes and swampland. The country has a tropical climate with temperatures moderated owing to its relatively high altitude. The natural vegetation is mainly savanna grasslands with areas of forests. Despite poaching, which has slashed rhinoceros and elephant herds, Zambia's land supports a large number of wild animals, many now in protected game reserves. The climate and some of the land support farming, which is the nation's biggest employer. Corn is the most frequently grown staple food, while large amounts of cassava, sugarcane, wheat, and peanuts are also harvested.

THE ZAMBEZI, ENERGY, AND MINERALS

Winding its way from northwestern Zambia to the Indian Ocean, the Zambezi river forms much of the country's southern border. The river drops 354 ft. as it flows over one of the world's most famous waterfalls, the Mosi-oa-Tunya, or Victoria Falls, on Zambia's border with Zimbabwe. Then 298 mi. east of Victoria Falls the river flows into Lake Kariba, a giant artificial lake built to generate hydroelectric power and shared by Zambia and Zimbabwe. Zambia derives 99 percent of its electricity from hydroelectric power. Zambia has traditionally relied on just two products to generate exports: copper and cobalt. Giant reserves in the north of the country saw the formation of an urban and industrial mining region, known as the Copper Belt, in which minerals are mined and processed. However, several decades of falling copper prices on the world markets and lower levels of production have caused serious economic problems.

CAMEROON

A heavily forested country, with the majority of its people living in the south, Cameroon has developed its industry and infrastructure since independence in 1961.

Area: 181,300 sq. mi.
Population: 16,184,748
Capital: Yaoundé (1,481,000)
Main languages spoken: English, French, 24 African languages
Main religions: indigenous beliefs, Christian, Islam
Currency: CFA franc
Main exports: crude petroleum, timber, cocoa, coffee, aluminum, cotton
Type of government: republic

Cameroon is a country of varied landscapes. In the south there are coastal plains, small wetlands, and a plateau mainly covered in rain forests. In the north dry grasslands continue northward until they reach the southern shores of Lake Chad. Along the country's northern and western borders with Nigeria the land is mountainous and rises to an elevation of 13,432 ft.—the peak of the Cameroon mountain volcano Fako. The western slopes of this mountain are some of the wettest places in the world, with an average annual rainfall as high as 400 in. Cameroon's population is very diverse, with over 210 different ethnic groups and no one dominant people. A large range of crops is grown for food and export, and for many years the country has been self-sufficient in staple foods. Over 90 percent of its electricity is generated through hydroelectric power, of which almost half is used to power a giant aluminum plant. Oil, although declining, still provides valuable export revenue, while commercial fishing is on the rise.

CENTRAL AFRICAN REPUBLIC

Since independence in 1960 the landlocked and poor country of the Central African Republic has been largely governed by dictators and the military.

Area: 204,500 sq. mi.
Population: 3,642,739
Capital: Bangui (666,000)
Main languages spoken: French, Sangho, Arabic, Hunsa, Swahili
Main religions: Protestant, Roman Catholic, indigenous beliefs, Islam
Currency: CFA franc
Main exports: diamonds, coffee, timber and timber products, cotton
Type of government: republic

Most of the Central African Republic consists of a plateau that ranges in elevation between 1,968–2,624 ft. The plateau is flanked by highland areas to the northeast and hill ranges to the north. Dense rain forests cover much of the south of the country, some of which are in reserves to protect wildlife, including gorillas and leopards. The remainder of the land is grasslands with some trees. Less than four percent of the country is cultivated, and subsistence agriculture dominates the lives of the people. Deposits of uranium, iron, and copper exist, but mining focuses on diamonds, which comprise just over half of the country's exports.

▶ These Baaka pygmies in the rain forests of the Central African Republic make simple shelters from bent tree branches covered in bark and foliage.

EQUATORIAL GUINEA

The small country of Equatorial Guinea consists of the mainland, called Rio Muni, and five islands, the largest of which, Bioko, is the site of the country's capital.

Area: 10,800 sq. mi.
Population: 498,144
Capital: Malabo (33,000)
Main languages spoken:
Spanish, French, Fang, Bubi
Main religion: Roman Catholic
Currency: CFA franc
Main exports: petroleum products, timber, cocoa
Type of government: republic

Surrounded by Gabon and Cameroon, the small mainland region of Equatorial Guinea is a land of few extremes in height. Inland from the coastal plain and hill ranges over half of the land is heavily forested. The country's varied wildlife includes elephants, gorillas, leopards, crocodiles, and chimpanzees. However, many creatures are endangered as a result of extensive and uncontrolled logging operations. In contrast to the landscape of the mainland, Equatorial Guinea's largest island, Bioko, has a dramatic and rugged terrain. Of volcanic origin, the island contains a number of crater lakes and extinct volcanic cones, one of which, Pico Basilé, is the country's highest point at 9,866 ft. Bioko is the center of the country's cacao bean production, the country's main export crop. Coffee is grown for export on the mainland, while rice, yams, and bananas are among the key staple foods. The country became independent in 1968 after a long period of Spanish rule and remained largely undeveloped until the discovery of oil in the late 1980s. Oil production today is around 115,000 barrels per day, small by Arab nation standards but enough to comprise almost 80 percent of its exports and two thirds of its GDP.

SÃO TOMÉ & PRÍNCIPE

Lying off the coast of west Africa, the smallest country in Africa consists of one large island, São Tomé, one smaller island, Príncipe, and a small number of islets.

Príncipe • Santo António

Gulf of Guinea

SÃO TOMÉ & PRÍNCIPE

São Tomé

Pico de São Tomé △ ■ SÃO TOMÉ
6,638 ft.

ATLANTIC OCEAN

Area: 371 sq. mi.
Population: 170,372
Capital: São Tomé (67,000)
Main language spoken: Portuguese
Main religion: Roman Catholic
Currency: dobra
Main exports: cocoa (over 95 percent of exports)
Type of government: republic

Separated by 89 mi. of ocean, both islands were formed by volcanic activity and have high mountains in the south and west and lowland areas in the north. Lying on the equator, São Tomé & Príncipe has a warm, tropical climate, and dense forests cover around half of both islands. A former Portuguese colony, the people are mainly of African descent, with a minority of Portuguese origin.

The majority are Roman Catholics, although some are Protestant or practice traditional African beliefs. The country is dependent on cocoa exports to pay for food and fuel imports and is also reliant on foreign aid. However, oil exploration, tourism, and fishing offer hope for future economic development.

CHAD

A poor, landlocked nation in northern central Africa, Chad lies more than 992 mi. from the ocean, and its northern region is part of the Sahara desert.

LIBYA

Tibesti

△ Emi Koussi 11,201 ft.

Sahara

NIGER

CHAD

Sahel

Lake Chad

Abéché • **SUDAN**

CAMEROON

■ N'DJAMENA

Chari

Sarh •

• Moundou **CENTRAL AFRICAN REPUBLIC**

Area: 486,200 sq. mi.
Population: 8,997,237
Capital: N'Djamena (735,000)
Main languages spoken: French, Arabic, Sara, Songo
Main religions: Islam, Christian, indigenous beliefs
Currency: CFA franc
Main exports: cotton, live cattle, meat, animal hides
Type of government: republic

Chad's landscape is dominated by the large basin that surrounds Lake Chad. This lake varies in size, swelling from an area of less than 3,900 sq. mi. up to 9,750 sq. mi. during a heavy rainy season. Stretching away from the basin are plateaus that rise to mountains in the north, south, and east. Chad's climate is hot and extremely dry in the north, where the land is desert, while rainfall is relatively heavy in the south, where the majority of the country's people live. The south is mainly savanna and is the chief farming region of the country. Since independence from France Chad has been beset by internal conflicts and civil wars, which have prevented the country's development. Oil reserves have recently been discovered in the southwest, which may improve the country's outlook.

▼ Located 490 mi. northeast of N'Djamena, Faya is one of the largest oasis towns in the Sahara desert and relies on underground water to grow dates, wheat, and figs.

GABON

Containing some of Africa's largest original rain forests and an array of wildlife, Gabon is a sparsely populated nation whose people are fairly prosperous.

Area: 99,500 sq. mi.
Population: 1,223,353
Capital: Libreville (573,000)
Main languages spoken: French, Bantu dialects
Main religion: Christian
Currency: CFA franc
Main exports: petroleum and petroleum products (accounting for over 80 percent of exports), wood, manganese ore, uranium
Type of government: republic

Gabon consists of a coastal plain that rises inland to form a series of mountains, valleys, and plateaus mostly covered in untouched rain forests. Unlike many African countries, Gabon has not been troubled by conflicts since independence from France in 1960. Although many Gabonese live in poverty, the country is wealthy in comparison to much of Africa, largely owing to its oil revenues—the country produces 325,000 barrels per day. Gabon has large, unexploited reserves of metals, including iron ore and manganese.

CONGO

The Republic of the Congo is a tropical country that was Africa's first communist state from 1970 to 1991. More than half of the land is covered in rain forests.

Area: 131,900 sq. mi.
Population: 2,958,448
Capital: Brazzaville (1,360,000)
Main languages spoken: French, Lingala, Kikongo
Main religions: Christian, animist, Islam
Currency: CFA franc
Main exports: petroleum and petroleum products, wood and timber products
Type of government: republic

Much of the country's northern region is part of the Congo river basin. This river flows along the country's eastern frontier, where it forms most of the border with the Democratic Republic of the Congo. The northern region of the country is covered with swamps and dense forests, while there are grasslands to the south. Oil, first discovered in the 1970s and largely found offshore, is the country's key resource and is responsible for 90 percent of its export earnings. Other major industries are mining, timber, coffee, and cocoa. Most farmland is devoted to producing food for local consumption, with women traditionally the farmworkers.

Congo's transportation, energy, and communications are underdeveloped, and much of the country is isolated, using only dirt roads or the large river network for transportation. Two hydroelectric dams have been built with aid from China. A third is under construction.

DEMOCRATIC REP. OF THE CONGO

The Democratic Republic of the Congo, formerly Zaire, is Africa's third-largest country. Despite rich natural resources, its people are among Africa's poorest.

Area: 875,500 sq. mi.
Population: 55,225,478
Capital: Kinshasa (5,064,000)
Main language spoken: French
Main religions: Roman Catholic, Protestant, Islam, Kimbanguist
Currency: Congolese franc
Main exports: diamonds, crude petroleum, coffee, copper
Type of government: republic

▼ A small settlement in the Democratic Republic of the Congo's Ruwenzori mountains. This rugged mountain range straddles the country's border with its neighbor, Uganda.

The Democratic Republic of the Congo is almost landlocked except for a thin strip of land on the north bank of the Congo river, which gives the country a 23-mi.-long Atlantic coastline. The Congo's giant river basin dominates the country's landscape, covering an area of almost 400,000 sq. mi., and is largely covered in rain forests. The basin rises to form mountain plateaus in the west, while in the south there are grassland plains. The country's highest mountains are found in the east. Lying on the equator, the country has a tropical climate, with the hottest temperatures in the central region. The southern highlands are cooler and drier, while the eastern highlands are cooler and wetter. Over 60 percent of this large country is covered in rain forests that account for approximately half of Africa's forests and around six percent of the world total. The country's underdeveloped transportation network has prevented large-scale clearance by big logging businesses. However, deforestation is occurring in order to supply local people with firewood and farmland.

Most of the population farm the land, growing rice, cassava, peanuts, and fruit trees. The Democratic Republic of the Congo is extremely rich in natural resources and is one of the world's leading producers of copper, cobalt, and diamonds. Yet the wealth from these resources has been squandered through decades of colonial exploitation, civil wars, and corrupt governments.

UGANDA

Uganda is a land of fertile uplands and mountains that border Africa's largest lake. It is recovering after 25 years of ethnic conflicts under dictators.

Area: 77,100 sq. mi.
Population: 24,699,073
Capital: Kampala (1,274,000)
Main languages spoken: English, Luganda, Swahili
Main religions: Protestant, Roman Catholic, indigenous beliefs, Islam
Currency: Ugandan shilling
Main exports: coffee (almost 70 percent of exports), cotton, tea
Type of government: republic

Much of Uganda consists of a plateau that rises gently from an elevation of around 2,952 ft. in the north to 4,920 ft. in the south. Surrounding this elevated plateau are large valleys or mountainous areas on most sides. The western mountain range is the location of the country's highest peaks. Uganda is a land of abundant freshwater sources. Many rivers flow through the country, while almost one fifth of the country's area is made up of lakes. These include Lake Kyoga in the center of the country and Lake Albert, which lies in the Great Rift Valley to the west. Uganda has a long shoreline with Africa's largest lake, Lake Victoria. This country has an essentially tropical climate, but average temperatures are cooler owing to its relatively high altitude. Rainfall varies, with the wettest areas in the south receiving around 60 in. per year and the driest in the northeast receiving just over half that figure.

UGANDA'S RESOURCES

Compared to some of its neighbors, Uganda is not heavily forested. The country had around 2,535 sq. mi. of forests in 1960, but today this has been reduced by over one fourth. While clearing land for farming has contributed to deforestation, the major cause has been the use of trees to burn as fuel by Uganda's mainly rural population. Around 85 percent of the country's total energy consumption is provided by wood fuel. Almost all of Uganda's electricity is generated by hydroelectric power. Uganda is not an oil producer, nor does it have large mining or manufacturing industries. The cost of transporting goods to seaports in Kenya and Tanzania is high.

The country is blessed with fertile farmland, and Uganda's largely rural population grows a range of crops for domestic use and also for export. Coffee beans provide over 70 percent of the country's export income.

▼ This Ugandan fisherman hauls in a freshwater fish from the waters of Lake Victoria. Uganda has one of the largest freshwater fishing catches in the world, almost all of which is consumed within the country. In 2001 the total fish catch was over 218,000 tons.

RWANDA

Called the "land of 1,000 hills," Rwanda is heavily populated, with about 90 percent of its people living in rural areas and involved in farming.

Area: 9,600 sq. mi.
Population: 7,398,074
Capital: Kigali (412,000)
Main languages spoken:
French, Kinyarwanda, English
Main religions: Roman Catholic, indigenous beliefs
Currency: Rwandan franc
Main exports: coffee (accounts for over 70 percent of exports), tea, hides and skins
Type of government: republic

A centuries-old conflict between two major ethnic groups, the Hutu majority and the Tutsi minority, has dominated Rwanda since independence from Belgium in 1962. In 1994 violence led to the deaths of around 500,000 people, while around two million fled the country as refugees. The economy was devastated. Attempts have been made to reconcile the two peoples, but poverty and diseases are widespread, and Rwanda depends on foreign aid. It plans to develop natural gas reserves under Lake Kivu and to increase tourism in the northern forests—home to the world's largest population of mountain gorillas.

BURUNDI

A small, landlocked, and mountainous country just south of the equator, Burundi has been troubled by ethnic conflicts between the Tutsi and Hutu peoples.

Area: 9,900 sq. mi.
Population: 6,373,002
Capital: Bujumbura (346,000)
Main languages spoken: Kirundi, French, Swahili
Main religions: Roman Catholic, indigenous beliefs
Currency: Burundian franc
Main exports: coffee, tea, cotton, animal hides
Type of government: republic

Lush hills and low mountains cover much of Burundi, while a large plain that borders Lake Tanganyika rises to form a plateau in the south. On the lake's northern shore is the country's capital city and chief port, Bujumbura. The fertile hill slopes are heavily farmed, with coffee the most important cash crop followed by tea and cotton. Tropical fruits are grown in the country's valleys. Burundi is one of the most densely populated countries in Africa, with 644 people per square mile. Birth rates are high, and families tend to have many children. Although the Tutsi comprise just 14 percent of the population, they retain much political and military control of the country. This has led to conflicts with the majority Hutus, resulting in over 200,000 deaths and as many as one million refugees.

KENYA

After independence in 1963 Kenya successfully developed its economy, but recent political and economic troubles have afflicted the country.

Area: 219,800 sq. mi.
Population: 31,138,735
Capital: Nairobi (2,343,000)
Main languages spoken: Swahili, English, indigenous languages
Main religions: Protestant, Roman Catholic, indigenous beliefs
Currency: Kenyan shilling
Main exports: tea, coffee, fruit and vegetables, petroleum products, cement
Type of government: republic

Kenya's dramatic landscape is dominated by the Great Rift Valley, which cuts through the country from north to south. The valley, which in some places is over 1,968 ft. deep, varies in width from 8.7 mi. to over 52 mi. A number of lakes are found along this valley in Kenya, including Lake Rudolf, the country's largest. The Great Rift Valley divides Kenya into two areas that are unequal in area. A narrower western area consisting of plains and plateaus borders Uganda and the northeastern shore of Lake Victoria. The much larger eastern region begins with a large area of central highlands in which Kenya's loftiest peak, the 17,052-ft.-high Mount Kenya (Kirinyaga), is located. This extinct volcano is the second-highest mountain in Africa. The highlands slope down toward grassy plains before reaching the coast, which is lined with long beaches and is the home of Kenya's major port and second-largest city, Mombasa. The former British colony of Kenya has 55 national parks and reserves that help protect large numbers of its rich array of native wildlife. Although numbers have declined since the 1980s, Kenya still receives close to one million visitors each year, and tourism remains Kenya's single largest foreign income earner.

Around two thirds of Kenyans are mostly from three ethnic groups: the Kikuyu, Luhya, and Kamba. Many other minority groups exist, including Kenyan Asians and Kenyan Arabs, who, although small in number, tend to hold much commercial power. Most Kenyans are employed in agriculture, with herding livestock important in the drier regions, especially in the north. Although they tend to be on a small scale, Kenya also has some of the most developed industries in east Africa. These include the processing of foodstuffs, textiles, beer brewing, furniture, plastics, and building materials.

▲ A group of Masai warriors in the Masai Mara National Park, Kenya.

▼ The Samburu National Reserve is one of many large nature reserves in Kenya. Animals that roam the Samburu include elephants, lions, giraffes, zebras, and leopards.

TANZANIA

Tanzania is home to some of the most
spectacular features on Earth, including
Africa's highest mountain, Mount Kilimanjaro.

Area: 342,100 sq. mi.
Population: 37,187,939
Capitals: Dodoma
(180,000)—legislative
capital and capital
designate; Dar es
Salaam 2,347,000)—
administrative capital
Main languages spoken:
Swahili, English
Main religions: Christian,
Islam, traditional beliefs
Currency: Tanzanian
shilling
Main exports: coffee,
cotton, cashews, tobacco
Type of government:
republic

▼ Located in northeastern
Tanzania, Kilimanjaro
consists of three separate
extinct volcanic peaks:
Kibo, Mawensi, and Shira.
Kibo, the youngest and the
highest, has a crater
around 1.2 mi. in diameter.
Despite lying near the
equator, Kibo's 19,332-ft.-
high peak has a year-round
cap of snow and ice.

Tanzania's landscape
varies from a low,
flat coastal plain that is
heavily covered in tropical
vegetation to rugged, volcanic
mountaintops. Much of the
country, however, is located on
a plateau averaging 3,936 ft. in
elevation that is largely covered in savanna
grasslands and forests but is more arid in the
north. Isolated mountain groups rise in the
southwest and the northeast, while both
branches of the Great Rift Valley run
through the country. The eastern branch
divides the northeastern highlands and
contains a series of small lakes. The
western branch contains Lakes Nyasa
and Tanganyika and acts as a natural
border separating Tanzania from
nations to the west. A little over half
of Africa's largest lake, Lake Victoria,
lies in the north of the country. Offshore
from Tanzania's Indian Ocean coastline
lie a number of islands, including Pemba
and Zanzibar. Many of these islands merged
with the mainland of Tanganyika in 1964
to form Tanzania. Around one third of the
country is protected

as either national parks or
game reserves. These include
the world-renowned Serengeti
National Park, which contains over 200
species of birds and 35 species of land
animals, including cheetahs, lions, elephants,
and the extremely rare black rhinoceros.
Tourists who are drawn to the country's parks
and reserves and its spectacular geography
number almost 500,000 every year. Although
Tanzania has gold and diamond mines and
around 44 percent of the country is forested,
farming provides most of the country's
exports and employs almost 80 percent
of the workforce.

MALAWI

The landlocked country of Malawi contains most of the giant Lake Nyasa (Lake Malwai) within its territory. It is one of the least developed and poorest countries in Africa.

Area: 36,300 sq. mi.
Population: 10,701,824
Capital: Lilongwe (523,000)
Main languages spoken: English, Chichewa
Main religions: Protestant, Roman Catholic, Islam
Currency: Malawian kwacha
Main exports: tobacco (which accounts for over 60 percent of exports), tea, sugar, cotton
Type of government: multiparty democracy

▼ Malawian fishermen bring in their boats and catch. Almost all of Malawi's 56,500 tons of fish caught every year are found in the waters of Lake Nyasa.

Malawi is bordered by Zambia, Mozambique, and Tanzania. The Great Rift Valley runs along the eastern region of the country from north to south. Contained within the valley and occupying almost one third of Malawi's territory is Africa's third-largest lake, Lake Nyasa. Much of the country consists of highland plateaus and mountains. South of Lake Nyasa lies the Shire Highland—home to the country's highest peaks. The large majority of Malawi's people live in the countryside, where farming is the chief occupation. An almost completely agricultural nation, Malawians rely solely on their domestic food crops, and when droughts strike, they devastate the country. When adequate rainfall does occur, Malawi is Africa's second-largest producer of tobacco behind only Zimbabwe. Other major exports include tea, sugar, and peanuts, while corn, sorghum, and a wide range of fruit and vegetables are grown for local food.

The country also has a growing fishing industry based on the shores of Lake Nyasa, which catches 56,500 tons of fish per year. Malawi has few industries beyond small local companies and few mineral resources. Over 90 percent of its electricity is generated via hydroelectric power programs. Malawi was formerly known as Nyasaland when it was ruled as a British colony between 1891 and 1964. Unlike some other countries in the region, Malawi has not been beset by serious conflicts between different ethnic or religious groups. Its people come from many different tribal groups, and around 55 percent are Protestants, 20 percent Roman Catholics, and 20 percent Muslims, with three percent following traditional African beliefs. High population growth has been curbed by the rise of AIDS, which, along with poverty and limited health care, has seen the average life expectancy drop to only 37 years of age. Forty-four percent of the country's population are under the age of 15.

ANGOLA

Rich in oil and diamonds, Angola suffered an almost continual civil war from its independence from Portugal in 1975 until 2002.

Area: 481,400 sq. mi.
Population: 10,593,171
Capital: Luanda (2,819,000)
Main languages spoken: Portuguese, Bantu and tribal languages
Main religions: traditional beliefs, Roman Catholic, Protestant
Currency: readjusted kwanza
Main exports: petroleum, diamonds
Type of government: republic

▼ The Benguela railroad is a vital transportation link connecting Angola to both the Democratic Republic of the Congo and Zimbabwe. It is currently undergoing renovation after being seriously damaged during the long civil war.

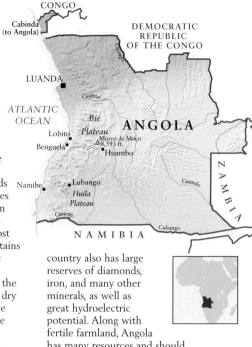

Angola's landscape is diverse. The land stretches from a coastal plain that varies in width from 15.5 mi. in the south to between 62–124 mi. in the north. Inland from the plain the land rises toward mountains and a plateau that covers almost two thirds of the country. The plateau undulates and varies in average height between 3,936–5,248 ft. Angola has no large lakes but does have many rivers, most of which begin in the central mountains and either flow west to the Atlantic Ocean or north. Angola's climate is essentially tropical but fairly dry. In the southwest the country is extremely dry and desertlike. Close to the coast the climate is more temperate, while the northern half of the central plateau is tropical and receives a little more rainfall. Large rain forests cover the northern part of the country, while grasslands are found in the central and south-central regions. Angola has large oil deposits, particularly offshore near the enclave of Cabinda, producing around 730,000 barrels per day. The country also has large reserves of diamonds, iron, and many other minerals, as well as great hydroelectric potential. Along with fertile farmland, Angola has many resources and should be relatively prosperous, but a civil war between two major groups, UNITA and the MPLA, was fought for many years. The result was a shattered economy with mines, industries, and transportation links destroyed and as many as ten million unexploded land mines left across its land.

BOTSWANA

Landlocked and dry, much of Botswana's territory is part of the red soil, sand, and scrubland of the vast Kalahari Desert.

Area: 226,000 sq. mi.
Population: 1,591,232
Capital: Gaborone (225,000)
Main languages spoken: English, Setswana
Main religions: indigenous beliefs, Christian
Currency: pula
Main exports: diamonds, copper, nickel, textiles
Type of government: parliamentary republic

Botswana's land is largely a broad, flat plateau with some hills in the east. In the northwest the Okavango river empties inland, creating the largest inland river delta in the world. The swamplands and floodplains of the Okavango Delta are a haven for wildlife, particularly birds. Farming is the main occupation, although water is often scarce. In 1967, one year after independence from Great Britain, enormous diamond reserves were discovered. Botswana is now the world's third-largest producer of diamonds and also has huge reserves of coal, copper, and nickel. The Tswana people make up over 95 percent of the country's population. Around 60,000 San people live a nomadic life in the Kalahari, hunting and gathering, as well as tending small herds of livestock. Despite much economic growth, the country's people are poor and beset by diseases, particularly AIDS. An estimated 40 percent of all Botswana's adults are believed to be HIV positive, the highest rate in the world.

NAMIBIA

Lying on the southwestern coast of Africa, sparsely populated but mineral-rich Namibia gained independence from South Africa in 1990.

Area: 317,900 sq. mi.
Population: 1,820,916
Capital: Windhoek (216,000)
Main languages spoken: Afrikaans, English, German, indigenous languages
Main religions: Lutheran, Christian
Currency: Namibian dollar
Main exports: diamonds, fish and fish products, copper, lead
Type of government: republic

Namibia consists of a central plateau region that occupies around half of the country, with an elevation of between 3,812–6,560 ft. Deserts lie on both sides of this plateau—to the east the Kalahari Desert extends into the country, while the whole western coast is occupied by the Namib Desert. Namibia's climate is hot and dry, and only the central plateau supports a large amount of vegetation. Despite the hostile environment, Namibia has much wildlife, some of which is protected in reserves. Eighty percent of the population are black Africans, with around six percent white.

▲ The Namib Desert is a dry, largely barren region where temperatures can reach 120°F.

ZIMBABWE

As a British colony the landlocked nation of
Zimbabwe was known as Southern Rhodesia
and, between 1965 and 1980, as Rhodesia.

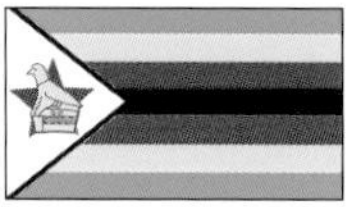

Area: 149,300 sq. mi.
Population: 11,376,676
Capital: Harare
(1,868,000)
Main languages spoken:
English, Shona, Sindebele
Main religions: Syncretic
Christian, indigenous
beliefs
Currency: Zimbabwean
dollar
Main exports: gold,
iron alloys, nickel,
cotton, asbestos,
tobacco, cut flowers
Type of government:
republic

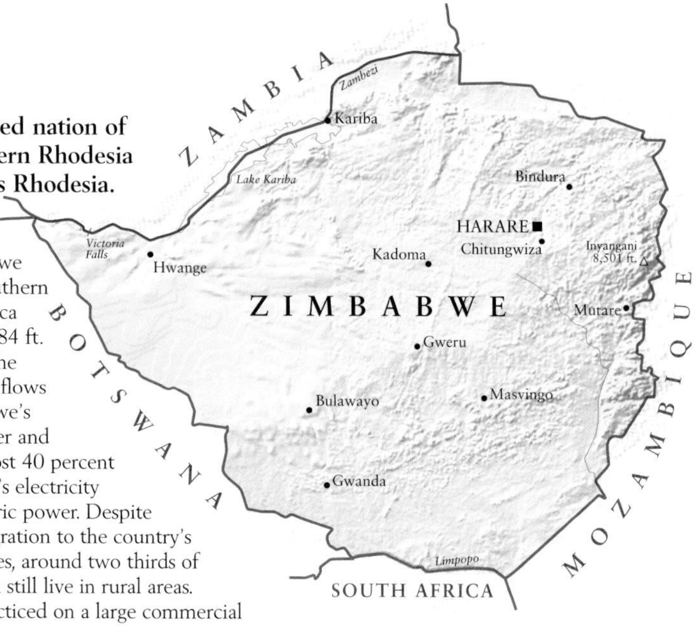

▼ Straddling the
border between Zimbabwe
and Zambia, Victoria Falls
(Mosi-oa-Tunya) is around
twice as high and twice
as wide as Niagara Falls
in North America.

Most of
Zimbabwe
lies on the Southern
Plateau of Africa
and is above 984 ft.
in elevation. The
Zambezi river flows
along Zimbabwe's
northern border and
generates almost 40 percent
of the country's electricity
via hydroelectric power. Despite
large-scale migration to the country's
towns and cities, around two thirds of
the population still live in rural areas.
Farming is practiced on a large commercial
scale, with tobacco the leading export crop.
Cotton growing and cattle raising are also
conducted on a large scale. In contrast
many Zimbabweans work their own
small farms, growing just enough to feed
their families. Huge mineral reserves exist
in Zimbabwe, including gold, nickel, and
asbestos. Zimbabwe also has one of the
widest ranges of industries in Africa—
from steel, chemicals, and cement to motor
vehicles, footwear, and textiles. Ruled by an
increasingly oppressive
government, Zimbabwe
has attracted international
criticism for human rights
abuses. Redistribution of
land and wealth from the
rich white minority to the
poorer black majority has occurred, sometimes
using force, but many black Zimbabweans are
still poor. Around one fourth of the population
are believed to be HIV positive.

MOZAMBIQUE

Mozambique is a large, ethnically diverse nation that is trying to rebuild after a long civil war and devastating droughts and floods.

Area: 302,700 sq. mi.
Population: 19,607,519
Capital: Maputo (1,134,000)
Main languages spoken: Portuguese, indigenous dialects
Main religions: indigenous beliefs, Christian, Islam
Currency: metical
Main exports: shrimp, cotton, cashews, sugar, copra
Type of government: republic

Two fifths of Mozambique's land is coastal lowlands that end in a 1,531-mi.-long shoreline with the Indian Ocean. Farther inland the land rises to a series of hill ranges, with mountains in the west and north. Mozambique has a tropical climate, but most of its soil is poor. Despite this, most of its people work as farmers growing corn and cassava for themselves or working on plantations growing coconuts, cashews, cotton, or sugarcane. The country's fishing industry is vital, with shrimp the most important export. Mining is underdeveloped, and the country is seeking investment to tap its large reserves of copper, iron, uranium, coal, and natural gas. Following independence from Portugal in 1975 a violent civil war erupted. Mozambique has struggled to rebuild after the war ended in the early 1990s.

Apart from the legacy of destroyed towns, transportation systems, and industries, there are between two and three million unexploded land mines. Clearing land of these weapons has been a slow process. In addition, the country has suffered from floods and droughts that have killed thousands of people, while diseases, especially AIDS, are common.

▲ Zebras are one of a number of large mammals that live within Mozambique's borders. A total of 15,600 sq. mi. of the country are part of the Greater Limpopo Transfrontier Park, which also extends into South Africa and Zimbabwe.

▶ A large cooking pot made from an oil drum is stirred at a Mozambique orphanage. Civil war, diseases including AIDS, and land mines have created approximately 1.2 million orphans in the country—one in six of all the country's children.

SOUTH AFRICA

South Africa occupies the southernmost part of Africa. A multiethnic society and a country of great mineral wealth, it has the largest economy in Africa.

Area: 471,400 sq. mi.
Population: 43,647,658
Capitals: Pretoria (1,590,000)—administrative capital; Cape Town (2,993,000)—legislative capital
Main languages spoken: English, Afrikaans, Ndebele, Pedi, Sotho
Main religions: Christian, traditional beliefs
Currency: rand
Main exports: gold, base metals, diamonds, food (particularly fruit and wine)
Type of government: republic

South Africa borders six nations, including Lesotho, which it completely surrounds, and is the only nation with both Atlantic and Indian ocean coastlines. Fishing in the coastal waters brings in over 500,000 tons of fish every year. The lands close to the coast are low-lying, fertile plains that tend to occupy a relatively narrow strip between 18.2–62 mi. in width. The coastal plains give way to a mountainous region, known as the Great Escarpment, that separates the coast from the high inland plateau on which most of the country is situated. The Drakensberg Mountains are the highest part of the Great Escarpment and run in an arc inland from the Indian Ocean coast.

THE VELDS AND WILDLIFE

Most of the plateau region of South Africa is called the Highveld and consists of rolling grasslands mostly above 4,920 ft. in elevation. The western portion of the plateau is known as the Middle Veld. Lying at an average elevation of 3,018 ft., the land there is dry and mostly used for herding

▲ A gold miner at work drilling in Savuka gold mine, approximately 50 mi. southwest of Johannesburg. Savuka, along with its sister mine, Mponeng, are among the deepest gold mines in the world at over 11,480 ft. in depth.

livestock. The Middle Veld merges with the Namib and Kalahari deserts to the west and northwest. To the northeast the High Veld descends into a large lowland area called the Bushveld that consists mainly of savanna grasslands and scattered trees. South Africa has highly varied wildlife, with over 200 species of mammals, including elephants, hippotamuses, zebras, and lions. Hunting has slashed herd numbers, but many

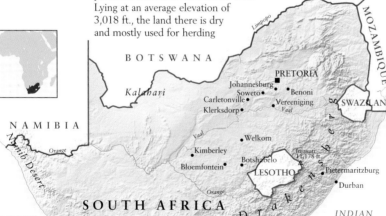

of these creatures are now protected in the country's 30 national parks and game reserves. In addition, South Africa is incredibly rich in flowering plants, with over 20,000 different species.

CLIMATE

South Africa lies in the temperate zone, but its climate varies greatly throughout the country. The highest temperature recorded was 125°F in the Kalahari Desert. Sutherland, 167 mi. northeast of Cape Town, regularly sees winter temperatures drop to 5°F. Elevation, wind, and ocean currents influence the regional differences in climate. For example, the cold Benguela Current, which flows northward along the west coast, cools temperatures and also reduces rainfall levels. South Africa is a semiarid country, and around half the land receives between 8–24 in. of rainfall per year, while a further one fourth receives less than eight inches. Rainfall levels tend to increase from west to east, with the eastern coast benefiting from the warm Mozambique Current, which raises temperature and rainfall levels.

WATER AND AGRICULTURE

South Africa has no large lakes and only a small number of major rivers. These include the Vaal and the Limpopo, which flow in the north and form much of the country's border with Botswana and Zimbabwe. South Africa's longest river is the

Orange, which travels around 1,296 mi. from Lesotho west through the Highveld before forming all of South Africa's border with Namibia and flowing into the Atlantic Ocean. With water at a premium, South Africa relies on large irrigation systems to water cropland. Despite only a small percentage of the land being suitable for crop growing, South Africa is usually self-sufficient in many crops, including cereals, vegetables, and sugarcane. The country is renowned for its high-quality fruit crops, including grapes, which form the basis of a large and profitable wine industry.

▲ Native bushmen in the Kgalagadi Transfrontier Park study animal tracks. This protected reserve has a huge area of 14,040 sq. mi.

▼ The rugged and spectacular Drakensberg Mountains are found in the Royal Natal National Park. Peaks in this mountain chain exceed 9,840 ft. in places.

▲ Founded in 1886 as a gold-mining town, Johannesburg has grown into South Africa's largest urban area with a population of 2.95 million.

▲ This family lives in Nyanga township close to the city of Cape Town. Township dwellers often have to contend with cramped living conditions, poor sanitation and water supplies, and high unemployment.

INDUSTRY

South Africa is the most industrially powerful country in the African continent. Cape Town, Johannesburg, Port Elizabeth, and Durban are large industrial centers producing a large range of goods—from chemicals, textiles, and paper to motor vehicles, electronic goods, and weapons. Much of South Africa's development has stemmed from huge reserves of valuable minerals that lie within its borders. Despite a decline in gold production, South Africa remains the world's biggest producer. It is also a world leader in platinum, manganese, chrome, and diamond production. The country has no major oil deposits but has huge reserves of coal. This is burned to generate most of the country's electricity. A huge challenge facing the country's government is how to provide electricity to the 80 percent of black South African homes that currently are not on the national electricity program.

THE "RAINBOW NATION"

South Africa is a multiracial nation in which there are 11 officially recognized languages, with many more spoken. Approximately three fourths of the population belong to one of nine black African ethnic groups. The Zulu people are the largest group, comprising around 21 percent of the country's total population. The next largest are the Xhosa, followed by the Tswana,

▼ Cape Town is the law-making capital of South Africa and one of its major ports and commercial centers. A fast-growing city, it is overlooked by the majestic Table Mountain.

Sotho, Venda, Tsonga, Ndebele, Swazi, and Pedi peoples. Around 12 percent of South Africa's people are white and are divided into two principal groups. Afrikaners, or Boers, are descendants of Dutch and sometimes German or French settlers. They speak Afrikaans and make up around 60 percent of the white population. Most of the remainder speak English and are of British origin. One in ten of South Africa's people has a mixed ethnic background, and three percent are of Asian, mainly

classified by race. Apartheid kept people of different racial groups apart on public transportation, in schools, jobs, and in most walks of life. Many black people were forced to live in townships outside of major cities or in "homelands" in rural areas. In these areas the growing land, schools, and facilities were often much worse than in white-only areas. Condemnation of South Africa's racist apartheid policy occurred around the world and was followed by trade sanctions and boycotts that prevented the country from taking part in many sports and cultural events. Apartheid's grip was finally loosened in the late 1980s and early 1990s, and in 1994 elections involving all people, regardless of race or color, occurred, returning a black president, Nelson Mandela, for the first time. Since then governments have tried to create a peaceful path to a multiracial society but with great difficulties. Large inequalities in education, income, and living conditions between many blacks and whites remain, and violent crime, especially in the cities, is among the highest in the world.

▲ Workers harvest grapes in the Nuy Valley vineyards in the Western Cape. South Africa is one of the world's leading wine producers. Approximately 260 million gallons are produced each year. The wine industry employs over 300,000 people.

Indian, descent. Over half of South Africans live in cities, and nine in ten live in the eastern half of the country or along the southern coast. Apart from the area around Cape Town, the west is very sparsely populated.

APARTHEID AND RECONCILIATION

South Africa's black population had been oppressed for decades before the government policy of apartheid was introduced in 1948. Meaning "apartness," apartheid was a country-wide policy, in place until the 1990s, designed to protect the interests of a white minority. Under apartheid people were

SWAZILAND

Landlocked between South Africa and Mozambique, Swaziland's traditional society and customs are in contrast to its more modern industries.

Area: 6,600 sq. mi.
Population: 1,23,605
Capitals: Mbabane (80,000)—administrative capital; Lobamba (6,000)—royal and legislative capital
Main languages spoken: Swazi, English
Main religions: Christian, indigenous beliefs
Currency: lilangeni
Main exports: wood and wood products, sugar
Type of government: constitutional monarchy

Swaziland is divided into three regions: the mountainous high veld in the west, the grassy middle veld in the center, and the low bushveld in the east. The high veld is humid and temperate, with warm, wet summers and cold, dry winters. Originally largely treeless, there are now large plantations of pine and eucalyptus trees—part of the country's extensive forestry industry. The middle veld has a subtropical climate with the most fertile soil. The majority of the population live in this region. Many herd cattle or grow corn or work on large plantations growing sugarcane and other crops. The low veld is dry and hot in the summer and receives less rainfall than other regions. To the far east mountains run along the border with Mozambique. Forestry, the mining of coal, gold, and diamonds, and manufacturing industries are major sources of work for the country's people, 95 percent of whom belong to the Swazi ethnic group. The people retain many of their ancient traditions and customs and are governed by an hereditary monarchy. Despite pressures for reform, political parties remain banned.

LESOTHO

Lesotho is surrounded by South Africa, from which it gained independence in 1966. Its people are mainly farmers and are reliant on South Africa for trade.

Area: 11,700 sq. mi.
Population: 2,207,954
Capital: Maseru (271,000)
Main languages spoken: English, Sesotho
Main religions: Christian, indigenous beliefs
Currency: maluti
Main exports: clothing, furniture, footwear, food, live animals, wool
Type of government: modified constitutional monarchy

▶ Like most of her country's population, this Lesotho woman makes a living from raising small herds of livestock and subsistence crop growing.

Known as the "roof of Africa," Lesotho is a mountainous land. Its lowest point is around 4,526 ft. in elevation, rising to almost 11,480 ft. in the mountains to the east. Rolling lowlands mainly in the west are the main agricultural areas. Corn, wheat, root vegetables, beans, and peas are grown, while more land is used as grazing pastures for cattle, sheep, and goats. Unrestricted grazing has caused much soil erosion. Apart from some diamond mining, the country has few mineral resources. Lesotho's rugged landscape does, however, allow it to generate all the electricity it needs from hydroelectric power. Large quantities of electricity are exported to South Africa. Lesotho has few industries, and many male adults move to South Africa to find work in mines and other industries. Its people are poor; 49 percent of the population are believed to live below the poverty line.

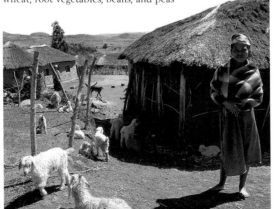

OCEANIA &
ANTARCTICA

OCEANIA

Oceania is a vast region of scattered islands lying across most of the Pacific Ocean. Covering approximately one third of the entire planet's surface, the Pacific occupies a total area of over 64 million sq. mi. The continent of Oceania has a land area of just over three million sq. mi. and consists of the continental landmass of Australia, larger islands including New Zealand's North and South islands, New Guinea and Tasmania, and more than 20,000 smaller islands. This latter group, often referred to as the Pacific islands, are often clustered in groups and separated by vast stretches of ocean. Most of the smaller islands have been created through coral formation or volcanic activity. Many of Oceania's islands lie on or near the edges of the Pacific tectonic plate, which is also the location of many of the world's volcanoes. The Pacific islands of Oceania are often divided into three distinct groups. Polynesia is the most easterly and consists of a huge, roughly triangular expanse of the Pacific, extending north of Hawaii, south of New Zealand, and eastward past Easter Island. Micronesia is the region west of Polynesia and closest to Southeast Asia, while Melanesia is considered the region containing New Guinea, Fiji, the Solomon Islands, Vanuatu, and a small number of other island groups. While aborigines reached Australia over 50,000 years ago and New Guinea has a long history of settlement, other parts of Oceania were the last places in the world to be settled by people.

In waves of migrations, which are estimated to have started between 6,000 and 7,000 years ago, different peoples from Southeast Asia reached the most westerly and northerly islands. Long voyages made in simple vessels saw peoples travel across much of the Pacific, reaching the most outlying islands between 2,000 and 1,000 years ago. Today Oceania's people number fewer than 32 million—less than half a percent of the total world population. Over half of the continent's people are found in Australia, a giant landmass and the most developed and economically powerful nation in the continent. In contrast neighboring Papua New Guinea and many of the smaller island nations are among the least developed countries in the world. The majority of the population of these countries are reliant on fishing and forms of agriculture that have not altered much for many centuries.

▲ The scattered Pacific islands of Oceania tend to experience tropical or subtropical climates with heavy rainfall. Many of the islands are covered in lush vegetation, including palm trees.

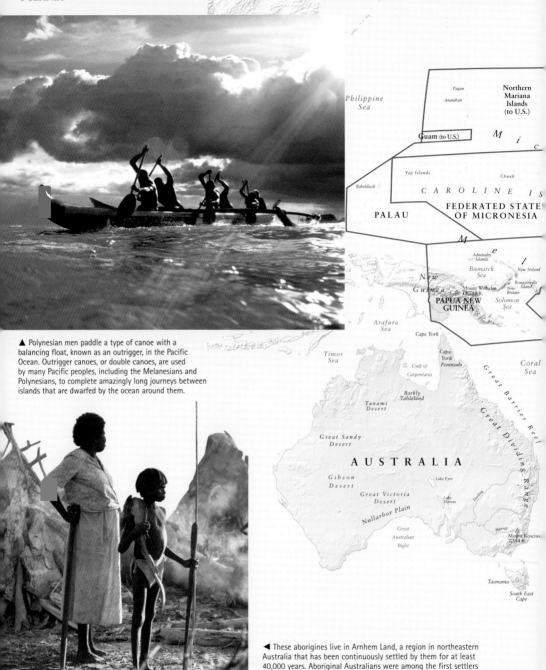

▲ Polynesian men paddle a type of canoe with a balancing float, known as an outrigger, in the Pacific Ocean. Outrigger canoes, or double canoes, are used by many Pacific peoples, including the Melanesians and Polynesians, to complete amazingly long journeys between islands that are dwarfed by the ocean around them.

Northern Mariana Islands (to U.S.)

Philippine Sea

Pagan

Anatahan

Guam (to U.S.)   M   i   c

Yap Islands   Chuuk

Babeldaob

PALAU

CAROLINE   IS

FEDERATED STATES OF MICRONESIA

M   e   l

Admiralty Islands

Bismarck Sea

New Ireland

New Guinea   Mount Wilhelm △ 14,789 ft.   Bougainville Island   New Britain

PAPUA NEW GUINEA   Solomon Sea

Arafura Sea

Cape York

Timor Sea   Cape York Peninsula   *Coral Sea*

Gulf of Carpentaria

Barkly Tableland

Tanami Desert

Great Barrier Reef

Great Sandy Desert

AUSTRALIA

Gibson Desert   Lake Eyre

Great Victoria Desert   Lake Torrens   Darling

Great Dividing Range

Nullarbor Plain

Great Australian Bight   Murray   Mount Kosciusko △ 7,314 ft.

Tasmania

South East Cape

◄ These aborigines live in Arnhem Land, a region in northeastern Australia that has been continuously settled by them for at least 40,000 years. Aboriginal Australians were among the first settlers in Oceania and are believed to have reached Australia at least 50,000—and possibly even 70,000—years ago.

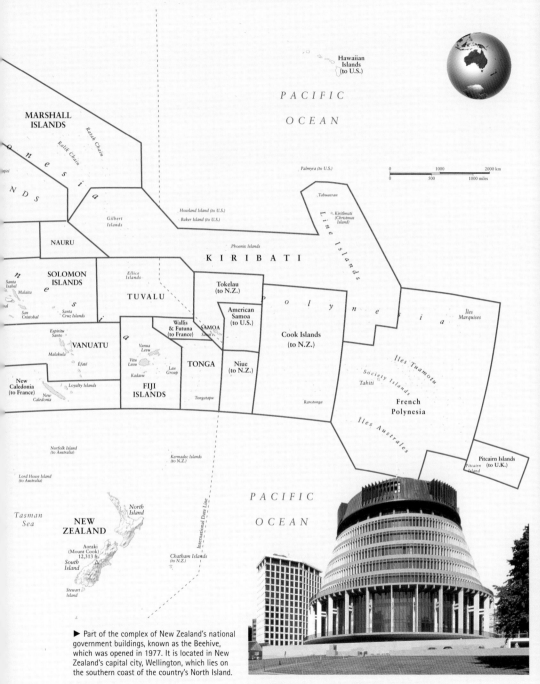

PACIFIC

OCEAN

Hawaiian
Islands
(to U.S.)

MARSHALL
ISLANDS

Ratak Chain

Ralik Chain

o n e s i a

Palmyra (to U.S.)

N D S

N A U R U

Gilbert
Islands

Tabuaeran

Kiritimati
(Christmas
Island)

Line Islands

Howland Island (to U.S.)

Baker Island (to U.S.)

K I R I B A T I

Phoenix Islands

SOLOMON
ISLANDS

Santa
Isabel

Malaita

Ellice
Islands

Tokelau
(to N.Z.)

P o l y n e s i a

Iles
Marquises

San
Cristobal

TUVALU

Santa
Cruz Islands

American
Samoa
(to U.S.)

Espiritu
Santo

VANUATU

Wallis
& Futuna
(to France)

SAMOA
Savai'i

Cook Islands
(to N.Z.)

Iles Tuamotu

Malakula

Vanua
Levu

Efaté

Vitu
Levu

Lau
Group

Society Islands

Tahiti

New
Caledonia
(to France)

Loyalty Islands

Kadavu

FIJI
ISLANDS

TONGA

Niue
(to N.Z.)

Rarotonga

French
Polynesia

New
Caledonia

Tongatapu

Iles Australes

Norfolk Island
(to Australia)

Kermadec Islands
(to N.Z.)

Pitcairn Islands
(to U.K.)

Pitcairn
Island

Lord Howe Island
(to Australia)

PACIFIC

OCEAN

Tasman
Sea

North
Island

NEW
ZEALAND

International Date Line

Aoraki
(Mount Cook)
12,313 ft.

South
Island

Chatham Islands
(to N.Z.)

Stewart
Island

1000   2000 km

500   1000 miles

► Part of the complex of New Zealand's national
government buildings, known as the Beehive,
which was opened in 1977. It is located in New
Zealand's capital city, Wellington, which lies on
the southern coast of the country's North Island.

277

PAPUA NEW GUINEA

A land of rich resources and traditional cultures, Papua New Guinea occupies half of the island of New Guinea, as well as numerous other smaller islands in the Pacific.

Area: 174,400 sq. mi.
Population: 5,171,033
Capital: Port Moresby (259,000)
Main languages spoken: English, Motu, over 700 other languages
Main religions: indigenous beliefs, Roman Catholic, Lutheran
Currency: kina
Main exports: petroleum, gold, copper, timber, coffee, cocoa, crayfish and shrimp
Type of government: parliamentary democracy

Papua New Guinea consists of over 600 islands. These include New Britain, its second-largest landmass, and the archipelago of islands located in the Bismarck Sea. Four fifths of its land area are made up of the eastern half of New Guinea. From a low-lying, often swampy coastline the land of New Guinea rises to rugged mountains. Although some of the country's smaller islands are formed from coral, many are of volcanic origin and feature mountainous interiors. Papua New Guinea's varied landscape provides habitats for large numbers of plants and animals. Recent surveys show that around five percent of the world's living species are found within its borders. Located just south of the equator, Papua New Guinea's climate is tropical, with its rainy season occurring between December and March.

▲ A Papua New Guinean tribesman paints his face in traditional decorations. Many highland tribes and groups were not discovered until the mid- to late 1900s and have lived in ways largely unchanged for thousands of years.

Ninigo Islands

Mussau

Manus Island

New Hanover

Bismarck Sea

PACIFIC OCEAN

Wewak

Sepik

Rabaul
Kokopo

New Ireland

Madang

Moint Wilhelm
14,789 ft.

Central Ra.

Mount Hagen
Goroka

New Britain

Arawa

INDONSESIA

New Guinea

Lake Murray

Lae

P A P U A
N E W
G U I N E A

Solomon Sea

Bougainville Island

Fly

Gulf of Papua

Trobriand

Woodlark Island

PORT MORESBY

Ra___

Fergusson Island

Alotau

Normanby Island

Coral Sea

Tagula

RICH IN RESOURCES

Over 80 percent of Papua New Guinea is covered in dense tropical rain forests, although this is declining owing to large-scale logging. One third of its forests is open to timber companies, and forestry is a major industry. This is eclipsed in importance, however, by the mining sector. Papua New Guinea is rich in many minerals, including copper, gold, silver, nickel, and cobalt, while oil and natural gas reserves are also exploited. The mining sector makes the largest contribution to the country's economy. Eighty-five percent of the workforce are subsistence farmers, despite less than two percent of the land being suitable for crops. Larger farms grow coffee and other export crops.

PEOPLE AND LANGUAGE

Settled for around 50,000 years, the geography of the country has acted as a barrier to movement, isolating many different groups of people who have developed their own languages and cultures. As a result, Papua New Guinea has one of the most culturally varied populations on Earth, with over 700 languages spoken. A distinction is often made between those people who live in lowland areas near the coasts and tend to have frequent contact with other groups and the more isolated highlanders. Although most of the population are Christians, traditional beliefs and customs are still widely practiced. Since independence in 1975 some of these ethnic groups have pressed for further change and to break away from the country.

▲ A highland area near Goroka, close to the highest point on Papua New Guinea, Mount Wilhelm. The highland areas are cooler than on the coast, where temperatures rise to 90°F or higher in the summer.

▼ Port Moresby, the capital of Papua New Guinea, is the manufacturing center of the country, with food processing the main industry.

AUSTRALIA

Australia's vast, arid interior is sparsely populated. But its rich mineral resources and highly developed agricultural base have made it a prosperous nation.

Area: 2,941,300 sq. mi.
Population: 19,546,792
Capital: Canberra (387,000)
Main languages spoken: English, aboriginal languages
Main religions: Anglican, Roman Catholic, other Christian
Currency: Australian dollar
Principal exports: food (particularly cereals and cereal preparations and meat and meat preparations), live animals, metallic ores, mineral fuels and lubricants (particularly coal and petroleum), basic manufactures
Type of government: democratic federal state system

▼ Sydney Harbor Bridge and Sydney Opera House are world-famous symbols of Australia's prosperity. The bridge was opened in 1932, and its total length is 3,769 ft., with a single arch span of 1,650 ft. It carries eight vehicle lanes, two railroad lines, a footpath, and a bicycle lane. The more modern opera house was completed in 1973, and its unique concrete roofs were designed by the Finnish architect Ove Arup.

Situated between the Indian and South Pacific oceans, Australia includes in its territory the large island of Tasmania and many other islands dotted along its 15,971-mi.-long coastline. Considered a continental landmass rather than an island, Australia has been geologically stable for over 300 million years, with few earthquakes, volcanoes, or upthrusts of land to create mountains. As a result, erosion by wind and water has created large, flat plains. Under seven percent of its huge area is above 1,968 ft. in elevation. Much of Australia is extremely dry; two thirds of the country are deserts or semideserts. Situated in the east of the country, the Great Dividing Range runs roughly north to south and separates the eastern coastline from the dry interior of Australia, known as the outback. Most of the population live in cities and towns along this eastern coast, including the country's largest and most cosmopolitan city, Sydney. Other major cities include Brisbane, Melbourne, Perth, Adelaide, and Canberra, the country's capital. Separating from other continental landmasses around 65 million years ago, Australia's isolation from the rest of the world has meant that many creatures have evolved there that are not found elsewhere. Most famous are

▲ Also known by its aboriginal name of Uluru, Ayers Rock is the world's largest monolith. Located in the Uluru-Kata Tjuta National Park, it rises 1,141 ft. above the desert floor and has a circumference of 5 mi.

creatures such as the kangaroo, koala, and duck-billed platypus. Australia's first human inhabitants arrived at least 40,000 years ago. The aborigines settled throughout much of Australia. They lived off the land and developed a rich culture before the arrival of European settlers in the 1700s onward. Today aborigines make up less than two percent of Australia's population, most of whom are of European descent.

AUSTRALIA

Cape York

Melville Island *Arafura Sea*

PACIFIC OCEAN

Cape York Peninsula

Joseph Bonaparte Gulf *Arnhem Land* *Gulf of Carpentaria*

Timor Sea

Mitchell

Coral Sea

Kimberley Plateau

Great Barrier Reef

INDIAN OCEAN

Barkly Tableland

Tanami Desert

Flinders

Great Sandy Desert

NORTHERN TERRITORY

Great Dividing Range

QUEENSLAND

North West Cape

Hamersley Range *Lake Disappointment* *Lake Mackay*

Georgina

Lake MacLeod

Gibson Desert

A U S T R A L I A

Macdonnell Ranges

Uluru △ (Ayers Rock) 2,844 ft.

Simpson Desert

Diamantina

Buckland Tableland

WESTERN AUSTRALIA

Lake Carnegie

Thomson

Lake Eyre North

Sturt Stony Desert

Cooper

Warrego

SOUTH AUSTRALIA

Lake Barlee

Great Victoria Desert

Lake Eyre South

Lake Torrens

Darling

NEW SOUTH WALES

Lake Frome

Flinders Range

Nullarbor plain

Lake Gairdner

Lachlan

Tasman Sea

Great Australian Bight

Dividing Range

SOUTHERN OCEAN

Kangaroo Island

Murray

■ CANBERRA
AUSTRALIAN CAPITAL TERRITORY
△ Mount Kosciusko
7,314 ft.

VICTORIA

| 0 | 300 | 600 km |
| 0 | 150 | 300 miles |

Bass Strait

Furneaux Group

TASMANIA

South East Cape

EASTERN AUSTRALIA

The region of Australia first settled by Europeans, eastern Australia is a land of rich mineral and natural resources and the centre of industry and commerce.

▲ The Royal Flying Doctor Service treats a patient in Queensland. Founded in 1928, its aircraft fly over 6.8 million mi. each year to isolated communities all across Australia.

Australia is divided into six states and two territories. Eastern Australia consists of the states of Queensland, Victoria, and New South Wales, as well as the Australian Capital Territory (ACT), in which the country's capital city, Canberra, is located. Australia became a federation of states on its independence in 1901, and Canberra was chosen as the seat of government shortly afterward. It is the only major Australian city that does not lie on the country's huge coastline. Australia has a 15,971-mi.-long coastline, of which Eastern Australia has 30 percent. Inland from eastern Australia's coast lie a series of coastal plains that form much of the region's farmland. Eastern Australia's most dominant land feature is the Great Dividing Range. This broken chain of mountains runs almost the entire length of eastern Australia from northern Queensland to the southern coast of Victoria. Averaging around 3,900 ft. in height, the Great Dividing Range has the highest peaks in the Snowy Mountains in New South Wales, with Australia's tallest, Mount Kosciuszko, rising to 7,314 ft. These highlands have some of the country's largest coal deposits, enabling Australia to be one of the world's largest coal exporters. West of the Great Dividing Range the land slopes down to plains heading westward into the country's mainly flat and dry interior. A major feature of this portion of eastern Australia is the Great Artesian Basin, one of the largest regions of underground water springs, many of which are tapped for irrigation. Eastern Australia's largest river system is the Murray-Darling river system to the south of the region. It has a total length of 2,325 mi. and drains an area of over 390,000 sq. mi.

THE GREAT BARRIER REEF

One of the natural wonders of the world, the Great Barrier Reef lies off the Queensland coast. It consists of more than 3,000 reefs, along with a number of small islands that extend around 1,240 mi. Covering an area close to 156,000 sq. mi., it is the planet's largest coral reef system. More than 350 species of coral make up the Great Barrier Reef, and the region provides habitats for a staggering array of wildlife, including 1,500 species of fish and more than 200 species of birds.

THE AUSTRALIAN PEOPLE

Australia was first reached by Dutch explorers in the mid-1600s. In 1770 James Cook claimed the land for Great Britain, and in 1788 a British prison colony was established in Australia where Sydney now stands. From that time until 1853 the policy of transportation saw aroound 160,000 British convicts moved to Australia. In 1851 gold was discovered in the state of Victoria, and a major gold rush attracted thousands of settlers hoping to make a fortune. After World War II the Australian government promoted an extensive immigration program, and around 5.5 million people emigrated to the country. Over half of the migrants who arrived were British, with large numbers of Germans, Dutch, Italians, Greeks, and Yugoslavs. Today over 90 percent of the population are of European descent, with growing minorities from Asia and the Middle East. The country's population of just under 20 million represents over 150 different nationalities. Around 68 percent of the population are Christians, while over 13 percent of the population are nonreligious.

▲ Parliament House lies in the center of Canberra and was completed in 1988. Canberra was chosen as the seat of government in 1908, seven years after Australia's independence.

▼ The tropical rain forests of Cape Tribulation National Park stretch right down to the shoreline facing Queensland's Great Barrier Reef. Most of the rain forests in the 624 sq. mi. protected area have existed unchanged for around 100 million years.

ABORIGINAL RIGHTS AND WELFARE

As many as one million aborigines lived in Australia before the arrival of European settlers. These immigrants brought new diseases with them against which the aborigines had no natural protection. Thousands died from smallpox, tuberculosis, and the common cold. Many more were killed in fights over land with the settlers, many of whom treated the aborigines as if they were savages. They were discriminated against, their lands were seized, and in many cases they were forced to change their way of life, moving to cities or housed in reservations. An estimated 100,000 aboriginal children, known as the "stolen generation," were taken from their families and placed in institutions or with white families. Until the mid-1960s adult aborigines were not even allowed to vote in elections. Since that time much progress has been made. Aboriginal culture has been increasingly embraced, welfare and education programs have been introduced, and native rights to land have started to be recognized. Despite many initiatives, aborigines still tend to be the most disadvantaged and poverty-stricken of all Australians, with a life expectancy over 15 years lower than the rest of the population.

▲ Australia has an illustrious sporting heritage, and the 2000 Oympics, held in Sydney, was the largest Olympics so far, with 10,651 athletes competing in 300 events.

▼ The Gold Coast is a 22 mi. stretch of resorts, hotels, and apartments in southern Queensland, attracting over two million tourists every year.

EASTERN AUSTRALIAN CITIES

Australia's three largest cities are found on eastern Australia's coast: Melbourne, the capital of Victoria, Brisbane, the capital of Queensland, and Sydney, the capital of New South Wales. Built on a spectacular natural harbor, Sydney has become the country's most populous city and is also its commercial center and the Australian city that draws more of the 4.9 million foreign visitors each year than any other.

TASMANIA

Separated from mainland Australia by the Bass Strait, the island of Tasmania is Australia's smallest state. Home to 473,500 people, it has a dramatic and beautiful landscape.

Tasmania's 26,200 sq. mi. territory, including the smaller islands of Flinders, King, and Cape Barren, is less than one percent of Australia's total land area. Tasmania was linked to Australia until as little as 9,000 years ago, and geologically it is part of Australia's Great Dividing Range. Much of the main island consists of a plateau over 2,952 ft. in height and a series of mountain peaks. The land is crossed with many fast-flowing streams and rivers, a number of which have been harnessed to provide hydroelectric power. Rolling farmland and meadows and many vineyards occupy large parts of the north, east coast, and the central midlands of the island. However, to the west the landscape is less cultivated and includes large tracts of native forests with many different trees, including the

▲ A small boat nudges a salmon pen into position at the Port Esperance fish farm, 30 mi. southwest of the state capital, Hobart.

▼ The New River Lagoon lies in the Tasmanian Wilderness World Heritage Area. This 5,000 sq. mi. national park is a world heritage site. More than one fifth of Tasmania is covered in national parks that are designed to protect its unique landscape and nature.

blue gum eucalyptus, the state symbol. Tasmania's logging and mining industries are economically important, but the state is now trying to conserve as much of the natural landscape as possible. Much of the workforce is engaged in farming, with apples, grapes, and livestock the key products. Most of the state's limited industries are based in the southeast close to Hobart, Australia's second-oldest city and the state's chief port. Tasmania was originally settled more than 35,000 years ago by aborigines when it was part of the Australian mainland, but after European settlement, diseases, and conflicts dramatically reduced the number of native people they now comprise no more than three percent of the population.

CENTRAL AUSTRALIA

Consisting of Northern Territory and the state of
South Australia, Central Australia is a largely flat and
arid land with isolated hill and mountain ranges.

▲ Goods are often moved
through central Australia
by road train—a high-
speed truck carrying a
number of linked trailers.

▼ A bush fire rages
in Kakadu National Park,
approximately 155 mi. east
of Darwin. Famous for its
aboriginal art sites and its
abundant wildlife, Kakadu
is home to 1,200 plant,
100 reptile, 200 bird, and
50 mammal species.

Much of central Australia
is part of the hot, dry
scrublands and deserts that
constitute the country's Great
Red Center. The Simpson,
Tanami, and Great Victoria
deserts occupy large areas
of the region. In the center lie
several mountain ranges—the
MacDonnell Ranges, which
extend over 124 mi. to the
west of Alice Springs and rise
to heights of over 4,920 ft.,
and the Musgrave Ranges just south of
Uluru (Ayers Rock). The northernmost
region of Northern Territory is known
as the Top End and is a region of savanna
woodlands and rain forests with swamps
along the coast. South Australia is mostly
low-lying with the forested Flinders
Ranges, the largest area of highlands.
Lying relatively close to the Flinders
Ranges is a series of huge lakes that are
salt basins most of the time and are only
occasionally filled with water. The largest
of these, Lake Eyre, sometimes covers
an area of over 3,470 sq. mi. South
Australia's major
river is the 1,562-
mi.-long Murray.

▲ Two aboriginal men wear ceremonial body
paint made from crushed rocks and soil. Aboriginal
gatherings, called corroborees, are held to celebrate
aboriginal culture and feature music and dancing.
Aboriginal peoples live throughout Australia, but
they make up a higher proportion of the population of
Northern Territory than any other region in the country.

CLIMATE AND FARMING

South Australia is considered the driest state in Australia. Inland around 80 percent of the state is arid, receiving less than 12 in. of rain per year. The same hot, dry conditions prevail throughout most of Northern Territory. However, on and near the coast the climate is tropical and can receive more than 64 in. of rain per year. Tropical vegetable and fruit crops are grown in the Top End of Northern Territory. With poor soil and a dry climate in the center and the south, farming there is largely restricted to cattle grazing. The south of its territory is more fertile, and large amounts of wheat, barley, and fruit are grown here, as well as oats, flax, and vegetables. Irrigation is widely practiced here.

SPARSELY POPULATED LANDS

Although Northern Territory is over 519,800 sq. mi. in area, it is only home to around 187,000 people—around one percent of the total Australian population. Small numbers of people are found in mining towns, farming communities, and aboriginal towns, but the majority of the region's population live in either Alice Springs or in Darwin. South Australia is smaller, at around 379,900 sq. mi., but its population is over seven times as large as Northern Territory's. Around 95 percent of South Australia's inhabitants live within 28 mi. of the coast. Most are concentrated in a small number of settlements, the biggest of which is the state capital of Adelaide.

WESTERN AUSTRALIA

The largest state of Australia, Western Australia has a mainly dry, desertlike landscape. The state has huge mineral resources and fertile lands in the southwest.

▲ A match between the Western Australian cricket team and a touring England team takes place at the WACA Ground in Perth.

▼ The sun sets over a beach at Broome in the Kimberley region of Western Australia. One of the few towns in northern Western Australia, Broome was once a traditional center of pearl fishing and now raises oysters on pearl farms.

Western Australia is a vast, arid land. The state has an area of around 975,100 sq. mi. Most of it is a sandy, dry plateau with an elevation of between 984–1,968 ft. and little vegetation. Three large deserts cover much of its territory: the Great Sandy, the Gibson, and the Great Victoria. All three contain scrub grasslands, salt marshes, and lakes. However, they are arid and hostile areas, with average annual rainfall below 8 in. and temperatures of over 86°F. There are high peaks in the Hamersley Range, while the most extensive area of uplands is the rugged Kimberley region. Damming in the Kimberley region has created Western Australia's largest lake, Lake Argyle.

CLIMATE AND FARMING

Western Australia is mainly hot and dry. The extreme north has a tropical climate and is sometimes affected by tropical cyclones, while the extreme south has a Mediterranean climate. Both these areas receive rainfall as high as 56 in. per year. A series of low-lying mountains just north of Albany is the only place that receives snowfall. To the southwest there is a fertile region where most of the state's crop growing is concentrated, on which oats, oilseeds, and wheat are grown. Western Australia is the country's biggest wheat producer. Livestock herding is also a major part of farming. Timber, largely from state-controlled forests in the southwest, and coastal fishing also make major contributions to the economy.

◀ Despite being one of the most remote cities in the world, Perth's business center flourishes, with office blocks dominating the skyline. Rapid growth since the 1970s has meant that Perth has overtaken Adelaide to become Australia's fourth-most-populous city.

MANY SMALL SETTLEMENTS AND ONE CITY

Western Australia is sparsely populated, with an average density of fewer than one person per square mile. Despite agriculture playing a large role in the region, less than 15 percent of the population live in rural areas. Perth, Western Australia's single major settlement and the state capital, is home to 1,340,000 of Western Australia's total population of 1,798,100. In contrast no other town in Western Australia has a population larger than 35,000.

▼ Aboriginal children sit in the flat, dry landscape of the Gibson Desert, which lies in the center of Western Australia and occupies an approximate area of 60,645 sq. mi.

NEW ZEALAND

Similar in size to Japan, New Zealand is geographically isolated from the rest of the world. Its small population lives in a varied and often spectacular landscape.

Area: 103,700 sq. mi.
Population: 3,908,037
Capital: Wellington (345,000)
Main languages spoken: English, Maori
Main religions: nonreligious (almost one fourth), Anglican, Presbyterian, Roman Catholic
Currency: New Zealand dollar
Main exports: meat and dairy products, wood and wood products, fish, machinery, basic manufactures, minerals
Type of government: parliamentary democracy

New Zealand lies around 992 mi. southeast of Australia. It consists of two large islands—North and South—divided by the 12-mi.-wide Cook Strait and a number of much smaller islands. Of these mountainous Stewart Island off the south coast of South Island is the largest, with an area of 657 sq. mi. New Zealand has strong links with a number of island territories. The Cook Islands and Niue, for example, are self-governing territories in free association with New Zealand. Tokelau is a separate territory but is dependent on New Zealand. It consists of three coral atolls more than 300 mi. north of Samoa. These islands provide homes to around 1,500 Pacific islanders who fish, farm, and export woven handicrafts.

VOLCANIC NORTH ISLAND, MOUNTAINOUS SOUTH ISLAND

For a fairly small nation New Zealand has an incredible variety of landscapes, including fjords, glaciers, mountains, beaches, plains, swamps, and gently rolling hills. New Zealand's North Island has been greatly shaped by volcanoes. The country's largest lake, Lake Taupo, extends to over 234 sq. mi. in area and is the crater of a huge extinct volcano. New Zealand's longest river, the Waikato, flows north and west from this lake before emptying into the Tasman Sea. Rising steeply from Lake Taupo is North Island's central plateau, on which there are four active volcanoes. The

▲ Located in New Zealand's Southern Alps in west-central South Island, Mount Cook is New Zealand's highest mountain at 12,313 ft. above sea level. Known to the Maoris as Aoraki, meaning "cloud piercer," the mountain is surrounded by a further 22 peaks exceeding 9,840 ft. in elevation.

central plateau is an area of great heat and activity beneath Earth's surface, with many hot springs, geysers, and frequent small tremors and occasional larger earthquakes. Away from the plateau North Island's landscape includes rolling plains and chains of low mountains with coastal lowlands. North Island's coast is heavily indented, and both of its largest cities, Auckland and Wellington, are built around large natural harbors. The Northland region, north of Auckland, has vast, sandy beaches, subtropical vegetation, and mangrove swamps. South Island's landscape is mostly mountainous and dominated by a large

▼ Auckland lies on a large natural harbor. Piercing the skyline is the 1,076-ft.-high Sky Tower, which, on its completion in 1997, was the tallest building in New Zealand and the entire Southern Hemisphere.

NEW ZEALAND

PACIFIC
OCEAN

North Cape

Whangarei

Great
Barrier
Island

Kaipara
Harbour

Hauraki
Gulf

Waitakere • North Shore
Auckland • Manukau
Manukau Harbour
Pukekohe

Coromandel
Peninsula

Waikato

Bay of
Plenty

East
Cape

North
Island

Hamilton • Tauranga
Cambridge
Tokoroa
Lake
Rotorua
Rotorua

Lake
Taupo
Taupo

North Taranaki
Bight

New Plymouth

Gisborne

Cape
Egmont

South Taranaki
Bight

Wanganui

Napier
Hawke
Bay

Mahia
Peninsula

Hastings

**NEW
ZEALAND**

Fielding
Palmerston North
Levin

Cape Farewell

D'Urville
Island

Cook
Strait

Porirua
Lower Hutt
WELLINGTON

Tasman
Bay

Nelson
Blenheim

Cape Palliser

mountain chain, the Southern Alps,
which runs almost the full length of the
island. The large Tasman glacier is located
in the Southern Alps on the slopes of the
country's highest peak, Mount Cook,
known to the Maoris as Aoraki.
The scouring action of glaciers
has created many features on
South Island, including long
lakes and deep valleys.
Much of the island's
rugged coastline is
broken up by many
fjords and bays.

Karamea
Bight

Cape
Foulwind

Greymouth

South
Island

SOUTHERN ALPS

Tasman
Sea

Aoraki
(Mount Cook)
12,313 ft.

Christchurch

Pegasus
Bay

Canterbury
Plains

Banks
Peninsula

Ashburton
Lake
Ellesmere

Lake
Tekapo

Timaru

Canterbury
Bight

PACIFIC
OCEAN

Lake
Wanaka

Lake
Hawea

Oamaru

Fiordland

Lakes
Te Anau

Lake
Wakatipu

Waiau

Dunedin
Otago
Peninsula

Resolution
Island

West
Cape

Cape Providence

Invercargill

Mataura

Foveaux Strait

South West
Cape

Stewart Island

▶ The Champagne
Pool is a crater lake filled with
bubbling mineral-rich waters at
temperatures of over 140°F. It
is found in Wai-o-tapu Thermal
Wonderland, an area of great
geothermal activity around
12 mi. south of Rotorua.

291

▲ Intricate wood carvings are an important part of Maori art. The Maori are of Polynesian origin, and their wood carvings are more complex than those of any other Polynesian people.

NEW ZEALAND'S PEOPLE

New Zealand is a country of old and new settlers. Around 12 percent are the oldest arrivals—the Maori who live predominantly in North Island. The Maori are greatly outnumbered by people of European, particularly British, descent, who arrived in New Zealand mainly after 1840. European people comprise three fourths of the population and have traditionally held most of the power and commercial positions in the country. Around six percent of the country's population originally come from other Pacific islands such as Tonga, the Cook Islands, and Samoa. They were drawn to New Zealand by the need to find work and the expansion of the New Zealand economy after World War II. Waves of more recent immigrants have come from parts of Asia, particularly Malaysia and Hong Kong. These more recent arrivals make up around six percent of the population. New Zealanders tend to enjoy a high standard of living, although the Maori suffer higher levels of unemployment and poverty. Changes to the economy since the 1980s have meant that welfare services are less generous than in the past. Despite the importance of agriculture, around 85 percent of New Zealanders live in towns and cities.

THE MAORI CULTURE

The Maori are the indigenous people of New Zealand and are of Polynesian origin. They are believed to have reached New Zealand, possibly from the Cook Islands, from the A.D. 900s. The Maori developed a rich culture that includes intricate wood carvings and full-face tattooing, called moko, common among male warriors. Dutch explorer Abel Tasman made the first European contact with the Maori in 1642, but it was the British explorer James Cook who first landed on New Zealand soil in 1769 and claimed the country for Great Britain. The arrival of waves of European settlers from the early 1800s onward resulted in wars and diseases that reduced the Maori population to under 50,000. The Maori were forced to give up large areas of land for no more than token payments. Conflicts between the Maori and Europeans continued throughout the 1800s. Recently New Zealand has begun to focus on its past and has awarded some compensation and land to the Maori, and their children now have access to education in their own language, Maoritanga.

POLITICS AND INTERNATIONAL RELATIONS

Although Auckland is the biggest and most populous city and the financial center of New Zealand, the seat of national government is in Wellington. Modeled along British lines, the country has no written constitution, and its head

▼ Located on the north coast of South Island, the beautiful 30-mi.-long Queen Charlotte Sound with its many bays is a popular haven for pleasure boating. The waterway was named by Captain Cook in the 1770s.

of state is the British monarch. In 1893 New Zealand was the first country in the world to give women the right to vote, and in 2003 the country's prime minister and the leader of the main opposition party were both women. Most New Zealanders are firmly in favor of staying in the Commonwealth and keeping strong ties with Great Britain, which is traditionally its most important trading partner. However, the U.K.'s entry into the European Union has forced New Zealand to strengthen its ties with other nations, particularly Australia, its largest trading partner, the U.S., Japan, and Southeast Asian nations. Around one fourth of the entire country is part of the 13 national parks and other protected areas. New Zealand strongly opposed French nuclear testing in the Pacific Ocean and has banned nuclear-powered ships and submarines from docking in its ports.

▲ The Wairakei Valley steam pipeline carries steam, heated by geothermal activity under Earth's surface, to a nearby geothermal power plant that generates electricity. Wairakei Valley lies just north of Lake Taupo, the largest lake on New Zealand's North Island.

▼ An international rugby match in progress between New Zealand, known as the All Blacks, and South Africa, held in Auckland. Rugby is the most popular sport in New Zealand, and the All Blacks have a long and illustrious history.

GUAM & NORTHERN MARIANAS

Territories of the U.S., Guam and the Northern
Mariana Islands are small island nations that have
both developed successful service industries.

Guam
(to U.S.)

Asan Hagatna
Agat Mount Lamlan
1,332 ft.

*PACIFIC
OCEAN*

Guam

Area: 217 sq. mi.
Population: 160,796
Capital: Hagatna (27,000)
Main languages spoken:
English, Chamorro, Japanese
Main religion: Roman
Catholic
Currency: U.S. dollar
Principal exports:
reexported petroleum,
construction materials,
foodstuffs, fish
Type of government:
dependency of the U.S.

Northern Mariana islands

Area: 189 sq. mi.
Population: 69,000
Capital: Garapan (77,311)
Main languages spoken:
English, Chamorro,
Carolinian
Main religion: Roman
Catholic
Currency: U.S. dollar
Principal exports:
clothing, agricultural
and fish products
Type of government:
self-governing dependency
of the U.S.

Guam was formed through the uplift of undersea volcanoes. The northern half of the island is a plateau of coral limestone. The southern half is a collection of volcanic hills and valleys. Guam's native wildlife, particularly its bird life, has been decimated by the brown tree snake, which has killed off the island's nine native bird species. A major military outpost for the U.S. in the Pacific Ocean, military bases cover one third of the island. Its palm-fringed beaches attract visitors, and tourism is the single largest industry on Guam, accounting for over half of the country's income. Along with the spending of U.S. military personnel stationed on the island, this has enabled Guam to develop its services and give its people one of the highest standards of living in the Pacific islands.

The Northern Marianas has also developed tourist resorts, particularly on the three largest islands of Saipan, Tinian, and Rota. Agriculture plays an important role in the Northern Marianas, which has a tropical climate. Cattle and pigs are raised, while sugarcane, taro, cassava, coconuts, and vegetables are grown in the fertile volcanic soil. A number of the islands' volcanoes are still active.

Agrihan

Pagan

*Northern
Mariana
Islands*
(to U.S.)

*Philippine
Sea*

Saipan
Tinian Garapan

Rota

*PACIFIC
OCEAN*

► Over 1.5 million
tourists, particularly
from Japan and some
from the U.S., visit Guam
every year. Visitors are
attracted by the island's
tropical climate and
duty-free shopping.

FEDERATED STATES OF MICRONESIA

A scattered collection of 607 small tropical islands, the Federated States of Micronesia was settled over 3,500 years ago and has a culturally diverse population.

Area: 271 sq. mi.
Population: 135,869
Capital: Palikir (33,372)
Main languages spoken: English, Trukese, Pohnpeian, Yapese
Main religions: Roman Catholic, Protestant
Currency: U.S. dollar
Principal exports: fish, clothing, bananas, black pepper
Type of government: republic

The Federated States of Micronesia consists of four states—Yap, Pohnpei, Kusaie, and Chuuk—that retain close ties and trade links with their former ruler, the United States. Part of the widely spread Caroline Islands archipelago, Micronesia experiences a tropical climate. The largest island, Pohnpei, is also the wettest, receiving as much as 220 in. of rainfall per year. Although the islands stretch across a vast area of the Pacific Ocean—over 620,000 sq. mi.—the total land area is small, no more than 271 sq. mi. Apart from deposits of phosphates, there are no mineral reserves and only 26 mi. of paved roads, while many homes outside of the small towns have no electricity or running water. The islanders rely on subsistence farming, growing crops, such as taro, coconuts, bananas, and yams, fishing, and raising poultry, pigs, and, sometimes, dogs for food. U.S. aid makes up more than half of the country's income. The islands have a variety of different Pacific peoples with their own distinct cultures and languages, despite Western customs being imposed by European whalers, missionaries, and traders from the early 1800s onward. Situated on Pohnpei, the giant ruins of Nan Madol are the largest ancient archaeological site found throughout the Pacific islands.

▶ A woman braids palm fronds into thatching for the roof of a home on Satawal Island. The most easterly of Yap's inhabited islands, with a population of around 560, Satawal had electricity installed for the first time in 2001.

Yap

C a r o l i n e   I s l a n d s

M I C R O N E S I A

Chuuk Islands

PALIKIR ■ *Pohnpei*

PACIFIC OCEAN

Kusaie

MARSHALL ISLANDS

Consisting of 1,150 coral islands, of which only 20 are inhabited, the Marshall Islands were United Nations Trust Territories under U.S. administration until 1986.

Area: 70 sq. mi.
Population: 73,360
Capital: Delap-Uliga-Darrit (16,000)
Main languages spoken: Marshallese, English, Japanese
Main religion: Protestant
Currency: U.S. dollar
Main exports: copra, coconut oil, handicrafts, fish
Type of government: republic

The Marshall Islands consist of two chains of coral islands and islets: the Ralik, meaning "sunset," to the west and the Ratak, meaning "sunrise," to the east. The chains lie around 125 mi. apart and are around 800 mi. long. Many of the islands are atolls consisting of a narrow fringe of coral-based land encircling lagoons. The largest atoll, Kwajalein, is one of the largest in the world. It encircles a lagoon of around 660 mi. in area, yet its actual land area is only 6 sq. mi. Several of the atolls, including Bikini atoll, were used for the testing of nuclear weapons in the 1940s and 1950s, and radioactive fallout made these and neighboring islands uninhabitable for many years. Kwajalein atoll is the current home of a U.S. missile-testing range, and rent from this base, along with U.S. aid, forms the

majority of the country's income. Around one in ten of the workforce is employed in tourism, while the atoll of Majuro is the commercial center of the Marshall Islands and home to 45 percent of its population. Life away from Majuro and Kwajalein is dominated by subsistence agriculture, growing coconuts, breadfruit, and taro, and fishing. Copra—dried coconut meat—is the island's major export, while many goods have to be imported.

NAURU

A small, oval-shaped, raised coral island and the world's smallest republic, Nauru's economy is based almost solely on phosphate mining.

Area: 8 sq. mi.
Population: 12,329
Capital: Yaren (700)
Main languages spoken: Nauruan, English
Main religion: Christian
Currency: Australian dollar
Main export: phosphates
Type of government: republic

A central plateau approximately 200 mi. in elevation covers the majority of the tropical island of Nauru. This plateau contains the island's phosphate reserves, with phosphate mining traditionally Nauru's sole industry. However, reserves are depleted, and attempts to diversify have led the economy into bankruptcy. Nauru has no natural harbor, docking is conducted offshore, and all drinking water, fuel, and many foodstuffs have to be imported. Most of the island's people live around the narrow but fertile coast of the island. The population includes groups of other Pacific islanders and people of Chinese and European origin. Many younger Nauruans migrate to Australia or New Zealand for work or education.

▶ Nauru has been mined for phosphates, used to make chemicals and fertilizers, for over 100 years. However, its reserves of phosphates are almost depleted.

SOLOMON ISLANDS

The third-largest island chain in the Pacific Ocean,
the Solomon Islands consist of a mixture of rugged,
mountainous islands and low-lying coral atolls.

Area: 10,600 sq. mi.
Population: 494,786
Capital: Honiara (78,000)
Main languages spoken:
English, Polynesian and
Melanesian languages
Main religions: Anglican,
Roman Catholic, Baptist
Currency: Solomon Islands
dollar
Main exports: timber
products, fish, palm oil,
copra, cocoa
Type of government:
parliamentary democracy

▼ Many of the islands in
the Solomon Islands group
are fringed by coral reefs.
The waters around the
islands are rich in marine
life, including many
brightly marked species
of tropical fish, sharks,
and dugongs—large sea
mammals also known
as sea cows.

The tropical islands of the Solomons are
a haven for plant life. The islands are
home to over 4,500 plant species, many of
which are used for building, food, medicine,
and clothing. Copra, cacao, and palm oil are
important cash crops, while people grow
sweet potatoes, yams, taro, rice, and tropical
fruits for food. The timber industry
is the country's largest,
and as a result, more
than one tenth of
the land has been
cleared of trees.
People have settled
on around one third
of the islands, with the
majority living on one of
the six largest islands: Malaita,
Guadalcanal, New Georgia, San
Cristobal (Makira), Santa Isabel,
and Choiseul. The larger islands are
volcanic and mountainous and have
vast forests. Guadalcanal is the biggest
of the islands and home of the capital,
Honiara, which is also the islands' major
port. First settled approximately 3,000

years ago, over the centuries the Solomon
Islands have seen waves of arrivals from
many parts of the Pacific. Different peoples,
societies, and cultures developed on many
of the islands with their own distinct
ways of life. Most Solomon Islanders are
Melanesian, and there are an estimated 115
different languages spoken. The differences
between certain ethnic groups spilled over
into conflict between 1998 and 2000 and
again in 2002.

VANUATU

Vanuatu consists of 80 islands located in a Y-shaped archipelago 1,345 mi. northeast of the Australian city of Sydney. The island group is renowned for its scenery.

Area: 5,700 sq. mi.
Population: 196,178
Capital: Port-Vila (31,000)
Main languages spoken: Bislama, English, French
Main religions: Presbyterian, Anglican, Roman Catholic
Currency: vatu
Main exports: copra, beef and veal, timber, cocoa, coffee
Type of government: republic

▼ A man from Tanna island prepares for a traditional ceremony involving the drinking of kava. The traditional drink of chiefs in many Pacific island cultures in the Melanesian part of the Pacific, kava is made from the root of a plant related to the pepper tree.

Vanuatu was formerly known as the New Hebrides and was ruled jointly by France and Great Britain until 1980. The islands experience a tropical climate, with rainfall averaging around 96 in. per year but as high as 156 in. in the northern islands. Tropical cyclones visit the islands from December to March. Vanuatu's islands are a mixture of coral and volcanically formed landmasses. They contain a number of active volcanoes and experience relatively frequent—but usually minor—earthquakes. Subsistence agriculture employs the majority of the workforce, but tourism and offshore banking services contribute the most money to the economy. Vanuatu's scenery, including deep ravines, heavily rain-forested mountains, clear seas, beaches, and cave systems, attracts an increasing number of tourists. Although almost all of Vanuatu's islands are inhabited, 80 percent of the population live on 11 main islands. The population is one of the most culturally diverse of all Pacific nations. The native Ni-Vanuatu people make up over 90 percent, but different languages—totaling 105—and cultures have developed separately on many islands. There are also small communities of French, British, Australian, New Zealand, Vietnamese, Chinese, and other Pacific island peoples. Ethnic strife is rare, but until very recently women tended to have a lower status.

NEW CALEDONIA

New Caledonia is a French overseas territory. It consists of one large island, New Caledonia, on which 90 percent of the population live, as well as many smaller islands.

Area: 6,530 sq. mi.
Population: 207,858
Capital: Nouméa (119,000)
Main language spoken: French
Main religion: Roman Catholic
Currency: French Pacific franc
Main exports: refined ferro nickel and nickel, nickel ore, fish
Type of government: dependency of France

The island of New Caledonia is a little over 198 mi. long and around 30 mi. wide and has a mountainous landscape with areas of grasslands. Tourism and agriculture are the biggest employers of New Caledonians, but mining, particularly of nickel, is the most economically important industry. New Caledonia has around 25 percent of the world's reserves of nickel, and over 85 percent of the islands' income comes from nickel exports. Discovered in 1774 by the British explorer James Cook, the island came under French control in the mid-1700s. The native Kanak people form over two fifths of the population, with a large and significant minority of French origin known as the

Caldoches. Tensions between the two groups have remained for many years.

▶ A traditional home on Lifou, New Caledonia's second-largest island. Lifou is part of the Loyalty Islands group, which also includes Ouvéa, Maré, and other smaller islands.

KIRIBATI

The republic of Kiribati is a series of 33 small islands spread out over almost two million sq. mi. of the Pacific.

Area: 277 sq. mi.
Population: 96,335
Capital: Bairiki (32,000)
Main languages spoken: English, Gilbertese
Main religions: Roman Catholic, Protestant
Currency: Australian dollar
Main exports: copra, reexports, fish and fish products
Type of government: republic

Kiribati's terrain is extremely low, with its highest point just 285 ft. and almost all of its land only a few feet above sea level. Rising sea levels, caused by global warming, are a major concern to Kiribati and other low-lying island groups in the Pacific. Kiritlmati (Christmas Island) is the country's largest island, making up over half of the land area, but Tarawa is the most populous. A part of the British Gilbert and Ellice Islands colony until 1979, the people of Kiribati still refer to themselves as Gilbertese, and almost all are Christian. Most are fairly poor, relying on farming and fishing to feed their families. The majority of the islands' soils are of poor quality and support little vegetation. Islanders grow a variety of

tropical crops, including bananas, papaw, and breadfruit. The islands can also suffer from low rainfall. This occurred in 1999 when a drought emergency was declared. Phosphate mining was the principal industry until reserves of this mineral ran out in 1980. Organized resettlement from densely populated Tarawa to other less populated islands occurred during the 1990s.

PALAU

The Republic of Palau consists of 260 islands, almost all of which lie in a large lagoon enclosed by a barrier reef that stretches a distance of over 62 mi.

Area: 4,177 sq. mi.
Population: 19,409
Capital: Koror (14,000)—a new capital (Melekeiok) is under construction on Babelthuap island
Main languages spoken: English, Palauan, Sonsorolese, Angaur, Japanese, Tobi
Main religions: Roman Catholic, Modekngei
Currency: U.S. dollar
Main exports: shellfish, tuna, copra, clothing
Type of government: republic

P alau is a small nation with the fourth-smallest population in the world. Many of its people live on Babelthuap, the largest island, or Koror, its administrative center. The two islands are linked by a concrete bridge. Palau has one of the smallest economies in the world. Its small population, however, has a higher-than-average standard of living among the Pacific islanders. Tourism is the fastest-growing part of the economy. Palau is considered to have some of the most spectacular underwater diving sites in the world. Agreements between Palau and the U.S. have allowed U.S. military bases to be located on the islands in return for aid and trade deals. While the majority of Palauans are Christians, around one third follow a native religion called Modekngei.

PALAU
Babelthuap
Peleliu   KOROR
Angaur

PACIFIC
OCEAN

Sonsorol Islands

Pulo Anna

Merir

▶ Palau's famed Rock Islands are humps of rounded, coralline limestone that are thickly covered with dense forests that have been undercut by erosion. The waters and reefs around Palau's islands are home to more than 1,400 species of fish.

TUVALU

Lying 620 mi. north of Fiji, the nine coral atolls of Tuvalu were formerly known as the Ellice Islands. In 2000 Tuvalu became one of the newest members of the UN.

Area: 10 sq. mi.
Population: 11,146
Capital: Fongafale (5,000)
Main languages spoken: Tuvaluan, English
Main religion: Congregational
Currency: Australian dollar
Main exports: copra, fish, clothing, fruit and vegetables
Type of government: dominion

T uvalu's land is low-lying with generally poor, salty soils in which only certain plants, such as coconut palms, flourish. The tending and harvesting of coconuts and raising ducks, pigs, and chickens are key farming activities. Copra—dried coconut meat—is the only agricultural export of importance, and even this is in limited quantities. Much food has to be imported, most arriving by ships at the islands' main port on Funafuti Atoll. Tuvalu's land is very low-lying and under severe threat from rising sea levels owing to global warming. Opportunities for work on these tiny islands are limited, and many younger Tuvaluans work overseas and send money back to help support their families. Tuvalu's major resources are the fish-rich seas around its islands, and the Tuvaluan

government has sold licenses to foreign trawler companies, particularly from Taiwan, South Korea, and the U.S. Foreign aid is also important, especially for new projects, including solar energy programs. Sales of postage stamps also support the economy. Tuvalu's Internet country identifying code is .tv, and rights to use this for web sites were sold to a Canadian media company, bringing in many millions of dollars. In contrast the islands themselves have no television service or daily newspapers—only a single radio service and bimonthly newspapers.

Nanumea Islands

Niutao

Nanumaga

Nui Atoll   Vaitupu
Vaitupu

TUVALU

PACIFIC   *Funafuti Atoll* ■FONGAFALE
OCEAN

Nukulaelae Atoll

WALLIS & FUTUNA ISLANDS

Made up of two volcanic island archipelagos, Wallis & Futuna Islands are a French overseas territory and are among the least developed of all Pacific island groups.

Mata'utu ● Wallis
(Uvéa)

Wallis and Futuna
(to France)

Futuna   PACIFIC
Alofi   OCEAN

Area: 106 sq. mi.
Population: 15,585
Capital: Mata'utu (1,100)
Main languages spoken: French, Wallisian, Futunan
Main religion: Roman Catholic
Currency: French Pacific franc
Main exports: copra and coconuts, construction materials
Type of government: dependency of France

The Wallis archipelago is made up of over 20 small islands and islets that are found on a barrier reef that encircles the main island of Wallis. It is a volcanic island but is fairly low-lying, with the highest point at 476 ft. Its terrain includes sharp sea cliffs and a number of water-filled craters. The Futuna archipelago is made up of two main islands, Futuna and Alofi, which is uninhabited. Futuna consists of a narrow coastal plain that rises sharply to heights above 1,640 ft. The islands have a tropical climate with heavy rainfall of over 120 in. per year. The Wallis islands take their name from English navigator Samuel Wallis, who claimed possession of them for England in 1767. Both the Wallis and Futuna island groups have been under French control since 1842 and became an

overseas territory of France in 1961. The economy is limited to traditional subsistence farming, growing mostly coconut palms, breadfruit, mangoes, and vegetables. Pigs and chickens are raised, and fishing from small boats is also important. These activities engage over 80 percent of the workforce. A further five percent are employed by the local government, which receives aid from France and sells licenses for fishing rights to Japan and South Korea. Over 15,000 Wallisians work in New Caledonia, another French territory, sending back part of their incomes to their families.

FIJI

Lying 1,240 mi. north of New Zealand, Fiji is the most populous and developed of all the Pacific island nations.

Area: 7,100 sq. mi.
Population: 856,346
Capital: Suva (203,000)
Main languages spoken: English, Fijian, Hindustani
Main religions: Christian, Hinduism, Islam
Currency: Fijian dollar
Main exports: sugar, clothing, gold, fish, timber, coconuts
Type of government: republic

▼ A casual game of rugby, one of Fiji's major sports, takes place in Albert Park in the capital city of Suva. Over 203,000 Fijians live in or around Suva, making it one of the largest settlements in the Pacific islands.

Fiji consists of around 330 islands, of which 106 are inhabited. The majority of the population live on the two largest islands: Viti Levu and Vanua Levu. These islands and a number of others are of volcanic origin and have mountainous interiors. Agriculture employs over 70 percent of the workforce, with major crops including bananas, cocoa beans, corn, coconuts, rice, and sugarcane. Fiji exports around one-and-a-half times the amount of food it has to import. Sugar processing is the country's biggest industry and is largely government controlled. Sugar accounts for over half of all exports. Forestry and fishing are important industries, while tourism was the fastest-growing industry until the country's troubles in 2000. Fiji has no fossil fuels, but a large hydroelectricity plant on Viti Levu generates over three fourths of the country's electricity. Viti Levu is also the location for Fiji's largest private industry— the Vatukoula gold mine, which employs around 1,600 workers. Fiji is sometimes known as the "crossroads of the Pacific" and has seen a number of waves of settlement stretching back to the Lapita people, who are believed to have reached the islands

around 3,500 years ago. The population today includes small minorities of Chinese, Europeans, and other Pacific islanders, but they are greatly outnumbered by two large groups: native Fijians and Fijian Indians. Most Fijian Indians were brought to the islands when they were a British colony to work on the sugarcane plantations. From World War II through independence in 1970 until the 1980s Fijian Indians, most of whom are Hindus, outnumbered native Fijians—almost all of whom are Christians. Tensions between the two groups have dominated Fijian politics, with civil disorder, outbursts of violence, and a series of military coups occurring between 1987 and 2000. This has led to economic problems, and a large number of Fijian Indians have left the country.

SAMOA

Consisting of nine islands and a number of small islets, Samoa is one of the most traditional of the Pacific island nations. It used to be known as Western Samoa.

SAMOA

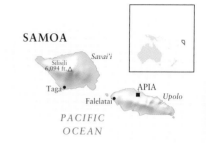

PACIFIC OCEAN

Area: 1,100 sq. mi.
Population: 178,631
Capital: Apia (35,000)
Main languages spoken: Samoan, English
Main religion: Christian
Currency: tala, local issue of New Zealand currency
Main exports: coconut oil, coconut cream, copra, fish, clothing, beer
Type of government: constitutional monarchy

▼ The interior of Samoa's major islands tends to be covered in lush plant life and cut by short, shallow, and fast-moving streams and rivers.

Samoa's land is dominated by two large islands—Savai'i and Upolo—and seven smaller islands, of which only two are inhabited. Savai'i and Upolo both have narrow coastal plains, coral reefs around their coasts, and volcanically formed, mountainous centers, much of which are densely covered in tropical forests. Samoa is a nation of farmers, with 78 percent of its people living in the countryside, mostly in the islands' 400 coastal villages. Agriculture is mainly on a small scale, although larger plantations of hardwood trees, coconut palms, and bananas provide products for export. Fishing is largely conducted using traditional outrigger canoes. Samoans tend to live in communal family groups who own 80 percent of the land—which they are not allowed to sell. Each extended family is headed by a *matai*, or elected male chief, who wields great power. Samoa faces major environmental problems, particularly deforestation and soil erosion.

More than half of its original forests have been cleared, destroying habitats of many native wildlife species. Government replanting programs and strict logging laws are helping keep the timber industry working while protecting some of the islands' land. Samoa generates over 35 percent of its electricity through hydroelectric power but has to import the remainder, along with many other goods and supplies. Despite a flourishing tourist industry, Samoa has large foreign debts and very high unemployment. Thousands of Samoans have migrated to other nations, particularly New Zealand, the U.S., and American Samoa, to seek a better living.

TONGA

Lying 397 mi. east of Fiji, the Kingdom of Tonga consists of 172 islands, many of which are covered in thick vegetation—but less than 40 are inhabited.

Area: 277 sq. mi.
Population: 106,137
Capital: Nuku'alofa (33,000)
Main languages spoken: Tongan, English
Main religions: Free Wesleyan, Roman Catholic, Mormon
Currency: pa'anga
Principal exports: squashes, fish, vanilla beans, root crops
Type of government: constitutional monarchy

▼ A sentry stands guard in front of the Royal Palace of the king of Tonga. Political power lies with the king, despite some Tongans pressing for more democracy. King Taufa'ahau Tupou IV has ruled since 1965 and oversaw Tongan independence from the U.K. in 1970.

Tonga's three main island groups—Tongatapu, Ha'apai, and Vava'u—lie just west of the Tonga Trench, the second-deepest part of the Pacific Ocean floor. The eastern islands are mainly low-lying and formed of coral. Many of the western islands were formed from volcanic activity and are more rugged and mountainous, with four active volcanoes. Tonga lies over 1,364 mi. south of the equator and has more variation in summer and winter temperatures than many Pacific islands. Winter temperatures average between 63°F–72°F, with summer temperatures between 77°F–91°F. The islands are located within the South Pacific's cyclone belt, and tropical storms regularly strike the islands. Tonga's largest island is called Tongatapu and is home to around two thirds of the islands' people. Over half of all Tongans work in agriculture, growing vanilla beans, coconuts, and squashes for export and vegetables, such as cassava, for food. Fishing, tourism, and the sale of handicrafts contribute to the economy. Tonga has no mineral resources and mostly generates its energy needs from imported fuel.

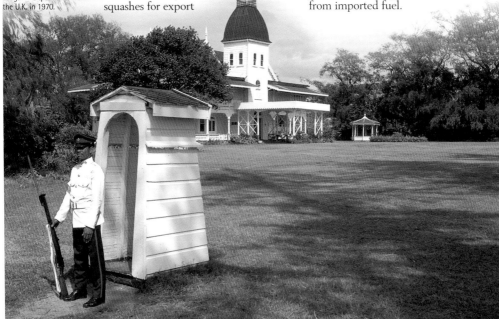

AMERICAN SAMOA

American Samoa consists of six volcanic islands and two coral atolls. The largest island is Tutuila, where the capital, Pago Pago, is located.

Area: 77 sq. mi.
Population: 68,688
Capital: Pago Pago (4,300)
Main languages spoken: Samoan, English
Main religions: Congregational, Roman Catholic
Currency: U.S. dollar
Principal exports: tuna, other fish
Type of government: dependency of the U.S.

American Samoa's volcanic-formed islands, which include Tutuila, Tau, and Olosega, have rugged landscapes rising to eroded mountains in their centers, with a mixture of cliffs and scooped out bays on their coasts. The mountain interiors of these islands are heavily covered in rain forests that provide homes for many bird species, as well as flying foxes, lizards, rats, and snakes. American Samoa experiences a tropical climate with heavy rainfall. Pago Pago tends to receive an average of 200 in. per year. The islands are susceptible to heavy storms between December and March. Unlike many Pacific island groups, American Samoa has relatively few tourists, and the economy relies on tuna canneries that process tuna caught in local waters. Textiles and handicrafts, such as woven mats, are also exported. The largest island, Tutuila, is where the majority of the territory's population live. The people of American Samoa often still live in large extended family groups, called *aiga*, but younger Samoans are becoming more Westernized and abandoning traditional ways of life.

▶ One of the finest deep-water harbors in the Pacific, Pago Pago harbor was formed from a volcanic crater that collapsed and was submerged millions of years ago.

NIUE

One of the largest coral islands and smallest self-governing states in the world, Niue is separately governed in free association with New Zealand.

Area: 100 sq. mi.
Population: 1,800
Capital: Alofi (620)
Main languages spoken: English, Niuean
Main religion: Congregational
Currency: New Zealand dollar
Principal exports: coconut cream and copra, honey, fruit
Type of government: self-governing dependency of New Zealand

Niue is a roughly oval-shaped island with broken and sharp cliffs facing the sea and an inland plateau rising to around 197 ft. The most fertile part of the island, where the majority of the people live, is the land near the coast, which contains wooded areas of palm and banyan trees. Almost one fourth of the island is capable of supporting some form of farming, although the soils are not of good quality. Niue lacks streams or rivers, and water tends to filter through the soil and the porous coral out into the ocean. Rainfall, which averages 80 in. per year, has to be collected and stored. Niue's economy is tiny, with the income from less than 800 tourists per year making a major contribution. The sale of postage stamps to foreign collectors and the exporting of copra, limes, and honey bring in further revenue. Aid, particularly from New Zealand, has enabled Niue to build a fairly extensive infrastructure, including television and telephone links. Yet opportunities for work on the island are limited, and around 15,000 Niueans have migrated to New Zealand to find work. Niue's people are mainly descended from Samoans and Tongans who settled on the island and have developed their own Pacific language, Niuean.

COOK ISLANDS

Lying east of Tonga, the Cook Islands consist of two groups of small volcanic and coral islands scattered over around 858,000 sq. mi. of the Pacific Ocean.

Tongareva
Rakahanga
Pukapuka
Nassau
Manihiki

Suwarrow

PACIFIC OCEAN

Palmerston

Aitutaki
Mitiaro
Atiu Mauke
Cook Islands
(to New Zealand)
Avarua
Rarotonga
Mangaia

Area: 100 sq. mi.
Population: 20,811
Capital: Avarua (3,000)
Main languages spoken: English, Cook Islands Maori
Main religion: Cook Islands church, Roman Catholic
Currency: New Zealand dollar
Main exports: copra, fresh fruit (particularly papayas), canned fruit, fish, clothing
Type of government: self-governing dependency of New Zealand

The Cook Islands are a self-governing dependency of new Zealand. They are made up of a northern group of six coral atolls and nine islands of volcanic origin in a southern group. The majority of the population live in the southern group, especially on the largest island, Rarotonga, where its capital, Avarua, is based. Surrounded by a coral reef, Rarotonga's land rises from a coastal plain to a volcanic peak. Cook Islanders are mostly descended from Polynesians related to the Maori people who settled in New Zealand. The Maori language, along with English, is widely spoken. While fishing and growing pineapples and other tropical crops occupy many in the small workforce, the most lucrative activities are tourism and offshore banking. Marine farms producing cultured pearls have recently been established. The expansion of New Zealand's economy has drawn many Cook Islanders to find work there. An estimated 32,000 Cook Islanders live

▶ Traditional dancers on the Cook Islands tell stories handed down from generation to generation. Usually accompanied by beating drums, the dancers wear traditional costumes made from palm fronds, tree bark, seashells, feathers, and flowers.

and work in New Zealand. The islands are self-governing but heavily linked to New Zealand, which donates aid and is the islands' major trading partner.

FRENCH POLYNESIA

A collection of island archipelagos made up of over 115 islands, French Polynesia sprawls across the Pacific and is the most eastern of the Pacific island nations.

French Polynesia *Iles Marquises*
(to France)

Iles Tuamotu

Bora-Bora • Papeete
Society Islands • Tahiti

Tubuai Islands

Gambier Islands

Area: 1,400 sq. mi.
Population: 257,847
Capital: Papeete (113,000)
Main languages spoken: French, Tahitian
Main religion: Roman Catholic
Currency: French Pacific franc
Main exports: pearls, copra and other coconut products, mother-of-pearl, vanilla
Type of government: dependency of France

▼ Scattered over an enormous area of the Pacific Ocean—there are over 1,240 mi. between the northernmost and southernmost islands—French Polynesia attracted over 200,000 tourists in 2001. Fringed by coral reefs, the tropical island paradise of Bora-Bora in the Society Islands group is a popular destination for wealthier tourists.

French Polynesia is divided into five island archipelagos: the Society Islands, the Gambier Islands, the Tubuai Islands, the Îles Marquises (Marquesa Islands), and the Tuamotu archipelago. The larger islands, which are of volcanic origin, support an array of natural life, including the large tiare flowers that are often worn by islanders. Many of the islands' plant and animal species, including wild pigs and sheep, were introduced by human settlers and have since flourished. The islands are also home to around 100 species of birds. While farming and fishing provide some employment on the outer islands, tourism is the most important industry. French Polynesia is the world leader in creating cultured pearls, particularly on the Tuamotu and Gambier islands. French Polynesia's economy, government, and transportation network are dominated by the island of Tahiti in the Society Islands. Encircled by a fertile coastal plain, Tahiti's land rises sharply to spectacular volcanic mountains. Over two thirds of the islands'

▲ Located in the Society Islands, Raiatea occupies 93 sq. mi. and is a mountainous island surrounded by palm-fringed beaches and coral reefs.

population live on Tahiti, which is also home to the main port of Papeete. A French military presence on the islands has provided a great deal of income and employment, but French nuclear tests on Muroroa atoll in the mid-1990s provoked opposition and outrage among the islanders, some of whom want more independence from France.

ANTARCTICA

L ying undiscovered until the early 1800s, the continent of Antarctica is a mostly icy wasteland whose interior has been barely touched by human impact or the activities of plants and animals. The continent, whose name means the opposite of Arctic, encircles the geographic South Pole. With an approximate land area of 5.5 million sq. mi., it is larger than the continent of Europe. The giant Transantarctic mountain range, almost 3,100 mi. long and containing peaks over 13,120 ft. in elevation, splits the continent into two regions: a larger eastern region and the western region, which includes the Antarctic Peninsula. This peninsula extends 800 mi. northward toward the southernmost tip of South America and is covered in mountain ranges. Its loftiest peak, the 16,062-ft.-high Vinson Massif, is also the highest point on the continent. Around 90 percent of the world's freshwater is contained in Antarctica, locked together as ice. All except around five percent of its land surface is covered by a thick ice sheet, averaging 1.4 mi. in depth. It is the coldest, windiest region on Earth and also one of the driest. With a temporary human population of around 4,000 in the summer and less than 1,000 in the winter, Antarctica is the most unspoiled and hostile environment on the planet.

South Orkney Islands (to U.K.)

South Shetland Islands

James Ross Island

Antarctic Peninsula

Anvers Island

Adelaide Island

Palmer Land

Alexander Island

Bellingshausen Sea

Ellswor Land

Thurston Island

Amunsden Sea

Carney Island

Siple Islar

◀ An ice-breaker ship travels slowly through an open but narrow sea-lane in the ice off the continent of Antarctica.

SOUTHERN
OCEAN

Fimbul
Ice Shelf

Riiser-Larsen
Peninsula

Riiser-Larsen
Ice Shelf

Queen
Maud
Land

Enderby
Land

W e d d e l l
S e a

Coats
Land

Kemp
Land

Cape Darnley

Berkner Island

Filchner
Ice Shelf

Amery
Ice Shelf

Ronne
Ice Shelf

Henry
Ice Rise

A N T A R C T I C A

Princess
Elizabeth
Land

Korff
Ice Rise

Ninson Massif
16,062 ft.

• South Pole

G r e a t e r
A n t a r c t i c a

Willhelm II
Land

Shackleton
Ice Shelf

D a v i s
S e a

L e s s e r
A n t a r c t i c a

Queen Mary
Land

Vincennes
Bay

Ross
Ice Shelf

Cape Poinsett

Roosevelt Island

R o s s
S e a

Victoria
Land

Ross Island

Adélie
Land

Porpoise Bay

SOUTHERN
OCEAN

Oates
Land

George V
Land

Cape Adare

• South Magnetic
Pole (1990)

D u m o n t
d ' U r v i l l e
S e a

| 0 | | 1000 | | 2000 k |
| 0 | 500 | | 1000 miles | |

of land are ice free, including most of the Antarctic Peninsula, Wilkes Land, southern Victoria Land, and much of Ross Island. The peaks and some valleys in parts of the Transantarctic mountain range and the Ellsworth Mountains are also exposed rock, and because of global warming, Antarctica's ice cap appears to be receding in places. Despite the harsh climate, the continent attracts around 13,000 tourists during its summer months, who travel on organized tours to experience Antarctica. Most visit the Antarctic Peninsula or travel through the Ross Sea, which contains Ross Island, the home of one of Antarctica's two active volcanoes, the 12,444-ft.-high Mount Erebus.

▲ The largest of all penguins, the Emperor penguin journeys up to 62 mi. inland on Antarctica to its breeding ground. Dense layers of fat and thick waterproof feathers enable these birds to survive the incredibly harsh Antarctic winter on land—the only large creature to do so.

▼ The rugged, icebound Mount Lister has a height of 13,202 ft. The mountain is part of the giant Transantarctic mountain range that cuts across the continent, dividing it into two distinct halves.

Antarctica is dominated by a giant ice cap that is over 13,120 ft. in depth in some places, while thinning to 4,920 ft. near the coast. The weight of the ice cap is phenomenal, enough to push parts of the continent's rocky base down below sea level. Antarctica doubles its effective size in the winter when a huge buildup of sea ice surrounds the coastline. Some of this ice calves, or breaks off, to form icebergs. In other places the floating sea ice stays attached to the land and builds up to form an ice shelf. Ice shelves make up around ten percent of the continent's area, with the Ross Ice Shelf and the Ronne Ice Shelf the two largest examples. Not all of Antarctica is covered in ice. Around 109,000 sq. mi.

COLD AND DRY

Antarctica is the location of the coldest-known temperature on Earth. In 1983 the former Soviet Union's Vostok scientific station recorded a temperature of -128.6°F. The warmest temperatures recorded on the continent are in the northern part of the Antarctic Peninsula, which has seen summer temperatures of 52°F. However, temperatures for the majority of the continent most of the time remain below 32°F. Average temperatures during the winter vary from between -40°F and -94°F in the interior to between -4°F and -22°F on the coast. These temperatures can feel

colder to creatures owing to the wind-chill factor brought about by the powerful, sweeping winds that scour the continent. In the interior winds as high as 198 mph have been recorded. The interior of Antarctica is a desert in which annual rainfall averages less than two inches per year. This increases at the coast to around 12 in. per year.

BARREN LANDS—FOOD-RICH SEAS

Antarctica's climate is so severe that few species of living things can survive there. The continent's plant life consists mainly of different types of simple algae, lichens, and mosses. These provide food for some small insects and microorganisms, as well as Antarctica's 43 different species of seabirds, including albatross and many species of penguins. In contrast to the barren land the waters around Antarctica hold large amounts of marine life. The ocean abounds with microscopic plants and animals, known as plankton, which are fed upon by a small shrimplike creature called krill. Krill live in giant swarms and provide rich feeding grounds for fish and larger marine creatures, including squid, seals, penguins, and whales. Many species of whales migrate to Antarctica in the summer to feed off the rich krill stocks. Trawlers from many nations fish the seas surrounding the continent, but a ban on whaling in the region was agreed in 1994.

▲ This 164-ft.-wide, 52-ft.-high dome covers part of the Amundsen-Scott research station located close to the South Pole. Named after the two explorers who memorably raced to reach the South Pole over 90 years ago, it is home to over 130 people in the summer months but only 28 people in the winter. Work on a new, enlarged South Pole research station is currently underway.

INDEX

The publishers wish to thank the following for their contribution to this book:

Photographs (*t* = top; *b* = bottom; *m* = middle; *l* = left; *r* = right)
Page i *b* Corbis; ii/iii *b* Corbis; iv *tl* NASA; iv *bl* Robert Glusic/PhotoDisc; iv *m* Philip Coblentz/Brand X Pictures; iv *mr* Philip Coblentz/Brand X Pictures; v *tl* David Lorenz Winston/Brand X Pictures; v *m* Corbis; v *mr* Corbis; v *b* Corbis; vi *tl* Herbert Maeder/Still Pictures; vi *m* Steve Allen/Brand X Pictures; vi *b* Corbis; vii *b* MediaFocus International; 1 NASA; 2 *b* NASA; 3 *br* Adalberto Rios Szalay/Sexto Sol/PhotoDisc; 4 *tr* MediaFocus Interrnational; 5 *tl* Emanuele Taroni/PhotoDisc; 6 *tr* Chris Madeley/Science Photo Library; 7 *tr* US Geological Surveys/Science Photo Library; 8 *b* Jeremy Horner/Panos Pictures; 11 *tl* Bernhard Edmaier/Science Photo Library; 11 *br* Rob Huibers/Panos Pictures; 12 *tl* Photo 24/Brand X Pictures; 13 *tl* Photo 24/Brand X Pictures; 13 *l* John Mead/Science Photo Library; 15 *tl* Photo 24/Brand X Pictures; 15 *b* Corbis; 16/17 MediaFocus International; 16 *tl* MediaFocus International; 16/17 *t* Lyndon Harvey; 17 *br* Bernhard Edmaier/Science Photo Library; 18/19 MediaFocus International; 19 *t* MediaFocus International; 19 *br* Photo 24/Brand X Pictures; 20 *tl* Glen Allison/PhotoDisc; 20 *b* Tom Van Saint, Geosphere Project/Planetary Visions/Science Photo Library; 22 *tl* Julian Holland; 22/23 *t* Photo 24/Brand X Pictures; 23 *br* MediaFocus International; 24/25 *t* MediaFocus International; 25 *br* MediaFocus International; 26 *tl* MediaFocus International; 26 *tr* MediaFocus International; 26 *b* MediaFocus International; 27 *tr* Charles O'Rear/Corbis; 28 *tr* NASA; 28 *b* NASA/Science Photo Library; 31 *bl* Photo 24/Brand X Pictures; 31 *br* Corbis; 32 *tl* Photo 24/Brand X Pictures; 32 *bl* MediaFocus International; 33 *bl* Amanda Clement/PhotoDisc; 33 *tr* David Lorenz Winston/Brand X Pictures; 33 *mr* Alain Le Garsmeur/Panos Pictures; 33 *r* MediaFocus International; 33 *br* Photo 24/Brand X Pictures; 34 *tl* Rouxaime & Jacana/Science Photo Library; 34 *tr* Philip Coblentz/Brand X Pictures; 35 *r* Julian Holland; 35 *b* NASA; 36 *tr* Bernhard Edmaier/Science Photo Library; 36 *b* Edouard Parker/Hutchison Library; 37 *t* Michael S. Yamashita/Corbis; 40 *tl* Trygve Bolstad/Panos Pictures; 41 *tr* Liba Taylor/Panos Pictures; 41 *br* John Mead/Science Photo Library; 42 *tr* Julian Holland; 43 *br* NASA; 49 PhotoDisc/Robert Glusic; 50 *b* B & C Alexander/Still Pictures; 51 *b* B & C Alexander/Still Pictures; 52/53 Photo 24/Brand X Pictures; 52 *tr* MediaFocus International; 52 *b* John Wang/PhotoDisc; 54 *b* Corbis; 54/55 *t* Corbis; 55 *r* Gerry Ellis/DigitalVision; 56 *tl* Ron Watts/Corbis; 56 *b* Steve Allen/Brand X Pictures; 57 *tl* David Lorenz Winston/Brand X Pictures; 58 *tl* Alain Le Garsmeur/Panos Pictures; 58 *bl* Bob Krist/Corbis; 58/59 *b* Glen Allison/PhotoDisc; 60 *tl* Gerry Ellis/DigitalVision; 60 *b* Steve Allen/Brand X Pictures; 61 *t* Corbis; 62 *tl* Trevor Page/Hutchison Library; 62 *b* Robert Glusic/PhotoDisc; 63 *tr* Gerry Ellis/PhotoDisc; 63 *bl* Staffan Widstrand/Corbis; 64 *tr* Gerry Ellis/PhotoDisc; 64 *b* Steve Allen/Brand X Pictures; 65 *t* Corbis; 65 *br* Photo 24/Brand X Pictures; 66 *tl* Steve Allen/Brand X Pictures; 66 *tr* David Lorenz Winston/Brand X Pictures; 66 *b* Steve Allen/Brand X Pictures; 67 *b* Jim Wark/Still Pictures; 68 *tl* Steve Allen/Brand X Pictures; 68/69 *t* Photo 24/Brand X Pictures; 68/69 *b* Jeremy Woodhouse/PhotoDisc; 69 *tr* Steve Allen/Brand X Pictures; 69 *r* Joseph Sohm; ChromoSohm Inc./Corbis; 70 *tl* Sandy Felsenthal/Corbis; 70 *tr* Photo 24/Brand X Pictures; 70 *bl* Jeri Gleiter/Still Pictures; 71 *tr* Gerry Ellis/PhotoDisc; 71 *br* Jeff Greenberg/Still Pictures; 72 *tl* Glen Allison/PhotoDisc; 72 *l* Photo 24/Brand X Pictures; 72 *b* Photo 24/Brand X Pictures; 73 *t* Photo 24/Brand X Pictures; 73 *br* Ken Redding/Corbis; 74 *tl* Bob Krist/Corbis; 74 *tr* Photo 24/Brand X Pictures; 74 *b* Corbis; 75 *b* Bob Rowan; Progressive Image/Corbis; 76 *t* Photo 24/Brand X Pictures; 76 *bl* Richard Weiss/Still Pictures; 77 *tr* NASA; 77 *b* Richard Hamilton Smith/Corbis; 78 *tl* Photo 24/Brand X Pictures; 78 *b* Steve Allen/Brand X Pictures; 78/79 *t* Robert Glusic/PhotoDisc; 79 *bl* MediaFocus International; 79 *br* Rick Doyle/Corbis; 80/81 Photo 24/Brand X Pictures; 80 *tl* Philip Coblentz/Brand X Pictures; 80 *l* Steve Allen/Brand X Pictures; 80 *bl* Jeff Greenberg/Still Pictures; 80/81 *t* Gunter Marx Photography/Corbis; 81 *tr* Gerry Ellis/PhotoDisc; 81 *br* Photo 24/Brand X Pictures; 82 *tl* Kevin Schafer/Still Pictures; 82 *r* Gerry Ellis/PhotoDisc; 82 *b* MediaFocus International; 83 *ml* Philip Coblentz/Brand X Pictures; 84 *b* Mark Henley/Panos Pictures; 85 *tr* Philip Coblentz/Brand X Pictures; 85 *bl* Philip Coblentz/Brand X Pictures; 86 *tr* Philip Coblentz/Brand X Pictures; 86 *b* Adalberto Rios Szalay/Sexto Sol/PhotoDisc; 87 *tr* MediaFocus International; 87 *br* Neil Beer/PhotoDisc; 88 *tl* IMS Communications; 88 *b* Edward Parker/Hutchison Library; 89 *tl* Phil Schermeister/Corbis; 89 *tr* Gerry Ellis/PhotoDisc; 89 *br* Adalberto Rios Lanz/Sexto Sol/PhotoDisc; 90 *b* Sean Sprague/Panos Pictures; 91 *tl* Nigel Dickinson/Still Pictures; 91 *bl* Gerry Ellis/PhotoDisc; 91 *br* Steve Allen/Brand X Pictures; 92 *ml* Philip Coblentz/Brand X Pictures; 92 *b* Mike Kolloffel/Still Pictures; 93 *r* David Reed/Panos Pictures; 93 *bl* S. Sprague/Panos Pictures; 94 *bl* Nik Wheeler/Corbis; 95 *ml* Philip Coblentz/Brand X Pictures; 95 *b* Philip Coblentz/Brand X Pictures; 95 *r* Philip Coblentz/Brand X Pictures; 96 *l* IMS Communications; 96 *br* Gerard & Margi Moss/Still Pictures; 97 Philip Coblentz/Brand X Pictures; 98 Philip Coblentz/Brand X Pictures; 99 *t* Mark Edwards/Still Pictures; 99 *b* Philip Coblentz/Brand X Pictures; 100 *tr* Klaus Andrews/Still Pictures; 100 *b* Mark Edwards/Still Pictures; 101 *mr* Rolando Pujol/South American Pictures; 102 *b* Marc French/Panos Pictures; 103 *m* Hisham F. Ibrahim/PhotoDisc; 104 *mr* Marc French/Panos Pictures; 105 *mr* Philip Wolmuth/Panos Pictures; 106/107 *b* Catherine Karnow/Corbis; 108 *b* Neil Cooper/Panos Pictures; 109 *mr* Philip Coblentz/Brand X Pictures; 110 *mr* Jonathan Blair/Corbis; 110 *br* Veronica Garbutt/Panos Pictures; 111 *tr* Philip Wolmuth/Panos Pictures; 111 *br* Philip Coblentz/Brand X Pictures; 112 *tr* Hubert Stadler/Corbis; 112/113 *b* Graham Neden; Ecoscene/Corbis; 113 *tr* Corbis; 113 *br* David Lorenz Winston/Brand X Pictures; 114 *tr* Corbis; 114/115 *b* Philip Coblentz/Brand X Pictures; 115 *bl* Philip Coblentz/Brand X Pictures; 115 *br* Philip Coblentz/Brand X Pictures; 116/117 *b* Tony Morrison/South American Pictures; 116/117 *t* Caroline Penn/Panos Pictures; 117 *br* Kevin Schafer/Still Pictures; 118 *t* Alfredo Cedeño/Panos Pictures; 118 *bl* IMS Communications; 119 *bl* Jonathan Kaplan/Still Pictures; 119 *br* Staffan Widstrand/Corbis; 120 *b* James L. Amos/Corbis; 121 *bl* Philip Coblentz/Brand X Pictures; 121 *br* European Space Agency; 122 *bl* IMS Communications; 123 *t* Jon Spaull/Panos Pictures; 123 *bl* Clive Gifford; 124 *bl* IMS Communications; 124/125 *b* Jeremy Horner/Panos Pictures; 125 *tl* Julian Holland; 125 *tr* Corbis; 126/127 *b* Tony Morrison/South American Pictures; 127 *tr* David Lorenz Winston/Brand X Pictures; 127 *br* Glen Allison/PhotoDisc; 128 *bl* Ron Giling/Still Pictures; 129 *tl* Mark Edwards/Still Pictures; 129 *b* Jeremy A. Horner/Panos Pictures; 130 *tr* MediaFocus International; 130 *b* Mark Edwards/Still Pictures; 132 *tl* Ricardo Azoury/Corbis; 132/133 *b* Richard T. Nowitz/Corbis; 133 *tr* Philip Coblentz/Brand X Pictures; 133 *br* MediaFocus International; 134/135 *t* Ernesto Rios Lanz/Sexto Sol/PhotoDisc; 134/135 *b* Chris Sattlberger/Panos Pictures; 136 *b* Tony Morrison/South American Pictures; 137 *b* Nick Haslam/Hutchison Library; 137 *mr* Philip Coblentz/Brand X Pictures; 138 *b* Philip Coblentz/Brand X Pictures; 138/139 *t* Jeremy Horner/Panos Pictures; 138/139 *m* Philip Coblentz/Brand X Pictures; 139 *br* Philip Coblentz/Brand X Pictures; 140 *bl* Philip Coblentz/Brand X Pictures; 141 *tl* Frank Nowikowski/South American Pictures; 141 *tr* Javier Pierini/PhotoDisc; 141 *b* MediaFocus International; 142 *tl* Kit Houghton/Corbis; 142 *b* MediaFocus International; 143 *tl* Gerry Ellis/DigitalVision; 143 *b* John Farmar; Ecoscene/Corbis; 144 *b* John Noble/Corbis; 145 Philip Coblentz/Brand X Pictures; 146 *bl* Charles & Josette Lenars/Corbis; 146 *tr* MediaFocus International; 147 *br* Ellerbrock & Schaft/Network; 148 *tr* MediaFocus International; 148 *b* Gavin Hellier/Robert Harding Picture Library; 149 *br* Steve Allen/Brand X Pictures; 150 *bl* Yann Arthus-Bertrand/Corbis; 151 *t* Galen Rowell/Corbis; 151 *b* Chris Lisle/Corbis; 152 *b* W. Herbert/Robert Harding Picture Library; 153 *t* Duncan Maxwell/Robert Harding Picture Library; 153 *mr* Pal Hermansen/Still Pictures; 153 *b* Bengt Andreasson/Robert Harding Picture Library; 154 *l* Dylan Garcia/Still Pictures; 155 *t* Wally Herbert/Robert Harding Picture Library; 155 *mr* K. Gillham/Robert Harding Picture Library; 155 *b* Robert Harding Picture Library; 156 *ml* MediaFocus International; 156 *b* MediaFocus International; 157 *tr* Adam Woolfitt/Corbis; 158 *ml* MediaFocus International; 158 *mr* Bob Krist/Corbis; 158 *b* Dave G. Houser/Corbis; 159 *b* Steve Allen/Brand X Pictures; 160 *ml* David Toase/PhotoDisc; 160 *b* Stephanie Maze/Corbis; 161 *tl* Christopher Tordai/Hutchison Library; 161 *tr* Christopher Tordai/Hutchison Library; 161 *br* Tuck Goh/Hutchison Library; 162/163 *b* Roger Ressmeyer/Corbis; 163 *ml* Julian Holland; 163 *bl* Julian Holland; 163 *t* Pawel Libera/Corbis; 163 *mr* Julian Holland; 164 *tl* David Toase/PhotoDisc; 164/165 *t* Robert Laberge/Getty Images; 164 *b* Michael St. Maur Sheil/Corbis; 165 *tr* Philip Coblentz/Brand X Pictures; 165 *mr* Philip Coblentz/Brand X Pictures; 165 *br* R. Rainford/Robert Harding Picture Library; 166 *ml* MediaFocus International; 166 *b* MediaFocus International; 167 *t* MediaFocus International; 168 *b* Sylvain Grandadam/Robert Harding Picture Library; 169 *t* Thomas Raupach/Still Pictures; 169 *br* MediaFocus International; 170/171 *b* Thomas Raupach/Still Pictures; 171 *t* MediaFocus International; 171 *br* MediaFocus International; 172 *tl* Emanuele Taroni/PhotoDisc; 172 *bl* John Wang/PhotoDisc; 172/173 *t* David Turnley/Corbis; 173 *tr* MediaFocus International; 173 *b* Hartmut Schwarzbach/Still Pictures; 174 *t* MediaFocus International; 174 *bl* MediaFocus International; 175 *b* Andy Williams/Robert Harding Picture Library; 176 *tl* MediaFocus International; 176/177 *b* MediaFocus International; 177 *tr* Martial Colomb/PhotoDisc; 177 *mr* Michael Busselle/Corbis; 178 *t* MediaFocus International; 178 *bl* Michael Short/Robert Harding Picture Library; 179 *tr* Philip Coblentz/Brand X Pictures; 179 *br* Martial Colomb/PhotoDisc; 180/181 *t* Tamas Revesz/Still Pictures; 180/181 *b* Ray Juno/Corbis; 182 *b* MediaFocus International; 183 *tr* Reuter Raymond/Corbis Sygma; 183 *b* Roy Rainford/Robert Harding Picture Library; 184 *b* S. Grandadam/Robert Harding Picture Library; 185 *t* Mike McQueen/Impact; 186/187 *b* Corbis; 187 *t* Barry Lewis/Corbis; 187 *br* Philip Coblentz/Brand X Pictures; 188 *b* Emma Lee/Life File/PhotoDisc; 189 *tr* Liba Taylor/Hutchison Library; 189 *b* Jan Hacad/Woodfall Wild Images; 190 *b* John Hatt/Hutchison Library; 191 *tl* Ron Giling/Still Pictures; 191 *tr* Phil Robinson/Robert Harding Picture Library; 191 *b* David Hoffman/Still Pictures; 192 *b* Liba Taylor/Hutchison Library; 193 David Lorenz Winston/Brand X Pictures; 194/195 *b* MediaFocus International; 195 *br* Edward Parker/Hutchison Library; 196 *bl* Philip Coblentz/Brand X Pictures; 197 *tr* Jose Fuste Raga/Corbis; 197 *b* Fin Costello/Robert Harding Picture Library; 198 *tl* Ryan MacVay/PhotoDisc; 198 *b* Philip Coblentz/Brand X Pictures; 199 *tr* Mark Henley/Impact; 200 *b* MediaFocus International; 201 *t* MediaFocus International; p.201 *r* Philip Coblentz/Brand X Pictures; 201 *br* Joerg Boethling/Still Pictures; 202/203 *b* Marco Cristofori/Still Pictures; 203 *t* Corbis; 203 *br* Explorer/Robert Harding Picture Library; 204 *tl* MediaFocus International; 204 *b* Martyn Goddard/Corbis; 205 *br* Philip Coblentz/Brand X Pictures; 206 *b* Janez Stock/Corbis; 207 *b* MediaFocus International; 208 *bl* Colin Paterson/PhotoDisc; 208 *tr* Marc French/Panos Pictures; 209 *b* MediaFocus International; 210 *b* Michael Short/Robert Harding Picture Library; 211 *b* Ed Kashi/Corbis; 212 *b* Leif Skoogfors/Corbis; 213 *b* Melanie Friend/Hutchison Library; 214/215 *b* Toma Babovic/Still Pictures; 215 *t* Mark Henley/Impact; 215 *br* Mark Henley/Impact; 216/217 *b* MediaFocus International; 216/217 *t* Christopher Bluntzer/Impact; 218 *ml* Gregory Wrona/Panos Pictures; 218 *b* Dean Conger/Corbis; 219 *bl* Steve Raymer/Corbis; 220 *b* Chris Lisle/Corbis; 221 *b* Nik Wheeler/Corbis; 222/223 *b* Peter Turnley/Corbis; 223 *tr* Gyori Antoine/Corbis Sygma; 224 *ml* Jeff Greenberg/Robert Harding Picture Library; 224 *b* Barry Lewis/Corbis; 225 *b* C. Bowman/Robert Harding Picture Library; 226 *b* Sandro Vannini/Corbis; 227 *tr* David B. A. Jones/Robert Harding Picture Library; 228 *tl* Dave G. Houser/Corbis; 228/229 *b* Michael Nicholson/Corbis; 229 *br* Janet Wishnetsky/Impact; 230 *tl* David Turnley/Corbis; 230 *b* Gregor Schmid/Corbis; 231 *tl* Wolfgang Kaehler/Corbis; 232 *tl* Bojan Vrecelj/Corbis; 232/233 *b* Christina Dodwell/Hutchison Library; 233 *tr* Paul A. Souders/Corbis; 234 *tr* Rhodri Jones/Panos Pictures; 235 *b* Heidi Bradner/Panos Pictures; 236 *b* Rhodri Jones/Panos Pictures; 237 *ml* Heidi Bradner/Panos Pictures; 237 *b* Jon Spaull/Panos Pictures; 238/239 *t* MediaFocus International; 239 *tr* Adam Woolfitt/Robert Harding Picture Library; 239 *b* Joan Klatchko/Hutchison Library; 240 *b* Philip Woolmuth/Hutchison Library; 241 Corbis; 242 *tr* Jochen Tack/Still Pictures; 242 *b* Giacomo Pirozzi/Panos Pictures; 243 *bl* Lindsay Hebberd/Corbis; 244 *tr* Jean-Léo Dugast/Panos Pictures; 244 *b* Robin Constable/Hutchison Library; 245 *br* MediaFocus International; 246/247 *t* K. M. Westermann/Corbis; 246/247 *b* K. M. Westermann/Corbis; 247 *mr* Dave Bartruff/Corbis; 248 *bl* Ricki Rosen/Corbis; 248/249 *b* Ricki Rosen/Corbis; 249 *t* Mike Schroder/Still Pictures; 250 *ml* Edward Parker/Hutchison Library; 250 *b* Alan Keohane/Impact; 251 *ml* Toby Adamson/Still Pictures; 251 *b* Charles & Josette Lenars/Corbis; 252 *ml* Caroline Penn/Panos Pictures; 252 *b* Michael S. Yamashita/Corbis; 253 *tr* Mohamed Ansar/Impact; 253 *b* John Isaac/Still Pictures; 254 *tr* Robin Laurance/Impact; 254/255 *b* Marcus Rose/Panos Pictures; 255 *tr* Charles & Josette Lenars/Corbis; 256 *tr* Hutchison Library; 257 *tr* Hutchison Library; 256/257 *b* Bernard Gerard/Hutchison Library; 258 *tl* Alex Majoli/Magnum; 258 *b* Mohamed Amin/Robert Harding Picture Library; 259 *b* Adrian Arbib/Still Pictures; 260 *mr* Guy Mansfield/Panos Pictures; 261 *ml* Romano Cagnoni/Still Pictures; 261 *br* MediaFocus International; 262 *b* Nick Haslam/Hutchison Library; 263 *tr* John Miles/Panos Pictures; 263 *ml* John Miles/Panos Pictures; 264 *tr* Klaus Reisinger/Still Pictures; 264/265 *b* Dieter Telemans/Panos Pictures; 265 *br* John McDermott/Panos Pictures; 266 *tr* Liba Taylor/Corbis; 266 *l* ESA/Starsem; 267 *tr* John Spaull/Panos Pictures; 267 *b* Marcus Rose/Panos Pictures; 268 *b* Brian Goddard/Panos Pictures; 270/271 *b* Dr Petocz/Still Pictures; 271 *tr* Joe Raedle/Getty Images; 272 *tr* Alain Le Garsmeur/Panos Pictures; 272/273 *b* Hartmut Schwarzbach/Still Pictures; 273 *br* Fred Hoogervorst/Panos Pictures; 274 *tr* Friedrich Stark/Still Pictures; 275 *tr* Henning Christoph/Still Pictures; 275 *br* Dermot Tatlow/Panos Pictures; 276/277 *t* Ingo Jezierski/PhotoDisc; 276 *b* Hutchison Library; 277 *tr* Jeremy Horner/Corbis; 277 *br* Gerry Ellis/DigitalVision; 278 *tl* Jeremy Horner/Panos Pictures; 278 *bl* Corbis; 278/279 Mark Henley/Panos Pictures; 278/279 *t* Bob Krist/Corbis; 278/279 *b* Wolfgang Schmidt/Still Pictures; 280 *tl* Daniel O'Leary/Panos Pictures; 280/281 *t* Piers Cavendish/Impact; 281 *tr* Jochen Tack/Still Pictures; 280/281 *b* Christopher Cormack/Corbis; 282 *b* Shehzad Nooran/Still Pictures; 283 *mr* David Lorenz Winston/Brand X Pictures; 284 *b* Chris Stowers/Panos Pictures; 285 *b* MediaFocus International; 286 *b* Thierry Thomas/Still Pictures; 287 *b* MediaFocus International; 288 *b* Sarvottam Rajkoomar/Still Pictures; 289 Corbis; 290 *b* Corbis; 291 *br* B.S.P.I/Corbis; 292/293 *t* Corbis; 292 *b* Corbis; 293 *tr* Gerry Ellis/DigitalVision; 294/295 *t* Corbis; 294/295 *b* Glen Allison/PhotoDisc; 295 *tr* Corbis; 295 *br* Ron Giling/Still Pictures; 296 *tl* MediaFocus International; 296/297 *b* Adam Crowley/PhotoDisc; 296/297 *t* Liu Liqun/Corbis; 297 *br* SETBOUN/Corbis; 298 *t* Adam Crowley/PhotoDisc; 298 *bl* Corbis; 299 *bl* Chris Stowers/Panos Pictures; 300/301 *t* Mark Henley/Impact; 301 *bl* Toby Adamson/Still Pictures; 301 *br* PERN/Hutchison Library; 302 *b* Friedrich Stark/Still Pictures; 303 *t* Jeremy Horner/Panos Pictures; 303 *b* Friedrich Stark/Still Pictures; 304 *b* R. Ian Lloyd/Hutchison Library; 305 *t* Jim Holmes/Panos Pictures; 305 *br* Friedrich Stark/Still Pictures; 306 *b* Corbis; 306/307 *t* Dean Conger/Corbis; 307 *br* Akira Kaede/PhotoDisc; 308 *tl* Roger Ressmeyer/Corbis; 308 *b* Corbis; 308/309 *t* Corbis; 309 *br* Akira Kaede/PhotoDisc; 310 *b* Philip Coblentz/Brand X Pictures; 311 *tl* Philip Coblentz/Brand X Pictures; 311 *tr* Philip Coblentz/Brand X Pictures; 311 *br* Chris Stowers/Panos Pictures; 312 *bl* Philip Coblentz/Brand X Pictures; 313 *t* Amanda Leung/Panos Pictures; 313 *b* Ingo Jezierski/PhotoDisc; 314 *bl* Jeremy Horner/Hutchison Library; 315 *t* Philip Coblentz/Brand X Pictures; 315 *br* Jean-Léo Dugast/Panos Pictures; 316/317 *b* Sarah Murray/Hutchison Library; 317 *tr* Caroline Penn/Panos Pictures; 318/319 *b* Glen Allison/PhotoDisc; 319 *tr* Hartmut Schwarzbach/Still Pictures; 320/321 *b* J. Holmes/Panos Pictures; 321 *t* Jorgen Schytte/Still Pictures; 321 *br* Jorgen Schytte/Still Pictures; 322 *bl* Jim Olive/Still Pictures; 323 *ml* R. Ian Lloyd/Hutchison Library; 323 *br* Corbis; 324 *tr* Steve Allen/Brand X Pictures; 325 *tl* Gerard & Margi Moss/Still Pictures; 325 *r* Macduff Everton/Corbis; 326 *tl* Fred Hoogervorst/Panos Pictures; 326 *bl* Mark Edwards/Still Pictures; 326/327 *t* Nigel Dickinson/Still Pictures; 327 *tr* Corbis; 327 *b* Robert Francis/Hutchison Library; 328/329 *t* Russell Gordon/Still Pictures; 329 *br* Chris Stowers/Panos Pictures; 330 *tl* Mark Edwards/Still Pictures; 330 *b* Philip Coblentz/Brand X Pictures; 331 *t* Dani & Jeske/Still Pictures; 331 *br* Michael Macintyre/Hutchison Library; 332 *tl* Johann Scheibner/Still Pictures; 332 *b* Mark Edwards/Still Pictures; 333 *t* Robert Francis/Hutchison Library; 333 *br* T. Turner/Times Picayune/Still Pictures; 334 *bl* Friedrich Stark/Still Pictures; 335 *bl* IMS Communications; 336 *tl* Dean Conger/Corbis; 336 *b* Yann Arthus-Bertrand/Corbis; 337 Herbert Maeder/Still Pictures; 338 *tr* Betty Press/Panos Pictures; 338/339 *b* M & C Denis-Huot/Still Pictures; 339 *br* Gerry Ellis/DigitalVision; 340 *tr* Adrian Arbib/Still Pictures; 341 *b* Ron Giling/Still Pictures; 342 *b* Georges Lopez/Still Pictures; 343 *bl* Mark Henley/Impact; 344 *b* Voltchev-Unep/Still Pictures; 345 *tr* Markus Matzel/Still Pictures; 346/347 *b* MediaFocus International; 347 *tr* Tibor Bognar/Corbis; 348 *b* Paul O'Driscoll/Impact; 349 *br* Dan Charlish-Christian Aid/Still Pictures; 350 *b* Maya Kardum/Panos Pictures; 351 *tr* Henning Christoph/Still Pictures; 352 *b* Mark Edwards/Still Pictures; 353 *mr* Clive Shirley/Panos Pictures; 354 *b* Ron Giling/Still Pictures; 355 *tr* Friedrich Stark/Still Pictures; 356 *b* Caroline Penn/Corbis; 357 *mr* Eldad Rafaeli/Corbis; 357 *br* Betty Press/Panos Pictures; 358 *b* Sebastian Bolesch/Still Pictures; 359 *b* Gallo Images/Corbis; 360/361 *t* Bruce Paton/Panos Pictures; 360/361 *b* Mark Edwards/Still Pictures; 362 *mr* Knut Müller/Still Pictures; 363 *tr* Julian Holland; 363 *bl* Liba Taylor/Panos Pictures; 365 *b* Genevieve Renson/Still Pictures; 366 *b* Edgar Cleijne/Still Pictures; 368 *b* James Sugar/Still Pictures; 369 *b* Ron Giling/Still Pictures; 370/371 *b* Fred Hoogervorst/Panos Pictures; 371 *ml* Anthony Bannister; Gallo Images/Corbis; 372 *b* Yann Arthus-Bertrand/Corbis; 373 *b* Brian Moser/Hutchison Library; 374 *bl* Michael Busselle/Corbis; 375 *tr* Trygve Bolstad/Panos Pictures; 375 *br* Gerry Ellis/DigitalVision; 376 *b* Hjalte Tin/Still Pictures; 377 *mr* Jeremy Woodhouse/PhotoDisc; 378 *b* Gerard & Margi Moss/Still Pictures; 379 *ml* Gerry Ellis/DigitalVision; 379 *b* Friedrich Stark/Still Pictures; 380 *tr* Michael S. Lewis/Corbis; 380/381 *b* Roderick Johnson/Panos Pictures; 381 *tr* Roger de la Harpe/Still Pictures; 382 *tl* IMS Communications; 382/383 *b* Jeremy Woodhouse/PhotoDisc; 382/383 *t* Friedrich Stark/Still Pictures; 383 *tr* Caroline Penn/Panos Pictures; 384 *b* Billie Rafaeli/Hutchison Library; 385 Steve Allen/Brand X Pictures; 386/387 Philip Coblentz/Brand X Pictures; 388 *tl* Bob Abraham/Corbis; 388 *bl* Penny Tweedie/Corbis; 389 *br* Paul A. Souders/Corbis; 390/391 *t* Corbis; 391 *tr* Michael Macintyre/Hutchison Library; 391 *b* Michael Macintyre/Hutchison Library; 392 *tr* Glen Allison/PhotoDisc; 392/393 *b* Steve Allen/Brand X Pictures; 394 *tl* Patrick Ward/Corbis; 394/395 *t* MediaFocus International; 394/395 *b* Corbis; 396 *t* Bill Ross/Corbis; 396/397 *b* Corbis; 397 *tr* Paul A. Souders/Corbis; 398 *tl* Nick Wilson/Getty Images; 398 *b* MediaFocus International; 399 *tl* Paul A. Souders/Corbis; 399 *b* Martin Hawes/Still Pictures; 400 *tl* O. Alamany & E. Vicens/Corbis; 400 *tr* Penny Tweedie/Corbis; 400/401 *b* Corbis; 402 *tl* Ted Spiegel/Corbis; 402/403 *t* L. Clarke/Corbis; 402/403 *b* Dave G. Houser/Corbis; 403 *tr* Gerry Ellis/DigitalVision; 404 *tl* Nick Wilson/Getty Images; 404/405 *t* Paul A. Souders/Corbis; 404/405 *b* Corbis; 405 *br* Robert Garvey/Corbis; 406 *t* Roger Garwood & Trish Ainslie/Corbis; 406/407 *b* Massimo Mastrorillo/Corbis; 407 *tr* Robert Garvey/Corbis; 408 *b* Steve Allen/Brand X Pictures; 408/409 *t* Pat O'Hara/Corbis; 409 *br* Steve Allen/Brand X Pictures; 410 *tl* Anders Ryman/Corbis; 410/411 *b* Corbis; 411 *t* Robert Dowling/Corbis; 412 *tl* Steve Allen/Brand X Pictures; 412 *b* Steve Allen/Brand X Pictures; 413 *t* Paul A. Souders/Corbis; 413 *br* Scott Barbour/Getty Images; 414 *b* J. G. Fuller/Hutchison Library; 415 *m* Anders Ryman/Corbis; 416 *br* Andy Crump/Still Pictures; 417 *b* Stephen Frink/Corbis; 418 *b* Roger Ressmeyer/Corbis; 419 *mr* Glen Allison/PhotoDisc; 420/421 Norbert Wu/Still Pictures; 422 *b* Jan Butchofsky-Houser/Corbis; 423 *b* Michael Macintyre/Hutchison Library; 424 *b* Patricio Goycoolea/Hutchison Library; 425 *mr* Jack Fields/Corbis; 426 *mr* Philipp Hympendahl/Still Pictures; 426/427 *b* Glen Allison/PhotoDisc; 427 *mr* Philip Coblentz/Brand X Pictures; 428 *b* W. Perry Conway/Corbis; 430 *tl* Fritz Polking/Still Pictures; 430/431 *b* Galen Rowell/Corbis; 431 *tr* Galen Rowell/Corbis; 432 *b* Mark Carwardine/Still Pictures; 434 *ml* Carl R. Sams II/Still Pictures; 434 *r* Gerry Ellis/DigitalVision; 434 *br* Mark Edwards/Still Pictures; 435 *mr* Corbis; 435 *bl* Diane Blell/Still Pictures; 436/437 *t* Bojan Brecelj/Still Pictures; 436/437 *b* Gil Moti/Still Pictures; 437 *br* Rui Vieira/Panos Pictures; 442 *ml* Kevin Schafer/Still Pictures; 442 *mr* Caron Philippe/Corbis; 443 *bl* Sabine Vielmo/Still Pictures; 444 *mr* Mike Schroder/Still Pictures; 445 *mr* Shehzad Noorani/Still Pictures; 445 *bl* Jorgen Schytte/Still Pictures; 446 *mr* Wolfgang M. Weber/Still Pictures; 446 *br* Ron Giling/Still Pictures; 447 *tl* Robert Holmes/Corbis; 447 *mr* Tom Wagner/Corbis; 447 *bl* Caroline Penn/Panos Pictures; 448 *bl* Pierre Gleizes/Still Pictures; 452/453 *t* Manfred Voller/Corbis; 452 *b* Claes Lofgren/Still Pictures; 453 *tr* Ron Giling/Still Pictures; 453 *br* Chris Stowers/Panos Pictures; 458 *tr* Ron Giling/Still Pictures; 458/459 *b* Heine Pedersen/Still Pictures; 459 *t* Nigel Dickinson/Still Pictures; 460 *tl* Bettmann/Corbis; 460/461 *t* Jorgen Schytte/Still Pictures; 460 *br* Robert Mulder/Still Pictures; 461 *tr* Sabine Sauer/Still Pictures; 461 *b* Hartmut Schwarzbach/Still Pictures; 462 *tr* Penny Tweedie/Panos Pictures; 462 *bl* Adrian Arbib/Still Pictures; 463 *tr* John Van Hasselt/Corbis Sygma; 463 *b* Catherine Karnow/Corbis; 464 *tr* Mark Henley/Panos Pictures; 464 *bl* Gordon Wiltsie/Still Pictures

Additional artwork: Julian Baker